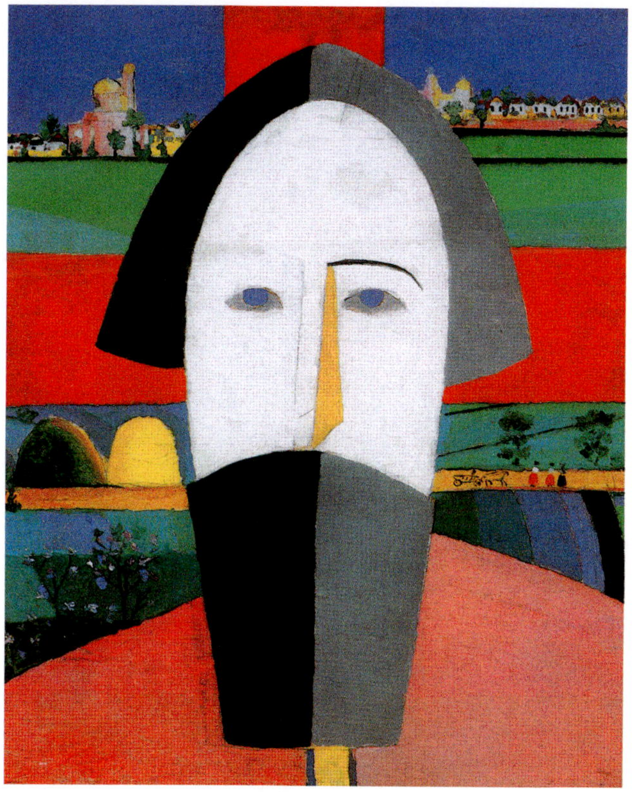

The Avant-Garde Icon

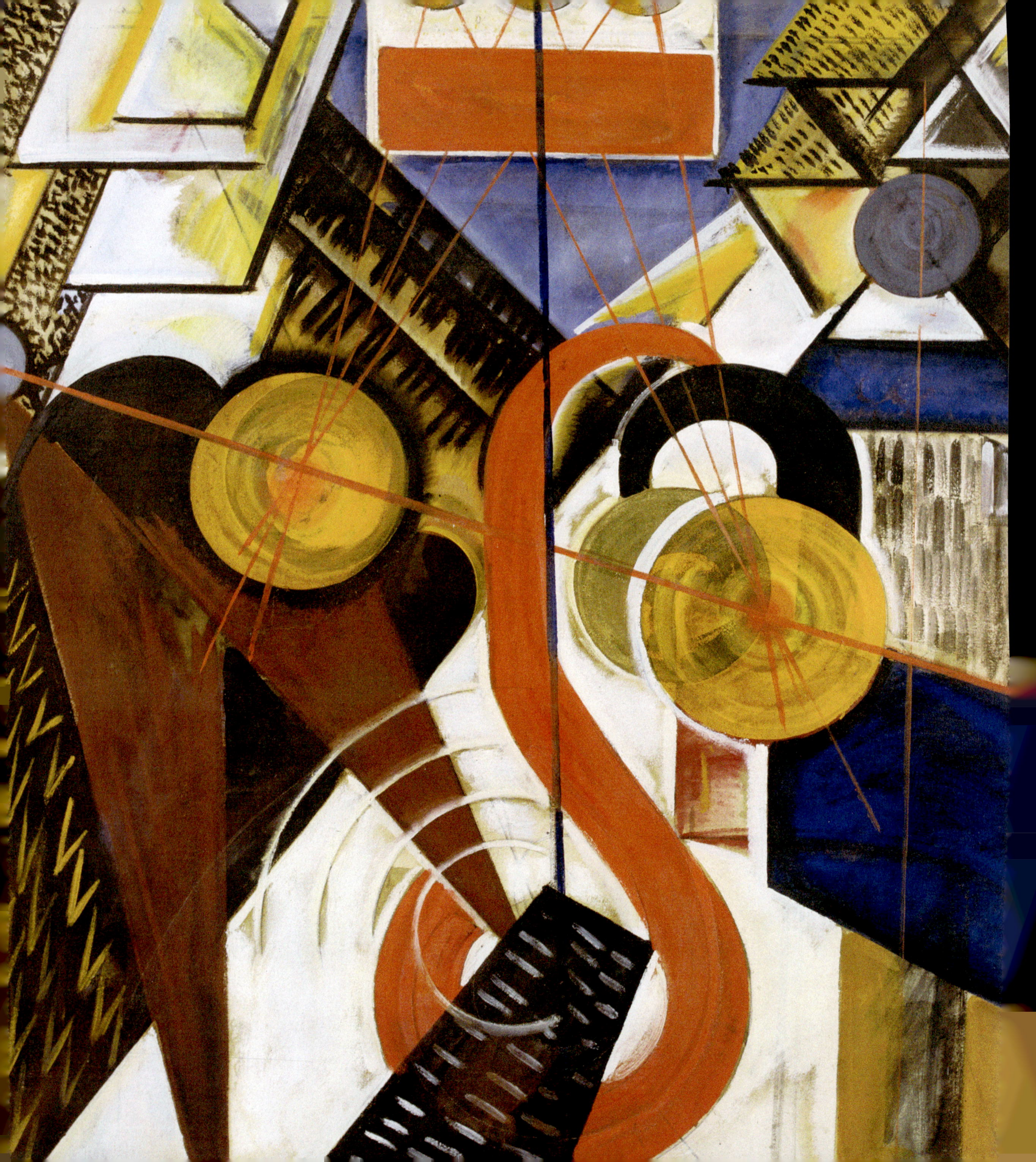

The Avant-Garde Icon

Russian avant-garde art and the icon painting tradition

Andrew Spira

Lund Humphries

First published in 2008 by

Lund Humphries
Gower House
Croft Road
Aldershot
Hampshire GU11 3HR

and

Lund Humphries
Suite 420
101 Cherry Street
Burlington
VT 05401-4405
USA

www.lundhumphries.com

Lund Humphries is part of Ashgate Publishing

British Library Cataloguing in Publication Data:
Spira, Andrew
The avant-garde icon
1. Art, Russian – 20th century
2. Art, Soviet
3. Avant-garde (Aesthetics) – Russia
4. Avant-garde (Aesthetics) – Soviet Union
5. Icons, Russian – Influence
I. Title
709.4'7'09041

ISBN-13: 9780853319757

Library of Congress Control Number: 2007938380

Edited by Howard Watson
Designed by Nigel Soper, set in Scala and Scala Sans
Printed in Singapore, by Kyodo

Cover: *St Parascevi and the Three Holy Hierarchs*, detail of Plate 103, and Liubov Popova, *Pictorial Architectonics*, detail of Plate 41
Frontispiece: Bela Uitz, *Iconanalysis with the Holy Trinity*, detail of Plate 56

DEDICATED WITH LOVE AND GRATITUDE
TO MY MOTHER AND FATHER

CONTENTS

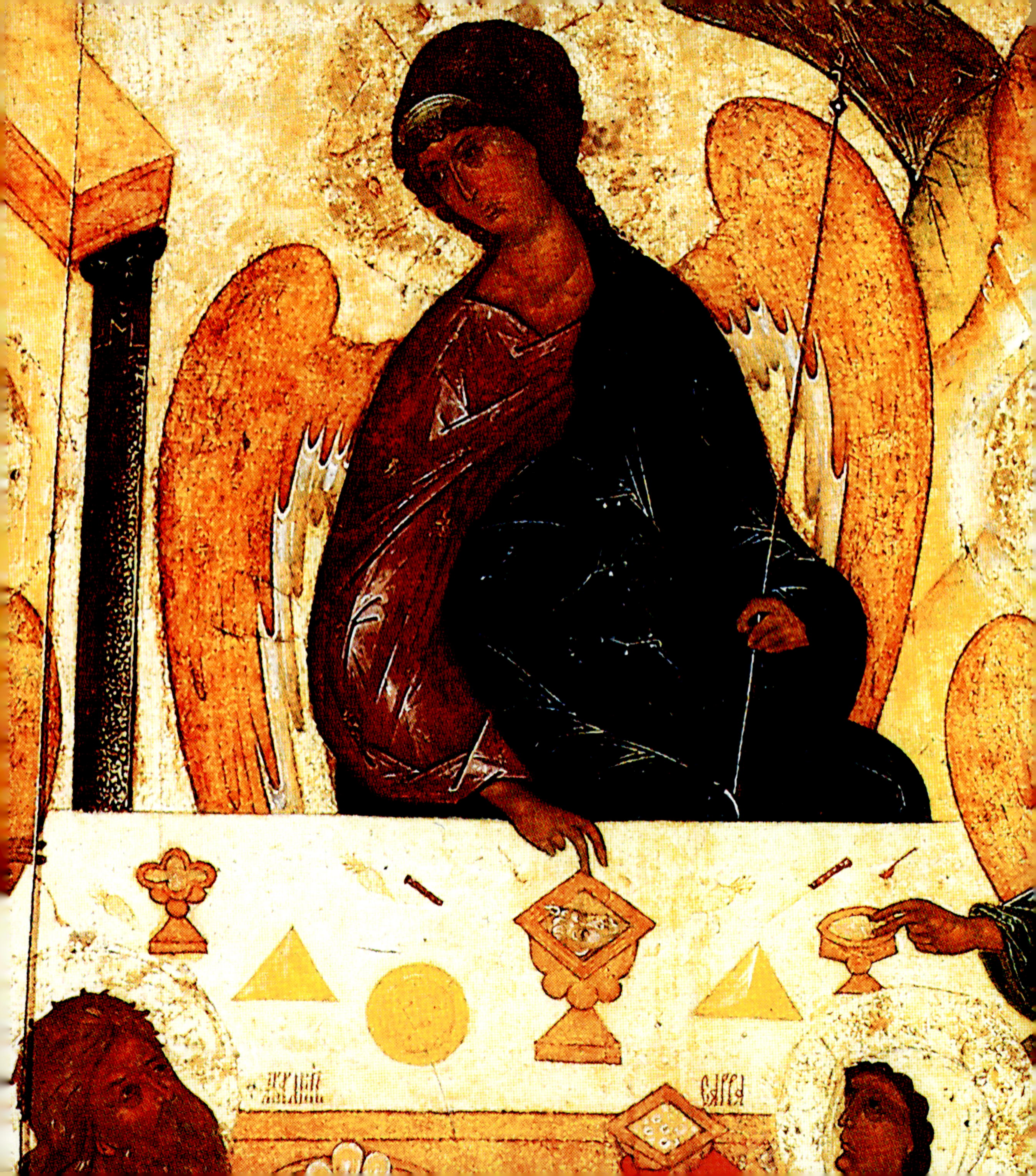

ACKNOWLEDGEMENTS

THIS BOOK STARTED LIFE as a proposal for an exhibition at the Temple Gallery, London, where I worked from 1988, spending many hours in the silent company of icons. It was then that the paradoxical modernity of icons slowly became apparent to me, as it must have done to artists at the start of the twentieth century. There seemed to be enough common ground between icons and Russian avant-garde art to warrant a modest show. However, the proposal could never reach a satisfactory level of completeness, as every discovery raised more questions than it answered. The exhibition never happened. Tapping away at a typewriter, with icons all around me, I had no idea that the resonances discovered then would lead to an abundance of connections resulting in a book 20 years later.

In the meantime, innumerable people have been supportive and helpful to me, at different times and in different capacities. I would like to express my gratitude towards them here. Among them, I extend special thanks to Ariadne Arendt, Lucy Daniels, Rosanna Kelly, Beatrice Oliphant, Malgosia Sady, Katherine Steel, Angelika Temple and Angelica von Hase for help with translations of Russian, Polish, Hungarian and German texts. I am also grateful to the very many people who have discussed and shared ideas with me, including Rosamund Bartlett, Eva Bajkay, Elena Basner, Colin Bearne, Tony Bond, Sue Compton, Michael Compton, Joy Law, Nina Lobanov-Rostovsky, Christina Lodder, Norbert Lynton, Gerard McBurney, Robin Milner-Gulland, Jonathan Powell, Edward Robinson, Dmitri Sarabianov, Simon Shaw-Miller and Evgenia Teslyuk. I am especially grateful to John Milner for offering valuable advice on the text.

I am immensely grateful to Sir Joseph Hotung and Evgeny Lebedev without whose support this book would have been a shadow of itself. I am deeply touched by their generosity. Their contributions have been integral to the realisation of the original concept of the book, allowing the visual argument to speak for itself, in conjunction with the text. Many individuals and institutions have been extremely helpful and co-operative in supplying images. David King has been particularly generous here, as have Alexander Lavrentiev, Dick Temple, Avdei Ter-Oganian and Barbara Thiemann. My thanks also go to Elvira Allocati, Olga Beloborodova, Jo Elford, Marat Guelman, Marina Ivanova, Anna Lovkacheva, Angela Minshull, Christina Peters, Marguerite Sablonnière, Tim Sanders, Emma Strouts and Hetty Wessels.

I would also like to thank staff at Lund Humphries, especially Laura Bolick and Miranda Harrison, who have taken great care over bringing the project to fruition, and Lucy Myers, Lucy Clark, and Alex Hitchins. I am also very grateful to Howard Watson for his considerate and painstaking editing of the text and to Nigel Soper for designing the book.

My family and friends have been hugely supportive and patient, never tiring of what must have seemed to them like a shaggy dog story. I bow to them. I owe huge thanks to Dick Temple for introducing me to the art and medieval sites of 'Holy Russia' in 1983 and for sharing his love of icons with me. Helen Brunner believed in the book from the very beginning; her care and support were empowering. Malgosia Sady's thoughtfulness and intuitive understanding of the book has been invaluable; her interest and support were always felt and her suggestions were spot on. David King has been hugely generous with time, knowledge, books, images and tea. The unique humaneness that he brings to the outrageous story of twentieth-century Russia has been, and continues to be, inspiring. Words do not really convey my gratitude to these friends.

Old Testament Trinity, detail of plate 84

PREFACE

The Avant-Garde Icon is about the influence of Russian icons on early twentieth-century Russian avant-garde art. At first glance there seems to be little in common between these two art forms. In many ways, they represent fundamentally different points of view – the sacred versus the secular, the traditional versus the revolutionary, the faith-based versus the self-righteous, the figurative versus the abstract. However, if one ventures beyond the immediate appearances of the two arts into their root causes and motivations, one finds that the differences are not as mutually exclusive as they seem. Avant-garde artists were passionate and vociferous in their denunciation of the credulity, passivity, manipulation and conservatism of conventional religiosity. Their antipathy towards religion should not be underestimated. Nevertheless, there were aspects of icon painting that resonated strongly in their work and, although evidence of their receptivity to icons is more hidden than evidence of their rejection of the Church and its trappings, it is arguable that the tradition of icon painting was integral to the shaping of their work. As with children who rebel against their parents but turn out to resemble them, the art of the avant-garde often showed striking similarities to icons in looks, mannerisms and even in deeper sympathies.

The avant-garde movement was an extraordinarily diverse phenomenon. Different artists were influenced by icons in different ways. Some were attracted to their popular and poetic associations, others by their aesthetic and technical qualities; many artists consciously identified with their social function. Inspiration of this kind was also found in other types of popular art in Russia – *lubki* (popular prints), children's drawings and painted shop signs, for instance. The definitive characteristic of icons, however, goes beyond artistic or sociological significance: it lies with their metaphysical identity. The influence of icons would have been relatively cosmetic if this uniquely metaphysical dimension had not also made a profound impact on a number of avant-garde artists. This level of impact is especially significant in the case of Kazimir Malevich whose Suprematist adventure led him to the threshold of the infinite in art. Malevich was not only influenced by icons; he was also influenced by the underlying principle of icons – the presence of an Absolute in the world – and he was interested in the way in which icons were set up to be transparent to this presence. Despite the many other areas of similarity that exist between icons and the work of other avant-garde artists, it was ultimately through Malevich's Suprematist aim – to realise the infinity of reality through art – that the relationship between the art of the icon and the art of the Russian avant-garde was finally consummated.

The Avant-Garde Icon is an investigation into this relationship. It operates on two levels. Firstly, it tells the historical tale of how the revival of interest in icons, beginning in the nineteenth century, became a working metaphor for the search for a uniquely Russian and contemporary form of culture in Russia. Secondly, by placing the art of the avant-garde (especially Suprematism) in the context of its spiritual heritage and icons in the context of the modern world, it attempts to elucidate the innate significance of both phenomena in ways that have not been fully explored before.

Since the tenth century, when ancient Rus converted to Orthodox Christianity, icons had formed a key part of Russian culture. But by the end of the eighteenth century they had become debased (from both a religious and artistic point of view), partly due to the westernising tendencies of the Romanov tsars. Chapter 1 summarises the history and theology of icons from their source in Byzantium up until this period. The revival of interest in icons first occurred in Russia as a function of the Romanticism that swept through Europe in the nineteenth century. It initially arose, in the first half of the century, in reaction to Enlightenment rationalism in general and the westernisation of

Russian culture by Peter the Great and his immediate successors in particular. In order to dissociate from these 'alien' values and to connect with a core of Russian-ness in Russian culture, members of the new intelligentsia began to seek the historical logic of their own past. These early enquiries gave rise to the first systematic historical and archaeological studies in Russia. In the second half of the nineteenth century, as historicism increasingly became a part of popular culture, identification with the Russian past became a more emotional issue. One of the most dramatic ways of gratifying the nationalistic appetite of contemporary society was the full-blown rehearsal of historical events in art. Artists both stimulated and satisfied this appetite by combining historical episodes with the massively emotive forms of not only vast canvases (Surikov, Vasnetsov), but also long operas (Mussorgsky) and epic novels (Tolstoy, Dostoevsky). The representation of biblical events as historical subjects, with moral rather than theological overtones, also became common at this time. The role of Christian iconography in the development of Realist and Romantic art in Russia is the subject of Chapter 2.

This desire to see contemporary art as the consummation of a historical tradition continued into the twentieth century. 'Neo-primitivist' artists rejected the evocative imaginings of Romanticism, partly because the naturalistic style of Romantic art was illusionistic – and therefore deceptive – and partly because it was associated with the aesthetic elitism of the West. In order to develop an art that was both popular and Russian, and yet had its own artistic integrity, these artists (including Mikhail Larionov, Natalia Goncharova and Malevich) introduced elements of the simplicity and directness of traditional Russian arts and crafts, including icons, into their work. The immediacy of traditional styles increasingly encouraged artists to invest the significance of their art in its optical impact, dispensing with conventional frames of reference. The very process by which the old world was fragmented and destroyed – as manifest in Cubo-Futurism – became the way in which the new world could be seen as a dynamic and multifaceted whole. The Constructivists, who picked up the pieces, were inspired by the fully integrated social function of icons, as well as the down-to-earth manner in which icons were traditionally constructed; both qualities resonated with their ideal of shared socialist workmanship. The way in which the artistic elements of icons were absorbed and transformed by avant-garde artists at the beginning of the twentieth century is addressed in Chapter 3.

Kazimir Malevich was influenced by icons at every stage of his career. During his life, his understanding of icons grew progressively deeper, moving from their poetic mystique, through their artistic and social significance, towards their metaphysical status. The essence of icons resonated at the heart of his work, as if guiding it from within itself towards its own perfection: as his sensitivity towards the significance of icons deepened, so his own art moved gradually towards an ever greater realisation of its own nature, until the true nature of Suprematism was completely realised – like that of icons – in self-transcendence. The transcendental nature of icons and Suprematism is the subject of Chapter 4.

Approaching its subject from this point of view, *The Avant-Garde Icon* explores the self-transcendence of Suprematism as the realisation of the spiritual significance of icons in a modern idiom – the integration of an ancient spiritual truth into a modern form of culture. By re-evaluating Malevich's work in the context of its spiritual implications, the study releases Suprematism from the context of cerebral idealism in which it is usually seen and which, by virtue of its dependence on rationalist categories, inherently obviates the possibility of spiritual awakening beyond the rational mind. At the same time, by exploring the potential of icons in the context of the modern world, it liberates them from a mass of traditional Christian conventions that frequently prevents contemporary western culture from fully appreciating their original significance.

The identification of icons with Suprematism (especially as realised in its most extreme form, Malevich's series of *White on White* paintings, Plate 91) is based on the intuition that God – or, in Malevich's case, a nameless absolute or ultimate reality – is already inherently incarnated in and as the world: that is to say, the spiritual nature of the world is already accomplished; it does not need to be facilitated in any way by human thought or action. It is not absent, therefore it does not need to be 'sought' or 'found'. In relation to icons, the present reality of the Divine was believed to have been completed 2000 years ago by the miraculous incarnation of Christ; in relation to Malevich, this reality is true on existential grounds. Reality is already maximally real; nothing can be done to make it more (or less) real. In both cases, the creative potential of life is not to be realised through the strategic production of works of art. It is to be found in a contemplative state of being in which the present fullness of reality is simply recognised and the mind, perpetually transcending itself and its self-defining need for a finite object, is multiplied by infinity. In this context, the value of art lies not so much in the works of art themselves, or even in the transformative impact they have on the passive viewer (as if they were magical objects), but in the enduring state of creative consciousness that pre-exists and generates them, and which is suddenly seen to pre-exist and generate the subjective mind of the viewer too.

The consummation of Malevich's work coincided with the Russian Revolution. Prior to this time, many artists conflated the revival of traditional Russian culture, the perfection of modern art and the promise of political change into one momentous ideal. In a mad moment of optimism, these hopes were somehow seen to necessitate each other and to prefigure the inevitable and total transformation of Russia (and eventually the whole world). After the Revolution, when that ideal was shattered and many artists became disenchanted, the peculiar logic that bound avant-garde art to icons was lost. However, icons continued to be invoked – partly ridiculed, partly exploited – in the early Soviet period. Initially, it was the narrative and didactic conventions of icon painting, subliminally associated with the transmission of truth by the Russian people, which were harnessed to the new ideology. From the 1930s, as Stalin rose to power, an interest in the narrative and didactic potential of icons was slowly superseded by an awareness of their potential as a focus for cultish psychology, which Stalin was quick to exploit in developing his own personality cult. The Soviet usurpation of icons, and of the suggestible psychology that existed around them, is the subject of Chapter 5.

Throughout the early Soviet period, when the conflicting values of the pre-revolutionary years became formally polarised, critics took it upon themselves to act as mediators for the new culture, with a vocational sense of responsibility to both the past and the present for 'revealing the hidden collective principles and organisational meaning of old art'.[1] Following the Russian Revolution, Anatolii Lunacharsky, the cultural minister from 1917 to 1929, attempted to strike a balance between the two worlds:

> We acknowledge the proletariat's absolute right to make a careful re-examination of all those elements of world art that it has inherited and to affirm the truism that the new proletarian and socialist art can be built only on the foundation of all our acquisitions from the past. At the same time we acknowledge that the preservation and utilisation of the genuine artistic values that we have acquired from the old culture is an indisputable task of the Soviet government. In this respect the legacy of the past must be cleared ruthlessly of all those admixtures of

> bourgeois degeneration and corruption; cheap pornography, philistine vulgarity, intellectual boredom, anti-revolutionary and religious prejudices – insofar as such admixtures are contained in our legacy from the past – must be removed. In those cases where dubious elements are linked indissolubly with genuine artistic achievements, it is essential to take steps to ensure that the new young, mass proletarian public evaluate critically the spiritual nourishment provided it. In general the proletariat must assimilate the legacy of the old culture not as a pupil, but as a powerful, conscious and incisive critic.[2]

The Soviet government exploited and undermined the religious heritage of Russia simultaneously. On the one hand, it destroyed old allegiances to the Church and Christianity by exposing the inconsistent, irrational and absurd forms of religious culture in Russia – particularly in relation to superstitious belief and the abuse of power by the clergy. On the other hand, it indulged the invisible dynamics of religious psychology – reducing an instinct for the transcendental source condition of life to a chronic dependency on an absolute political authority – by directing it towards itself and its own programmes of salvation. Although a tendency towards collectivism and passivity has, for many years, been considered by some to be an innately Russian quality,[3] the impossibility of containing and controlling the 'Russian soul' in a closed political form has also been widely recognised – long before it re-manifest itself as the dissolution of the Soviet Union in 1991. Shortly before he died in 1881, Dostoevsky wrote of the 'ceaseless longing which has always been inherent in the Russian people, for a great, general, universal union of brotherhood in the name of Christ' and how 'it is not in Communism, not in mechanical forms that we find the socialism of the Russian people: they believe that salvation is ultimately to be found in worldwide union in the name of Christ': 'And if this union does not yet exist, if the Church has not yet been fully established – not merely in prayers alone but in fact – then the instinct for this Church and the ceaseless longing for it is still to be found in the hearts of the millions of our people'.[4]

Following the death of Stalin in 1953 and the subsequent demise of his personality cult, icons ceased to set a consistent precedent, however distorted, for the expression of a cultural life in Russia. Since the fall of communism, they have however become the focus of new interest in Russia, albeit partly as an expression of dissociation from the Soviet regime. How they might contribute, once again, to the regeneration of contemporary culture in Russia remains to be seen.

NOTES

1. Bogdanov, A., *Proletariat i iskusstvo* (*The Proletariat and Art*), 1918, quoted in Bowlt (1988), p.177.
2. Lunacharsky, A. & Slavinsky, Y., *Tesizy khudozhestvennogo sektora NKP i TsK Rabis ob osnovakh politiki v oblasti iskusstva*, 1920, quoted in Bowlt (1988), p.184. Together with Alexander Bogdanov and the writer Maxim Gorky, Anatolii Lunacharsky was instrumental in the emergence of 'God-building', an intellectual orientation that attempted to liberate the spiritual instinct of the Russian people from its conventional religious accretions and reconcile it with the revolutionary vision of the Bolsheviks. The movement developed from 1905. See Stites and Kline.
3. See, for example, Rancour-Laferriere.
4. Dostoevsky, F., *A Writer's Diary*, trans. K. Lantz, London, 1994, vol.2, p.1351, quoted in Figes (2002), p.340.

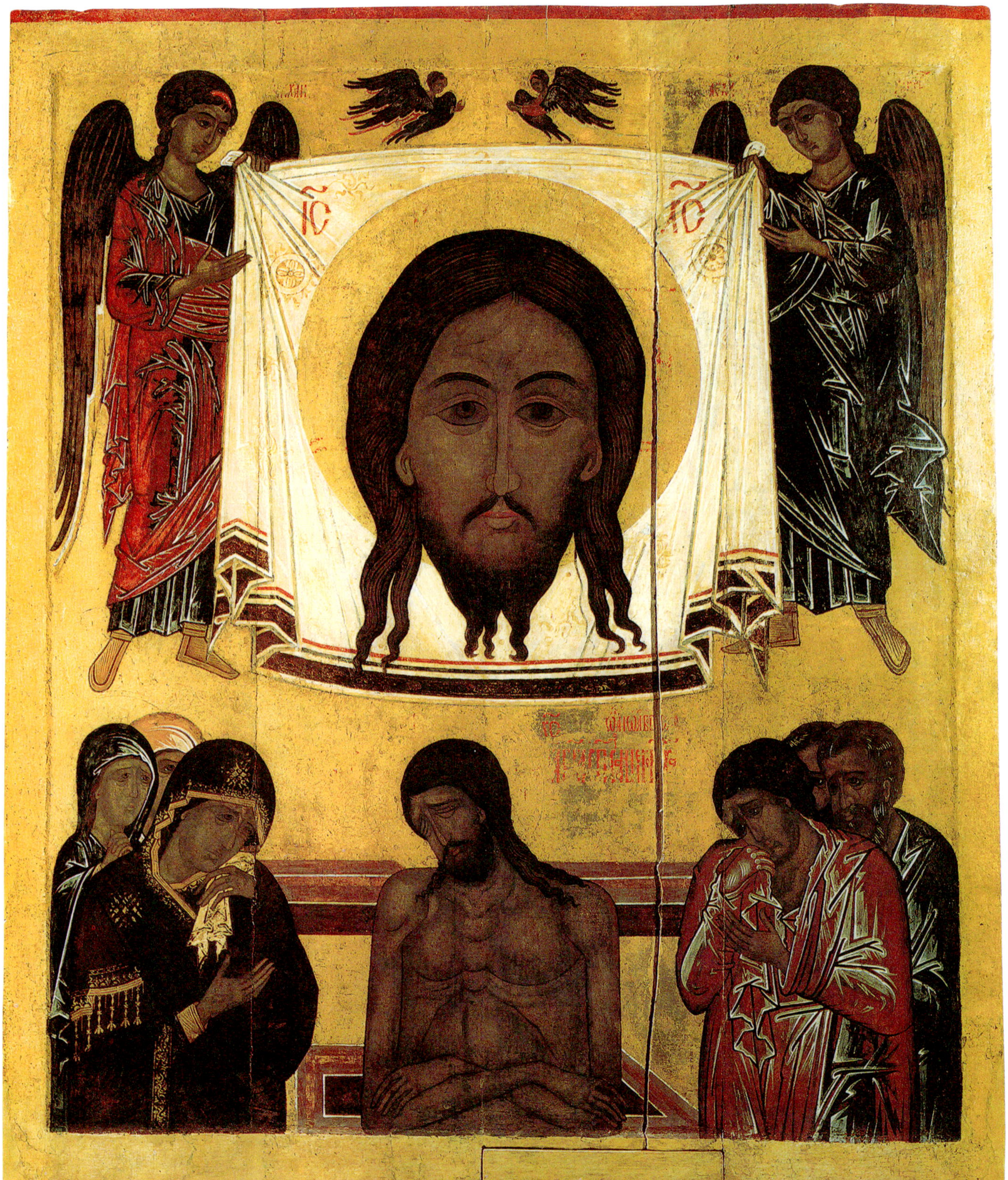

1

Icons: An Introduction

By the time Christianity was introduced to Russia in the tenth century, the status of icons as a form of sacred art had already been established for several centuries. The struggle to create a form of art that could communicate the mystery of the incarnate God had taken place in the context of the Eastern Church, independent of the Western Church since Constantine's foundation of Constantinople as an alternative imperial capital to Rome in the fourth century. From the outset, the idea of religious images had been tainted by their association with pagan idolatry, though, ironically, the earliest Christian images were heavily indebted to their Classical precedents. Over the years, numerous arguments both for and against images were developed. From a philosophical point of view, any attempt to represent the Infinite in a finite form was considered illogical and therefore deluded. From a religious point of view, representations of the Divine contravened the biblical commandment against 'graven images' and were therefore blasphemous. The development of a purely symbolic tradition of Orthodox iconography, which could have deflected such accusations of idolatry as it did in the West, was also thwarted. In the year 692, a Church council in Constantinople (the Quinisext Council in Trullo) decreed that it was inappropriate to represent Christ as, say, a lamb because he was *not* a lamb; he should be depicted as a man.[1] In retrospect, this fervent espousal of literalism, rather than symbolism, anticipated the later sacramental approach that maintained that icons do not so much represent Christ – as if he were their 'subject matter' – as actually realise him in an extended material form. Although icons are of course replete with symbolic meanings, this adherence to their sacramental significance, over their symbolic significance, is crucial to their true identity and accounts for the comparatively limited range of iconographic subjects in Orthodox art.

The dialectical process of challenging and justifying Christian imagery continued for decades, eventually coming to a head in the 'iconoclastic controversy' in the eighth and ninth centuries when figurative representations of religious figures were forbidden and countless sacred images were destroyed. One of the reasons for the timing of the crisis was the influence of Islam, a new and iconoclastic religion which had been spreading throughout the Byzantine Empire since its origin in the seventh century. Some

1
Mandylion, 1570
Tempera on wooden panel
140 x 118 cm (55⅛ x 46½ in)
Kolomenskoye District Museum

commentators surmised that imagery angered God, associating the success of Islam with its rejection of images.[2] Nevertheless, the iconodules (supporters of religious imagery) eventually prevailed over the iconoclasts (opponents of religious imagery – literally 'image-breakers'), and a theology of icons was drawn up at the Seventh Ecumenical Council of 787 (the second Council of Nicaea); it was confirmed at the end of the iconoclastic controversy in 843.[3] Despite this victory – known as the 'Triumph of Orthodoxy' – the development of Orthodox iconography was profoundly influenced by iconoclasm in ways that differentiate it significantly from western art. Reservations about representing the Infinite in finite form resulted in the total absence from Orthodoxy of images of God the Father (with lapses from the fifteenth century onwards when European influence began to assert itself).[4] God had chosen to incarnate Himself as Christ the Son, but not as the Father; the incarnation of God as Christ, therefore, legitimised the representation of God *as Christ* but not as the Father.

As far as images were concerned, the important principle was that arbitrary subjectivity, the source of all error, should be avoided at all costs; a supernatural precedent and justification had to be found for all traditions. For this reason, it also came about that the Resurrection of Christ was never represented in traditional Orthodox iconography. As the moment of the Resurrection had not been witnessed by human eyes, it was considered inappropriate to 'imagine' it. Icons of the Anastasis (the apocryphal descent of Christ into hell after the Crucifixion and before the Resurrection, believed to have been witnessed by Adam and Eve, Plate 2)[5] and the Three Marys at the Tomb were seen to refer to the Resurrection without actually addressing it, and were used instead. A similar compromise with the iconoclasts' reservations about religious imagery lies behind

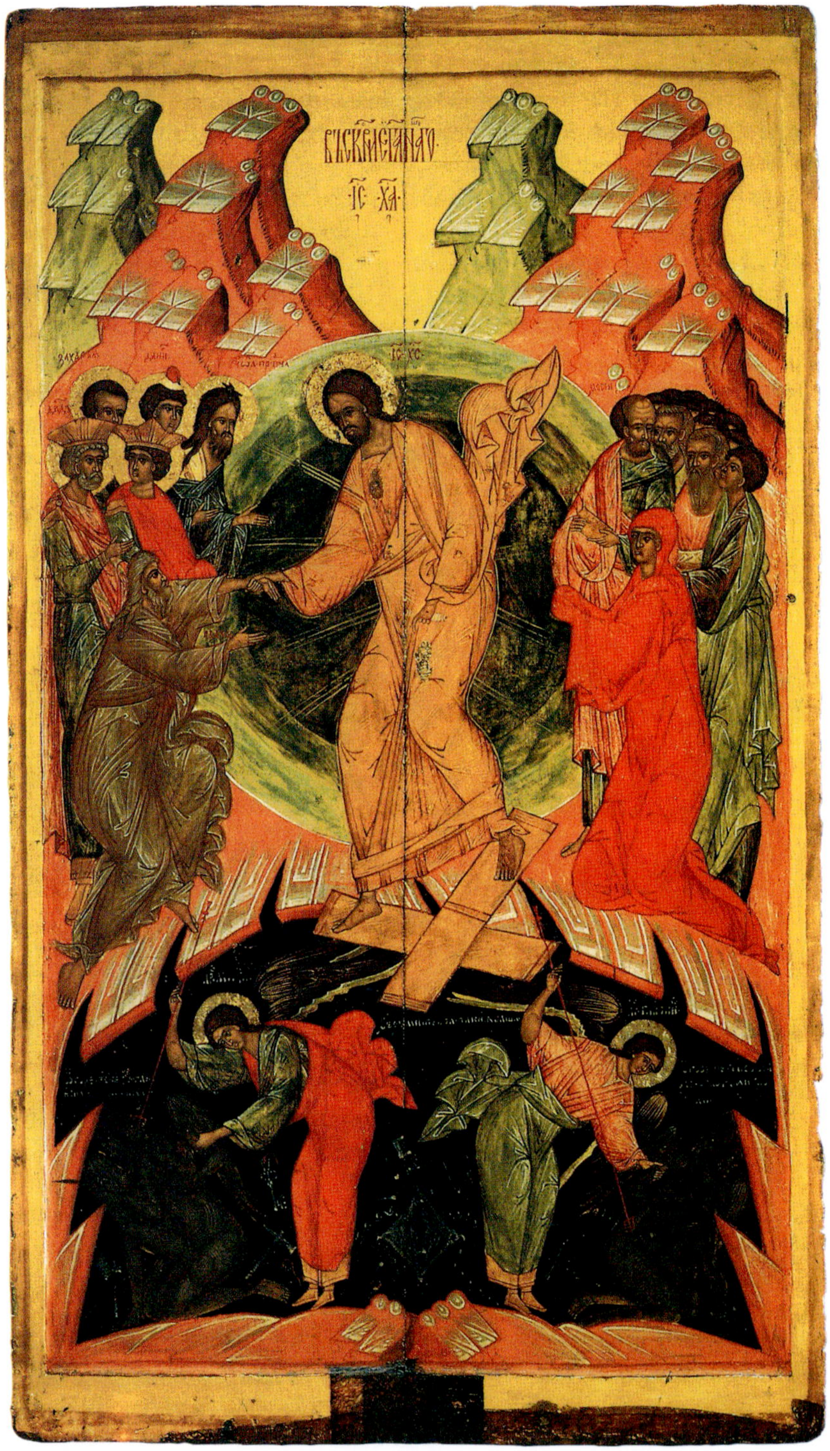

the absence of three-dimensional sculpture from the Orthodox Church. The only exceptions to this rule are low reliefs, mostly made of precious stone, ivory, wood or metal (Plates 58, 94). Besides contravening the Old Testament commandment that man should not create 'graven images', three-dimensional sculptures were believed to be physically inhabitable by pagan demons. The same was not true of flat – or shallow – images which were too thin to accommodate them.[6]

Due to the primarily sacramental status of images, there is – again, in contrast to the West – very little strictly narrative art in the post-iconoclast Orthodox Church. One of the reasons for this was that it was typical in the Eastern Church to translate the scriptures and liturgy into the language of the converted people. Alphabets were created where necessary – an Armenian alphabet, for instance, in the fifth century and the Cyrillic alphabet, drawn up by St Cyril and St Methodius for the Slavonic world, in the tenth century. As a result, the scriptures were immediately comprehensible to the entire community (only becoming obscure in later centuries when spoken languages began to diverge from written traditions) and it was unnecessary to use icons for story-telling. Although scenes from the life of Christ and the Mother of God were frequently represented in icons, these are primarily approached as celebrations of church festivals, with their own feast days, rather than as a means of telling stories. In the West, by contrast, although the scriptures were translated into Latin – the native tongue of the Romans – they were not understood by most of the inhabitants of the Roman Empire who spoke indigenous languages. Latin became the preserve of the educated clergy in the West, continuing to be used for scriptural and liturgical texts until the Renaissance. As a result, an alternative tradition of popular story-telling – narrative iconography – had to evolve. Subsequently a tradition of didactic, symbolic, narrative and emotive imagery developed in the West, in strict contrast to the sacramental tradition of the East which western theologians considered to be cultish and idolatrous.

Despite the various conditions that arose around the Orthodox use of imagery, an official theology of icons was eventually developed on the basis of the fundamental belief of Christianity – that the Divine was and is incarnated in the world as Christ. This theology maintained that, by incarnating in matter as Christ, God established a principle on the basis of which it was subsequently lawful and appropriate to represent the Divine in material form. Icons were said to be an application of this principle. Like the eucharist, they were regarded as extensions of the body of Christ. Their aesthetic impact was of no great significance; even their symbolic meaning was secondary. It was their sacramentality that counted. One witness, Paul of Aleppo, Archdeacon of Antioch, who visited Russia in the middle of the sixteenth century, wrote: 'As all Muscovites are known for their great affection and love of icons, they consider neither the beauty of the image nor the art of painting. For them, all icons, beautiful or not, are the same'.[7] One hundred years later, Joseph Vladimirov, a friend of the controversial, westernising icon painter Simon Ushakov and one of the first Russian writers to value and defend artistic quality in icons, accused 'unscrupulous merchants' of telling buyers of icons that 'salvation cannot be gained by good painting and that among the miraculous icons there were many that were badly painted'.[8] On some occasions, such as when cult images of saints were made of edible substances for the purpose of healing, the distinction between icon and eucharist became blurred.[9] According to theologians, the

2

Anastasis, Vologda,
early 16th century
Tempera on wooden panel
125 x 71 cm (49¼ x 28 in)
Russian Museum,
St Petersburg

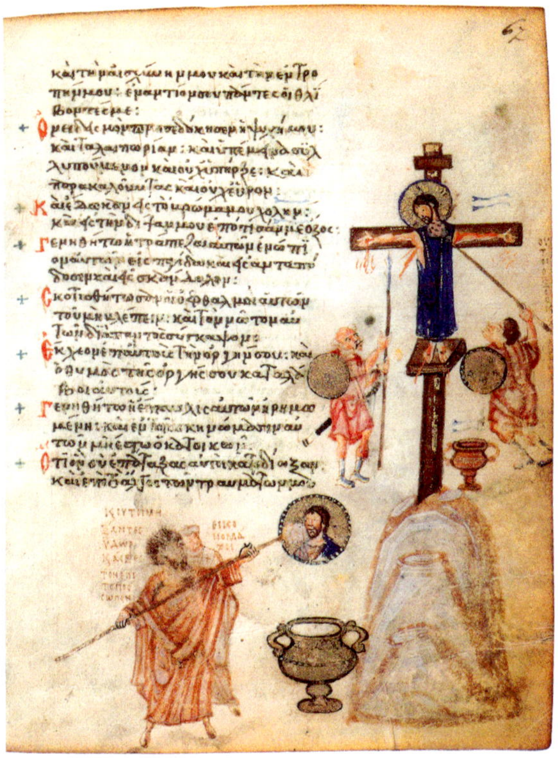

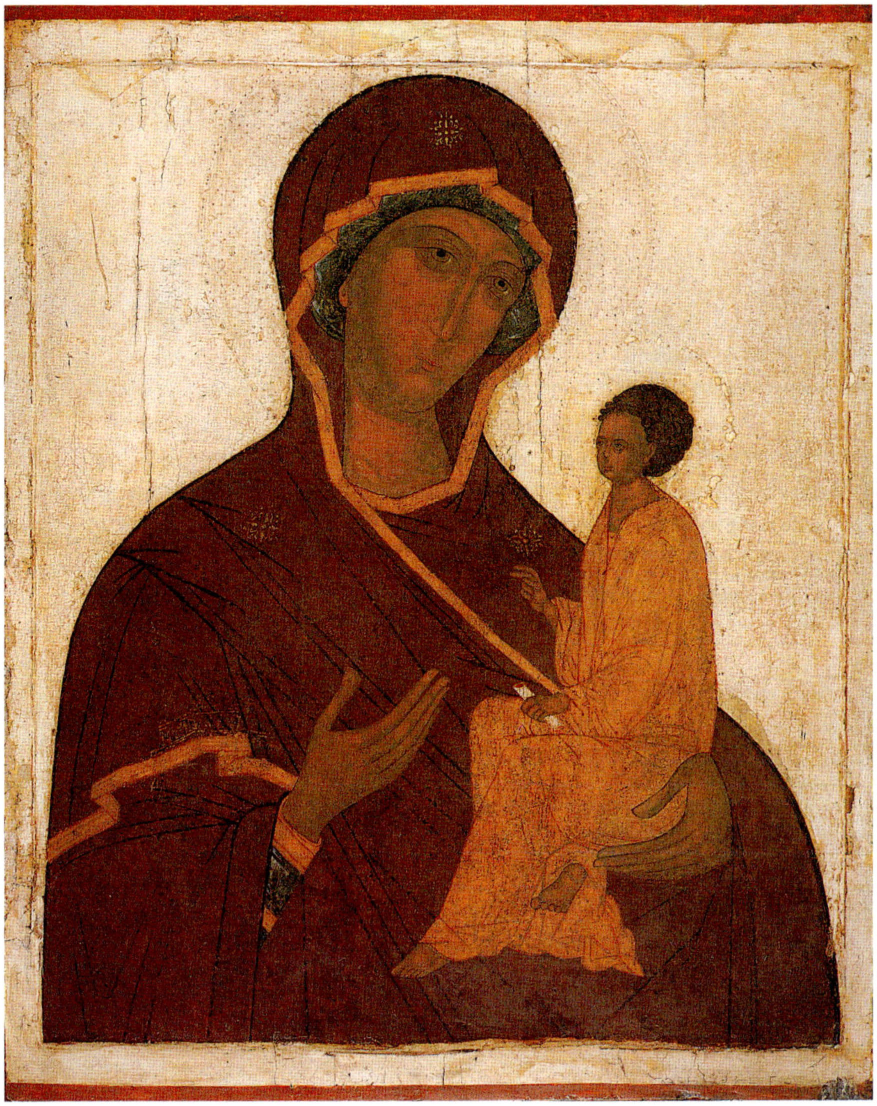

3.

Khludov Psalter, *c.*850-900
19.5 x 15 cms (7¾ x 6 inches)
State Historical Museum,
Moscow

4

Tichvin Mother of God with Christ ('Hodigitria'), Moscow,
16th century
Tempera on wooden panel
111 x 88 cm (43¾ x 34⅝ in)
Temple Gallery, London

inherently spiritual nature of icons was 'proven' by the fact of the incarnation. Icon painting came to be recognised as an innately sacred form of art that originated, and continued to subsist, in the incarnation of Christ. Conversely the wholesale destruction of icons by the iconoclasts was actually equated with – and not simply compared to – participation in the Crucifixion. A ninth-century monk, St Theodore the Studite, described an occasion at which Jews subjected an icon of Christ to exactly the same torments as Christ himself had suffered – mocking, nailing, beating, sponging with vinegar – and how the icon bled when it was finally pierced.[10] The same point is made on a contemporary psalter (plate 3) where an image of an iconoclast whitewashing an icon is juxtaposed with an image of the Crucifixion. Ironically in this case, an indignant reader has angrily erased the face of the iconoclast (but not those of the two men crucifying Christ), further reflecting the iconophiles' belief in the power of images to actually incarnate what they represent.[11]

For theologians and scholars the theology of icons was formulated as a rational proposition. However, for the vast majority of people, to whom such ideas were either unknown or incomprehensible, the same teaching was communicated through legends about the historical origins of icons. According to one tradition, dating from the sixth century, the first ever icon was 'not made by human hands' but was miraculously created by Christ himself. This tradition maintains that during the lifetime of Christ there was a king, Abgar of Edessa (in Syria), who was taken ill and whose physicians could not cure him. On hearing of the extraordinary healing powers of Christ, King Abgar sent a messenger, Ananias, to Christ asking him to come to Edessa to heal him. Christ is said to have refused the invitation but, rather than send the messenger away empty-handed, he wiped his face on a piece of cloth and gave it to the messenger to give to the king. When Christ returned the cloth to Ananias, his facial features were miraculously imprinted on it – as in the western legend of the veil of St Veronica (*vera icon* – literally, a 'true image'). Ananias returned to Edessa with the cloth and the king was duly healed by it. This sacred relic, called the mandylion (Plate 1), is represented in innumerable icons; it is both the subject and exemplar of the icon-painting tradition.[12]

A second story, also dating to the sixth century, maintains that the first ever icon was painted by the Evangelist Luke. The icon is said to have been painted from life and it represented the Mother of God with the Christ Child on her lap. Subsequent icons of the Virgin and Child (Plate 4) are said to have stemmed from this image and are believed by the faithful to be accurate representations of the holy couple.[13] As late as the nineteenth century, an elderly monk on Mount Athos, saved from the Greek War of Independence as a small child in 1821, could claim that he had never seen a woman in his entire life and that he presumed that all women resembled the Mother of God as depicted in icons.[14] The occasion of Luke's painting of the Mother of God and Christ itself became a subject for illustration at least as early as the eleventh century – since which time St Luke has been revered as the patron saint of painters.[15] The purpose of these legends, like that of the theological explanations that paralleled them, was to confirm that the tradition of icon painting was inaugurated and sanctioned by Christ himself and was not merely an arbitrary invention of the human imagination – an orientation towards the transpersonal source of authority that would re-emerge in Orthodox Russia in years to come, in many different ways.

It was not until the fifteenth century that icon

painting came into its own in Russia. This was facilitated by a number of developments that had taken place in the previous century. From a political point of view, the gradual rise of Muscovy and the decisive (although not final) victory by the Russians over the occupying Tatars at the Battle of Kulikovo in 1380 had paved the way for a resurgence of national self-esteem. In 1453, Constantinople, the capital of the Byzantine Empire, fell to the Ottoman Turks and the seat of Orthodoxy moved to Moscow, which came to be known as the 'Third Rome'. From a spiritual point of view, the influence of the monastic disciplines of hesychasm, an ancient tradition of unceasing prayer that was revived on Mount Athos in the fourteenth century, led to a period of intense mystical and religious fervour in Russia, especially following the legitimisation of the teachings of St Gregory Palamas in 1341 and 1351.[16] This new fervour was paralleled by the development of the iconostasis (Plates 5, 86) – originally a simple rail demarcating the sanctuary area in Byzantine churches – to a wall-to-wall, floor-to-vault screen of icons that completely separated the sanctuary of a Russian church from its congregational area. The screen served both to conceal the consecration of the sacraments from the view of the laity and to provide a theophany of the divine order through the tiers of icons that adorn it. At a practical level, it adapted the iconographic programmes of Byzantine churches, usually executed in mosaic or fresco on stone or brick walls, to the all-wood environment of most Russian churches.

The peak of the icon-painting tradition is usually associated with Andrei Rublev (*c.*1370–1430). Although little information about Rublev survives, his legendary status is sufficient to have led to his canonisation in 1988, an achievement which now makes it legitimate in the Orthodox Church to paint and venerate icons of him. Rublev is known to have worked with Theophanes the Greek (a Byzantine painter from Constantinople) at the Cathedral of the Annunciation in the Kremlin, Moscow, in 1405 and the icons that are attributed to him are clearly indebted to his master's genius. They achieve the same combination of monumental grandeur and tender simplicity, penetrating directness and abiding patience. His icon of the *Old Testament Trinity* (Plate 6), painted for the iconostasis of the Cathedral of the Trinity at Sergeev Posad (where he was a monk), differs from Theophanes' fresco of the same subject in the Church of the Transfiguration in Novgorod in that it omits all reference to the narrative context of the image. The image represents the 'three men in white' (shown as angels) who came to Abraham and Sarah to tell them that they would have a child, despite their age, and to whom the couple showed hospitality under the tree of Mamre (Genesis, chapter 18). It came to be used as the key image of the Trinity in the Orthodox tradition, partly because it was believed to be the first visible revelation of Divinity to man but also because it provided an image through which to represent the Godhead without representing God the Father specifically – significantly, the individual angels were not, at this stage, associated with specific persons of the Trinity, an imprecision that enabled the image to remain mystically unknowable. Rublev characteristically passes over the inessential details of the subject, reducing the image to its contemplative essence – the Unity and Trinity of the Godhead. The icon is imbued with the contemplative spirit of hesychasm. Although it has subsequently given rise to endless debate regarding its meaning, it is not primarily a theological statement. In this important respect, it epitomises Russian icon painting at its most pure and intense, silently revealing the triune God to the inner eye, or heart,

5

Interior of the Annunciation Cathedral in the Moscow Kremlin (1489) with late 14th- and early 15th-century icons on the iconostasis and 16th-century frescos

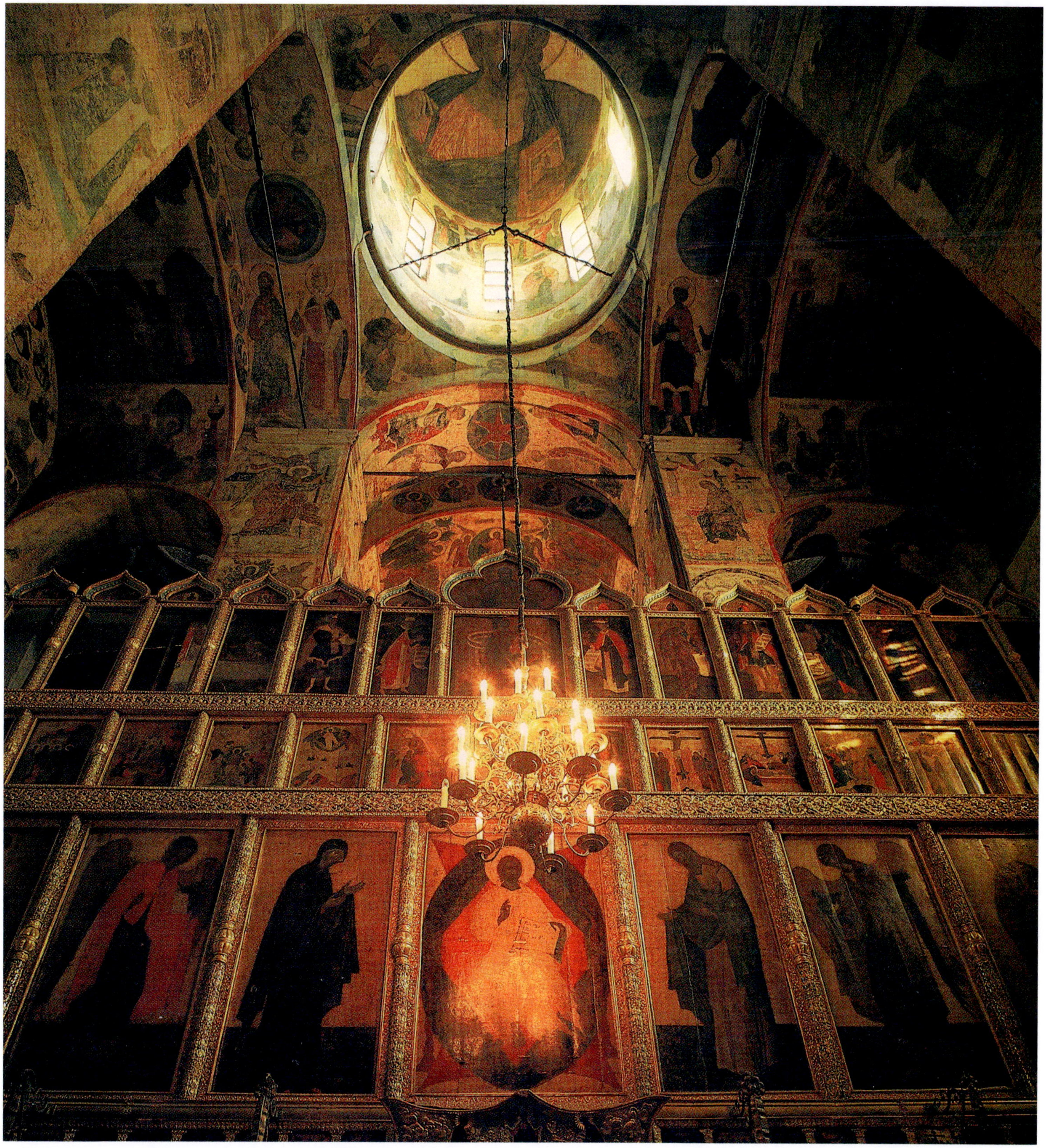

of the faithful. The theologian-philosopher Pavel Florensky said of the icon that it is, in itself, 'proof of the existence of God'.

In contrast to the luxury materials that were available to Byzantine craftsmen, the one material that was accessible to Russian craftsmen, almost exclusively, and that had been worked locally for centuries, was wood. For most of the peasant population, all manufactured objects, from buildings and bridges to household utensils, were made of this material; wooden churches were assembled without nails; peasants' shoes were made of bark, well into the twentieth century. Russian icons were also made of wood, and painted with natural pigments from the earth, unlike Byzantine icons which were made in a wide range of materials (silver, enamel and precious stones, as well as wood). In contrast to objects made of other materials which, together with the craftsmen skilled at working them, often had to be imported, the materials and craftsmanship of icons was entirely indigenous, a characteristic that gave them a special integrity and a unique affinity with the motherland. While the influence of western styles can be seen in medieval Russian architecture, sculpture and manuscript illumination, western European icon painters and paintings are unheard of.[17] This remained the case even when icons first began to show signs of European influence. Such conservatism was not merely a practical matter; it also became a matter of religious and national pride, a means of articulating belief in the unique spiritual mission and destiny of Russia. The particular sanctity ascribed to painted wooden icons – in contrast to other religious artefacts in other media – continued untouched long after the circumstances that first determined their physical appearance ceased to apply. It was not until the seventeenth century that the rigidly traditional status of icons came to be seen as an anomaly, causing the icon painter Joseph Vladimirov, touched by the liberal rationalism of the West, to ask:

> Canst thou possibly say that only Russians are capable of painting icons, that only icons of Russian painting should be venerated, and that those of other lands should neither be accepted

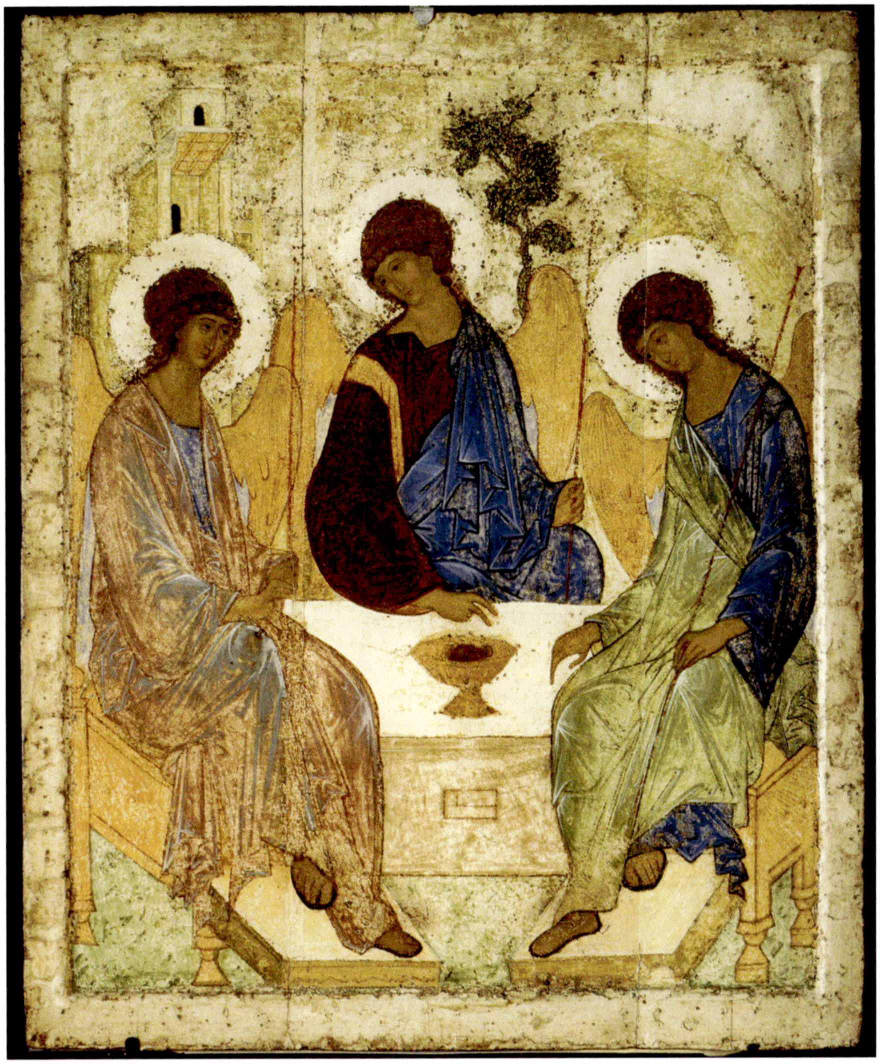

6
Andrei Rublev

Old Testament Trinity, from the Cathedral of the Trinity, Sergeev Posad, *c.*1411–20
Tempera on wooden panel
142 x 114 cm (55⅞ x 44⅞ in)
Tretyakov Gallery, Moscow

> nor honoured? Ask thy fathers or the elders, and they will tell thee that in all our Christian Russian churches the church plate, chasubles, omophoria, altar cloths and palls, ornamental and gold cloths, precious stones and pearls – you receive all these from foreigners and bring them into church to adorn the altar and icons with no thought of their being good or bad.[18]

The questioning of traditional values associated with the sacred tradition of icon painting signals the beginning of its decline. This shift corresponds to the waning of the Middle Ages in Europe, but unlike medieval culture in Europe, the equivalent in Russia was not displaced by a Renaissance. There were some attempts to rationalise Christian belief (often manifest as outbursts of heretical iconoclasm) and there was growing concern over the level of political motivation in the Church, particularly with regard to landownership, but nothing resembling a secularising western-style Renaissance took place in Russia. This divergence from the West was reinforced by the fact that the Classical values reworked during the Renaissance in Europe and especially Italy – the home of those values – had no historical root in the collective memory of the Russian people. This was partly due to the eastern tradition, already mentioned, of translating the scriptures and liturgy into the language of a new people as soon as they were converted. One side-effect of this tradition was that the clergy did not have automatic access to the literature and learning of the Classical world – as they did in the West – and, as a result, the Classical tradition did not become a natural part of their heritage. Consequently, there was no nostalgic or nationalistic motive in sixteenth-century Russia for a revival of Classical values, despite some attempts to trace the ancestry of the tsars (from the word 'Caesar') back to the Roman Emperor Augustus. Although signs of European influence did penetrate into Russia in the sixteenth century, it was not until Peter the Great began his systematic westernisation of Russian culture towards the end of the seventeenth century that the country began to undergo anything approaching a Renaissance – and even then, the change was initially cosmetic, prompted more by the appeal of western autocracy than by the virtues of Renaissance humanism.

Despite the absence of a Renaissance in sixteenth-century Russia, a disintegration of the typically medieval interrelationship between spiritual life and popular culture did begin to take place. This is immediately apparent in icons of the period which become more aesthetically self-conscious and decorative in their appearance (Plate 128), and more rationalised in their iconography – in both cases subject to the influence of western art. The contemplative awareness that characterises the expressions of the saints in medieval icons, and which calls for a corresponding orientation on the part of the viewer, is strangely lacking. Moreover, in the absence of such awareness, the attitude of the people became increasingly polarised between credulous superstition on the one hand, and rationalising doubt and atheism on the other.

Attempts to preserve the pure tradition of icon painting by formalising it were made but, ironically, they had the opposite of the desired effect. In fact, they further undermined the principle of insight and experience on which the tradition was based. The tendency towards formalisation crystallised at the Hundred Chapters Council or *Stoglav* of 1551, convened to address the growing laxity of religious life in the Church. Following the destruction of many churches and icons in the great fire that swept through the wooden city of Moscow in 1547, the Council also took advantage of the opportunity to regulate Orthodox policy on icons.[19] The cerebral attitude of the councillors may have reflected a degree of influence from Renaissance rationalism, but as they approached each inconsistency on its own terms, without regard for the broader implications, they created as many problems as they solved. For instance, controversy arose again over the question of representing God the Father in figurative form, as it had centuries earlier in Byzantium. In strict contrast to the mystical and contemplative approach of Andrei Rublev, some theologians attempted to solve the riddle of the Old Testament Trinity by identifying each of the angels with a specific person of the Trinity. It was suggested that the building behind the left-hand angel represented the Temple of the Old Testament, or the Heavenly Jerusalem, and should therefore be associated with God the Father; the tree behind the central angel symbolised the cross, identifying that angel as Christ (in such interpretations, the central angel is given a cruciform halo, as in Plate 84); and the rocky ascent behind the angel on the right was symbolic of monastic retreat and spiritual ascent and was therefore associated with the Holy Spirit.[20]

This attempt to develop a rational programme for the Old Testament Trinity met with immediate opposition. Conservatives believed that even the slightest suggestion that one of the angels might represent God the Father was to contradict the principle, established at the Triumph of Orthodoxy in 843, that the Incarnation of God in Christ set a precedent for representations of Christ in icons, but not of God the Father. The problem was made worse by the fact that a new, untraditional representation of the Trinity, known as the New Testament Trinity (or the Paternity of God), in which God the Father is explicitly represented as an old man with a white beard, was becoming popular at this time.[21] The image of God the Father (which was common in the West) was excused in these cases because it represented a prophetic *vision* of God (as 'the Ancient of Days' or 'Lord God of Sabaoth'), as narrated in the apocalyptic book of Daniel (chapter 7, verse 9), rather than an actual optical sighting of him; it was therefore considered to be illustrative rather than idolatrous. Similarly, depictions of the Holy Spirit as a dove were defended against the charge of illegitimate imagined symbolism on the grounds that the Spirit was actually described as a dove in the biblical narration of the baptism of Christ and therefore had divine sanction. The same case was made for the hand of God, represented in one of the top corners of many icons, symbolising God's blessing. Though it could be wrongly understood by some to imply that God has a body, the 'hand of God' is mentioned many times in the Bible and was therefore also considered 'precedented' and legitimate (Plates 53, 75).

To discover an iconography of the Trinity that did justice both to the incarnate Christ and the disincarnate Godhead simultaneously was of course an impossible and illogical task. In the absence of a conclusive rational solution, the Hundred Chapters Council simply agreed that icons of the Old Testament Trinity were to be painted 'according to the ancient models', mentioning by name Andrei Rublev, renowned for his mystical fervour and piety as well as his gifts as an icon painter. *Podlinniki* (iconographic manuals) were also introduced in order to formalise and regulate canons of iconography. Above all, subjective invention, which appeared to threaten and undermine the antiquity and objectivity of Christian truth, was strictly forbidden.[22] Although this stipulation was entirely consistent with traditional attitudes towards icon painting, which had always been based on copying models, the need to rationalise the process reflected the fact that the contemplative spirit that had spontaneously supported the tradition from within itself for centuries no longer prevailed. A subtle shift had taken place. Icon painters continued to copy prototypes as instructed, but it was as if they now copied them (focusing on their physical attributes) because they had lost touch with the spirit of the tradition, rather than because they were engaging with that tradition as a sacramental medium for the transmission of the incarnate God to the world.

The movement away from the traditionally contemplative function of icons towards a more rational approach was also reflected in the development of a new canon of theological and didactic iconography. Verse-by-verse illustrations of the Creed and other scriptures, encouraging credulity over devotion, became commonplace. Apart from sacrificing the simplicity of design characteristic of so many earlier icons (and so conducive to their contemplative function), much of the later iconography was so abstruse (though decorative) that it could not be understood without explanatory inscriptions – even by monks, who are known to have complained about their obscurity.[23] Some didactic examples, in which each verse of a text is represented in its own compartment with its own inscription, resemble diagrams more than cult objects and may be indebted to Protestant sources.

In the light of this, it is not surprising that, although icons did continue to be painted in traditional styles as well as westernised ones until the communist era, post-sixteenth-century icons often lack the depth of feeling that is characteristic of earlier icons. This was partly due to the fact that the main source of icon painting had shifted from a widely dispersed network of monasteries to the Armoury Chamber in the Kremlin – the tsar's court workshop in Moscow – in which it had to compete with secular arts. By the end of the sixteenth century, the distinctive sanctity of the iconic form had become so corrupted that the technique and style of icon painting was being used for secular portraiture, the earliest form of the genre in Russia. Such portraits (or '*parsuna*') were posthumous funerary images, and were no doubt expected to bless if not to sacralise their subjects.[24] In due course, signs of Classical and naturalistic influence from western Europe (perspective, illusionism, chiaroscuro, Classical architectural details etc.) began to appear in Russian painting, undermining the traditional impression of gravity, austerity and otherworldliness. An illusion of three-dimensional depth was created and backgrounds were furnished with luminous skies and trees, stimulating the imagination – in strict contrast to the traditional orientation, according to which the possibilities of the aberrant imagination were to be rigorously submitted to the revelation of certain truth. Human features were realistically modelled, and a quality of personal self-consciousness and charm crept into the facial expressions. In the 1660s and 1670s, the icons of Simon Ushakov, in which the facial features and hands of the figures are naturalistically modelled for the first time, albeit in a primitive way, were criticised for their lusciousness and sensuality. Archpriest Avvakum, founder of the ultra-conservative Old Believers (assembled in the late 1650s in reaction to Church reforms), commented on the puffy faces, red lips and curly hair of such figure types, considering them to have been made, under foreign influence, 'for carnal reasons, because the heretics love sensuality and do not care for higher things'.[25] Emotive imagery showing scenes from the Passion of Christ, a staple ingredient of Catholic piety since the late Middle Ages but relatively understated in the Orthodox tradition, became widespread.[26] Such iconography reflected the newly evolved tendency away from Orthodox conformity to a triumphant, resurrected divinity, and towards personal feeling and sentimentality. By the end of the eighteenth century, although many of the conventional routines of church life continued to be rehearsed, the awareness of the presence of the Risen Christ that had informed and sustained the ancient tradition of icon painting appears to have almost entirely vanished from the religious life of Russia.

As a result of the phenomenal ambitions of Tsar Peter I and Catherine the Great, the increasingly secular style of the West spread rapidly throughout the country. Royal portraiture became common, initially retaining the hieratic formality and regalia of ecclesiastical presentations, but eventually opening up to the self-consciousness of European models. Peter's decision not to replace Patriarch Adrian (head of the Church in Russia) on his death in 1700 was deliberately intended to undermine the political power of the Church, a process that was furthered when the leadership of the Church was reconvened as a Synod – effectively a department of the state – in 1721. Peter's stipulation that ships should have no more than one icon on board, serving an entire crew, was typical of his rationalised approach to icons and dramatically undermined the demand for sacred art. In 1698, he reduced the number of icon painters working in the Armoury Chamber from 65 to just two. It should be mentioned, however, that although Peter dismissed the Church as a political and cultural presence in his new vision of Russia, he did not reject religion out of hand; in fact he had an extremely active, if contradictory, attitude towards religion, which in some ways anticipated avant-garde travesties of the Church in the twentieth century. While minimising the public profile of religion, he dramatised his own form of religiosity privately, duplicating and exaggerating the rituals and nomenclature of the Church among his entourage.[27] In 1764, Catherine the Great further undermined the influence of the Church by appropriating its property, its main source of revenue, for the state. By the beginning of the nineteenth century, Christianity in Russia was at its lowest ebb. In relation to icons, what had once been an actively sacred form of art had now become an ineffectual sop to a demoralised people.[28] By the end of the century, cheap, artless icons, mechanically printed on paper and stamped from tin sheets, were being produced in their hundreds of thousands.[29]

The decline of icons represents a turning point in the history of Russian spirituality. It was not terminal, nor was it totally unproductive. In relation to the sacred culture of Russia, it represented a kind of Anastasis or 'Descent into Hell', prior to a rebirth of the sacred in a new form. Although this moment reflected the end of a cycle in the cultural history of the country, it was also the seedbed of a new era. It was not until the outmoded conventions of Christian religiosity had been recognised and released that the more fundamental principles of its spirituality could be revitalised in contemporary form. It is precisely at this point – a death at the heart of Russian culture – that our story begins.

NOTES

1. This principle was established in Canon 82 of the Council. Translated in Mango, p.139. See also Cormack, pp 98–102. The principle was re-affirmed at the Great Moscow Council of 1667; see Ouspensky & Lossky, p.165, note 4.

2. Cormack, p.111.

3. For the text and translation of the council decrees, see Tanner, N. (ed.), *Decrees of the Ecumenical Councils*, Sheen & Ward, 1990, vol.I, pp 131–56. See also Mango, p.172.

4. For instance, an early fifteenth-century Novgorodian icon of the Paternity in the Tretyakov Gallery, Moscow, inv. no.22211, illustrated in the *Complete Catalogue of the State Tretyakov Gallery*, vol.I, Moscow, 1995, no.25, p.86.

5. See Ouspensky & Lossky, p.185, and Kartsonis, p.131.

6. See Bevan, p.51; also Barnard, pp 7–13, and Rodley, p.34.

7. *The Journey of Patriarch Macarius in Russia*, translated from the Arabic into Russian by G. Murkos and published in Moscow in 1889; quoted in Ouspensky (1992), vol.2, p.336.

8. 'Letter of a Certain Iconographer Joseph to the Iconographer of the Tsar, the Wise Simon Theodorovich (Ushakov)', quoted by Ouspensky (1992), vol.2, p.330. See also Hamilton, p.241, and Cracraft (1997), p.81.

9. Belting, p.60.

10. St Theodore the Studite, *On the Holy Icons*, translated in Roth, p.55.

11. *Khludov Psalter*, *c.*850–75, State Historical Museum, Moscow. Reproduced in colour in Lowden, p.181. See also Cormack, p.134ff.

12. Belting, pp 208–24.

13. The legend of St Luke as the painter of the first icon is recounted in Belting, pp 342–8. This legend and that of the mandylion were cited as arguments in renewed support of icons by St Joseph of Volokalamsk (1439–1515) whose *Message to an Iconographer* was written in response to the outburst of iconoclastic heresies that occurred in Russia towards the end of the fifteenth century. Ouspensky (1992), vol.2, p.266.

14. See Curzon, R., *Visits to Monasteries in the Levant*, John Murray, London, 1849. Mount Athos is an all-male colony of Orthodox monasteries which has, according to legend, banned women and all other female species (except bees, for honey) from its shores for 2000 years.

15. Belting, p.53.

16. Meyendorff (1989), p.96ff.

17. In the absence of skilled architects in Vladimir, Prince Andrei Bogoliubsky employed German architects, sent by the Emperor Frederic Barbarossa, to work on the Church of the Intercession on the River Nerl, built in 1166. See Hamilton, p.58 (and note 11). The portals and corbels of this church were clearly influenced by Norman architecture; the low relief decoration that covers the exterior walls may be due to Armenian influence. Likewise, the bronze doors of St Sophia in Novgorod, made in Magdeburg in the middle of the twelfth century, were brought to Russia in around 1336. See Lasko, p.218. The exuberant intertwined birds and monsters that surround the figures in the late fourteenth-century psalter of Ivan the Terrible are of Romanesque derivation and would have been inconceivable in contemporary icons. See Popova, plate 26.

18. Hamilton, p.253.

19. Hamilton, p.161; Ouspensky (1992), vol. 2, p.289; Cracraft (1997), p.49. See also Tarasov (2002).

20. This iconography was only novel in Russia at this time. Rare Byzantine precedents for it, unlikely to have been seen by Russian icon painters, are known from the tenth and eleventh centuries: Ouspensky (1992), vol.2, p.292; also Ouspensky & Lossky, p.200. In reaction to the over-specific implications of this interpretation, and in order to re-equalise the three persons of the Trinity, some icon painters attempted to restore order by giving all three angels cruciform haloes – leading to accusations of the 'theopaschite' heresy: the heretical belief that God the Father suffered on the cross as well as Christ; see Ouspensky (1992), vol.2, p.292.

21. Ouspensky (1992), vol.2, p.371ff.

22. The *Pedalion* (or 'Rudder'), an ancient collection of ecclesiastical canons inherited from the Byzantine Church and used at the 1551 *Stoglav*, states: 'Let the iconographer's skills resemble those of the ancient models, the first painters, men of divine wisdom... Let him not add anything new himself, not even an iota; even if he thinks he knows many things, let him not dare transgress the tradition of the Fathers.' Ouspensky (1992), vol.2, p.299.

23. Ouspensky (1992), vol.2, p.303ff.

24. For example, Prince Mikhail Vasilievich Skopin-Shuiskii, Tretyakov Gallery, Moscow, *c.*1620–30. Reproduced in Cracraft (1997), plate 16. Sixteenth-century *parsuna* of Ivan the Terrible and his son Fedor Iannovich also survive in the Tretyakov Gallery. See *Russki Istoricheski Portret: Epocha Parsuni (Historic Russian Portraits: The Epoch of the Parsuna)*, Moscow, 2004.

25. Hamilton, p.253.

26. The *Man of Sorrows* below the mandylion in Plate 1 is not unusual in Byzantine art but is exceptional by Russian standards.

27. Hughes, p.249ff. See also Zitser.

28. Ouspensky (1992), vol.2, p.411ff.

29. Nichols, p.135.

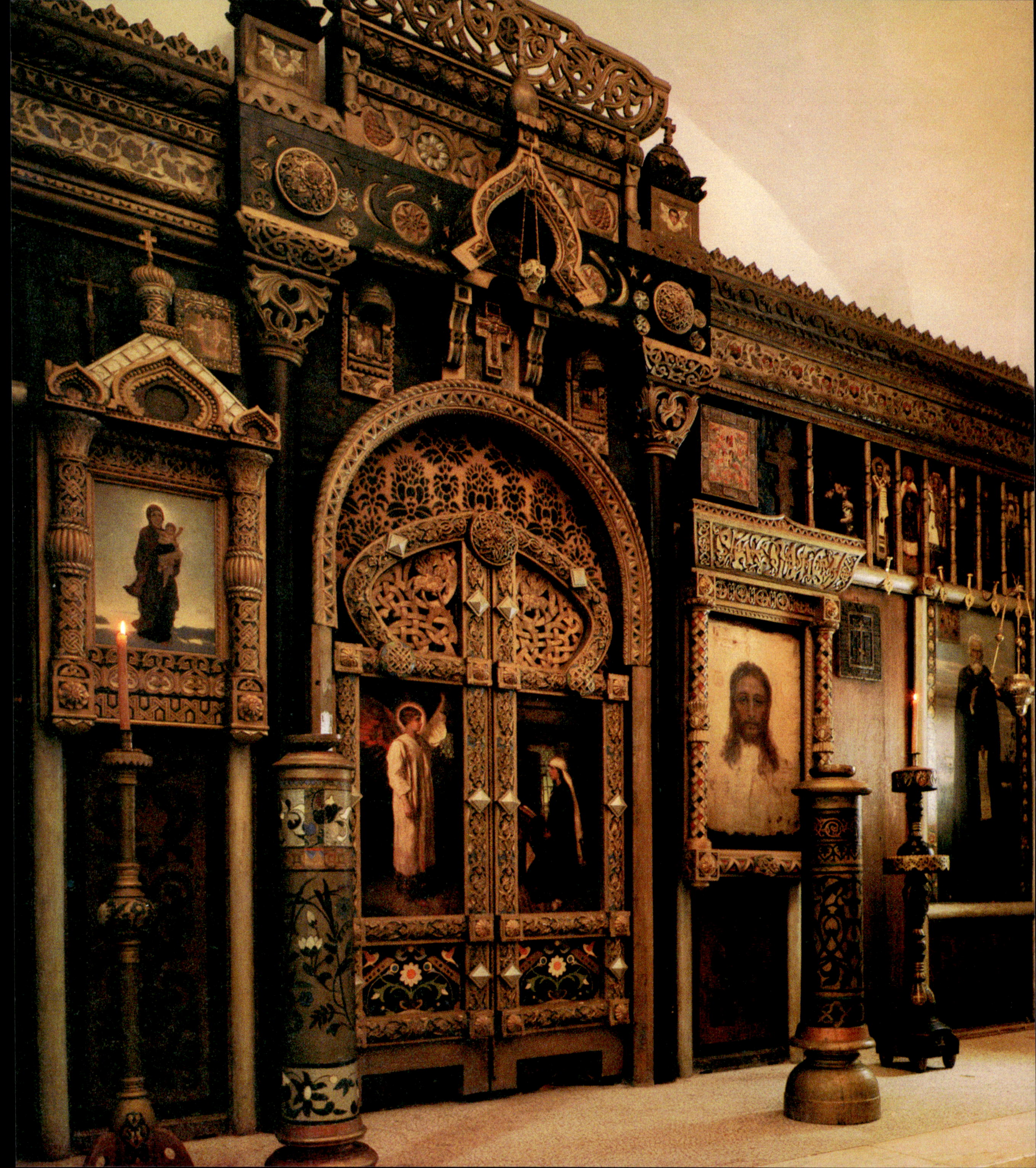

2

Background to the Avant-Garde: The Romantic Associations of Icons

THE AIM OF THE RUSSIAN avant-garde movement was to create an intensely contemporary national culture. It is ironic therefore that its seeds lay in a Romantic and nostalgic quest, which gathered momentum throughout the nineteenth century, to rediscover the cultural integrity of the past – the cultures of ancient Rus and pre-Petrine Russia. This quest took on national proportions following the failure of Napoleon's invasion of Russia in 1812. The December uprising of 1825 – traditionally regarded as the first revolutionary act in modern Russian history – developed in direct response to contact made with revolutionary France. This confrontation clearly drew energy from the vigorous nationalism that arose in reaction to European interference in Russian affairs but it was also significantly influenced by French revolutionary ideas which were witnessed at first hand by officers who had been sent abroad to be educated or who studied with foreign tutors in Russia. The fact that the uprising received support from the new intelligentsia was especially important because it reflected, for the first time, an ideological call for political and social change, beyond the more immediately practical demands (and ineffectual revolts) of the oppressed peasantry. Although it was unsuccessful on its own terms, it set in motion an avalanche that culminated in the Revolution of 1917.

One of the most immediate signs of this growth of nationalistic anti-European sentiment was the revival of interest in the traditional arts of Russia. Although this development also represented a desire to shift the criterion of culture away from the westernised style of the imperial court towards a more popular idiom, it was supported at the highest levels. Ironically, Tsar Nicholas I (*d.*1855), who quashed the 1825 uprising, took an active interest both in icons and in the restoration of the ancient churches of Moscow and Kiev, albeit partly with a view to turning the potential of cultural nationalism to his own ends. The investment of new interest in Orthodox culture was quickly manifest at an institutional level. The first major church to be built in Russia in a nationalistic form of medieval style was the Church of Christ the Redeemer in Moscow, built to commemorate the Russian soldiers lost in the victory over Napoleon in 1812, and completed in 1832. An interest in medieval style had already reached Russia from Europe by the end of the eighteenth century when such Gothic revival buildings as the Chesme Church in St Petersburg (1777–80)

7

Interior of the church at Abramtsevo showing the iconostasis, 1882. From left to right: ***Mother of God with Christ*** (Viktor Vasnetsov), ***The Annunciation*** (on the Royal Doors, Vasily Polenov), ***The Saviour*** (Ilya Repin), ***St Sergius*** (Viktor Vasnetsov) and Petrovsk Palace in Moscow (1775–82) were built. However, whereas the Gothic style had ideological implications in Europe, in Russia, where it had no history, it was no more than a decorative alternative to the Classical style. The Church of Christ the Redeemer was the first major medievalising Russian building, built in a grave Orthodox mode rather than an elegant Gothic one, to be imbued with nationalistic and political significance.

In 1856, when the decoration of the interior of the church was underway (several years after the completion of the structure of the building), classes in icon painting were offered at the St Petersburg Academy of Arts to prepare artists for the work.[1] To inspire and instruct them, a collection of traditional Old Believer icons was put on display at the Academy for the first time. In the same year, Dimitrii Rovinskii's *Survey of Icon Painting in Russia to the End of the Seventeenth Century*, the first significant study of icon painting, was published. In 1862, the Slavist critic Fedor Buslaev recommended that students of painting study the artistic traditions of ancient Russia rather than European models. He advocated a return to the simplicity and directness of church frescos and icons, making particular mention of the Sevastianov collection of icons in the Rumiantsev Museum, now in the Russian Museum, St Petersburg.[2] In the following year the Society of Lovers of Spiritual Enlightenment, which offered academic and practical studies of icon painting, was founded by the Orthodox Church.

The rise of nationalism in mid-nineteenth-century Russia coincided with a gradual shifting of the seat of Russian culture from St Petersburg to Moscow. While St Petersburg was the centre of a highly Europeanised form of Russian culture that, since its foundation in 1703, had regarded all aspects of traditional Russian life as uncivilised and undesirable, Moscow was the capital of ancient Muscovy and had a tradition that stretched back to the twelfth century. The shift of attention towards Moscow reflected a shift of interest to the values it represented. The revival of Moscow as a cultural centre was further aided by the rise of the merchant classes whose influence on European politics in the nineteenth century developed directly at the expense of the aristocracy. Whereas it had been the aristocracy that patronised the arts throughout the eighteenth and early nineteenth centuries, promoting the imperial values associated with the Classical style, the expansion of industry and commerce saw the development of wealthy merchants as the principal patrons of the arts at this time. Significantly, many of the most successful of the merchant entrepreneurs from this period were from conservative Old Believer families, renowned for their independence, resourcefulness, self-sufficiency and self-discipline. Considering how the Old Believers had begun collecting ancient icons in the eighteenth century – albeit for religious reasons (in order to steer clear of stylistic and iconographical innovations) – it is perhaps not surprising that the first great collections of icons were also developed by wealthy merchants. The fact that the Old Believer Church was formally suppressed until 1905 may also have contributed to the way in which wealthy individuals took responsibility for their religious heritage.

The first signs of secular interest in Orthodox culture appeared at the beginning of the nineteenth century and were primarily archaeological and literary. For this reason the earliest collections of Orthodox material consisted largely of chronicles and charters. The earliest collecting of icons *per se* was closely related to the creation of a national school of contemporary Russian painting. Its beginning marks the point at which interest in the past ceased to be a matter of purely academic appeal, but became a vital function of contemporary Russian culture. In the West, by contrast, the few literati who were aware of icons in the nineteenth century tended to judge them narrowly – devoid of cultural value and incompatible with their own Classical–Romantic frame of reference. One exception was Johann Wolfgang von Goethe, whose depth of interest in nature, history and culture took him beyond the transient and self-referential conventions of taste, enabling him to see icons as part of a bigger picture. Goethe was fascinated by icons, recognising that they belonged to a pictorial tradition that was unbroken since early Christian times. His interest in Orthodox culture stemmed from 1808 at the latest when a choir on its way to the Russian consulate in Paris stopped in Weimar and sang in the 'beautifully decorated' Orthodox chapel there. The chapel, serving a community of 20 Greek Orthodox Christians, was established in the basement of a private house by one of Goethe's admirers and supporters, the Grand Duchess Maria Pavlovna (daughter of the Empress Maria Feodorovna) who had lived in Weimar since 1804 as the wife of Carl Friedrich of Saxe-Weimar. Goethe attended services at the chapel and befriended the provost and chaplain; he is also presumed to have known Russian clergymen in Weimar, Yasnovsky and Yegorev, among the countless other Russians visiting the consulate in Weimar between the Russian and Prussian victory over Napoleon at Leipzig (1813) and the Congress of Vienna (1815). Letters in a private collection in St Petersburg indicate that, in 1814, Goethe asked the Grand Duchess for information about icons. His notes on 'Russian Pictures of Saints' reflect the nature of his interest:

> In the town of Suzdal which once was the centre of a government, as well as in the villages of the surrounding districts, there are the kinds of pictures being painted which are not the object of the Russian Church service but its external motivation. These sacred pictures are being painted on to little wooden squares, poured from metal in half relief, chiselled into stone, enamelled, probably even engraved in wood. Whether there are also free-standing statues of saints being fashioned is doubtful as Peter the Great forbade statues in his churches. About these objects one would like some detailed information as to what is the purpose of their fabrication, how many people are involved in it and whether this work represents an important branch of trade. How long has this institution been there? Are there any old Greek [Byzantine] pictures left to serve as models? Are there any especially excellent artists among the painters of Suzdal? Is everything still done according to the old sacred style? Or are different subjects pictured in a modern way?[3]

Maria Pavlovna conveyed Goethe's interest to her mother, the Empress dowager, who passed it on to O.P. Kozodavlev, the Russian Minister of Interior Affairs. Kozodavlev in turn spoke to Nicholas Karamzin, writer of the first modern history of Russia, *The History of the Russian State*, and A.N. Suponev, Governor of the Province of Vladimir. In April 1814, Goethe was informed that:

> the painting of icons in Suzdal copies the Byzantine, which was brought to Russia with the Greek creed at the time of Vladimir… This style of painting has not changed in the course of the centuries because the Russian clergy demanded that our painters make exact imitations of Byzantine models, and innovations were seen as sacrilege. The figures, their attitudes, colours, robes, everything had its laws. A religious

> congress in Moscow in the 16th century confirmed that pictures of saints had to be painted according to the example of Andrei Rublev and not otherwise.[4]

In a letter of May 1814, Suponev wrote to Kozodavlev saying that the tradition of icon painting had almost completely ceased to exist but that three villages in the Suzdal region – Palekh, Kholui and Mstera – were still producing icons, adding that 'even if there are holy pictures being painted partially according to the Greek originals found in the Cathedral and in some other churches, this work is of no significance'.[5]

Goethe also attempted to build up a collection of his own, writing: 'It would be appreciated to receive models of each kind of these pictures even in the smallest format, if possible from the best of contemporary artists, as it has to be enlightening for a friend of the Arts to know how a branch of the Arts, originating from the ancient times of Constantinople, reached our times unchanged by means of perpetual imitation.'[6] Suponev also complied with this request, informing Kozodavlev that he was sending him four icons to be sent on to Goethe: 'Of the two smaller icons, one shows the Twelve Holy [Feast] Days of the year, and the other one shows the Mother of God; they are works by the greatest of the masters, Andrei and Ivan Kaureev from the village of Palekh. The other two pictures, which are larger, show the Redeemer and the Mother of God and are from the village of Kholui, also painted by the greatest masters of the art'. The icons were to be sent to Goethe by courier, as they were too heavy to be sent by post, but they were apparently never received, waylaid by the long absences of Maria Pavlovna from Weimar, the Congress of Vienna and Goethe's own travels.

One of the first writers in Russia to appreciate the broad cultural value of icons was Nikolai Leskov whose short story, *The Sealed Angel*, published in 1873, made a significant contribution to the revival of interest in icons among the general public. Leskov was renowned for his sensitivity to the details of daily life in provincial Russia and in this story he gives a sympathetic impression of the position of icons in the life of a community of peasants. The story tells of a community of Old Believers who are converted to mainstream Orthodoxy through the miraculous agency of an ancient icon of an angel. Although Leskov implicitly suggests that Orthodox beliefs are superior to the ultra-conservative beliefs of the Old Believers (albeit unconvincingly, according to some contemporaries),[7] he does cast the Old Believers in a benign light, showing them a tolerance – itself a sign of the new appreciation of traditional values – that had largely been withheld from them since they seceded from the official Church in the seventeenth century. The story goes into considerable detail about the way icons were made, used and treasured in the middle of the nineteenth century. Much of Leskov's information came from an icon-painter friend of his, Nikita Racheiskov, in whose St Petersburg studio the story was written. The story was popular both at the imperial court, where it was read aloud to the royal family, and among the general public. As a reflection of the role it played in the regeneration of interest in icons, Leskov recalled that Nikita 'received many orders for icons of angels' after its publication.[8]

In Russia, the serious and systematic collecting of icons was closely connected with the desire to create a museum of Russian art. Significantly, two of the most important early collectors of icons became curator-directors of the first national collection (now part of the Tretyakov Gallery, Moscow). The transformation of their private interests into concern for popular culture corresponded directly to a deepening of desire by a growing number of individuals to realise their sense of identity on a national scale.

Best known among the earliest collectors of icons was Pavel Tretyakov (1832–98), whose comprehensive collection of Russian art became the corner-stone of the Tretyakov Gallery. The opening of the Tretyakov Gallery to the public in 1892 not only made individual national treasures accessible to the public, it was also a consummate celebration of self-esteem on the part of the Russian nation. The idea of a museum of Russian painting had interested Tretyakov since his youth and throughout his life he collected work by contemporary artists (Ilya Repin, Mikhail Nesterov, Valentin Serov), many of whom became his close friends. It was not until 1890 that Tretyakov began to buy icons. Having shown little interest in sacred art up to this point, it seems likely that his appreciation of icons as part of the history of Russian painting was partly due to the broader vision of the artists he mixed with. His collector's desire for comprehensiveness may also have been provoked by an 1890 public exhibition of icons belonging to other private collectors, many of whose icons were later acquired for his own collection. Following Tretyakov's death in 1898, the directorship of the Tretyakov Gallery passed to I.S. Oustroukhov. He was also a private collector and the Tretyakov Gallery received some of its finest pieces from him. Like Tretyakov, his passion for icons not only epitomised the growth of interest in national art but eventually came to articulate it on a national scale. A sense of national responsibility motivated a third collector, the Old Believer Stepan Riabushinsky, who was instrumental in the early development of a tradition of icon restoration. Besides running an icon restoration workshop in his own home, Riabushinsky had a number of churches built in Moscow according to Old Believer principles.

Such enlightened and literary attitudes towards Orthodox culture were by no means universal in Russia. The growth of interest in traditional Orthodox culture took place largely among the intelligentsia, an elite minority, and occurred more as a function of the overall development of Russian nationalism than a specifically historical or Orthodox phenomenon. One of its underlying purposes was to bring historical authority to the quest for popular national identity. It is scarcely surprising therefore that, despite the movement's admiration for the past, its combination of liberalism and traditionalism – the sense of a 'return to the future' – frequently brought it into conflict with the Orthodox Church which was becoming increasingly distant from the new cultural and spiritual ideals. On one hand, the Church was conservative – in defence of its political security – and therefore resistant to change; on the other hand it had become untraditional in that certain aspects of its routine life, including the style and iconography of its icons, were already highly westernised. Neither of these stances served the search for national identity.

The highly critical and dissociated attitude of many mid-nineteenth-century artists towards the Orthodox Church is reflected in the early works of the Muscovite painter Vasily Perov (1834–82), a graduate of the Moscow School of Painting, Sculpture and Architecture. While typifying the social realism that was developing throughout Europe, his paintings derive special significance from their Russian context. Unlike other European nations, where open expression of new political ideas was becoming increasingly possible and tolerated, the forbidding autocracy of tsarist Russia made it difficult and dangerous for ordinary people to make direct challenges to political authority. Throughout the 1860s, therefore, the voice of social dissent came to be increasingly associated with the more oblique forms of literature and painting. At the same time,

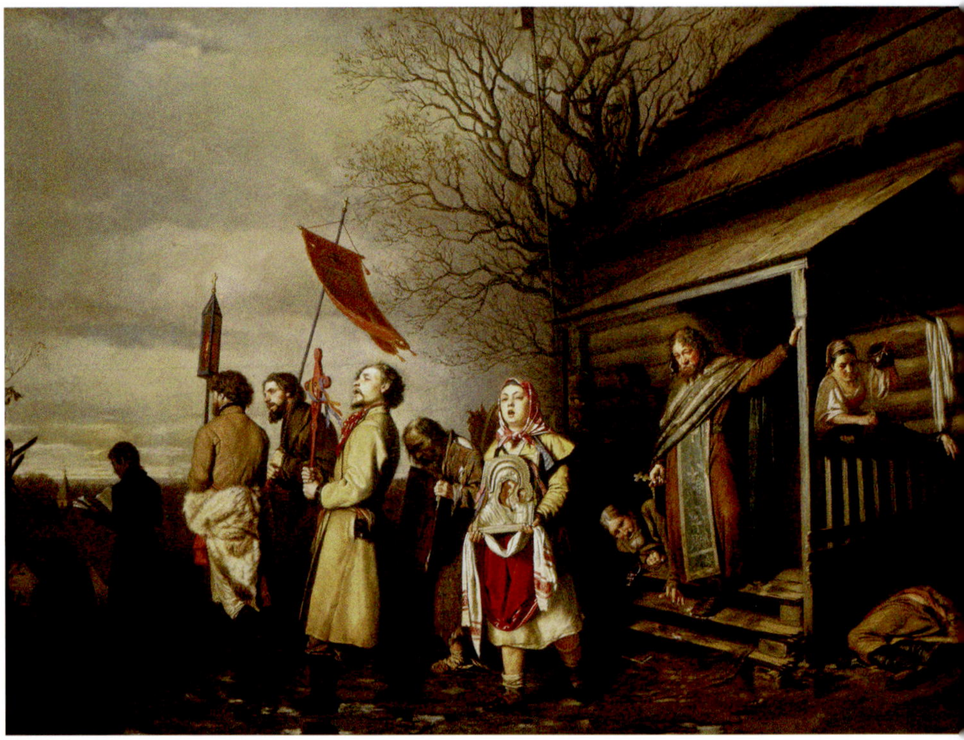

8
Vasily Perov

Easter Procession, 1861
Oil on canvas
71.5 x 89 cm (28⅛ x 35 in)
Tretyakov Gallery, Moscow

the arts were expected to perform a social function. This drive to invest the arts with the power of social, political and ultimately spiritual transformation became a fundamental aspect of the new Russian culture and it set an important precedent for the avant-garde movement.

Perov's *Easter Procession* (Plate 8) of 1861 openly exposes the depraved state of the clergy, demonstrating the low esteem in which icons were held in the middle of the nineteenth century among the unreformed. At the same time, it shows how deeply divorced institutionalised religion had become from contemporary culture. The painting depicts a religious procession setting out from a house towards a distant church. The procession's leaders have already begun to leave the picture, to the viewer's left. Straggling along at the back of the procession – the focal point of the painting – is a distracted woman casually carrying an icon. Beyond her is a dishevelled beggar holding an icon without noticing that it is upside down; the dimness of the light around him fully conveys his confused state of mind. Last in the procession is a drunken priest, clutching a cross and propping himself up on the porch of the house, hardly able to support himself. A grasping simpleton lies sprawled out at his feet. In the corner of the painting another figure lies insensate in a heap. The new spirit in Russian art was to arise from these ashes: it was as if it was necessary for the degenerated forms of Orthodoxy to be seen as mechanical and empty before the essence of Orthodoxy could be distilled and conducted into the future in a form that was compatible with contemporary culture.

Perov's style was sufficiently conventional for his mildly satirical *Village Sermon* of 1861 to win the Gold Medal, the most prestigious award offered by the St Petersburg Academy of Arts, enabling him to travel abroad. However, the generally mundane and critical subject matter of his work conflicted with the Classical and dramatic tone of the Academy. In the following year the Academy Council withdrew the condition of the competition that allowed students to select their own subject matter. The Academic Council's rigorous prescription of subject matter, and its refusal to allow award-winning students to deviate in any detail from the design they submitted as their initial application for the prize, was characteristic of academic idealism throughout Europe. However, it may also have been subtly underwritten in Russia by the traditional belief that to deviate from the sanctified canon of subject matter and composition in icon painting was a form of blasphemy. Significantly, it was the Council's censorious enforcement of its stand against the free choice of subject matter that prompted the action now commonly associated with the beginning of the modern movement in Russian art. As a direct result of the decision, 14 students seceded from the Academy in 1863 and set up their own circle of independent artists. This epoch-making gesture of defiance was made in reaction to the excessively academic and conservative tendencies of the Classical tradition then prevailing in the arts; yet it also reflects the feeling of discontent and desire for change that were endemic throughout Russia and Europe at the time. In keeping with the spirit of change that saw the abolition of serfdom two years earlier, this defection was one of an increasing number of events to occur in reaction to the suppressive and controlling regimes of imperial Russia.

In 1870 a number of the seceding group of artists, joined by Perov and others, formed themselves into a new association whose mission was to take art 'to the people' by organising exhibitions of their work in towns all over Russia. The *Peredvizhniki* or 'Wanderers' – named after their touring exhibitions – rejected the current understanding of art as a luxury for the aristocracy and engaged it as a medium of wider social contact and cohesion. Their style and subject matter were basically realist, most comparable among well-known western artists to the work of Gustave Courbet. In direct contravention of the principles of the Academy, which demanded that students paint set pieces, the Wanderers depicted everyday scenes in a loosely handled style.

Over a period of two decades, the process initiated by the Wanderers developed into a powerful movement of alternative culture in Russia. Although it was not originally motivated by feelings of nationalism, the movement soon came to be associated with a search for a truly Russian national identity that had originated in literary and archaeological circles in the 1840s and 1850s. Throughout northern Europe, the revival of medieval Christian traditions served as a vehicle for national self-renewal. In England and Germany, for instance, this relationship gave rise to the Pre-Raphaelites and Wagner's medievalising operas respectively. In Russia, it was reflected in an enthusiasm for emotive subject matter, executed in the realist style of the Wanderers, that glorified moments of significance in early Russian history and legend. Religious scenes, including scenes from the life of Christ, were also painted, partly because they evoked the mysterious and fervent atmosphere of the Middle Ages but also because, taken at the most simple level, they constituted historical drama. In many cases, such as Vasily Polenov's *Christ and the Woman taken in Adultery* of 1886–7,[9] great pains were taken to ensure that they were historically 'correct' and therefore dramatically convincing (rather than doctrinally pure). There were, however, significant differences between East and West. Whereas the Pre-Raphaelites' and Wagner's visions of Christ as 'Saviour of the World' tended to reflect a degree of national self-esteem in their respective countries, the fact that Christ – representative of the quest for true justice – was frequently depicted in Russian art as the selfless victim of philistine forces in the world reflected a quality of internal conflict in Russian society that would eventually lead to a national collapse.

This state of internal conflict was idealised to the point of resembling an inescapable destiny in the religious works of Ivan Kramskoi (1837–87) and Nikolai Ge (1831–94), who both studied at the St Petersburg Academy of Arts. Both artists were realists and were represented at the first Wanderers exhibition in St Petersburg in 1871. Unlike Perov, who was concerned with the state of the Orthodox Church as a contemporary social ill, Kramskoi and Ge ignored the Church as a social institution. Following the example of Tolstoy, they looked directly towards its spiritual source, the human person of Jesus, who they represented as a moral and psychological being rather than a doctrinal truth, as in icons. Their images of Christ are iconic in the sense that, both artistically and conceptually, they concentrate on the magnetic figure of Christ as the focus of the viewer's attention. However, despite their return to Christian subject matter and the fact that reproductions of their Christian works were displayed as 'Tolstoyan icons', the relationship of these works to icon painting as such is indirect. Indeed, their mood of defeated disenchantment and alienation from the world is fundamentally at odds with the Orthodox theology of icons which maintains that icons are inherently triumphant and celebratory as they are an extension of the incarnation of Christ, demonstrating the triumphant presence of Christ in the world, and thereby undermining any cause for doubt and sorrow. Moreover, unlike icons, the majority of Kramskoi and Ge's paintings of (or about) Christ depict scenes from the period immediately preceding his Passion (Christ before Pilate, doubting Peter, the betrayal by Judas). In this respect they relate to the Catholic tradition of emotive Passion iconography, rare in Russian icon painting until the eighteenth century, though unlike Catholic art they do not represent Christ's physical suffering with a view to evoking pity and compassion. Indeed, they rarely show action *per se*, let alone physical suffering. They tend to represent psychological states that relate to dramatic actions which have either just happened or are about to happen; they are implicitly dramatic. The absence of personal contact between Christ and the viewer, while being highly effective in its attempt to transmit the desired sense of moral dilemma and intense desolation, is also fundamentally alien to icons.

Kramskoi's *Temptation of Christ in the Wilderness* (1872, Plate 9) is a case in point. The subject matter of the work is novel but the unflinching focusing of attention on Christ is not; it is the equivalent – if also the opposite – of an icon of *Christ in Majesty* (Plate 42). The impact of the rocky landscape as a place of total barrenness is also informed by the renunciate associations of rocks and caves in icons (such as Plates 2 and 125) but, in this case, it does not complement the ordeals of sacrifice and death with the promise of birth and regeneration, as icons do. When the painting was first exhibited at the second exhibition of the Wanderers in 1872, it attracted very mixed responses ranging from praise of its seriousness, sincerity, courage and emotional depth to disapproval of its hopelessness and joylessness, considered by many to be inappropriate in an image of Christ. However, as Kramskoi himself wrote of the work, 'This is no Christ, it is an image of the sorrows of humanity, which are known to all of us'.[10] That is to say, it was not intended to be an image of Christ as he is in his abstract perfection (in relationship to which Kramskoi spoke of himself as an atheist),[11] but of humanity projected onto and transformed by – and even into – Christ. Kramskoi painted the image not as a celebration of the incarnation of Christ – the 'objective truth' that is celebrated by icons – but as a self-purificatory and therapeutic necessity, an act of sublimated subjectivity. Reflecting on the genesis of the work, he

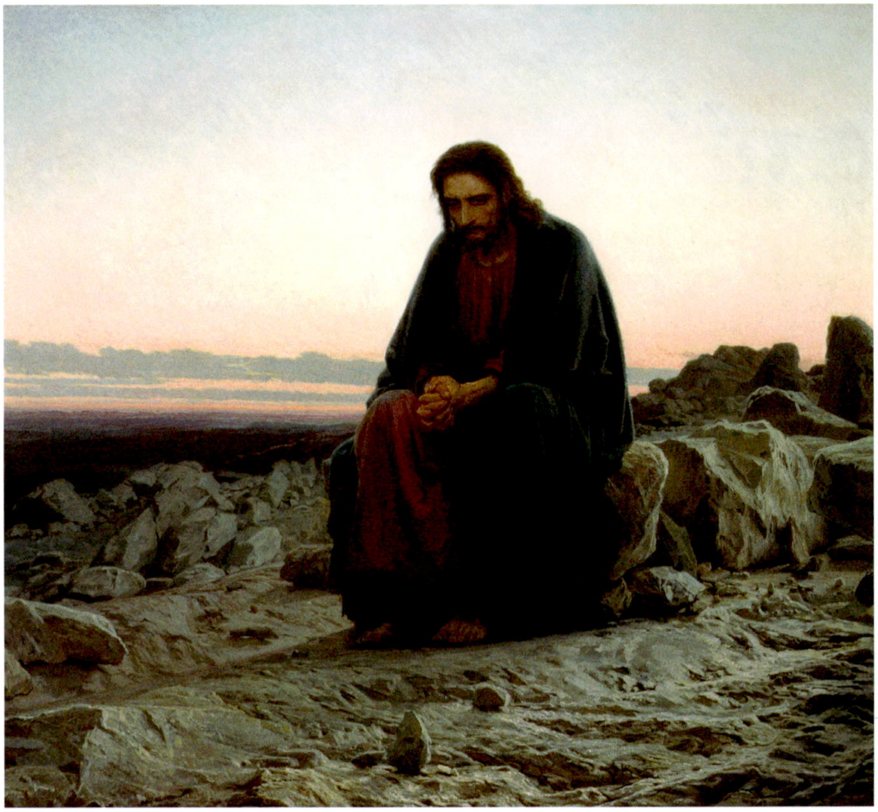

9
Ivan Kramskoi
Temptation of Christ in the Wilderness, 1872
Oil on canvas
180 x 210 cm (70⅞ x 82⅝ in)
Tretyakov Gallery, Moscow

10
Nikolai Ge
What is Truth?, 1890
Oil on canvas
233 x 171 cm (91¾ x 67⅜ in)
Tretyakov Gallery, Moscow

wrote: 'the image stood before me continually for five years. I had to paint it, in order to be rid of it. During work on the painting, I mused, prayed and suffered a great deal... I have perhaps committed sacrilege but I couldn't help but paint him. I couldn't, if you like, not do it.'[12]

Nikolai Ge's religious works express the same sense of the intense isolation of Christ. His most controversial work, depicting Christ before Pilate and entitled *What is Truth?* (1890, Plate 10), does not represent Christ as the transcendent and victorious revelation of Orthodox Christianity; it represents him as the embodiment of human vulnerability. Although Christ's facial expression in this work conveys something of the quality of quiet penetrative insight that one associates with some medieval icons, it is difficult to maintain, with George Heard Hamilton, that 'it is as if the religious emotion of medieval art had been recreated in modern terms'.[13] On the contrary, the work is quintessentially Romantic and fatalistic, dramatising the dissonance between the innocence of the human soul and the cruel and indifferent imperfections of human nature with a peculiarly Russian intensity. By pitching the impoverished and unjustly victimised figure of Christ, as political prisoner, against brutal authority, he is drawing attention to the oppressive and autocratic role that he considered the Church to be playing in relation to both the mystical essence of Christianity and the peasant population. Perhaps predictably, the religious authorities found the work unacceptable and demanded that it be withdrawn from exhibition, unwittingly reproducing the authoritarianism of its subject matter in real life. Given Ge's commitment to Tolstoy's ideal of returning to the renunciate Christ-like values of early Christianity and his disenchantment with the established Church, it seems likely that the iconography of the despondent Christ corresponded to his own sense of distance from the world. As with Kramskoi's *Temptation of Christ in the Wilderness*, his work suggests a degree of personal identification with the figure of Christ and, arguably, a tendency to spiritualise his own predicament.

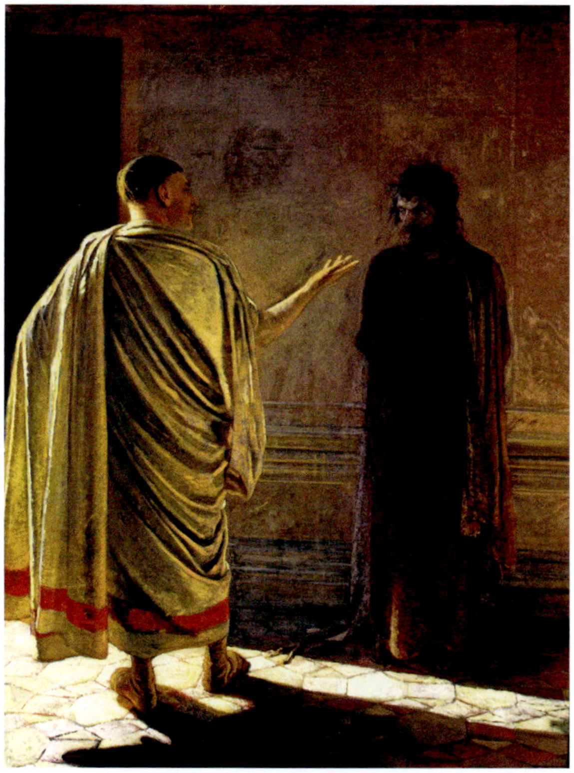

The iconography of Christ as a helpless and disaffected victim before Pilate is found again in Mark Antokolsky's life-size sculpture, *Christ Bound Before the People*, of 1874 (Plate 11). As a young man, Antokolsky was involved in the construction of iconostases and he participated in the first of the Wanderers' exhibitions in 1871. In this work, Christ is bound by cords, as if being interrogated by Pilate before the flagellation – a position that the viewer is made to assume. His glazed expression indicates his introverted disengagement from the world. The representation of Christ in a three-dimensional

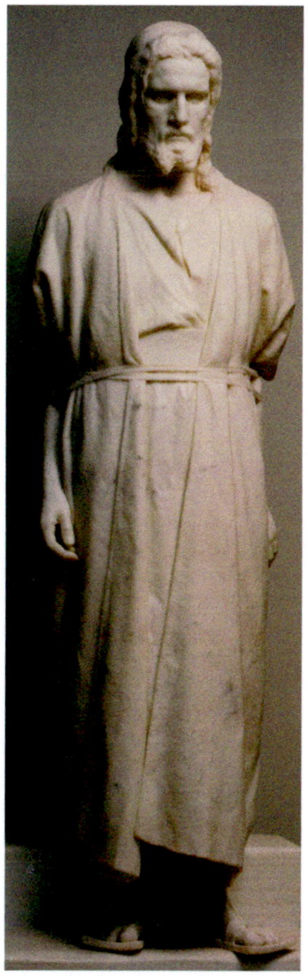

11
Mark Antokolsky
Christ Bound Before the People,
1874
Marble
190 cm (74¾ in) tall
Tretyakov Gallery, Moscow

sculpture is fundamentally contrary to the theology of icons (on the grounds that sculpture constitutes 'graven imagery') and, at a purely artistic level, the naturalistic concept of the work belongs as much in a western European context as in a Russian one. The unyielding frontality of the work and the artist's focus on the ironic impotence of the all-powerful, however, is typically Russian. Most importantly – and in keeping with the Christ-orientated works of Kramskoi and Ge – Antokolsky's *Christ* elevated the state of personal deprivation to the level of a spiritual state by identifying it with the incapacitated, suffering Christ. In representing Christ in this way, Antokolsky enables the viewer to transform a destiny that seems inescapable and forsaken into one that feels necessary, meaningful and even redeemed.

Interestingly, Christ's humiliating confrontation with Pilate continued to reappear as a motif in Russian literature throughout the Soviet period – to such an extent, in fact, that fascination with this particular dynamic can be said to have become an autonomous form of discourse, with its own internal references. Just as the Romantic image of 'Christ as victim', in the 1870s and 1880s, had located suffering in the context of salvation, so the complementary image of 'Pilate as perpetrator' framed the tendency of individuals to 'wash their hands' of the responsibility to stand up for people they knew to be innocent for the sake of their own personal safety or political power. In the Soviet period, there was a significant shift of emphasis in the evaluation of the dynamics at work here. Mikhail Bulgakov, who coined the term 'pilatism' in *The Master and Margerita* (written in the 1930s but not published until 1966), highlighted Pilate's ambivalence about the innocence of Christ, providing a model for the reconsideration and even partial redemption of moral cowardice at a time when such an archetype or precedent was especially needed by many. The lack of sympathy extended to Pilate by later writers suggests that, as the scope for dissenting from the party line increased in the 1960s, tolerance of 'moral cowardice' diminished and, as a result, Pilate came again to be seen more unambiguously as a target for recrimination, rather than as a source of potential reconciliation and understanding.[14]

The biblical narrative of Christ before Pilate provides the ideal vehicle for the profoundly Russian tendency to romanticise and spiritualise – and therefore tolerate rather than conquer – the passive 'victim-disposition'. This tendency to romanticise passivity is arguably a fundamental part of the Russian psyche. There is a case for suggesting that the 'Russian soul' was moulded into this disposition by its long experience of the extreme climate and the landscape, towards which it was chronically forced, over many centuries, to assume a position of patience and passivity. It is as if it became dependent on activation from without and habitually inclined to project the possibility of activation on to an 'other'. The tendency towards passivity manifests in both negative and positive ways, ranging from stultifying inertia – so clearly identified by some Russians as a function of the Russian psyche that it acquired a name of its own, 'Oblomovism', after a protagonist of this disposition in a nineteenth-century novel – to extraordinary feats of endurance and renunciation.[15] On one hand, it has been said to lay Russians open to abuse by their own authoritarian regimes, leading to a chronic state of submissiveness and conformism; on the other hand, it has prepared them to endure the powerful forces of extreme natural conditions, long journeys over vast distances, political adversity and war – for instance, during the Siege of Leningrad (1941–4) – as well as self-imposed disciplines such as intense monastic life. And travellers to Russia today will be familiar with the Russians' extraordinary capacity to wait in long queues! At a religious level, the tendency has been rationalised for centuries by the notion that the individual is powerless to save himself; he is entirely passive to Christ. It is also present in the concept of the 'icon not made by human hands', according to which human beings are considered to be incapable of making authentic holy icons. The true prototypes of icons are conceived as miraculous God-created objects, and it is a privilege for man to be passive to their grace. In the same way, widespread belief in superstitious and magical practices reflects a wish, or even a need, to find the rationale for personal action in external signs rather than in the individual will. In pagan Russia, words ritually overheard outside a wooden cottage at night, the sound of a squeaking gate or the patterns made by a handful of twigs thrown into the snow were frequently consulted for their mysterious ability to reveal the temperament of a future husband or some other possible destiny.[16] And as we shall see, even among the avant-garde, artists tended to create systems, manifestos and credos, investing them with autonomous logic, as if in order to collectively take up a submissive position in relation to them – in keeping with the notion that spiritual freedom required the sacrifice and sublimation of personal freedom.

The 'holy fools' of medieval Russia attempted to sacralise the state of powerlessness – embracing it consciously rather than submitting to it unwillingly or fatalistically – by living as renunciates. Ironically, these parallels between total freedom and total sacrifice (or loss) of freedom are reflected in the unsettling way in which Russian monasteries and convents, originally conceived as havens of spiritual freedom, were so easily and frequently used as prisons. In the seventeenth century, several high-ranking women, including the first wife of Peter the Great, were banished to the Pokrovskii Convent in Suzdal and in 1698 Peter had his half-sister, his rival to the throne, incarcerated in Novodevichy Convent in Moscow. Solovetsky Monastery in the far north of the country was converted into a notorious prison camp in 1923. Similar uncomfortable resonances were also promoted by perceptions of the Russian landscape, which was increasingly seen in the nineteenth century as a symbol of infinite freedom but which could also accommodate the incapacitating fantasy of 'too much' freedom. In such cases, the open space of the Russian landscape was seen to resemble a prison because it was simply too vast to escape from; it became a place of 'inescapable freedom'. From the point of view of internal exiles in Siberia, the distances were so great, the conditions so poor and the weather so inhospitable that prison walls were scarcely necessary. This impression is amply given by Isaak Levitan's *Vladimirka Road* (1892), along which many prisoners journeyed east, never to return, and is powerfully suggested in psychological terms in Kramskoi's *Temptation of Christ in the Wilderness* (Plate 9), couched in a landscape of limitless barrenness.

The Christ-oriented works of the Wanderers operate at many levels, in each case sacralising – or *sacrificing* (if one considers the origin of the word: to 'make holy') – the feeling/disposition of endurance and passivity. What was instilled in the Russian soul by long experience of nature was sacralised, or redeemed, by the example of Christ. Indeed, when used to refer to the events leading up to the death of Christ, the word 'Passion' also incorporates this cluster of meanings (intensity, passivity, suffering, redemption). At a religious level, the works represent the human soul's defiance of mortality, paradoxically and mystically realised in the person of the suffering Christ; at a political level, they sacralise the freedom of the individual, as pitched against the oppressive conventions of the imperial state and Church hierarchy; and, at a personal level, they surely ennoble the feelings of the artists themselves, distanced from the Academy and the establishment. This conflation of spiritual, social and personal ideals helped to consolidate and deepen the significance of the nationalist debate. Its existence was to set an important precedent for several artists of the younger generation who continued to aim for the ultimate reconciliation of these ideals in their own way.

By the end of the nineteenth century, the nationalism and populism of the Wanderers had become sufficiently accepted as a cause to be systematically espoused by the tsar. Realism ceased to be regarded as having a destabilising effect on the political *status quo* and began to attract imperial patronage. Tsar Alexander III (1881–94) became an active collector of the Wanderers' works and, finding himself in competition with Tretyakov for the finest pieces, he requested private previews to the Wanderers' exhibitions from 1886. However, his interest in contemporary art was largely engaged as a vehicle for his nationalism, as indicated by the fact that, having bought Antokolsky's *Christ* in 1874, he later expressed reservations about the cosmopolitanism of the sculptor's style. As a further sign of his subjection of the Wanderers' activism to his own conservatism, he was instrumental from 1889 in the appointment of several members of the Wanderers to senior teaching posts at the Academy.[17]

Alexander III was particularly committed to capitalising on the growing sense of identification with the past. With regard to the ancient tradition, he promoted a revival of the early Muscovite style of architecture in place of the more academic and less exclusively Russian neo-Byzantinism of the middle of the century. For instance, in commemoration of his father Alexander II, assassinated in 1881, he required the Church of the Spilt Blood to be built in St Petersburg in the early Russian style of St Basil's Cathedral in Moscow. In 1884, he was responsible for the highly traditional style of decoration at the Cathedral of St Vladimir in Kiev, a building project which had been initiated in 1862 to commemorate the first millennium of the existence of the Russian nation. He also worked for several years on a plan to open a museum in St Petersburg, dedicated to Russian art. His plan was delayed for over a decade until a suitable building could be found. It was finally realised after his death (in 1894) in the form of the 'Russian Museum of Alexander III' (subsequently called the State Russian Museum) which was opened to the public in the former Mikhailovsky Palace in 1898.

While imperial patronage secured recognition for the Wanderers, it also had the subtle effect of disempowering them, for it was ultimately impossible for a genuinely popular art of the people to flourish under imperial patronage. Consequently, it was more in the context of support from disinterested merchants, rather than the tsar, that the traditional art of the Russian Orthodox Church was first recognised as having an active cultural value of its own, an impact that transcended its purely historical interest. The first practical revival of interest in icons *per se* took place among a group of artists, descended from the Wanderers, who gathered around the wealthy industrialist-patron Savva Mamontov. Their interest in icons was awakened in 1880 when the flooding of a river, not far from Mamontov's estate at Abramtsevo near Moscow, made the local church inaccessible to its congregation. To prevent such a situation from arising again, the colony of artists living at Abramtsevo resolved to build a new church on the estate grounds. All the work, from the construction of the building down to the smallest decorative details, was to be executed in a traditional manner by artists on the estate. The church was originally to be built in the medieval

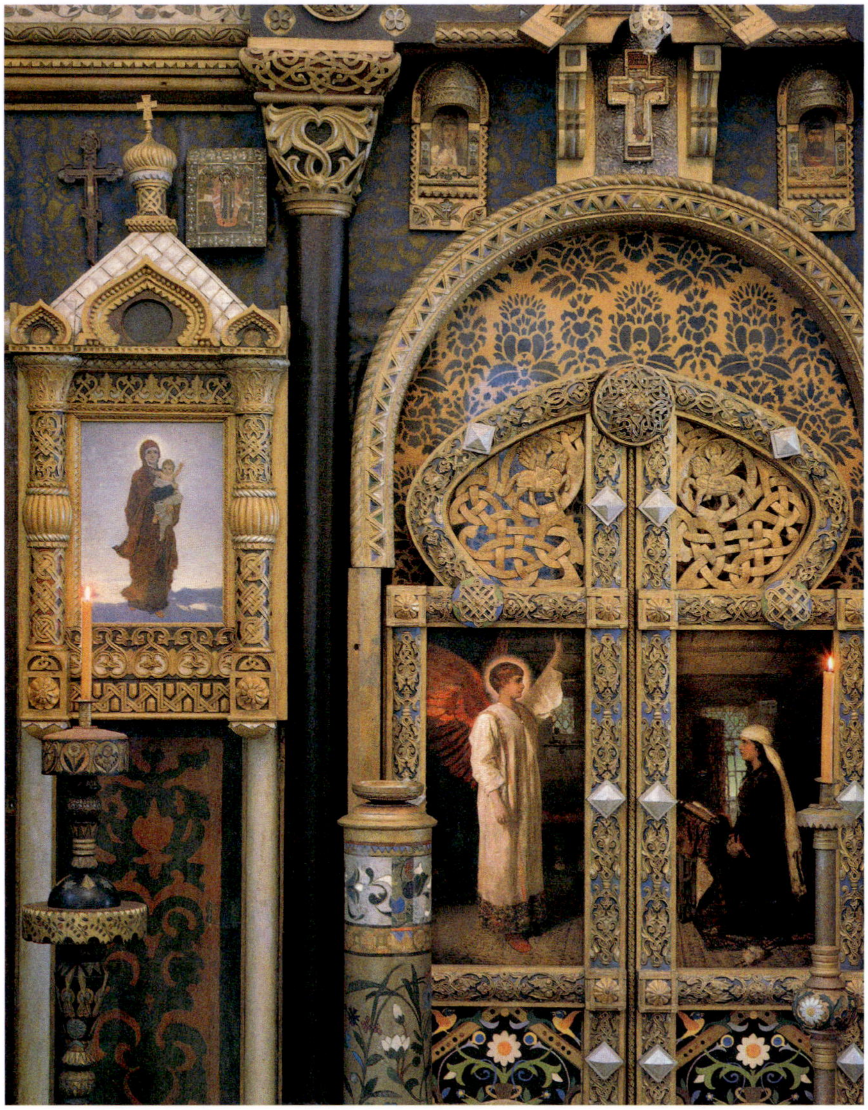

12.

Detail of the inconostasis in the church at Abramtsevo, 1882, showing (left) *The Mother of God with Christ* (Viktor Vasnetsov) and (right) *The Annunciation* (Vasily Polenov)

Novgorodian and Pskovian styles but its details were eventually based on ancient prototypes from a variety of sources. A vast amount of research was required for the project and as a result some of the best-known artists of the day were exposed with a new depth of purpose to the ancient traditions of Russian sacred art.

The church at Abramtsevo was completed in 1882. Its iconostasis (Plates 7, 12) was created by Vasily Polenov, Ilya Repin, Mikhail Nesterov and the Vasnetsov brothers and the work varies significantly in quality and style. Polenov was largely responsible for the overall structure of the iconostasis, faithfully reproducing the ornamentation and deep undercutting of ancient Russian woodwork. His contribution to the icons, however, was less traditional. His *Annunciation* is divided over the two Royal Doors in the traditional manner but its attempt to combine the hieratic stillness of icons with the emotional accessibility of the realists results in a stiffness and sentimentality that is reminiscent of the Pre-Raphaelites. The numinous immediacy of Repin's *Saviour* is significantly closer to the spirit of ancient icons. The image is clearly based on traditional representations of the mandylion (Plate 1); however, the intense personal charisma of the figure of Christ also associates the image with the high romanticism of Kramskoi and Ge which, as we have seen, departs dramatically from the spirit of icon painting in several respects. In a similar way, *Mother of God with Christ* and *St Sergius* by Viktor Vasnetsov (1849–1926) capture something of the austerity and otherworldliness of icons but, unlike traditional icons, these works also exploit the emotive and atmospheric potential of resplendent dusky skies. The icons at Abramtsevo were clearly conceived within the context of an ancient tradition and some of the artists working on the project were later seen to have 'reinstated a national style in religious art'.[18] Although they were in many ways at odds with the spirit of that tradition, the total commitment and thoroughness with which they embraced the work is an indication of how they considered the language of their ancient religious culture to be expressive of their own feelings.

The building and decoration of the church at Abramtsevo was followed by many other projects involving the restoration of ancient churches or the building of new churches in the medieval style. In 1886, Viktor Vasnetsov was commissioned to design a Byzantine interior for the Cathedral of St Vladimir in Kiev, a project which was supported by Alexander III. Vasnetsov had studied at the Academy in St Petersburg and was originally known for his genre and history paintings. He joined the Wanderers in 1878 and formed an indispensable part of the colony at Abramtsevo, where he came to associate the responsibility of contemporary artists with the example of 'artists of old'. In a letter to Yelizaveta Mamontova, the wife of Savva Mamontov, Vasnetsov wrote:

> How the artists of old amaze us by the depth and immediacy and sincerity of their depiction. How fully and fearlessly they accomplish their tasks. Where do they get it all from, this warmth, this sincerity and courage? Not all of them are geniuses by any means! ... There is a simple answer to the question. We have to picture to ourselves how, in earlier ages and in his own age, all the people surrounding the artist, great and small, educated and ignorant, profound and simple, believed in the same things as he did. All of them lived and drew sustenance from the same aspirations. That is how artists great and small could find work to satisfy them heart and soul; how every heartfelt word they uttered was received with joy and gratitude. What passionate love they put into the churches they built, and the picturesque poems they wrote, and the entire worlds they hewed out of stone. And the whole crowd was agog, and waited eagerly, and rejoiced in the creations of its artists.[19]

Vasnetsov's growing desire to revive the traditional values of Russian art and culture was reflected in the shift of his subject matter away from social history towards episodes from ancient folklore and legend. This shift coincided with his move in 1878 to Moscow, the heart of traditional Russia, where, he said, 'I felt I had come home ... The Kremlin. St Basil's Cathedral ... almost reduced me to tears, so much did I feel in my heart that this was part of me, and never to be forgotten'.[20]

Vasnetsov's passionate interest in ancient Russia naturally brought him into contact with Russia's Byzantine heritage and rich tradition of icon painting. Besides assembling his own collection of sixteenth- and seventeenth-century icons, he also travelled to Venice, Ravenna and Sicily to study original Byzantine monuments *in situ* in preparation for the commission for frescos in the Cathedral of St Vladimir in Kiev. In direct response to these precedents, his massive painting of *The Mother of God with Christ* in the dome of the cathedral's apse (a duplicate of an earlier version of the image that he produced for the iconostasis at Abramtsevo) is ultimately derived from the twelfth-century mosaic of the same subject in the apse of the cathedral in Torcello.[21] Many of the painting's features are typical of the icon-painting tradition, and its expansiveness and wide-eyed simplicity are reminiscent of the eleventh-century mosaic of the Mother of God in the Cathedral of St Sophia, also in Kiev. However, despite the number of similarities, Vasnetsov did not attempt to capture the austere spirit of these Byzantine originals. This intensity and rigour would come with a later generation; in their place, he infused his work with the airy fullness of a Raphael *Madonna*. In conservative circles, his art was seen to adapt the religious purity of orthodox iconography to the sophisticated realism of academic art. By shedding the primitive stylisations of medieval icons, Vasnetsov was judged to have brought orthodox iconography to an unprecedented level of perfection. It was only in subsequent years that the dramatic worldliness of his style was seen to be at odds with the sacramental and quasi-existential nature of icons.

Although Vasnetsov was instrumental in the

13

Mikhail Nesterov

Photograph of the artist's second wife Ekaterina Nesterova and their daughter Natalia, 1908–11
David King Collection, London

14

Vladimirskaya Mother of God with Christ ('Hodigitria'), *c.*1500
Tempera on wooden panel
32 x 25 cm (12 5/8 x 9 7/8 in)
Temple Gallery, London

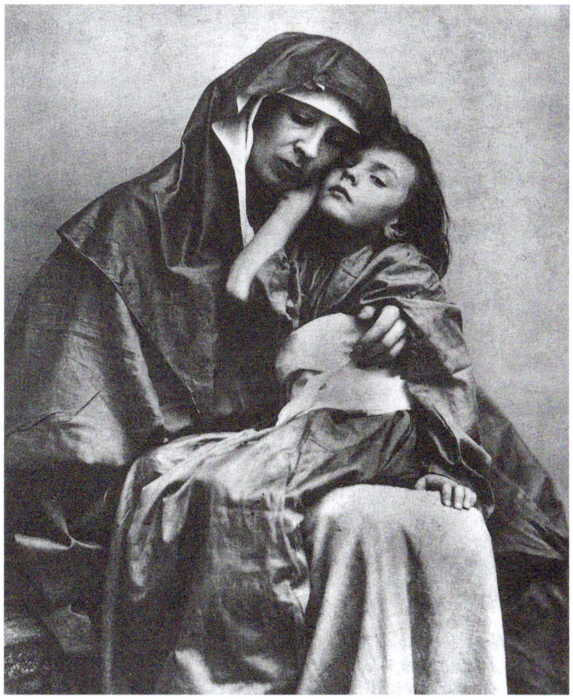

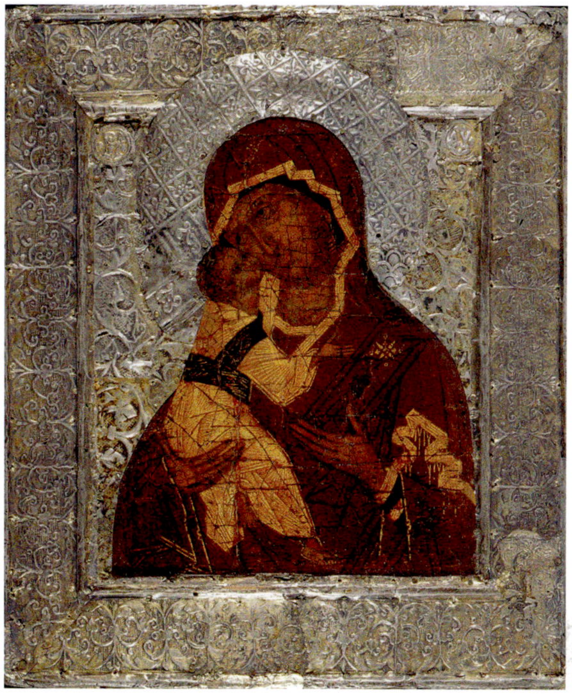

revival of religious art in Russia, he was more interested in it as an agent for the continuity of the Russian tradition than as a religious medium in its own right. Alongside the saints that were habitually represented in icons, a number of semi-legendary national heroes – Princess Olga, Andrei Bogoliubsky, the chronicler Nestor – were also included in his iconographic programme, elevating the very evolution of the Russian nation to the status of sacred history. Mikhail Nesterov (1862–1942), who worked alongside Vasnetsov at Abramtsevo, was more deeply interested in the fundamentally religious appeal of sacred Russian art. Nesterov had trained as a realist under Perov in Moscow but, especially after the death of his wife in childbirth in 1886, was influenced by Vasnetsov's ability to evoke a rich and potent sense of atmosphere. Unlike Vasnetsov's saints, however, which, though relatively traditional in design, are conventionally romanticised in mood, Nesterov's representations of religious figures are naturalistic and intimate. This difference in approach is underlined by the fact that even for his traditional iconic compositions he worked from life as much as from imagined ideals. A photograph, dating from between 1908 and 1911 (when he was working on the frescos of the Convent of SS Mary and Martha in Moscow for which he also painted the iconostasis), shows his second wife posing with their daughter in the highly intimate positions of the *Vladimirskaya Mother of God with Christ* (Plates 13 and 14). The couple's pose, set against a plain pale background, follows its iconic prototype down to the finest details: the monumental pyramidal form of the Mother of God; her tilted head and downcast eyes, in contrast to the outward and somewhat distracted glance of the twisting child; the strictly rectilinear folds in the mother's head-dress – made from a deliberately stiff material – and the glimpse of white veil beneath it; the two faces pressed together; the mother's large left hand emerging in the midst of a wealth of dramatic drapery-folds and curving protectively round the child. The photograph reflects Nesterov's wish to reconcile traditional iconography with the artistic integrity of observation, bringing a modern way of seeing to an image of universal significance.

Many of Nesterov's works are infused with a strong feeling of nature mysticism. In his *Vision of* the *Boy Bartholomew* (Plate 15) of 1889–90 – the first of a series of paintings based on the exemplary life of St Sergius of Radonezh – the bright figure of an innocent young boy, worked up from a photograph of the artist's son, is counterpoised with the darkly shrouded and faceless figure of the old saint. The scene is characteristically set beneath a pallid, washed-out sky and the two figures are absorbed into the static quiescent mood of the Russian land around them. The work focuses on the subtle transmission of spiritual energy. The viewer's attention is initially drawn to this quality by the narrative of the wise old man helping the boy, but it is subtly kept there – and deepened – by the bewitching and elusive mood of the surrounding landscape. In keeping with Nesterov's quest for 'the living soul of living forms, of living beauty in nature, in thoughts, the heart and everywhere',[22] the entire picture is suffused with religious feeling. As in most of Nesterov's early landscapes, the natural world is silent and still; it is multilayered and translucent, luminous without being bright; it borders on the rapturous without ever being sensational. The fact that the overall setting of the vision is so profoundly ordinary and undramatic only serves to intensify the impression that the quality of awareness momentarily captured between the two figures is always latently present in the very landscape of Russia.

Like Vasnetsov, Nesterov became involved in reconstructions of churches in the medieval style.[23] His *Vision of the Boy Bartholomew*, painted at Abramtsevo, prompted Adrian Prakhov, who had acted as consultant on the Abramtsevo church project, to invite him to work on the frescos for the Cathedral of St Vladimir in Kiev which he was also supervising. Again like Vasnetsov, who had begun working on this project in 1886, Nesterov travelled in Italy to acquire first-hand experience of Byzantine art before embarking on the work. He also travelled widely in Russia, visiting monasteries and hermitages where he became thoroughly immersed in the traditional use of images in Orthodox spirituality. He is known to have painted icons on a number of occasions, including for the iconostasis at St Vladimir's. However, because his priority was to convey his religious feelings rather than sustain a tradition *per se*, his interest in historic styles was more a matter of expedience than principle. He wrote:

> The Byzantine style is closest to us ... but may serve as a model only with severe reservations... In itself no one style, artificially evinced, can fully satisfy the aesthetic sense, and even less can it satisfy the seeking for faith itself... What fascinates me in Byzantium is not what is not there, or was there once upon a time, but what is there and has survived to our day in all its pristine purity. I am fascinated by the life force in it.[24]

It has been said of Nesterov that he succeeded, 'more than any other master of these years ... in creating a truly artistic interpretation of Russian pietism and medieval faith'[25] and, certainly, his

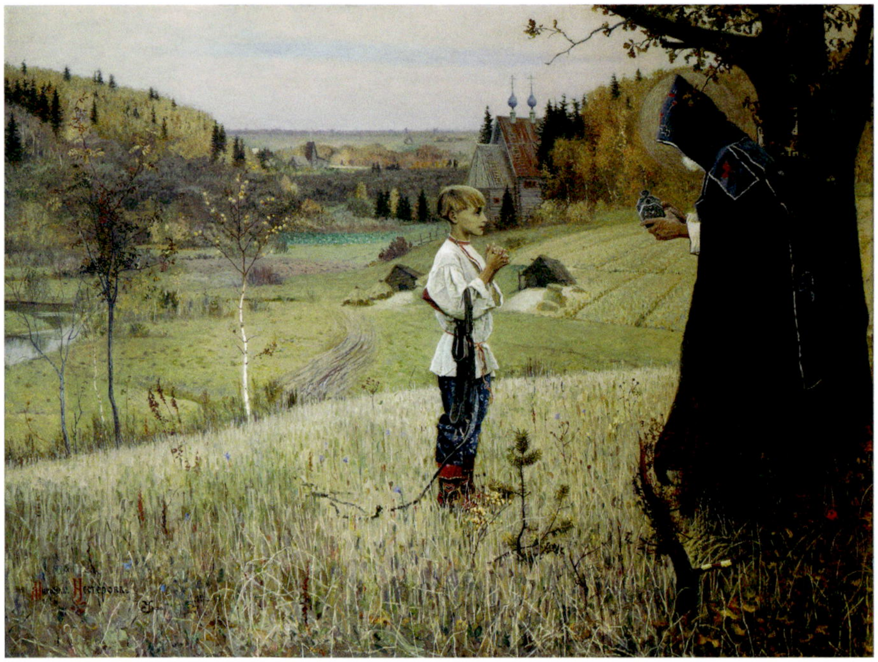

15
Mikhail Nesterov
Vision of The Boy Bartholomew, 1889–90
Oil on canvas
160 x 211 cm (63 x 83 ⅛ in)
Tretyakov Gallery, Moscow

religious works evoke something of the purity and fervour of Holy Rus. However, his work also retains an element of mystique and sentimentality that is entirely foreign to traditional Russian sacred art. In this respect, his work was more indebted to the poetics of the French painters, Jules Bastien-Lepage and Puvis de Chavannes, whose work he saw when he visited Paris in 1889.

Although Slavophile artists were sincere in their efforts to recreate a genuinely medieval and Russian atmosphere, their impressions of ancient Rus were often distorted by the limited availability of accurate archaeological and historical information. What they saw was rarely as ancient and authentic as they believed. As icons had always been seen to serve a spiritual rather than aesthetic function, facilitated by the clarity of the image rather than its beauty, many of the most ancient examples had been repainted over the centuries, sometimes several times, in order to 'improve' their condition. When some early icons were reworked, they were updated into the decorative styles of later centuries which, from the late sixteenth century onwards, became increasingly ornamental, naturalistic and romanticised in mood. In the imperial Stroganov and Palekh schools, for instance, there was a movement away from the simplicity and immediacy of the visual impact of medieval icons towards a miniaturist style of greater complexity and refinement (Plate 128). In these schools, the simplified architectural settings of earlier medieval icons became enchanted clusters of galleries, towers and domes – reminiscent of fairy-tale palaces – in which every surface is enriched by minute decorative detail. Although architectural ensembles in this extravagant style did actually exist in Russia from the sixteenth century onwards – St Basil's in Moscow is only the most famous example – the impression conveyed by these icons is one of otherworldly fantasies. Such icons came to be seen in a haze of legend and mythology, as glimmers of light in a deep and mysterious past, though they were not as ancient as many people believed. The medieval ideal was further distorted by the fact that the influence of naturalism from Europe, following the westernising reforms of Peter the Great in the eighteenth century, led to a proliferation of illusionistic, 'charismatic' Baroque icons that contributed to a thoroughly false impression of icons as sentimental images of sensational visions. Icons that were not reworked were encased in jewel-encrusted silver frames (called *rizas*, Plate 14), or simply became concealed beneath thick layers of darkened varnish, giving the misleading impression that authentic icons are dark and complex, exotic and obscure.

Up until the 1890s, it had been the Romantic and nationalistic potential of icons, rather than their aesthetic appeal or theological significance, which had attracted the attention of contemporary artists. By the end of the nineteenth century, this overtly nostalgic attitude had served its purpose as an agent of nationalistic development and several decades of Romantic attachment to the past came to be challenged by other agendas. The academic historicism of the Slavophile pioneers and the motive to create a modern Russian culture began to disentangle. With regard to historicism, the continuing process of research and restoration gave rise to an increasingly accurate and objective picture of the history of icon painting. Conservatives were further motivated to pursue this end by the mass-production of cheap uncanonical tin and printed-paper icons, which threatened to corrupt the integrity of the craft of icon-making and was met with widespread disapproval and a determination to preserve the 'authentic' spiritual heritage of the country. Under Tsar Nicholas II, who ruled from 1894, the Orthodox Church initiated a programme of 'preservation and protection of the ancient manner of icon painting and its traditions, as well as the strict reproduction of ancient icon painting images without any alteration, whatever it might be, in favour of modern artistic requirements'.[26]

The process of restoring icons to their original condition, often remarkably well preserved under layers of overpaint, became a metaphor for discovering the true nature of icons, itself obscured beneath layers of misconception and which, newly understood, was re-incorporated into contemporary debate about the role of art. In 1901, a 'Committee for the Guardianship of Russian Icon Painting' was founded, under the tsar's patronage, as part of a broad revival of the traditional religious culture of Russia. Led by Count Sergei Sheremetev and Nikodim Kondakov, the commission aimed to instil traditional centres of icon painting with the organic and integrated ethics of the Arts and Crafts Movement. Besides reconciling aesthetic sensibility with manual skill and application, icons were believed to unite all levels of society and to express the soul of the nation and of the people. In particular, the moral and social values associated with icon painting – communal, creative, integrated – were to be revived and continued as a form of popular culture. In 1902, Kondakov published a report, entitled *The Contemporary State of Russian Folk Icon Painting*, describing the condition of icon-painting workshops in the villages of Palekh, Mstera and Kholui in Vladimir province and Borisovka in Kursk province. In the same year, a number of schools were established with a view to raising the artistic quality of icon painting. These schools taught the techniques, iconography and regional styles of historic icons, but also instructed students to follow the example of contemporary revivalist masters such as Viktor Vasnetsov, whose works in St Vladimir's, Kiev, were copied in provincial churches all over Russia. Academic life-drawing, considered by contemporary art theorists to be one of the mainsprings of artistic quality, was also taught – by graduates from the St Petersburg Academy of Arts. Students were encouraged to copy icons by hand, using graph paper, rather than transferring designs from tracings. Courses in the conservation of medieval icons were also offered. Besides familiarising students with the techniques and styles of historic icons, which they were frequently required to copy, the new interest in icon restoration led to numerous icons being seen in their original condition, hitherto concealed beneath layers of overpaint and darkened varnish. A five-volume collection of copies of historic icons and frescos, entitled *The Iconography of Our Lord God and Saviour Jesus Christ*, was among the commission's earliest resolutions, though only the first volume was published, in 1905.

While the craft of icon painting was being regenerated from within, in keeping with the general revitalisation of the tradition of folk craft, a new demand for icons was also developed. The canonisation of new saints aroused public piety and created new subjects for icon painters. Seraphim of Sarov, for instance, was canonised in 1903 and was immediately represented in icons. Vasnetsov's icon of Patriarch Germogen, who was canonised in 1913, typically attempted to refresh Orthodox tradition by introducing traditional principles of art and church piety to forms of contemporary culture – a contemporary artist representing a contemporary saint in a style that was related to contemporary aesthetics but which was nevertheless clearly rooted in tradition. Shops selling traditional crafts and icons were established in towns all over the country and icons were promoted as the epitome of Russian art at trade fairs at home and abroad. Local ecclesiastical authorities were asked to help monitor the quality of icons that were available in their regions in the belief – widely discussed in art journals – that the ethical and aesthetic dimension of icon production did actually have a subtle influence on the morality of the people.

Throughout the second half of the nineteenth century, the revival of traditional Russian values and artistic styles was engaged as a quest for national identity. By locating themselves firmly within the context of Russian history, artists hoped to realise something of the sense of necessity that they believed to inform the evolution of the Russian nation as a whole. Towards the end of the century, however, the nationalist cause became increasingly institutionalised, both politically and by the Church, and it lost its cutting edge. Despite an improvement in the quality of craftsmanship, religious art tended to become stereotyped and uninspired. At the same time, recognition of the cultural status of Russia began to gather momentum abroad, relieving Russian artists of the impulse to justify themselves on purely nationalistic terms. Prophets of popular culture ceased to require art to function as an articulation and consummation of the past; they felt free to look at the content of contemporary culture on its own terms and to allow it to determine its own forms. For several decades, the Romantic associations of the past had served as an effective vehicle for the development of a national self-consciousness. Now that that self-consciousness had evolved, it was necessary for it to sustain itself from its own resources.

NOTES

1. Kirichenko, p.88. The icons from the St Petersburg Academy Museum later became the core of the collection of icons in the Russian Museum.
2. Buslaev's *General Concepts in Icon Painting* was published in 1866. See Stavrou, p.161.
3. Alexeyev, p.61. See also Wahl.
4. Alexeyev, p.61.
5. Ibid, p.62.
6. Ibid, p.63
7. Dostoyevsky, F., *The Diary of a Writer*, 1873, translated by Boris Brasol, Haslemere, 1984, pp 57–60. See McDuff, pp 19–20.
8. See McDuff, p.20.
9. Russian Museum, St Petersburg.
10. Hamilton, p.376.
11. 'My God – Christ – is the greatest of atheists, a person who has destroyed God in the universe and shifted him directly to the centre of the human spirit and who, therefore, goes calmly to his death'; letter to Ilya Repin, 30 January 1874, Lang, p.5.
12. Kramskoi letter to Fedor Vasilev, 10 October 1872, in Goldstein, N.G., *Ivan Nikolaevich Kramskoy, Pisma Statji*, vol.1, Moscow, 1955–6, pp 132–3, quoted in Lang, p.3.
13. Hamilton, p.380.
14. Wright, pp 163–76; and Ziolkowski, pp 164–81.
15. Ivan Goncharov's *Oblomov*, published in 1855. See Batchan, p.329.
16. See Ryan, passim.
17. Valkenier (1989), p.123.
18. Ibid, p.125.
19. Kirichenko, p.146.
20. Ibid, p.146.
21. Illustrated in Beckwith, no.242, p.278.
22. Nesterov, M. V., *Letters*, selection, introduction and commentary by A. Rusakova, Leningrad, 1968, p.134, quoted in Kirichenko, p.229.
23. See Kirichenko, p.228; Rusakova, 1990.
24. Kirichenko, p.229.
25. Hamilton, p.398.
26. Quoted in Nichols, p.139.

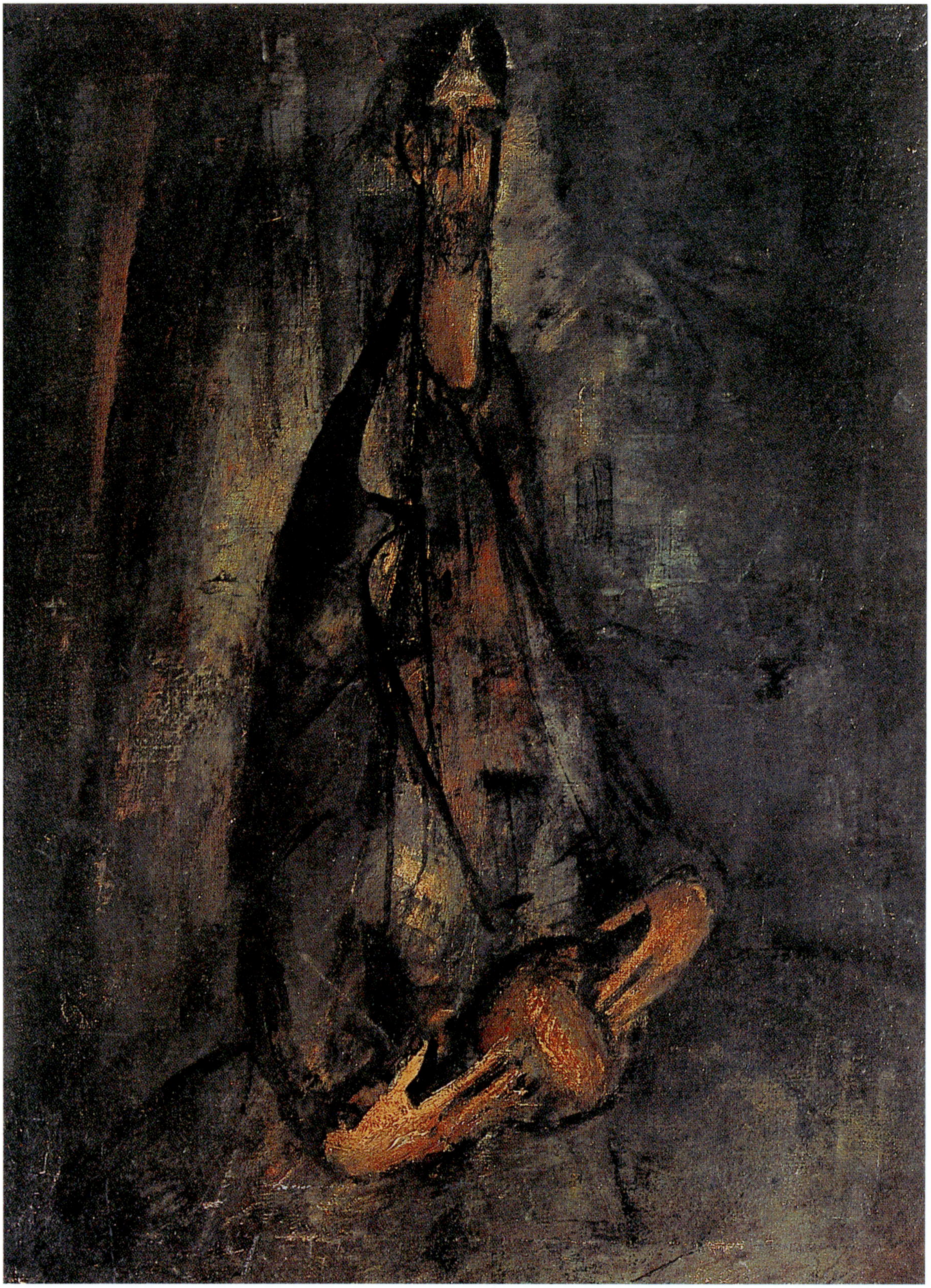

3

The Iconic Techniques of the Avant-Garde

16
Vasily Chekrygin

Portrait of Tatlin, 1913
Oil on canvas
68.5 x 52 cm (27 x 20 ½ in)
Private collection

THROUGHOUT THE NINETEENTH CENTURY, revivalism served as a medium for the realisation of a contemporary Russian culture. Towards the end of the century, attitudes towards the past became increasingly academic and less immediately concerned to influence contemporary society. At the same time, the search for a contemporary form of culture became less dependent on the Romantic potential of the past and more directly in touch with modern life. From the 1860s, an increasing number of Russian artists became attracted to the technical advances occurring in the West and travelled abroad. For several decades, prize-winning artists from the Academy had already been travelling to Rome to study the ancient and modern classics, with a view to bringing what they learned back to their homeland. Well known painters such as Karl Briullov (1799–1852) and Alexander Ivanov (1806–58) spent most of their careers in Rome, though they continued to be seen as intensely national artists. The monumentally ambitious and grandiose masterpieces of both artists (*The Last Days of Pompeii*, 1830–3, and *Christ's Appearance to the People*, 1832–7, respectively) were both painted in Rome and sent home. After the uprisings in various European cities in 1848, many Russian artists were recalled to Russia, for fear that they would be tainted by corrupt revolutionary ideas.

In 1873–6, Ilya Repin, the most influential painter of the period, took advantage of a scholarship from the Academy in St Petersburg to spend three years in Rome, Naples and especially Paris where he was able to experiment with purely formal artistic issues at the expense of social and critical subject matter. Ivan Kramskoi, who Repin regarded as his mentor, disapproved of Repin's apparent abandonment of the nationalist cause for the sake of empty aestheticism (although he had also spent some time abroad) and he exhorted Repin to return to Russia where his painting could honour its true purpose of social criticism and moral edification. Unlike European artists, he maintained, Russian artists should not feel 'free as birds'. Repin was relieved to have shed the burden of responsibility that weighed on artists working in Russia, but he did also feel unsatisfied with the 'meaninglessness' of French Impressionism, saying it was 'merely brushwork, nothing more'. Interestingly, he was aware that his ambivalence was tied up with his physical absence from Russia, accepting that a sense of the social responsibility of the artist was innate in his land, climate and culture, and that it would impose itself on him again on his return home. Replying to Kramskoi's criticism in 1874, he wrote, from Paris, 'I have now completely forgotten how one reflects or passes judgement, and I do not regret having lost a capacity by which, previously, I was completely devoured. On the contrary, I would prefer it never to return. But something tells me that, once I am back in my dear mother country, it will be there again – it is simply part of the climate. May God preserve Russian art from devouring analyses!'[1]

The relationship between Russia and the West had always been a vexed one. The thoroughly exclusive westernising reforms of Peter the Great and the anti-European reaction to the influence of Napoleon were just two of the causes of the profound ambivalence towards the West that became increasingly characteristic of Russian culture as a whole during the nineteenth century. The Slavophile movement was the first coherent expression of a conscious intention to formulate a national identity distinct from that of western Europe and, as we have seen, it led to a progressive revival of traditional values throughout Russia. It is a persistent irony that the great artistic forms through which the cultural elite of Russia came to express the nation's sense of identity – the novel, the symphony, the oil painting – were derived from the West. While writers, composers and painters were able to infuse these forms with a quality that was so uniquely drawn from the landscape and climate of Russia that no other country could imitate it even if it wanted to – namely its scale, physical size, intensity and breadth – there remained a profound need to realise a form of cultural expression that was distinctly Russian. Alongside the growing search for a thread of cultural continuity in Russian history, there existed a passionate oscillation between receptivity to new artistic discoveries from the West and a total rejection of the westernising implications of those discoveries, which were perceived as demeaning.

The Slavophile debate raged for several decades. By the 1890s, its vision, once urgent and experimental, had become parochial and formulaic. In reaction to the narrow, stifling atmosphere that it created, a new generation of artists turned away from nationalistic interests towards the more hedonistic aestheticism of *fin-de-siècle* Europe. Unlike the Romantic culture from which they emerged, these artists, broadly associated with the 'World of Art' movement, initiated by Alexander Benois, Sergei Diaghilev and Leon Bakst in 1898, were neither religious nor traditional. The aim of the movement was to liberate the arts from the variety of formalities that had been imposed upon them by historical and social convention. At a purely functional level, it provided an artists' association, an exhibiting organisation and a magazine. The movement was not concerned, like its predecessors, to continue and consummate a historical tradition; it was concerned to develop an artistic culture that was a genuine reflection and product of contemporary society. Rather than strive to renew and revitalise the traditional content of Russian culture – its history and legends – members of the circle were intent on creating a new and contemporary language which would allow the content of contemporary culture to manifest itself spontaneously and freely. In principle, the heritage of Russia was of interest to the extent that it served this cause. Diaghilev, who began his entrepreneurial career as an organiser of exhibitions of 'old Russian art', certainly saw the seeds of cultural renewal in the past. Referring to the excessive influence of western naturalism, he maintained that 'as long as the Russian national art misses a consciously composed harmony, a majestic simplicity and a unique beauty of colours we will not have real art. You only have to look at our great pride, the old time of Novgorod and Suzdal'.[2] In practice, however, the momentum of the historicising tendency in Russian culture was felt to be so limiting that the World of Art movement increasingly turned its attention to the revolution in artistic techniques taking place in the West. In 1898, for instance, the reproduction of a nostalgic work by Viktor Vasnetsov in the first issue of the society's magazine provoked an outcry from some of its members who claimed that to include a work in such a conservative style was to 'confuse purely artistic standards of value ... with a cultural-historical phenomenon'.[3]

From 1903 the functions of the World of Art movement were dispersed among new artistic groups and associations. In its wake, there appeared a new generation of artists led by Mikhail Larionov, Natalia Goncharova, Kazimir Malevich and Vladimir Tatlin. Although these artists – the avant-garde proper – ultimately dissociated themselves from the elitist literary aestheticism of the World of Art movement, the westernising orientation that the World of Art initiated remained the most active influence on Russian modernism until around 1911. Throughout this period, Russian artists were exposed to European influence in a number of different ways. Many of them travelled in Europe, especially to Munich and Paris, where they met their European counterparts; exhibitions of contemporary European art were organised in Moscow and St Petersburg; a growing number of Russian journals provided artists with a constant supply of articles on European artists with reproductions of their work; and, most importantly of all, the magnificent collections of the two great merchant-collectors Sergei Shchukin and Ivan Morosov, comprising a wealth of paintings by the Post-Impressionists and Nabis as well as by the ultra-moderns Pablo Picasso, Henri Matisse and others, were opened to the public on a weekly basis.

The rejection by pioneers of the avant-garde of sentimental nationalism, in favour of a more dynamic cosmopolitanism, was a crucial step in the evolution of Russian art. On the one hand, it enabled artists to purify their art of elements that they regarded as a distraction from the true potential of art as an expressive medium, such as illusionism and deceptively emotive, nationalistic subject matter. On the other hand, it enabled them to investigate the expressive potential of artistic techniques on their own terms. For many artists, an encounter with the West served as a catalyst through which to bring about this purification. Natalia Goncharova, for instance, acknowledged that it was her experience of western art that awakened her to the significance and value of the art of her own country. She could have been speaking for the avant-garde movement as a whole when she said that it was through the West that she came to see the possibility of an art that was both truly Russian and truly contemporary.[4] However, she was also very quick to point out that, once it had served its purpose, the example of the West should be rapidly dropped. From around 1910, both she and her partner (later husband) Mikhail Larionov became increasingly outspoken in voicing their disapproval of Russians who exposed themselves to what they regarded as the superficially aestheticising influence of modern art in Munich and Paris, at the expense of traditional sources within the national tradition. In January 1912, they refused to participate in the second Jack of Diamonds exhibition because it included works by German and French painters; in its place, they set up their own group, The Donkey's Tail, which excluded the work of foreign artists or of artists working abroad (with the significant exception of Chagall) from its exhibitions.[5] Goncharova's own work epitomised the relationship between a practical interest in western techniques and an ideological rejection of western artistic values. She strongly maintained that the West opened her eyes not to a wisdom of its own but to the wisdom of her own tradition, to which she subsequently returned:

> At the beginning of my development I learned most of all from my French contemporaries. They stimulated my awareness, and I realised the great significance and value of the art of my country... Now I shake the dust from my feet and leave the West, considering its vulgarising significance trivial and worthless – my path is towards the source of all arts – the East...
>
> Similarly I find those people ridiculous who advocate individuality and who assume there is some value in their 'I' even when it is extremely limited. Untalented individuality is as useless as bad imitation, let alone the old-fashionedness of such an argument.
>
> I express my deep gratitude to western painters for all they have taught me.
>
> After carefully modifying everything that could be done along these lines and after earning the honour of being placed alongside contemporary western artists – in the West itself – I now prefer to investigate a new path.[6]

With these words, she expressed a characteristically Russian ambivalence towards both individualism and aestheticism in art, albeit in a radically contemporary form. In her work, Goncharova was not seeking so much to express herself as to express a reality that she believed to be greater than herself, with which the national identity of Russia was profoundly intertwined. Her belief in a popular transpersonal role for art, which had been a definitive characteristic of Russian nationalism since the middle of the nineteenth century, was reflected throughout the avant-garde movement in the tendency of artists to formulate collective political aims and to subscribe to them in passionately committed groups of exhibitors (however loose, short-lived and torn by rivalries these commitments might be). Her efforts to revive folk traditions served not only to historicise, popularise and politicise her ideals, and to lend them the expressive force of simplicity, but also to aggressively dissociate from the exclusive elegance and sophistication of aestheticism, and the arbitrariness of subjectivity.

As these ideals gathered momentum, becoming ever more closely tied up with revolutionary politics, the scope for subjectivity became more limited, charged with the negative associations of elitism and self-indulgence. Artists disinclined to subject their art to the new ideals became increasingly marginalised until, after the October Revolution, the notion of art for art's sake became, to all intents and purposes, blasphemous. As a result, many artists of a 'subjective' disposition emigrated to the West which was clearly more conducive to the development of a kind of art that was based on poetic effect and physiological impact rather than political meaning. Significantly, despite their nationalism, Goncharova and Larionov both emigrated in 1915, settling in Paris in 1919. Wassily Kandinsky and Marc Chagall – both of whom were highly subjective and idiosyncratic artists – emigrated in 1921 and 1922 respectively. For many such artists of course, the idea of Russia remained deeply affecting – powerful and pure, ancient and mysterious – but, in contrast to their compatriots at home, it was less politicised and less collectivised. In many cases, it was deeply personal and poeticised, in keeping with the tradition of individualism and genius that had been celebrated in the West (in contrast to Orthodox conformity) since the time of Vasari; it was aesthetic and physiological (subject to personal experience) rather than doctrinal (subject to an overriding objective truth). As a result, it served as a mainspring for personal visualisations and insights, rather than a communication of political ideology.

The development of the avant-garde in Russia was inspired by contact with the West but it was also precipitated from within by the example of the highly idiosyncratic artist Mikhail Vrubel (1856–1910), who worked on the fringe of the World of Art movement but whose work also anticipated some of the fundamental innovations of the avant-garde movement. Vrubel was unique among Russian artists in bridging the gap between the Romantic naturalism of the 1880s and the modernism of the beginning of the twentieth century, although the weight of this change proved too great and in 1905 Vrubel went tragically mad. He died at an asylum in 1910 at the age of 54.

In 1880 Vrubel entered the St Petersburg Academy where he received an academic training. While still a student at the Academy, he was invited to work on the restoration of the twelfth-century frescos in the St Cyril's Church in Kiev. This involved both the restoration of damaged originals and the replacement of lost originals with new works painted in a fitting Byzantinesque style. Before executing the work, Vrubel immersed himself in the study of icons and Byzantine art, copying and making designs from ancient models. In 1884, he travelled to Venice, Ravenna and Rome where he was deeply impressed by the richness and splendour of the Byzantine mosaics. Some of the panels he painted for St Cyril's were executed during this trip. Two years later, he worked on the new frescos of the Cathedral of St Vladimir, also in Kiev. Although his designs were eventually rejected on account of their incompatibility with Orthodox tradition (they were finally realised by Viktor Vasnetsov), these experiences were to leave an indelible mark on all his subsequent work.

Vrubel particularly admired the way Byzantine artists took advantage of the flatness of a picture surface for aesthetic purposes. Rather than attempt to create an illusion of depth, imitative of the kind of space occupied by the viewer, Byzantine artists had evolved a technique that was expressive on its own account. They achieved this through the stylised use of lines and flat planes in the treatment of draperies and through a masterly use of colour to create the effect of surface movement. It was in response to the influence of Byzantium that Vrubel first formulated his interest in the potential of art as an expressive medium rather than as an occasion for deceptive illusionism. Following the example of Byzantine art, he became increasingly preoccupied with the formal two-dimensional properties of the picture plane. In 1890, he wrote, 'The chief mistake of the contemporary artists who try to revive the Byzantine style is their lack of appreciation for the Byzantine artists' use of drapery. They make of it a mere sheet where the Byzantine artists revealed so much wit. Byzantine painting differs fundamentally from three-dimensional art. Its whole essence lies in the ornamental arrangement of form which emphasises the flatness of the wall.'[7]

Vrubel's understanding of the expressive potential of surface design is already apparent in his *Descent of the Holy Spirit*, painted in 1885 for St Cyril's in Kiev (Plate 17) where his pointillistic technique is clearly based on Byzantine mosaics. The highly linear treatment of the draperies in this work – another typically Byzantine feature – creates a curiously abstract effect. Vrubel's non-commissioned secular works take his fascination with the aesthetic potential of artistic technique, especially the use of line and colour, to unprecedented extremes. Many of his later paintings – for instance, *Lilacs* of 1900

(Plate 18) – are composed of frenetic swarms of luminescent brushstrokes that seem reluctant to settle on the picture surface. This impression of dynamic surface movement is created by the minute fragmentation of line (in a way that anticipates Cubism), a proliferation of visual detail, often facilitated by the presence of rich textiles, and passages of pure abstract pattern. Glassy highlights are scattered loosely over a dark and evenly toned ground. Despite creating an impression of space – albeit a thoroughly obscure and ambiguous one – Vrubel often seems loath to commit himself to any mark that might seem to penetrate the picture plane at all. In some cases, if it was not for the presence of a diminutive human face or figure to create a sense of scale and context, the picture would dissolve into a turbulent mass of swirling colour-points.

Besides his many portraits and religious commissions, Vrubel's iconography was also highly personal and subjective – more closely related to the visionary subject matter of the Romantics than to the realist concerns of the avant-garde. Towards the end of his life, his iconography became increasingly manic and all-consuming. He became particularly identified with an androgynous love-death figure, called the Demon (after a poem by Mikhail Lermontov), and he painted a series of pictures on this theme culminating in the catatonic *Demon Downcast* in 1902. Although Vrubel himself was unable to resist the vortical pull of his own visions, their combination of linearity, dynamism, opalescence and abstraction was to live on in a new form in the work of the younger artists who followed him. Vrubel's work was instrumental in the creation of an avant-garde movement in Russia. Its importance lay in the fact that it explored the worlds of colour, form and line for their own sakes. Like Post-Impressionism in western Europe, it released the techniques of art from their subservience to

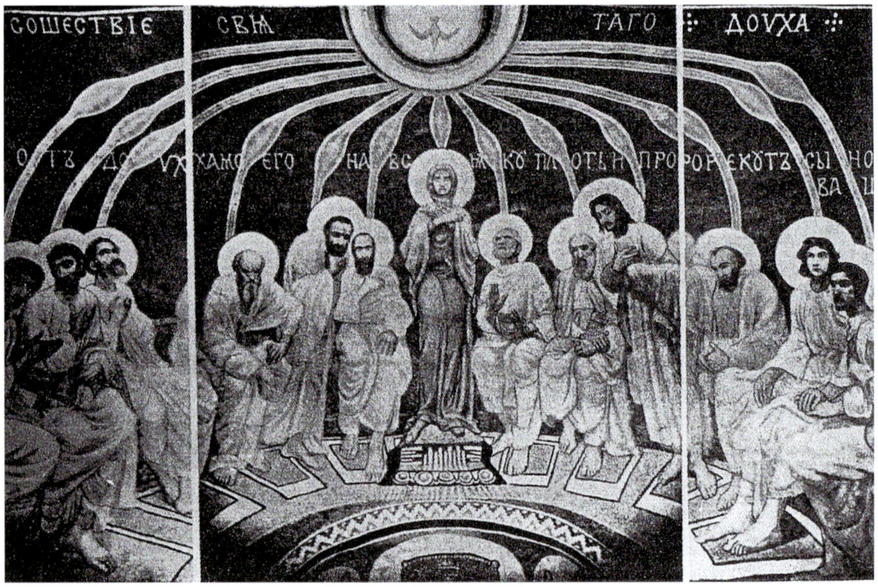

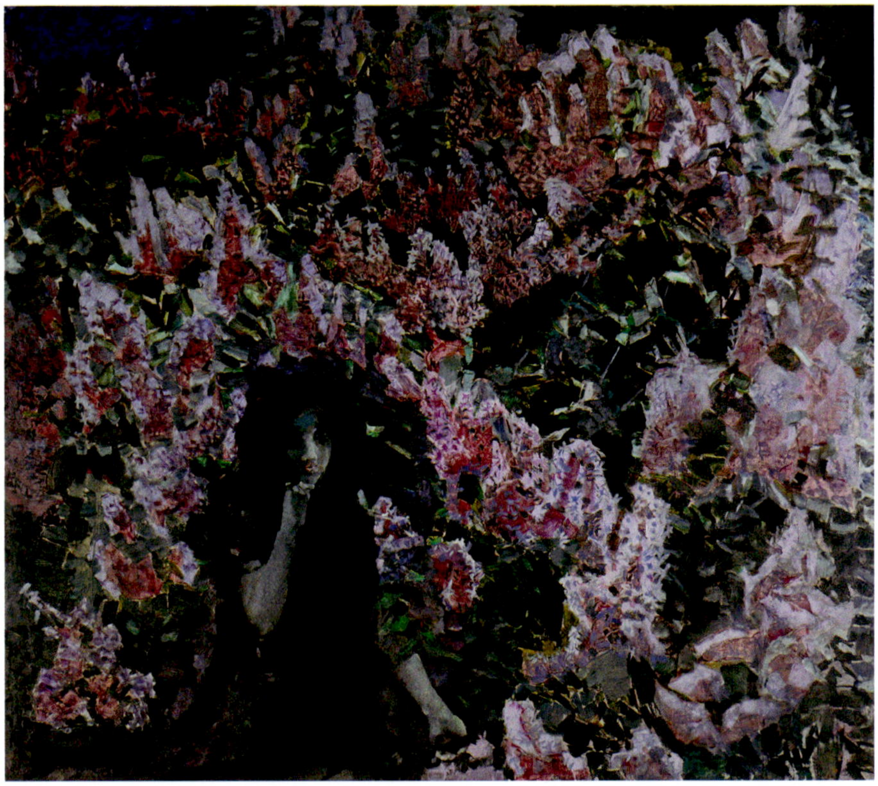

17 *(opposite, top)*
Mikhail Vrubel

Descent of the Holy Spirit, St Cyril's Church, Kiev, 1885
Oil on stucco
6 x 9.25 m (6.5 x 10 yd)
David King Collection, London

18 *(opposite, bottom)*
Mikhail Vrubel

Lilacs, 1900
Oil on canvas
160 x 177 cm (63 x 69 ⅝ in)
Tretyakov Gallery, Moscow

subject matter and imbued them with an expressive potential of their own.

For a number of artists, experimentation with the Symbolist aesthetic of Vrubel represented the first step away from conventional representation towards a specifically avant-garde style. In 1913, the writer Vsevolod Dmitriev wrote, in the journal *Apollon*, that:

> A significant re-evaluation of ancient Russian icon painting ... has also changed our tastes and attitudes towards Vrubel... The mural paintings at St Kirill's, the studies for St Vladimir, and the late 'Byzantine' works of Vrubel which used to appear as the prelude and conclusion to the more important Moscow period of the artist's activity, now emerge as his fundamental and vital aspect... For the contemporary artistic movement, Vrubel's whole heroic life leads the way to an authentic revival of ancient Russian *ikonopis* [icon painting].[8]

The early work of Mikhail Larionov (1881–1964), for instance, which explored the semi-abstract potential of representing iridescent and light-pervaded objects (fish, water and sun-filtering trees) with minutely fragmented surfaces of coloured brushstrokes, was clearly indebted to Vrubel. The shimmering lights of Larionov's *Peacock* (1908) both connect him with Vrubel (whose *Demon Downcast* lies strewn over a bed of crushed peacock feathers) and anticipate the dynamic and interacting light effects of his own fully developed Rayist works, as described on page 61. While Larionov was adapting the extreme Impressionism of Vrubel, Kazimir Malevich (1878–1935) was exploring the dusky, introverted imagery of the Symbolists. The sinuous lines and uniform tones of Malevich's fresco studies may seem contrived in the light of his future development, but they played an

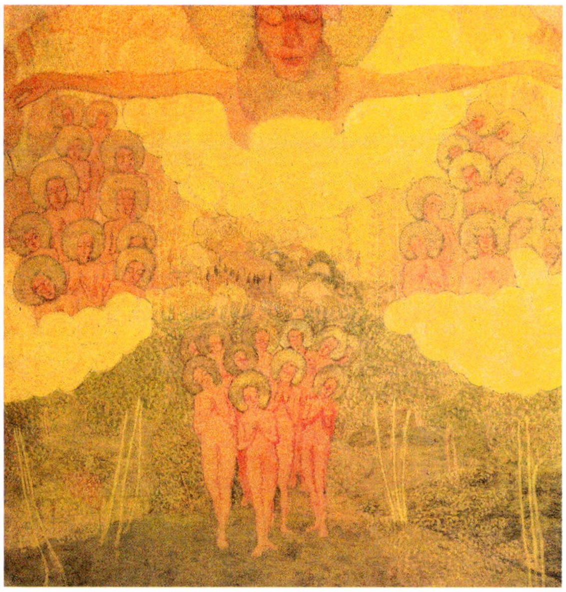

19 *(this page, top)*
Kazimir Malevich

The Triumph of the Heavens, 1907
Tempera on cardboard
72.5 x 70 cm (28 ½ x 27 ½ in)
Russian Museum, St Petersburg

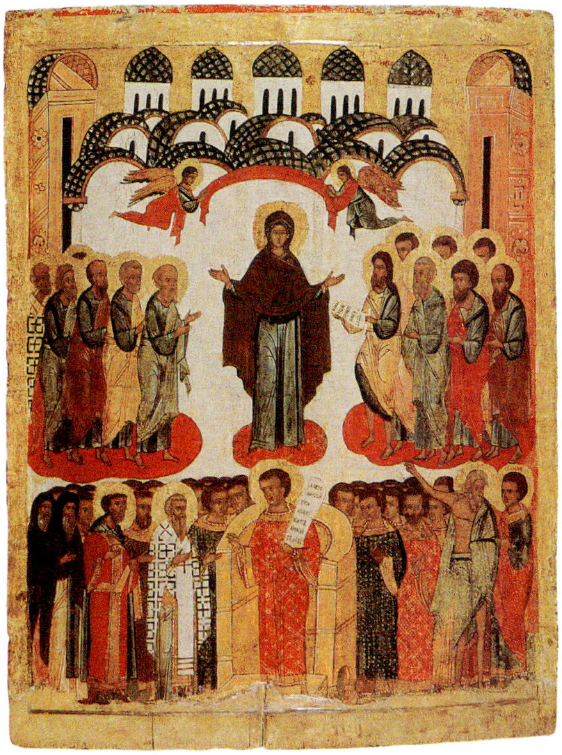

20 *(this page, bottom)*

Intercession of the Mother of God (Pokrov), Novgorod, 15th century
Tempera on wooden panel
107.4 x 82.7 cm (42 ¼ x 32 ½ in)
Temple Gallery, London

important part in liberating him from the shackles of objective naturalism. The symmetrically placed groups of haloed figures in *The Triumph of the Heavens* (1907, Plate 19), so tightly packed together that some of the figures' haloes eclipse their neighbours' faces, surely indicates an early awareness of icons where the faces of onlookers and saints are commonly obscured in this way (Plate 20). The pervasive amber light, which intensifies the image's inscrutable and exotic atmosphere, may also have been inspired by the tendency of varnish on ancient icons to darken over time.

The liberation of art from conventional illusionism, first deliberately investigated in Russia by Vrubel, also found support from within the Russian tradition. Just as Picasso and André Derain in France were attracted to African and Polynesian art on account of its primordial simplicity of means and directness of expression, so young Russian artists were becoming increasingly inspired by the simplicity and immediacy of the traditional and primitive arts of Russia. These arts included painted signboards, *lubki* (plural of *lubok*, a popular Russian print), peasant arts, crafts and costumes, shamanistic objects, children's art and icons. In relation to icons, the art historian Dmitri Sarabianov has written:

> Ancient Russian enthusiasms were especially typical of the early 1900s. It was then that the first efforts were made to exhibit, collect and clean icons; for the first time art experts could inspect the Russian icon in its primordial splendour. The icon was coming to be recognised as the primary source of the national tradition. Kuzma Petrov-Vodkin and Pavel Kuznetsov, Mikhail Larionov and Natalia Goncharova, Vladimir Tatlin and Kazimir Malevich, Alexander Shevchenko and Alexei Grishchenko – each of these artists in his or her own way mastered that legacy.[9]

It is ironic that the first acknowledgement of the aesthetic value of icons to be widely influential should have come from a Frenchman and not a Russian. Henri Matisse visited Russia in October 1911. It seems unlikely that this was the first time that he saw icons, as Diaghilev had included 36 examples from the Likhachev Collection, dating from the fifteenth to seventeenth centuries, in his exhibition of Russian art held in Paris in 1906. This exhibition was organised alongside the Salon d'Automne, to which Matisse contributed several works. But the experience may have made little impression on him as the true brilliance of icons was still mostly hidden under layers of darkened varnish and overpainting at this time. On the second evening of his visit to Moscow five years after this occasion, his host, the collector Sergei Shchukin, took him to see the Oustroukhov collection of icons. On the following day, Ilya Oustroukhov wrote to a friend:

> Yesterday evening Matisse visited us. And you should have seen his delight at the icons. Literally the whole evening he would not leave them alone, relishing and delighting in each one. And with what finesse! ... At length he declared that for the icons alone it would have been worth his while coming from a city even further away than Paris, that the icons were now nobler for him than Fra Beato [Angelico]... Today Shchukin phoned me to say that Matisse literally couldn't sleep the whole night because of the acuity of the impression.[10]

Matisse's feelings about icons were published in the daily press. He described them in his own words, as follows:

> Yesterday I saw a collection of old Russian icons. They are really great art. I am in love with their moving simplicity which, to me, is closer and dearer than Fra Angelico. In these icons the soul of the artists who painted them opens out like a mystical flower. And from them we ought to learn how to understand art.[11]

> The icon is a very interesting type of primitive painting. Nowhere have I ever seen such a wealth of colour, such purity, such immediacy of impression. It is the best thing Moscow has to offer. One should come here to learn because one should seek inspiration from the primitives. Their colours, their understanding, their simplicity – all these elements are in the primitives. The modern artist should apply them with a sense of measure so as to create a work of high artistic value.[12]

Although Matisse was deeply touched by icons, his art was not clearly influenced by them, though they may have strengthened his enjoyment of bold, flat expanses of colour contained within firm outlines. The seeds of his appetite for icons may have been sown by his experience of Byzantine mosaics, to which he had been exposed in 1904 by Paul Signac (whose own exposure to mosaics in Venice led to his squaring up and emboldening of the dotted colour-points that he was using in his pointillism at that time). The example of Byzantine colourism inspired Matisse throughout his life; photographs of Hagia Sophia adorned the walls of his home in Nice until he died. For artists of the Russian avant-garde, however, the example of icons served a completely different purpose. Signs of their direct influence began to appear in the work of Mikhail Larionov from 1909. Up until this time, Larionov's career had unfolded in a fairly unremarkable way. He was born in Tiraspol, Moldova, in 1881, and baptised into the Russian Orthodox Church. In 1893, his family moved to Moscow and five years later, at the age of 17, he enrolled at the Moscow School of Painting, Sculpture and Architecture where he learned to paint in a decorative neo-Impressionist style, influenced by Vrubel and the Symbolists. As we have seen, his earliest works consisted mostly of outdoor scenes where he could pursue his marked interest in the elusive hovering of light in the interstices between leaves and blades of grass, and where the delicate shimmering of light over the surfaces of opalescent forms could be most easily observed. After a period of reactivity against the potentially elitist aestheticism of this style and iconography, manifest in the aggressive anti-aestheticism of his neo-primitivist works, Larionov would return to his interest in the dynamics of light and base a new pictorial language on it.

In 1909 Larionov began to develop his neo-primitivist style. His neo-primitivist works were clearly indebted to the expressive colourism of Vincent van Gogh, Paul Gauguin and the Fauves which he knew from the ground-breaking exhibitions of modern French art that were organised under the auspices of the *Golden Fleece* journal between 1908 and 1910. But, more importantly, they also reflect the powerful influence of Russian folk artefacts. The ideological appeal of such artefacts, including icons, was that they stood as national precedents for rejecting conventional naturalism. As such, they gave moral support to the development of Larionov's impressionistic Symbolist style into the deliberately crude and simplified manner that began to characterise his work. But they also provided him with a spontaneous, visceral and expressionistic pictorial language, using bright unmodulated colours and bold descriptive outlines – like many ancient icons – in

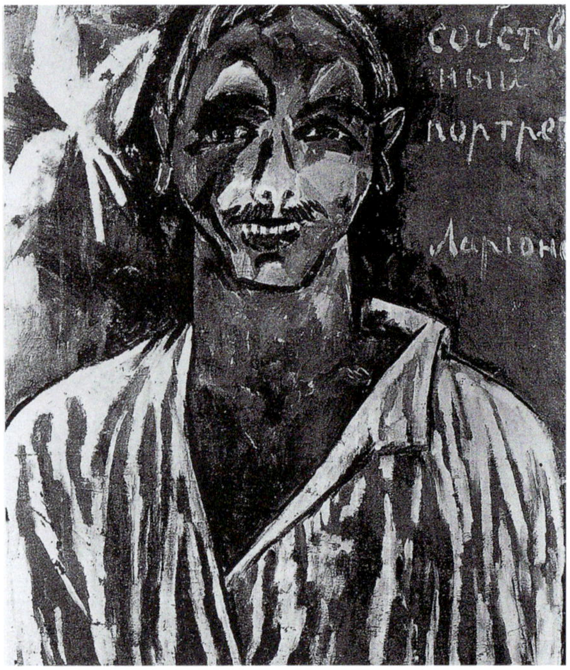

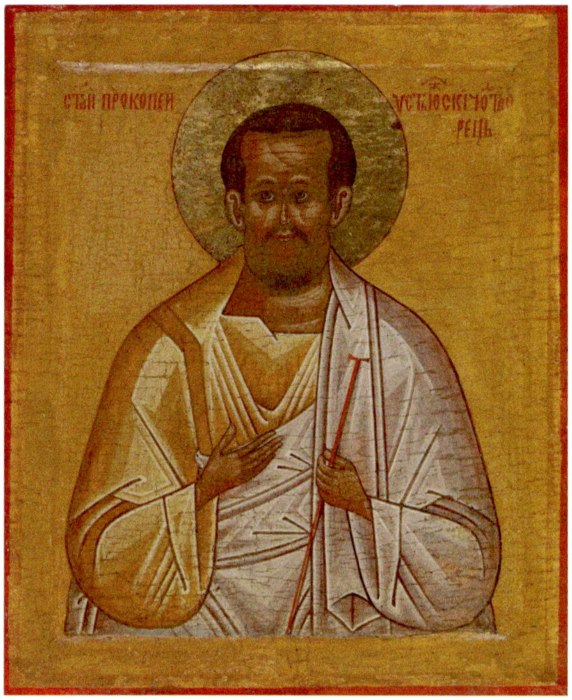

21 *(this page, left)*
Mikhail Larionov

Self-portrait, 1910–12
Medium and dimensions unknown
Whereabouts unknown (Ex-Tomilina-Larionova Collection). Reproduced in Eli Eganbyuri's monograph, *Natalia Goncharova, Mikhail Larionov*, Moscow, 1913

22 *(this page, right)*

St Procopius of Ustiug, Veliki Ustiug, early 16th century
Tempera on wooden panel
49 x 39 cm (19 ¼ x 15 ⅜ in)
Tretyakov Gallery, Moscow

23 *(opposite, top)*
Natalia Goncharova

The Four Evangelists, 1910–11
Oil on canvas
204 x 58 cm (80 ⅜ x 22 ⅞ in) each panel
Russian Museum, St Petersburg

24 *(opposite, bottom)*
Mikhail Boichuk

Inert Life, 1909
Medium and dimensions unknown
Private collection

place of subtly shaded forms. The growing tendency towards angularity, particularly in the stiff treatment of draperies, is also extremely common in icons (Plates 21, 22) and is especially significant at this time in the light of Larionov's future evolution.

It was not until 1911 that, encouraged by Matisse's views on icons, Larionov's general interest in traditional Russian folk art became a more pointed and strategic aspect of his work. His first major statement in this direction was his decision, with his companion Natalia Goncharova, to break away from the exhibiting circle, the Jack of Diamonds, to set up a rival group, The Donkey's Tail. The Jack of Diamonds group had itself been founded, in 1910, as an alternative to established artistic groups which its members (the Burliuk brothers, Aristarkh Lentulov, Ilya Mashkov, Pyotr Konchalovsky and Robert Falk) considered to be shackled by the outdated values of the Symbolists and World of Art. The group was set up to exhibit the work of the European moderns (Wassily Kandinsky, Alexei von Jawlensky, Ernst Kirchner, Franz Marc, Fernand Léger, Robert Delaunay, Pablo Picasso etc) beside their Russian contemporaries but Larionov and Goncharova considered its members to have capitulated to western values. Exactly as Kramskoi had said of Repin, they believed the Russian members of the Jack of Diamonds, who worked, broadly speaking, in an expressionistic Fauvist style, to be over-concerned with purely aesthetic and artistic matters. While acknowledging that their own eyes had been opened to the riches of their own tradition by the 'primitivist' example of western artists, both artists now called for an independent school of Russian art and, as already stated, refused to include the work of artists working abroad in the exhibitions they organised. In order to highlight their allegiance to a Russian tradition, both artists intensified their identification with its material signs.

Larionov and Goncharova's attraction to Russian folk art had two interdependent aims: to inspire an authentic and expressive contemporary style in art (neo-primitivism) and to affirm the continuity of Russian tradition. While traditional models provided

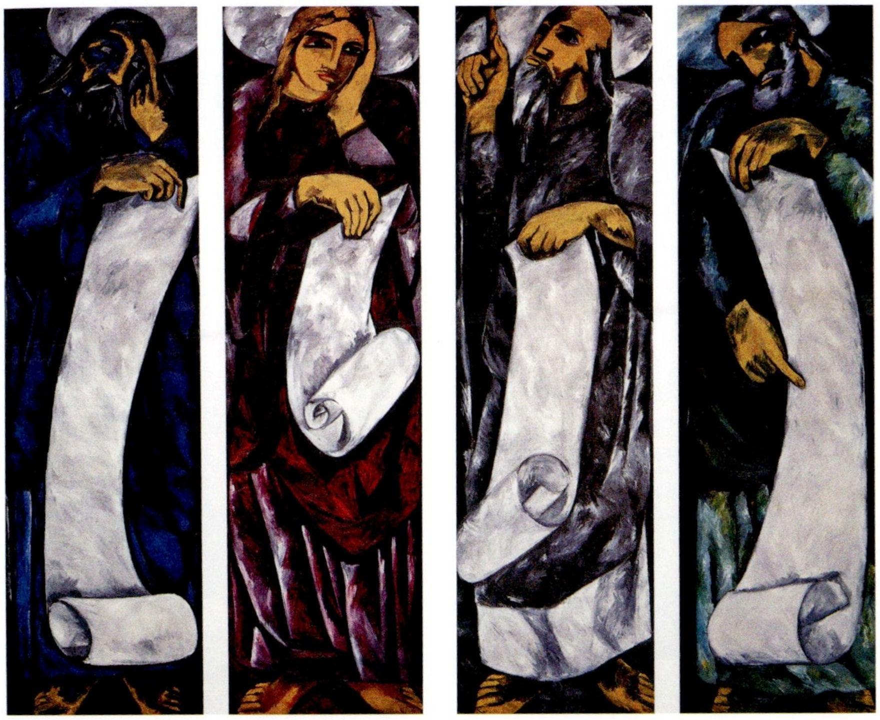

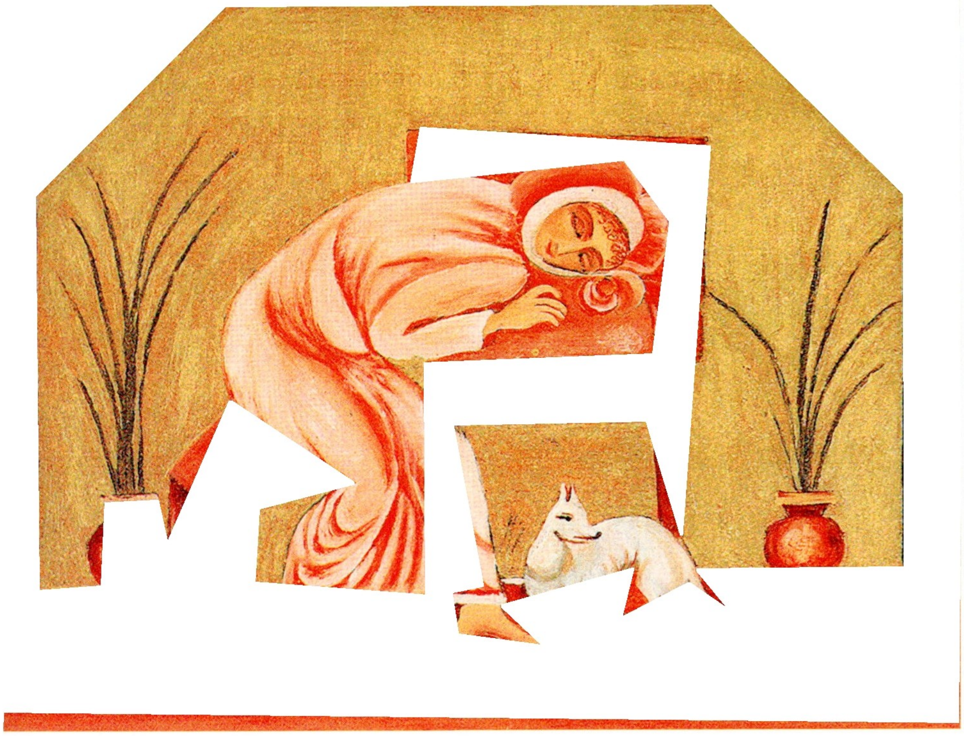

them with examples of a very direct and sensory means of expression, rather than a sophisticated illusionistic one, they aimed through their art to provide that tradition with a new form for its own continuation. The neo-primitivists were quick to point out that they were not merely imitating traditional forms for the sake of their associations. They were attempting to understand how such forms operated as the vital elements of a primordial language of art and to use them as the basis for a new and ultra-contemporary cultural language. Goncharova's *The Four Evangelists* (1910–11, Plate 23), discussed in Chapter 4, is a case in point. In this respect, the neo-primitivists differed radically from the 'neo-Byzantinists', who were commonly seen to use Byzantine prototypes for their purely decorative and sentimental effect. The Ukrainian artist Mikhail Boichuk, for instance, who had been involved in the restoration of icons in Lvov in 1907 and who created a neo-Byzantinist workshop in Paris from 1908 to 1911, was criticised for imitating iconic forms without either capturing their inner spirit or using them to elicit the spirit of modern art (Plate 24). Boichuk had exhibited two works at the Salon d'Automne in 1909, and his entire group of 'Boichukists' was represented at the Salon des Indépendants in 1910. Reviewing the latter exhibition, Guillaume Apollinaire praised the group's use of traditional models but tempered his admiration by adding, 'it is a pity that, by voluntarily limiting themselves to pastiches, they are not skilful enough to adapt to a modern temperament; despite their good intentions, when they depict a man with a shirt collar, their byzantinism vanishes and all that remains is the clumsy painting of a minor Russian artist who has everything to learn about modern art, which is quite different and ultimately more exacting than the gilded icons of the cathedrals in the Ukraine'.[13]

Possibly under the influence of Diaghilev's Ballets Russes, which had mesmerised Paris from the time of their first visit to France in 1909, Apollinaire later qualified this view by suggesting that French artists could benefit from the neo-Byzantinists' ability to 'cheat with the centuries'.[14] The Ukrainian sculptor Alexander Archipenko, who emigrated to Paris in 1908, was even more critical of the neo-Byzantinists for the superficiality of their interest in icons. Archipenko had always admired the frescos and mosaics that he been brought up with in Kiev, acknowledging that he was himself influenced by Byzantine art,[15] and he had an intimate knowledge of icons from his grandfather who was an icon painter. His *Prayer* of 1907 clearly reflects his sympathy for both the muted sensibility of icons and their ambiguous three-dimensionality.[16] The integration of poetic effect with an extremely refined sense of composition, pursued on its own terms, became an abiding characteristic of his later work. In an edition of the Russian journal, *Parizhskiy Vestnik*, published in Paris in 1911, he commented on the neo-Byzantinists: 'Seeing these works, one can see how their creators have returned to the traditions and principles of periods in which art was at the peak of its evolution. But there are also errors and deviations among these byzantinists who exhibited their icons and who think that it is sufficient to preserve the aesthetic forms of the works of previous ages without the interior essence that has made them immortal.'[17]

Similarly, in his booklet *Neoprimitivism: Its Theory, Its Potential, Its Achievements* (1913), Larionov's friend the painter Alexander Shevchenko strongly criticised the purely decorative designs of the neo-Byzantinist artist Dmitri Stelletsky (1875–1947). Stelletsky had been a student at the Academy of Arts in St Petersburg from 1896 to 1903, and became a well-known painter, illustrator and designer of stage

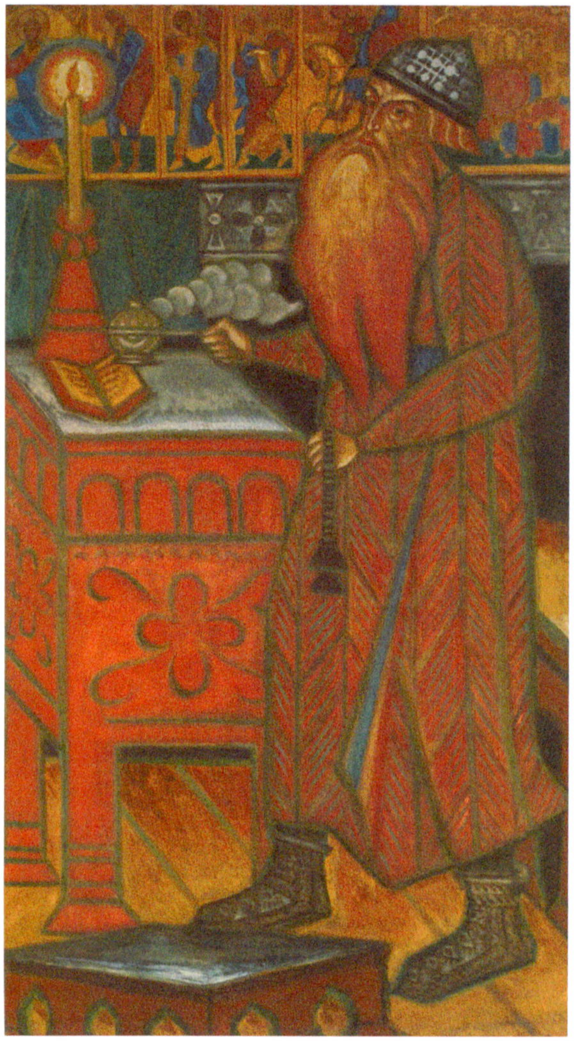

25
Dmitri Stelletsky

Praying Boyar, before 1921
Pencil and gouache on board
161 x 88.9 cm (63 3/8 x 35 in)
Private collection (Courtesy Christie's)

sets. His pictorial language was fundamentally developed from the decorative impact of schematism, as found in illuminations from historical chronicles of Russia and in Russian folk art (Plate 25). He was deeply influenced by frescos and icons, which he studied in Novgorod in 1903, as well as by the sixth-century mosaics in Ravenna which he visited with a fellow Byzantinist and icon-collector Boris Anrep.[18] Some of his works were made with paints using medieval recipes. Although Stelletsky did make use of the expressive brightness and angularity of icons, his oeuvre fits more comfortably within the aesthetic parameters of the World of Art than of the avant-garde and, as a result, his works were looked upon by modernists with contempt, prompting Shevchenko to write that they 'in no way reveal old Russia, Byzantium or icons. They are mere historicity – a resolution of high ideas by home-made, amateurish means, an imitation devoid of perception – whereas icons are saturated with the East, with Byzantium, and at the same time remain entirely original.'[19]

Significantly, while evolving his own primitivist style, Larionov also assembled a personal collection of traditional Russian artefacts and books on traditional art. In some cases, the naive objects and imagery that inspired avant-garde artists – including children's drawings, primitive carvings and icons – were displayed alongside their own work in their exhibitions. Icons and *lubki*, for instance, as well as gingerbread moulds and examples of lace work, were exhibited at the third and last Golden Fleece exhibition (1909–10), one of the major antecedents of neo-primitivism. Children's drawings were exhibited at the second Salon exhibition organised by the sculptor Vladimir Izdebsky in Odessa in 1910, alongside works by Larionov, Goncharova and the Burliuk brothers. In 1913, Larionov highlighted the complementary nature of traditional Russian art and modernism by organising an exhibition of Genuine Icon Painting and Lubki – which included 129 icons from his own collection – to run concurrently with a show of his own most recent work. This exhibition, organised to celebrate the 300th anniversary of Romanov rule in Russia, had a profound and lasting impact on a number of avant-garde artists.[20] Over 50 years later, Berthold Lubetkin, who studied architecture under Alexander Rodchenko, Vladimir Tatlin and Alexander Vesnin in Moscow and St Petersburg but who left Russia in 1922, spoke of the range of styles and types represented in the exhibition, which he saw, highlighting how multifaceted the influence of icons could be:

> All of a sudden the sheer splendour of this art burst on us like a revelation, summing up the entire course of Russian art. Some were 13th century ones from Novgorod, some 15th century, produced by the monks of Novodevichy Monastery. Others were Baroque ones of the 17th century Moscow School of Stroganov. But some had been made only yesterday by the village signwriter or some itinerant craftsman, and they combined centuries-old traditions with authentic inventiveness and originality, saying what no-one had dared to say before.[21]

As far as Larionov's art was concerned, it was particularly in relation to the visual techniques of the icon painters that he was inspired by icons. He was interested in the way icon painters used unnaturalistic artistic devices to capture the attention of the viewer and communicate spiritual and philosophical meanings. In the 1920s, Larionov wrote a short essay on icons in which he described this phenomenon in the following way:

> There are two artistic principles. The first: to copy nature on the basis of acquired knowledge and to use naturalistic forms in various ways for the composition. ... The second: to study life in itself, regardless of the manifestations of the surrounding world and, based on these always moving and changeable forms, to render only the most expressive aspect of the object or situation...
>
> Russian icon painters were inspired by the second principle and were strongly drawn towards abstraction. This abstraction manifested itself in the use of schemas and formulas related to a predetermined style through which they expressed the mystical and abstract sense of life... It is through the nuances of colour and the

> finesse of the graphic forms that the religious and mystical state we experience when contemplating icons manifests itself… It is a kind of spiritual realism. Idealised faces, conventionalised folds, the schematised perfection of the drapery: none of this exists in [ordinary] life … you really believe that they concern another life.[22]

Significantly, Larionov even distinguished between Russian icons, which he considered to be spiritually abstracted and stylised, and Greco-Byzantine icons, which he saw as more representational, illusionistic and densely painted, 'deriving more from the first principle'.[23] He believed that Russian artists inherited the Greco-Byzantine style as an exterior form that needed to be impregnated with mystical spirit. His distinction highlights many of the aspects of Russian icons that he admired:

> Outwardly, Russian icons are distinguishable from Greco-Byzantine examples by their graphic form, and above all by their very clear and delicate colours; also, by the nuances on the picture plane that make the surface vibrate and confer a sense of infinite depth on Russian icons. Greek and Byzantine icons have a dense and opaque sense of colour, with unbroken surfaces that relate to each other without colour-vibration; they attempt to realise a sense of relief and depth – not infinite depth as in Russian icons, but a depth that is subject to perspectival space… The saints in Greek and Byzantine icons are not deprived of flesh and blood, as they are in Russian icons. The latter are abstract symbols of another life. They are not human beings transformed into saints, as in Greek and Byzantine icons; they are saints that have taken on a remote and symbolic human appearance, without crossing the limit of verisimilitude, in order to be recognised, and to be seen to be of human origin. They preserve their human forms but these forms are transposed into a rhythmic style through which life – spiritual and mystical life rather than naturalistic 'real' life – expresses itself, flows and is held before the human eye.[24]

The association of icon painting with anti-naturalism was crystallised in a bizarre episode that took place in January 1913 when a 'mentally deranged' icon painter, Avram Balashev, visited the Tretyakov Gallery in Moscow and slashed Repin's famous painting of *Ivan the Terrible*, painted in 1888. Balashev's reasons for slashing the painting, which happens to depict a crazed act of destruction (the tsar having just killed his son in a fit of rage), are unclear. Besides the various possibilities of political and psychological estrangement, it is not inconceivable that, as a conservative icon painter, he considered its depiction of worldly characters – especially a secular autocrat – and the use of a sensuous naturalistic style to be blasphemous. The fact that, by 1913, the painting had come to be revered as a 'secular icon' of the revolutionary values promoted by the Wanderers, of which Repin was a member, suggests that Balashev may also have felt alienated from 'high culture' in general. Whatever the case, the incident caused a furore, principally because Repin blamed the damage on Futurist 'innovators' who, just one month earlier, had proclaimed their 'insurmountable hatred for the [Classical and naturalistic] language' of their predecessors in their manifesto, *A Slap in the Face of Public Taste*. To the indignant Repin, Balashev's action seemed so consistent with the views of the Futurists, who did indeed consider it to be a 'service to art', that he must have been influenced by them; he even went so far as to suggest that Balashev may have been bribed to attack the work. Such was his perception of the interests shared by icon painters (albeit disturbed ones) and Futurists! The controversy culminated in a public debate, organised by the Symbolist artist Maksimilian Voloshin and members of the Jack of Diamonds group, which became so acrimonious that Repin, aged 70, had to leave before the end. Ironically, the Futurists were acting rather as Repin had in the 1860s, so it is perhaps not surprising that when the First World War began in 1914, the two factions were able to settle their differences and spend weekends together drinking and sketching.[25]

If neo-primitivism placed modern art in the context of traditional culture, Larionov's Rayism, which developed in 1912, represented a consummation of traditional culture in the context of contemporary art. Rayism emerged from – and perfected, in its founder's view – the fragmentation of French Cubism and the dynamism of Italian Futurism. While aggressively dissociating itself from the self-conscious 'background of old and new art',[26] the aim of Rayism was to render visible the four-dimensional world 'beyond time and space', in which the limited reality that human beings conventionally perceive was ultimately believed to exist, in its fullness. The theory of the fourth dimension had been popularised in Russia by the writer and philosopher, Pyotr Ouspensky, whose works *The Fourth Dimension* and *Tertium Organum*, published in 1909 and 1911 respectively, developed the theoretical works of the English and American writers Charles Hinton and Claude Bragdon while also standing in line with a tradition of non-Euclidean geometry in Russia. Ouspensky reconciled mathematical models of the fourth dimension with the possibility of higher states of consciousness, suggesting that the consciousness of an ordinary man is presently limited to a perception of three-dimensional objects in the context of a fourth dimension – linear time. If a human being's level of consciousness was to evolve, he would grow to perceive the fourth dimension (linear time) as a finite 'object' in the context of a higher fifth dimension – planar time, in which all points on the 'line of time' would be experienced simultaneously, i.e. in an experience of infinite time beyond thinking. From this point of view, the incomprehensible nature of infinite linear time, as we perceive it, is simply an illusion arising as a result of man's currently limited state of consciousness. Ouspensky valued the arts as a medium of insight into this higher knowledge but he was conservative in his taste, as he was in his politics, and he appears to have been ambivalent about contemporary developments. As the editor of a daily newspaper, *Nov'*, he published an illustrated article about Larionov's shamanic face-painting (which Larionov and Goncharova considered to be the 'first speech to find unknown truths'),[27] but he also criticised unspecified 'Futurist painters' for falsifying the theory of the fourth dimension, suggesting that they were using the term metaphorically and that their understanding was not rooted in practice and experience.[28]

Larionov's means for accessing the four-dimensional world was by visualising the otherwise invisible light rays that he understood to be emitted by physical objects. It is the light rays emitted from objects, rather than the objects themselves, that he believed to be seen. To this end, he wrote: 'We do not sense the object with our eye, as it is depicted conventionally in pictures and as a result of following this or that device; in fact, we do not sense the object as such. We perceive a sum of rays proceeding from a source of light; these are reflected from the object and enter our field of vision.'[29] By describing his work in this way, Larionov was unwittingly echoing the beliefs of the fourteenth-century monk Gregory Palamas, who re-invigorated the mystical 'hesychast' dimension of Orthodox monasticism. As part of a widespread revival of mystical practice within the Orthodox Church, Gregory advocated that God be contemplated directly without the mediation of the Church, the priesthood or even the sacraments; all that was required was total, perpetual immersion of contemplative attention in the presence of God. While the Church authorities were fearful for their power and rejected the notion that God could be perceived unmediated in this way, the hesychasts discriminated between the essence and emanations of God, maintaining that although God cannot be perceived in his essence, which is ineffable, he can be known in his emanations or energies. The necessary precedent for this revelation was found in the Transfiguration of Christ on Mount Hermon, at which the disciples Peter, James and John witnessed Christ transformed into light – 'and his face did shine as the sun and his raiment was white as the light' (Matthew 17, 2; Mark 9, 2). As Gregory Palamas said, quoting Dionysius the Areopagite: 'When we become incorruptible and immortal, and attain to the blessed state of conformity with Christ, we will be ever with the Lord, gaining fulfilment in the purest contemplations of His visible theophany which will illuminate us with its most brilliant rays, just as it illumined the disciples at the time of the most divine Transfiguration'.[30]

Icons of the Transfiguration were seen to extend this revelation of divine energy into the material world. The mystic, philosopher, priest, scientist and teacher Pavel Florensky expanded on their ability to do this (in his *Iconostasis* treatise of 1918–20) by saying that 'because an icon makes the light of an illumined person *appear* to us, it is an energy'.[31] To the extent that Larionov talks of seeing the rays emitted by an object rather than the object in itself, he too is speaking of transfigured objects – objects revealed as their energy – and duplicates the structure of the hesychast argument. This is borne out by the visual

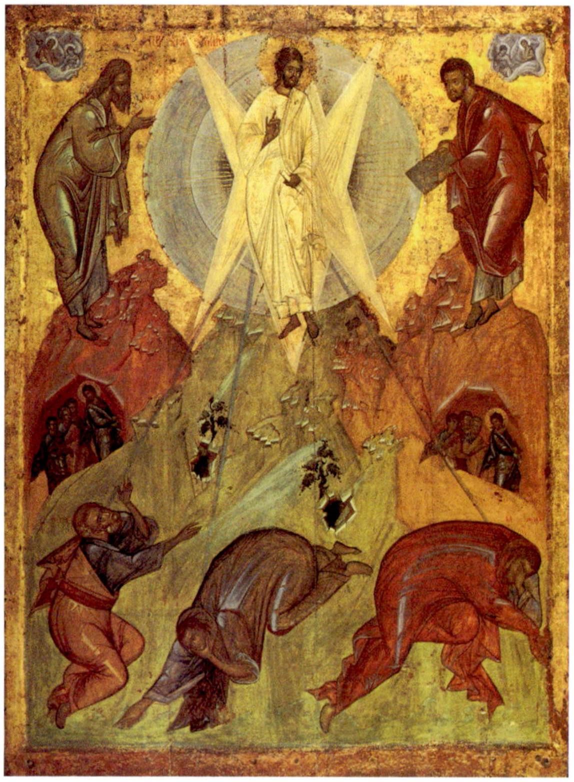

26
Theophanes the Greek

The Transfiguration, 1403
Tempera on wooden panel
184 x 134 cm (72 2/5 x 52 4/5 in)
Tretyakov Gallery, Moscow

language of his works. Just as the figure of the transfigured Christ is frequently represented in icons against a shining star, with dynamic white beams radiating in all directions, Larionov's Rayist works are largely composed of dynamic inter-penetrating shards of white and blue-white light (Plates 26,27).

Until the end of the sixteenth century, when a decorative style of icon painting began to develop, the sense of form in icons was largely indicated by networks of lines superimposed over expanses of unmodulated colour, rather than by shading or colour gradation. This effect is especially clear in the representation of draperies, where the ridges of folds are frequently lined with white highlights (Plate 22). The visual effect of this technique – a dynamic web of bright angular lines superimposed over a monochromatic ground – frequently appears in Larionov's work, though in the latter case it is used for its own sake, expressive of dynamic relationship, rather than as a sign of three-dimensional form. Furthermore, the networks used by icon painters of the fifteenth and sixteenth centuries tended to consist

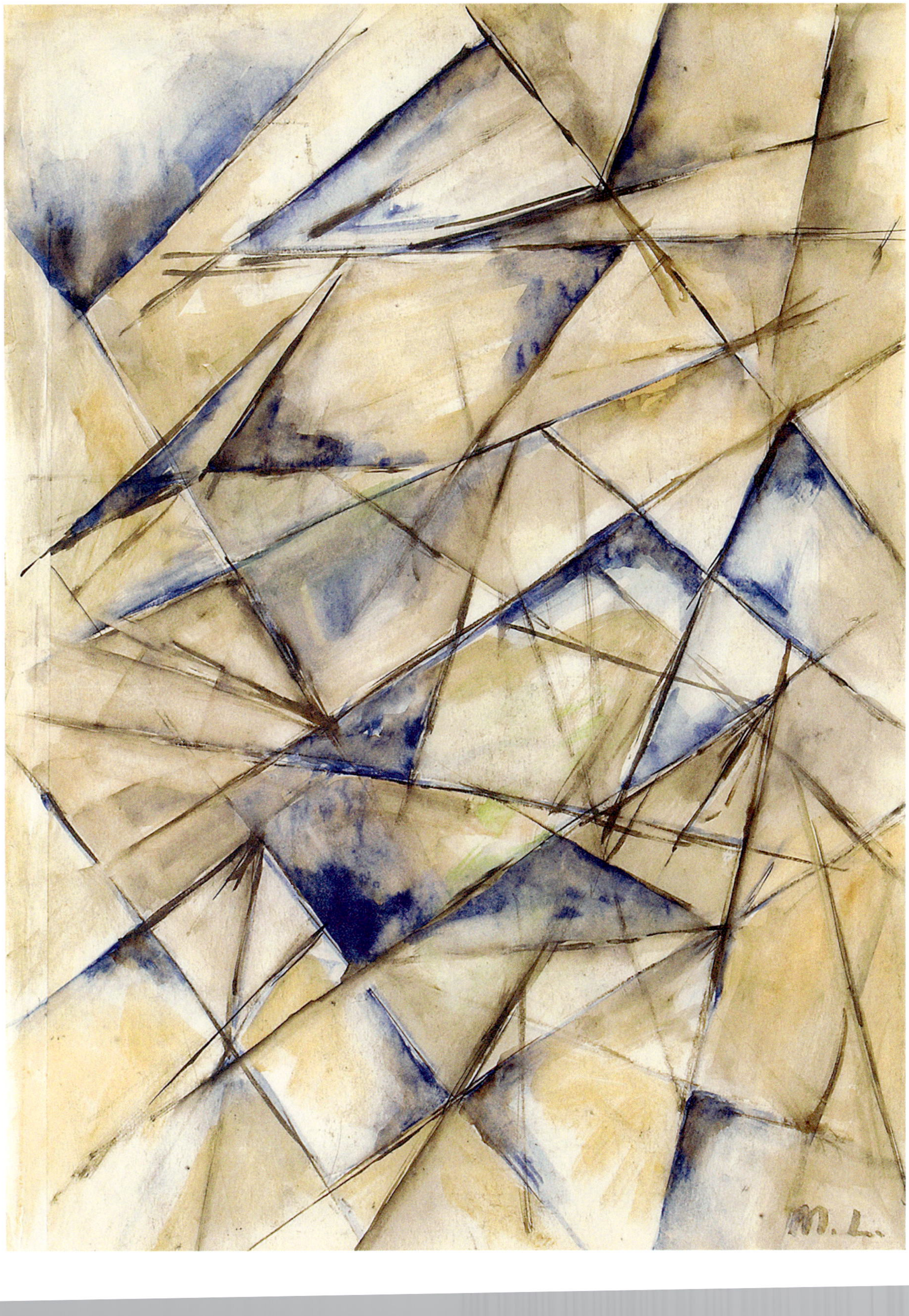

27
Mikhail Larionov

Rayist Composition, 1912
Gouache and watercolour on tracing paper
34.3 x 24.2 cm (13 ½ x 9 ½ in)
Private collection (Courtesy Christie's)

of fragmented straight lines, rather than flowing curves. The use of continuous curves was generally limited to outlines and silhouettes. When a line was required to change direction within a single colour field, it tended to be broken rather than curved. The complex and dynamic web of flattened ridges and striated white highlights that resulted from this system surely influenced Larionov's Rayist paintings. Several of these works are loosely representational. In such cases (for instance *Blue Rayism*, 1912, or *Sea Beach with Woman*, 1913, in which figures are just discernible),[32] the impression of substantial form is greatly weakened by the absence of curves. In others, the artist has dispensed with the three-dimensional object-source from which invisible light rays are emitted, and focuses on the emissions alone, existing transcendentally in a higher dimension. In these latter examples, it is as if the work has closed in on a single area of pure drapery-description in an icon, obviating the need for an outline. It also adapts the radiating white lines that were used by icon painters to highlight the raised ridges of drapery folds, but which serve equally well to dematerialise the figure, to give an impression of empty space penetrated by light as if through broken glass (Plate 27).

The impression of dematerialisation has iconographic and symbolic significance that links Rayism to icons in other ways. The fact that icon painters reserved a special gilding technique for areas of particular sacredness (Plate 14), such as the robes of Christ, thereby investing the technique – resplendent fans of golden rays, called *assist* – with a special spiritual significance, may have inspired Larionov to seek spiritual significance in his own work with light rays. Interestingly, a description of the sacred working of *assist*, recounted by Pavel Florensky in his treatise, *Iconostasis*, written between 1918 and 1920, provides a close parallel to the kind of 'structural dynamics' that Larionov was attempting to achieve with Rayism. Despite the very real differences between the two minds, they both reflect the existence of an impulse – fundamental to the cultural life of the time – away from the cool detachment and subjectivity of western-style aestheticism towards an art of transformative power, rooted in a metaphysical source; and they both express it, in this instance, in the same way. The passage in question is written in the form of an imaginary conversation:

> Are you saying that the golden strokes of assist accomplish a metaphysics in highlighting what is depicted? Is the ontology of (say) clothes, or books, or footstools – that is, the ontology of everything that is – being revealed this way? I'm understanding you to say that, in the lines of gold-highlight (*assist*), one sees the invisible realm somehow become comprehensible to us and, further, its primary energies become actualised into sensory images, energies whose interactions constitute the ontological skeleton of a thing. For yes, then we can say that the assyst-lines are the lines of energy constituting the force-field that is the thing itself.[33]

Pavel Florensky (1882–1937) was one of the most influential thinkers of his time though, partly due to the range and complexity of his interests, the scope of his influence has yet to be fully explored.[34] He was deeply interested, experienced and experimental in many different aspects of the sciences – physics, mathematics, biology, geology, meteorology, physics and others – but was also well versed in literature, philosophy and the arts, regularly attending the soirées of the Symbolists in St Petersburg when he was a student at the Moscow Theological Seminary between 1905 and 1907. Following a crisis of confidence in the self-sufficiency of physics in 1899, he intensified his commitment to the Orthodox faith, finally becoming a priest in 1908. Although aesthetic experience formed a key part of his theology, as perfected in icons, he did not seek to apply his ideas to art as an end in itself. On the contrary, he continually sought to realise them in the context of a Christian truth, a factor which may have limited their ability to be explicitly influential.

Although Florensky was working on subjects that would certainly have interested Larionov (his thesis on graduating from the Department of Physics and Mathematics at Moscow University in 1904 was 'On the Peculiarities of Planar Curves as Loci of Disruptions of Continuity'),[35] there is no evidence to suggest that the artist was familiar with his work when he was developing Rayism. However, such ideas were being discussed in Moscow and St Petersburg at the time and it seems highly likely that Larionov was exposed to them in fragments (he was certainly influenced by the latest discoveries about radioactivity and electromagnetism).[36] Nor is Larionov likely to have felt any sympathy for Florensky's profoundly unfashionable attitude towards the world as a mystical revelation of Christ. However, had he known it, he would surely have been fascinated by Florensky's description of the spiritual operation of icons, so couched in the technical terminology of a mind trained in the material sciences. With regard to Larionov's own attempt to represent the immaterial emissions of light in visible form, as a kind of higher science rather than as a symbolic or mystical revelation, Florensky's analogy between icons as visualisations of the invisible and the possibility of representing the physical, but invisible, force field of a magnet is even more pertinent:

> If an artist in depicting a magnet were to be satisfied with showing merely the visible aspect, then he would be depicting not a magnet but merely a piece of steel; the real essence of the magnet – that is, its force-field – would go not only unrepresented but also unindicated.
>
> Clearly in depicting a magnet, both the field and the steel must be shown; but their depictions must also be incommensurate, showing that the magnet's two dimensions belong to two different planes. The steel could be shown in colour while the field must be depicted abstractly... I dare not try to instruct the artist in how actually to represent this unmingled mingling of two planes of existence; but I am entirely certain that figurative art has the capacity to do it.[37]

Although Florensky was not equating his hypothetical representation of a magnet with an icon, his use of an analogy from the physical world to expose a dynamic in the metaphysical world throws incidental light on the inner dynamic of Rayism – on Larionov's theory (developed several years before Florensky published on the subject) that the essence of an object lies not in its inert material reality but in the dynamic structure of its force-field. Returning to the question of representing the invisible force-field of the divine in the world, Florensky continued: 'Analogously, then, we can say this: the form of the visible is created by these invisible lines and paths of divine light'.[38]

Florensky not only established the principle that icons conduct the invisible into the visible world; he also described in detail how the very technicalities and visual forms of icon-painting have specific spiritual significances. In this respect, his theory resembles Larionov's theory of Rayism extremely closely. Stylised fan-like patterns, for instance, were not merely pictorial conventions for indicating the folds of drapery; they had a deeper meaning. Firstly, the very fact that the saints wore clothes at all was imbued with spiritual significance (as there could be no other reason for their needing them in heaven):

> we can call their clothes the covering woven by their acts of spiritual discipline, or *podvig*; and this is not mere figure but the exact expression of the idea that the saints, in and through ascetic *podvigs*, actually generate in their physical bodies new tissues of light-bearing organs so that their bodies may be brought continually closer to the great sphere of spiritual energies; and in terms of visual perception, this spiritual expansion of the body is symbolised by the clothes.[39]

While Florensky considered draperies to be embodiments of specific spiritual truths, he also found subtle differences of significance in the various styles that were used over the centuries to represent them. He explains the ability of meaning to be transmuted into visual forms – not merely symbolised – in the following way:

> With a unique exactness, the long tradition of Russian icon painting reveals the entire history of ecclesiastical spirituality by the characteristic folds in iconic garments, so that one need only glance at the folds to know when the icon was done and to understand the whole spirit of the culture reflected in it.
>
> From the fourteenth to sixteenth century, there is a process of growing spiritual self-consciousness (including a self-consciousness in and of Russia herself), a process wherein all of Russian life is organised to co-inhere with the spirit through the collective ascetic disciplines of the emerging nation... Furthermore, the folds in this period grow intentionally straight and stylised, becoming rationally abstract yet with a strikingly abstract tendency to naturalism. If we knew nothing at all about the second half of the sixteenth century ... then – if we had the icons, or even only the *folds* in the icons – we could understand what happened in the great spiritual transformation of medieval Rus into the Renaissance Kingdom of Muscovy.[40]

Larionov's interest in icons at this stage was artistic, ideological and spiritual – it was not religious and certainly not Christian. The same was largely true of Kazimir Malevich who was influenced by icons more radically than any other avant-garde artist. Malevich was born in Kiev to Polish-speaking parents, and spent much of his childhood in a part of the Ukraine that had been assimilated into the Russian Empire. He studied briefly at the School of Art in Kiev in 1895–6, until the family moved to Kursk where both he and his father worked for the railway industry. In 1904 he moved to Moscow where he continued to study art at the Stroganov School of Art and at the Moscow School of Painting, Sculpture and Architecture where Larionov had also studied. Although his parents were Catholic, and he and all his siblings were baptised in a Catholic church (St Alexander's in Kiev), Malevich remarked that his parents kept an icon in their home 'more for the sake of tradition and society than from some religious feeling'.[41] However, one of his uncles was a Catholic priest – and according to his sister, Wictoria Zaicev, their parents also wanted Kazimir to become one.[42] She maintained that their family was more religious than Malevich admitted and that he had understated the case in his autobiographical writings for philosophical and political reasons.[43] Malevich's earliest experience of artists was, at the age of 12, a feeling of intense fascination with three painters who had come from St Petersburg to his home town to paint icons in a local church. It is not inconceivable that his interest in Christian iconography, which surfaces in his work throughout his career (regularly, if not frequently), was engendered by this experience. The occasion certainly made a great impression on him. He describes the drawn-out search to discover more about the mysterious strangers in vivid detail and with great relish in his *Chapters from an Artist's Autobiography*, written in 1933.[44]

During his neo-primitivist years (1911–13), Malevich's feelings towards the Church were sufficiently sympathetic for him to regard the subject of *Peasant Women at Church* (1911) as a suitable medium for promoting the cause of a traditional, Russian and modern style of art. His respect for icons at this stage was two-fold. From a socio-political point of view, he valued icons as a sign that the traditional and authentic art of Russia was deeply connected to 'the people', mostly peasants; from an artistic point of view icons were seen to set a precedent for the entirely new aesthetic of directness that he and the artists he mixed with were looking for. In his *Chapters from an Artist's Autobiography*, Malevich describes how he was influenced by both these aspects of icons. Of their social implications he wrote:

> In spite of my naturalistic leaning, of my feelings towards nature, I was strongly moved by icons. I felt some kinship and something splendid in them. I saw in them the entire Russian people with all their emotional creativeness. I'd then recall my childhood: the horses, flowers and roosters of the primitive murals and wood carvings. I sensed some bond between peasant art and icons: icon art is a high-cultural form of peasant art. I discovered in them the whole spiritual side of the 'Peasant Age'; I came to understand the peasants through icons, saw their faces not as saints, but as ordinary people.[45]

Regarding the techniques of icon painting and their significance for him, he continued:

> Through icon art, I understood the emotional art of the peasants, which I had loved earlier, but whose meaning I hadn't fully understood. In what way did this art overturn my striving for lifelikeness and the sciences – anatomy, perspective, the study of nature through the drawing of sketches? All of the Wanderers' convictions regarding nature and naturalism were overturned by the fact that the icon painters, who had achieved a great mastery of technique, conveyed meaning outside of spatial and linear perspective. They employed colour and form on the basis of a purely emotional interpretation of theme. They painted without regard to any of the rules established by the classics and especially the academy of V. Makovsky and Repin.[46]

The social and artistic impact of icons on Malevich's early work can be seen in his neo-primitivist paintings, painted from around 1911. Up until that time, Malevich had been largely preoccupied with scenes of middle-class life – bathing women, ladies in city parks, summery cottages seen through blossoming trees – using a cool palette, rich in blues, greens and white. These works allowed him to experiment with the airy techniques of the Impressionists. However, in 1911 – the year he became involved with Larionov and Goncharova's all-Russian neo-primitivist group The Donkey's Tail – Malevich's work changed dramatically. His palette warmed up, intensifying the relationships between colours. His drawing technique became more simplified, minimising the use of modelling and perspective, thus giving rise to flatter, bolder forms and reducing the illusory sense of space. His subject matter also began to change, coming to focus on labour rather than leisure. Titles such as *The Gardener, Floor Polishers* and *Woman Reaping* became common. Regarding his break with an impressionistic style, Malevich wrote, 'I stayed on the side of peasant art and began painting in the primitive spirit. In the first period, I imitated icon painting. The second was purely a "labour" period: I drew peasants at work, harvesting, threshing. In the third period, I grew closer to the "suburban genre" (carpenters, gardeners, vacation resorts, swimmers). The fourth period was the "city faces" (floor washers, maids, lackeys, servants).'[47]

It is conceivable that, on at least one occasion, Malevich based a neo-primitivist work directly on a specific icon or icon-type. Despite the significant differences, his gouache, *Chiropodist at the Baths* (1911–12, Plate 28) is sufficiently close in composition and in some details to Andrei Rublev's famous icon of the *Old Testament Trinity* (Plate 6) to suggest that the artist may have had the icon in mind when working on the painting. In 1904, Rublev's icon was stripped of centuries of metallic accretions, cleaned and put on public display to great acclaim. Malevich's work, which may have intended to capitalise on the *Old Testament Trinity*'s new aura and popularity, is comparable to the icon in a number of sometimes irreverent ways. Besides the overall arrangement of three figures – two at the sides, facing inwards, and one at the centre – the focal point of both images is located at the centre of the composition on a table that is rendered in inverted perspective and unnaturalistically tipped up towards the viewer. The two bathers at the sides of Malevich's work, draped in large white towels, resemble the two angels, also draped in shining white robes, at the sides of the icon. The prominence of the right-hand bather's left foot in the *Chiropodist* may also relate to the curious disposition of the feet of these two angels. The fingers of the chiropodist's right hand – two of them folded back towards the palm – can be likened to the right hand of the central angel raised in blessing. However, it may be the chiropodist's scissors (one of Malevich's favourite motifs) that are intended to correspond with the angel's fingers. If this is the case, then it is the banal act of nail-clipping, rather than the sanctified sign of the hand with two fingers extended, that becomes the surrogate form of blessing, introducing an element of absurdity to the work. Furthermore, if Andrei Nakov's contention that the central figure is a self-portrait of Malevich is accepted, then the painting takes on yet another meaning: the angelic agent of blessing is replaced by the artist in the act of transgressing the sacred; transgression becomes a form of blessing because it liberates the mind from the binding structure of prescribed thought-forms.[48] This was a theme that Malevich would return to. The wry references in the *Chiropodist* certainly attempt to demystify the icon of the *Old Testament Trinity* (reputedly one of the most mystical and incomprehensible of images), but whether they amount to a 'destruction' of it, as Alan Birnholz suggests, is debatable.[49]

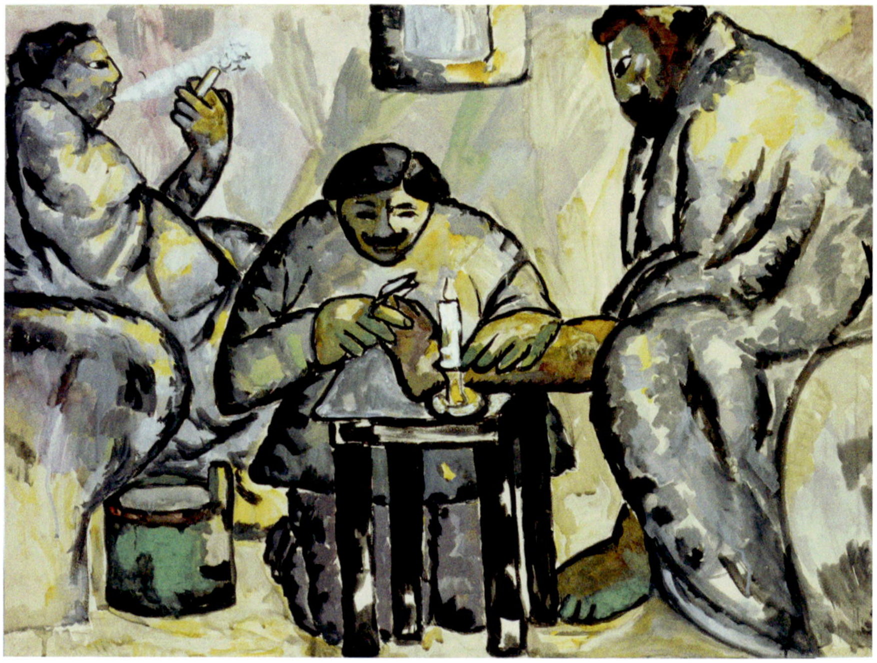

28
Kazimir Malevich
Chiropodist at the Baths, 1911–12
Gouache on paper
77.7 x 103 cm (30 ⅝ x 40 ½ in)
Stedelijk Museum, Amsterdam

The undiluted brilliance of the colours, the simplified forms of the figures and the minimisation of the illusion of depth are features of Malevich's neo-primitivist works that are typically characteristic of icons. The preponderance of figures from this period with heads bowed in submission as they work also recalls icons of saints in which the figures characteristically bow their heads in deference to Christ. Although they were inspired by a totally different vision, Malevich was attracted to these qualities because they provided him with a formal language through which to express his feelings for the social function and responsibility of art with immediacy and passion. His sympathy for icons led Anatolii Lunacharsky, head of the People's Commissariat of Enlightenment (Narkompros) from 1917–29, to describe him as 'strong and true like his models, the icon and the woodcut ... a classic at heart'. Of his early work, Lunacharsky wrote:

> Malevich began by imitating icons with fervent, saintly Russian faces which, while retaining their icon-like sternness, were also painted in a simplified but expressive, slightly wooden toy-like manner, with a suitable range of primitive, simple colours, for example red and blue. Malevich went on to make his icons even more like toys. But at the same time, under the influence of the Cubists (Malevich most closely resembled Picabia at this period), the small figures he painted in two or three primary hues began to lose their human shape in his pictures and turned into rods, elongated prisms etc.[50]

The effect of the neo-primitivists' appropriation of the social implications of icons was dependent on the emotive associations of their imagery. These associations, however, were not integral to the avant-garde vision and they did not continue to feature in its art. They served more in a transitional capacity – as romanticised ideals through which to dissociate from the autocratic cultural values of the time – without offering a vision of their own. The primitive techniques of icon painters, on the other hand – as distinct from their imagery – had a profound and lasting impact on the avant-garde movement. This was due to the fact that the communicative power of these techniques does not depend on their relationship to the outside world. On the contrary, they have an expressive value of their own and consequently they set a precedent for the pioneers of abstract art in Russia.

We have seen how Malevich echoed the postures of iconic figures in his neo-primitivist works for poetic effect. In his Cubist works, painted from 1912–14, he went a step further, adapting new aspects of icon-painting techniques to his search for an inherently expressive visual language. In these semi-abstract images he renounced the Romantic associations of subject matter (sometimes opposing them, in fact, with deliberately incongruous juxtapositions of seemingly unrelated images) and concentrated on the expressive potential of technique itself. Like icons, his Cubist works do not represent excerpts from everyday life but exist independently as transfixing centres of energy and attention. Their sense of depth is ambiguously shallow or non-existent, strategically pressing the content of the image up against the picture surface. In the *Knife-Grinder* of 1912, the impression of surface activity is further intensified by the use of elements of inverted perspective, concealed as the banister rail and steps in the top left- and right-hand corners of the picture.[51] This device was habitually used in the architectural backgrounds of icons where it frustrates the desire of the eye to relax into the illusion of depth (Plate 29). It has been suggested, somewhat unconvincingly, that the use of inverted perspective in icons promotes the attitude of contemplation that is appropriate to sacred art. By causing the vanishing point to be located in front of the image rather than within it, it places the point of natural rest within the viewer, thereby intensifying the viewer's awarenes of himself and the opportunity of spiritual awakening rather than relieving him of it.

The notion of inverted or reverse perspective as a necessary characteristic of sacred or 'pure' art was strongly advocated by Florensky, who traced its use back to pre-Christian times. As we have seen, Florensky's explanation of the way in which the invisible power of saints represented in icons is transmitted to the viewer – not simply by virtue of the sanctity of the represented figure but also by virtue of the purely material and formal properties of the icon itself – provides a close parallel to Larionov's Rayism. Florensky's thoughts on perspective add further substance to the elusive notion that, in searching for a new model of artistic culture that was both objective and absolute, some avant-garde artists may have become sensitive to universal or archetypal forms and configurations that lay dormant in the national sub-consciousness. Such forms may have evolved in ancient times but, according to Florensky, they were only sacralised by the icon painters of the Orthodox Church through whom they were invested with the sanctity of Christ. By virtue of their alignment to a metaphysical ideal, some artists may have become receptive to the influence of such archetypes, enabling them to resonate in their work and to exert their own power.

In his treatise *Reverse Perspective* (first conceived as a lecture in 1919 and presented in 1920, but not published until much later), Florensky described how the use of reverse perspective in icons corresponds to a metaphysical perception of reality *as it is*, in contrast to the naturalistic perspective of western art which attempts to rationalise the world, reducing it to the level of a human being's ability to perceive it. Florensky considered naturalistic 'linear' perspective, as formulated by Leon Battista Alberti, to be an illusory form of representation that is fundamentally worldly, limited and conditional in its scope; it merely reproduces the physical appearance of objects. He maintained that objects depicted in this way (as if they are fully real and complete) cause men to become mere observers of

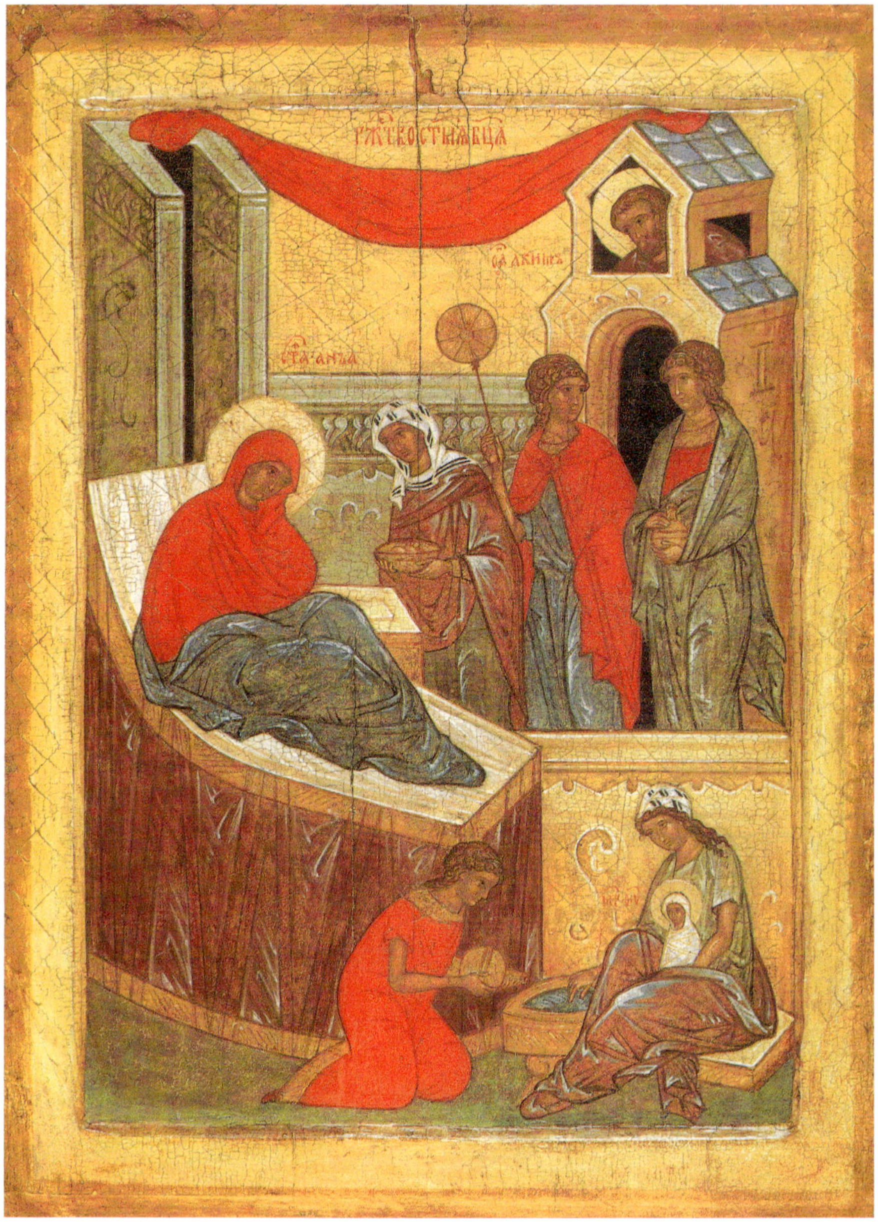

29

Nativity of the Mother of God,
Novgorod, late 15th century
Tempera on wooden panel
55 x 40 cm (21⅝ x 15¾ in)
Temple Galley, London

life, rather than participants who engage with life with the help of life-enhancing art. On the other hand, images that do not pretend to be coterminous with the space of this world do not compete with life; on the contrary, they can enhance it, depicting a transpersonal world, mysteriously inviting the viewer beyond the possibilities of optics and into the possibilities of vision, to a realm that lies beyond the scope of his ordinary perceptual faculties. Such art has existed since the most ancient times. Florensky did not believe the absence of perspective in ancient art to be a sign of its immaturity; he believed it to be a conscious expression, on the parts of its makers, of its engagement with a higher sacred principle. He also believed that the fact that icon painters also used reverse perspective for an explicitly religious purpose is reflected in the fact that they highlighted the areas in which the 'rules of perspective' were most obviously contravened with extreme unnaturalistic colour. For instance, the gospel book that is held by Christ, and some saints, in icons is not only flattened up against the picture surface so that the viewer can see the sides and the top of the book simultaneously; its edges are also often coloured with cinnabar in order to intensify its visual, and thereby spiritual, appeal, a practice that never occurs with real gospel books (Plate 42).[52]

Although there are clear parallels between his views and avant-garde theories of space, Florensky did not condone the abandonment of figurative content in contemporary painting, which he believed would lead to the ultimate destruction of art, and there is no evidence to suggest that he had a direct influence on the analytical, reductive and Constructivist avant-garde of the time.[53] On the contrary, Florensky's priority was manifestly spiritual and he did not invest the formal properties of art with an ability to transmit spiritual energy on their own account, without a relationship to a higher 'reality'. For him, reality was not simply what, if anything, was left behind when all illusions were stripped away (let alone the representation of human hardship or the surface appearance of material objects). It was a living engagement with religious truth, an absolute that ultimately transcended the material and aesthetic aspects of art. His realism was not primarily concerned with the object, or non-object in the case of abstract artists, of artistic representation (though his ideas did generally have the effect of steering those mostly conservative artists that were influenced by him – the Makovets group – in the direction of figurative work). Florensky's realism was concerned with the visionary condition of artistic practice – for which icon painting provided a perfect precedent.

As with Malevich, the early paintings of the Constructivist artist Vladimir Tatlin (1885–1953) were significantly influenced by the visual impact of icons. Unlike Malevich and other neo-primitivists who allowed the ethos of neo-primitivism to justify crude craftsmanship, Tatlin was independently concerned with the artistic value of his work from the outset of his career. His most expressionistic works, for instance, are not uninhibited celebrations of the expressive potential of shape and colour, as those of the neo-primitivists tend to be. They are also disciplined studies in the art of seeing and drawing, revealing the artist's sensitivity to the structural basis of forms. This feeling for the tightly knit and integrated structure of forms was later to eclipse his interest in representation and lead to the development of Constructivism.

Tatlin was the son of a railway engineer and he trained and travelled as a merchant sailor. His knowledge of mechanics, rigging and sails was reflected throughout his life in his tactile approach to his work. However, he also trained as an icon painter in Moscow and Yaroslavl from an early age

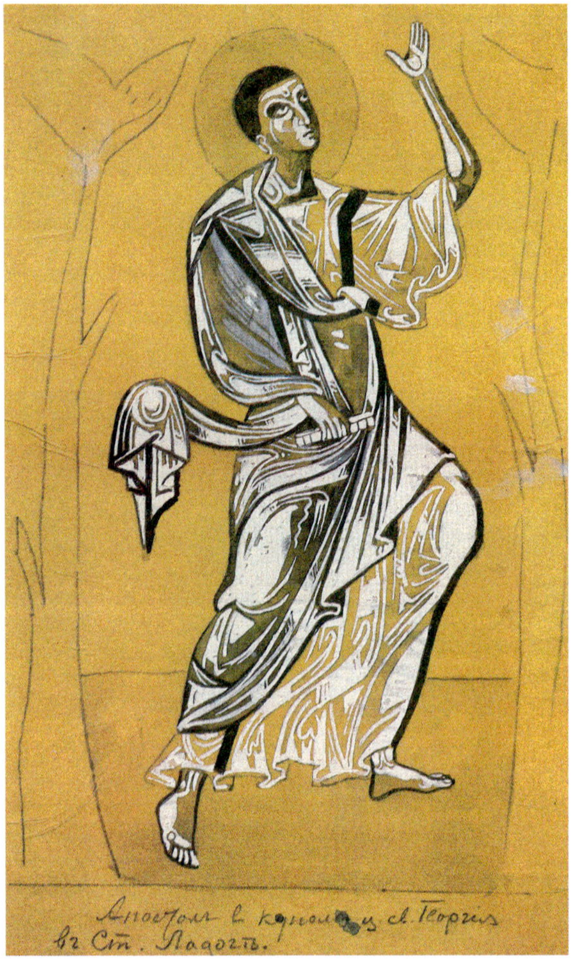

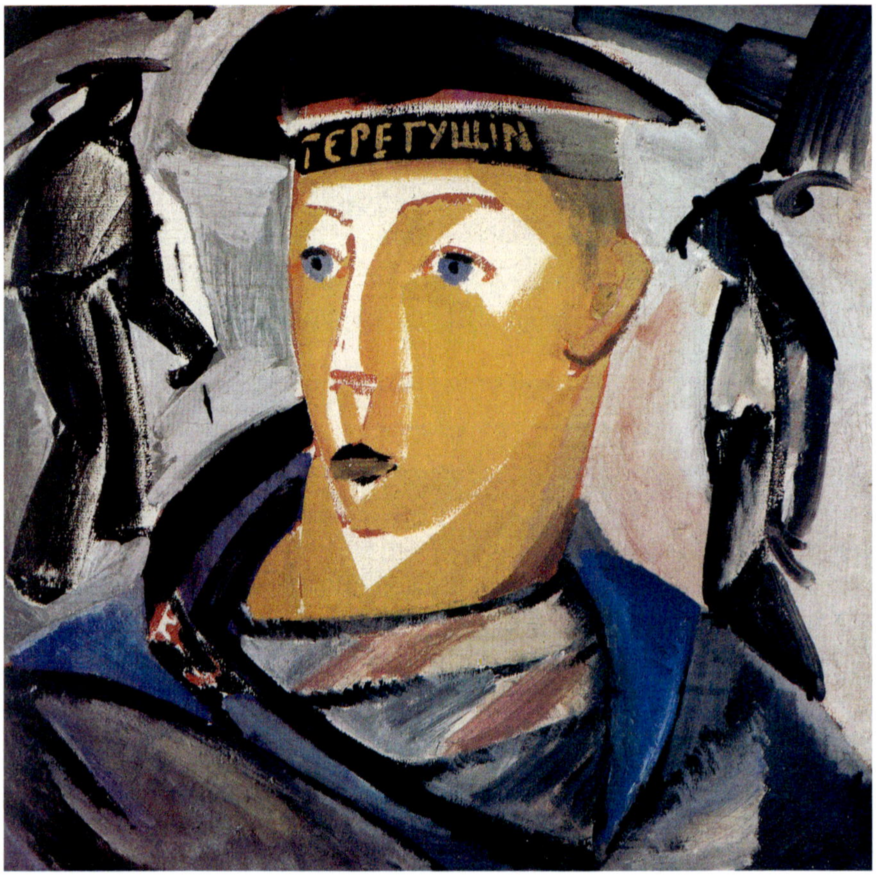

(his first contact with art) and then again between 1900 and 1910 when he worked in a number of icon-painting workshops.[54] Several examples of his early copies of frescos, made in Novgorod churches and elsewhere, still survive (Plate 30).[55] Tatlin was familiar with the neo-primitivists and exhibited with them at the Jack of Diamonds exhibitions, but unlike Larionov and Malevich, whose works from this period capitalise on the simplicity, directness and even crudeness of icons, he was drawn to the tightness and elegance of their compositions, 'allying himself' (in the words of Dmitri Sarabianov) 'not to the popular variant of Russian icon painting, as did Goncharova and Larionov, but to the classical one'.[56] Many of his works were designed with a compass and ruler. His appreciation of the figuration and techniques of icon painters is reflected in his earliest work. In his *Sailor*, for instance (1911, Plate 31), the rather wooden delineation of the nose and eyebrows, defined with a single curved line, is reminiscent of the highly simplified treatment of the facial features in some icons. The dark butterscotch colour of the face and the simple technique of placing white highlights over a monochrome ground to indicate a sense of form are also commonly found in icons. The sailor's costume closely resembles the flatly represented folds often found in the tunics of the Virgin and saints, and the two figures to the left and right of the sailor's face call to mind the presence of the Mother of God and Christ in icons of St Nicholas (Plate 70).

A thoroughly simplified treatment of the same iconic figuration is evident in Tatlin's series of nudes, painted in 1913 when he joined the loudly

30
Vladimir Tatlin

Study of an apostle on the cupola of the Church of St George, Staraia Ladoga, 1905–10
Watercolour and white paint on tracing paper
24 x 15.5 cm (9 ⅕ x 6 ⅛ in)
TsGALI, Moscow

31
Vladimir Tatlin

Sailor, 1911
Tempera on canvas
71.5 x 71.5 cm (28 ⅛ x 28 ⅛ in)
Russian Museum, St Petersburg

32
Vladimir Tatlin

Nude, 1913
Oil on canvas
143 x 108 cm (56 ¼ x 42 ½ in)
Tretyakov Gallery, Moscow

33
Vladimir Tatlin

Composition – Analysis, 1913
Pencil, gouache, watercolour on paper
49 x 33 cm (19 ¼ x 13 in)
Private collection

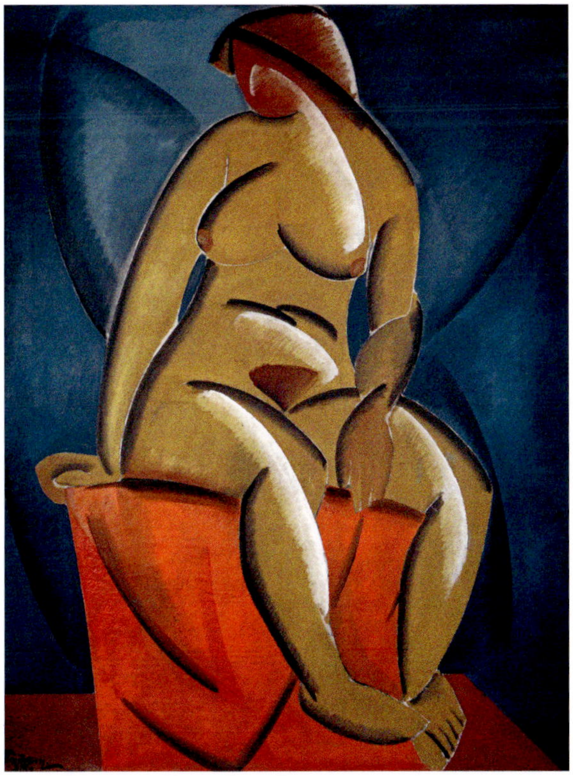

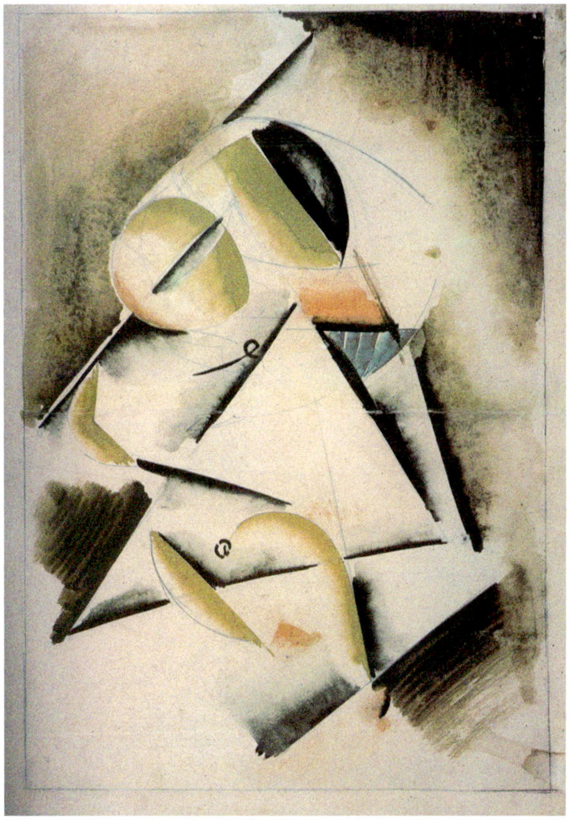

pro-Russian Donkey's Tail group. In one example (Plate 32), the quality of fullness and maternity in the figure and the rather melancholy impression of wilting in the lines recall icons of the Tichvin *Mother of God with Christ* (Plate 4) in which the sinuous yielding outlines of the Mother of God enhance the expression of sorrow in her face. In both images the monumental form of the woman conveys a sense of placid strength while her slightly tilted head and averted gaze introduce an element of vulnerable reflectiveness to her expression. Already in this work, however, Tatlin's debt to icons can be seen to be shifting away from their poetic mood towards the more purely artistic effect of their fragmented and flattened technique. One of the primary functions of the figure in his *Nude*, for instance, is to provide a basic form from which to generate a dynamic interplay of semi-abstract arcs. The form of the figure is painted in a single colour, outlined by dark arcs and highlighted by light arcs. This system of articulating a monochromatic shape by overlaying it with a network of descriptive lines can be closely compared to the stylised representation of facial and bodily features in numerous icons. The unity of the *Nude* as a whole is assured by the continuation of the play of arcs beyond the confines of the figure. The abstracting effect of this treatment – submitting the entire picture surface to a web of inter-connecting arcs – results in the impression that the form of the model is differentiated from its surroundings more by its distinct colouring than by any attempt at linear definition (this effect becomes especially clear when the image is seen in black-and-white reproduction). Indeed, the rather indirect

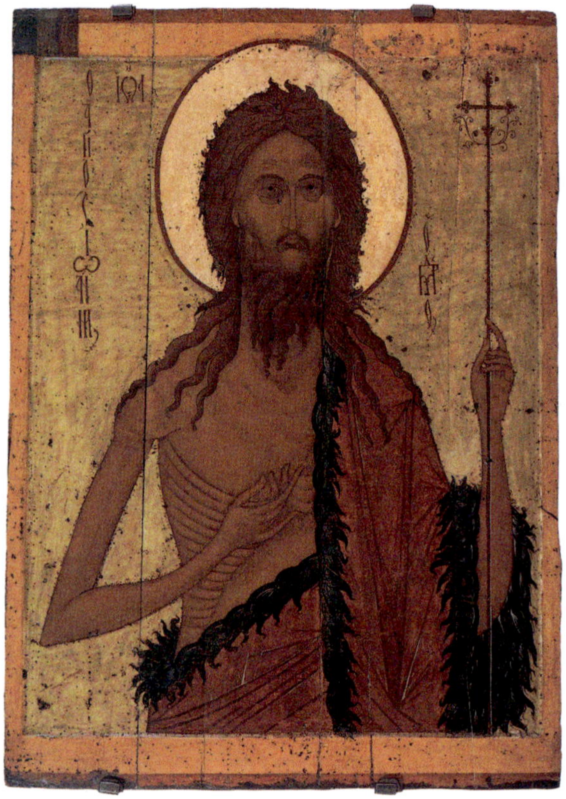

and abstracted way in which the figure is defined enables the opened-up structure of the model's form to interact with the structure of the surrounding space in a way that further anticipates Constructivism.

Tatlin's growing interest in the impact of artistic technique – in contrast to the emotive potential of imagery – is most amply demonstrated by an analytical sketch he made, also in 1913, of an unidentified painting of the Virgin and Child by the sixteenth-century Flemish master Lucas Cranach, though it also compares closely to icons of the Vladimirskaya Mother of God with Christ (Plates 33, 14).[57] Because the compositional structure of the original was designed to enhance its narrative content – the tender but dynamic relationship of the Virgin and Christ – the subject lent itself particularly well to compositional analysis. In his sketch, Tatlin has rid the image of its extraneous references and associations, reducing it to its most basic compositional elements. He has broken the composition down into a series of interrelated curves and lines without undermining its structural coherence. Although the sketch was based on a western European model, it epitomises the way in which Tatlin consistently used the artistic wisdom of icons as a basis for his own compositional experiments. Ultimately, he did not put importance on the specific model, which merely served as a springboard for a new composition that had its own internal rationale:

> It is unimportant to a true artist whether to portray a Madonna or a strumpet because he solves his own artistic problems through their creation. So the outside of the model may be almost anything. In their time, people who placed the commissions [just] wanted Madonnas ... I, however, see Cranach's idea before me. He was obliged to create a composition out of triangles, and he was able to solve the problem brilliantly. And to make this even clearer ... he drew the young lady and child into a triangle – touchingly enough to produce tears![58]

Tatlin clearly acknowledged the expressionistic and socialist potential of icons (as exploited by Larionov and Malevich) but at this stage in his career it was primarily the melancholy poetry of their pictorial style to which he kept returning. Something of this sad beauty can also be seen in the work of Vasily Chekrygin who knew and painted Tatlin and whose early training as an icon painter at the Pechersky Monastery in Kiev clearly left its mark on his attitude towards art and especially on his early work. Commenting on an exhibition of icons that he saw in Moscow, probably the 1913 exhibition, he said: 'Alters my philosophy or rather, or strengthens it'.[59] He considered himself to be a pupil of Andrei Rublev and, according to Lev Zhigin, he once made an abstract 'copy' of Rublev's *Old Testament Trinity*. Chekrygin was particularly drawn to monumental

34.
St John the Forerunner, *c.*1570
Tempera on wooden panel
135 x 97.5 cm (53⅛ x 38⅜ in)
History Museum, Yaroslavl

fresco-painting which remained the dominant influence on his work until his untimely death at the age of 25 in 1922. His *Portrait of Tatlin* (1913, Plate 16) captures the mood both of the sitter and of the icon-painting tradition. Its weary lines, flattened representation of form and spaceless (though atmospheric) background are reminiscent of Tatlin's work from this period but they are also typically iconic features. It is the extreme attenuation of the figure, however, that takes the work's connection with icons beyond the purely technical level. The tendency to stress the vertical axis – as if to connect the inner world of the individual with the 'higher' world of feeling at the expense of the expansive worldliness of the horizontal – was characteristic of Moscow icons from the fourteenth and fifteenth centuries, when monastic practice of the profoundly inward discipline of hesychasm was at its most intense (see plate 34). In icons, exaggerated verticality was used to convey an impression of otherworldliness, renunciation and interior connection with God through unceasing prayer; in Chekrygin's portrait, it serves as a visual metaphor for moral economy, uprightness and rigour in exactly the same way.

Although Chekrygin's early work reflects the influence of his Cubo-Futurist and neo-primitivist contemporaries (with whom he exhibited in 1914), he never minimised the poetic potential of imagery. Throughout his life, this remained at the heart of his work, much of which was concerned with religious subject matter: *Adam and Eve*, *The Transsubstantiation of the Flesh into the Spirit* and *The Resurrection of the Body*. His commitment to the religious potential of art came to the fore in 1921 when he co-formed the Makovets (Summit) group of artists, named after the hill at Sergeev Posad, the spiritual centre of the Russian Orthodox Church, under the spiritual guidance of Pavel Florensky who was living at Sergeev Posad at the time. Florensky had begun teaching 'Analysis of Space' in the Department of Monumental [fresco] Painting at the VKhUTEMAS (Higher State Artistic and Technical Workshops) school that year. The following year, Makovets published his essay on the Orthodox liturgy as an exemplary synthesis of the arts.[60]

As the art of the Russian avant-garde became ever more abstract, it sacrificed its dependency – which it shared with icons – on the emotive potential of stylised figure-types. However, as avant-garde art became increasingly free of reference to the outside world, growing to depend ever more exclusively on its own resources, it came to resonate with icons at a deeper level. By 1913, a significant number of artists had ceased developing technique as a means for communicating or commenting on a preconceived content and began to explore the expressive potential of technique on its own terms. An image ceased to be significant on the basis of its relationship or reference to subject matter but became significant purely as a source and centre of energy and experience, conveyed exclusively through artistic technique. As the contemporary painter, Liubov Popova, commented, 'We do know instances of distortion for formal and painterly achievements – Russian and Byzantine icon painting, the art of primitive peoples, Romanesque, Gothic, Cézanne and other examples. But transformation for the sake of painterly or sculptural construction – that is the revelation of our artistic revolution'.[61]

Kazimir Malevich, who coined the term 'Suprematism' in 1915 to refer to the supremacy of his *non-objective* art over merely *abstracted* art (which could be highly abstract but was nevertheless based on an object), explained his own development towards abstraction in relation to the tradition of nineteenth-century Russian figurative painting. He clearly indicated a degree of sympathy for the feeling-orientation of some of his predecessors, but he dissociated sharply from their means of expressing such feeling and from their overall concept of art. Significantly the subject matter of the paintings he chose for comparison with his own work is both abstract – in the sense that it does not simply involve the representation of an actually perceived reality – and Christian:

> The preceding schools and the 'Wanderers', whom I admired, did as follows: they chose an appropriate subject ... and the painting developed in the mould of this subject... These masters regarded subject matter as the principal content to be expressed through a painting. My approach was different. I did not want painting to act as a means, but only as its own content. Ge, in his *Crucifixion*,[62] invested the feeling of his painting in its subject matter. In the same way, in *The Last Supper*, he used the figure of Judas as a means through which to create a light effect. I gained a further insight from this picture: I saw that it was possible to use subject matter as a means. Strictly speaking, Ge and several other artists had a feeling for pure painting, but they could not imagine the existence of painting as such, as non-figurative. They sensed the non-figurative, but they produced figurative work. I also found myself in this position; it still seemed to me that painting in its pure aspect was empty and that it was absolutely necessary to give it a content. On the other hand, however, the emotional power of painting would not allow me to see images as purely representational... Naturalism could not stand up to my criticism, and I began looking for other possibilities – not outside painting, but within the very core of the emotion of painting, expecting that painting itself would sooner or later generate the form from its own painterly qualities, and would escape the magnetic attraction of objects and non-painterly associations. This position led me further and further away from an academic study of nature, from naturalism, from illusionism. My knowledge of icons convinced me that it is not a question of mastering anatomy and perspective, nor of reproducing nature exactly, but that it is necessary to have an intuition of art and of artistic realism. I saw that it is necessary to transform reality or content into an ideal form arising from the depths of aesthetics. In this way, anything can become beautiful in art. Even that which is not beautiful in itself can become beautiful, once realised at an artistic level.[63]

The 'feeling for pure painting' and sense of the 'non-figurative' that Malevich detected in Ge's work may have been magnified by the influence of Tolstoy, whom Ge knew well and whose ideals of Christian simplicity made a significant impact on the artist. In a perceptive and sympathetic article on 'Lev Tolstoy's Suprematist Icon-Painting',[64] Ksana Blank evokes Tolstoy's own feeling for pure perception and his sense of the non-figurative by drawing attention to the uncanny resemblance between the way the author describes his characters' insights into the shaped and coloured essences of people and objects seen in the world, and Malevich's Suprematist work. Tolstoy's description, in *War and Peace*, of the soldier Petya Rostov sitting in a forest on the eve of his death is particularly suggestive:

> Petya had every reason to know that he was in a forest, in Denisov's band, a verst [a unit of distance] from the road, sitting on a wagon

35
Kazimir Malevich

Painterly Realism: Boy with Knapsack – Colour Masses in the Fourth Dimension, 1915
Oil on canvas
71.1 x 44.5 cm (28 x 17 ½ in)
Museum of Modern Art, New York

captured from the French near which horses were tethered; that the big dark patch (*chernoe piatno*) to the right was the watchman's hut, the red spot (*krasnoe piatno*) below to the left the dying campfire; yet he neither knew nor wanted to know anything of all this. He was in an enchanted kingdom where nothing resembled reality. The big dark patch might be a hut, it is true, but then it might be a cavern leading to the very depths of the earth. The red spot might be a fire or it might be the eye of some prodigious monster. Perhaps he really was sitting on a wagon, but it might very well be that he was not sitting on a wagon at all, but on a marvellously high tower from which, if he fell, he would go on flying for a whole day, a whole month, before he reached the earth – or he might fly forever and never reach it.[65]

Blank's comparison of this passage with Malevich's *Painterly Realism: Boy with Knapsack – Colour Masses in the Fourth Dimension* of 1915 (Plate 35) is strangely apt. Entirely in keeping with Malevich's vision of Suprematism as feeling-vision, Petya's perception of the scene is gradually overwhelmed by the impression of the 'big dark patch' and the 'red spot' which become like momentous centres of potency, suspended in his consciousness and divorced from any sense of objective reality. They become emptied emblems of infinity.

Tolstoy evoked the essence of individual people in a similar way, as pulsating impressions of form that pre-exist personal appearance and articulations of character. He also suggested the transrational nature of such perceptions, subtly conveying how incomprehensible they are to the rationalising mind. For instance, Natasha Rostov (also in *War and Peace*) describes Boris Drubetskoy to her mother as, '"very sweet, really very sweet. Only not quite to my taste –

he's narrow like the dining-room clock... Do you understand? Narrow, you know, grey – pale grey..." "What nonsense, you're talking!" said the Countess. "Don't you understand?" Natasha continued. "Nikolai would understand. Bezhukov, now is blue – dark blue and red, and foursquare (*chetverougol'nyi*) ... dark blue and red – how can I explain it to you?"'

Just as Tolstoy reveals what Blank calls 'the iconic image of the feeling' evoked by Bezhukov in Natasha's soul – coloured shapes of 'intense feeling' against the white 'void beyond feeling' – so Malevich's Suprematist works were not only independent abstractions, but could also exist as forms of feeling-vision into the nature of things, some of which were specifically identified in their titles, as peasant women, football players etc. On one occasion, in a notebook of 1923, he wrote that 'when people stand up in their equality, then their shape will be rectangular, square' – presumably when they are no longer identified by their external, 'objective' attributes but by their inner natures as pure feeling.[66]

Although there is no evidence to suggest that Malevich knew of Tolstoy's 'Suprematist' insights into the nature of things, Tolstoy's descriptions are important and relevant in the present context because they offer a close parallel for the 'feeling for pure painting' that Malevich saw in Ge. They give a rare impression of Suprematist vision in its natural habitat – as a natural and spontaneous state of being, rather than as an 'art experience'. The paradox of intuiting the infinite, without attempting to induce it artificially through strategic effort or art, was one that preoccupied Malevich throughout his maturity. One can only speculate how he would have responded to Tolstoy's descriptions – given the circumstantial differences that separated the two artists.

Because icons were primarily conceived as objects of contemplation, they were designed to attract and hold the attention of the viewer. Moreover, because the object of their contemplation was a single noumenal truth – ultimately Christ – rather than a complex system of referential ideas, they tended to have a minimum of narrative and symbolic content, preferring to absorb the attention of the viewer than to stimulate his or her mind. The process of contemplation was facilitated at an artistic level by presenting the viewer with an image of almost hypnotic appeal. From a psychological point of view, this 'hypnotic' quality is largely concentrated in the remote but penetrating expressions of the figures' eyes. However, it is also conveyed at a purely technical level through the uncompromising centrality and stability of their compositions, the static grandeur of their forms and the flat immobility of their decorative motifs.

For their own revolutionary reasons, avant-garde artists were also keen to monopolise the attention of the viewer, forcefully distracting him beyond the illusory safety of the familiar world. Many of them

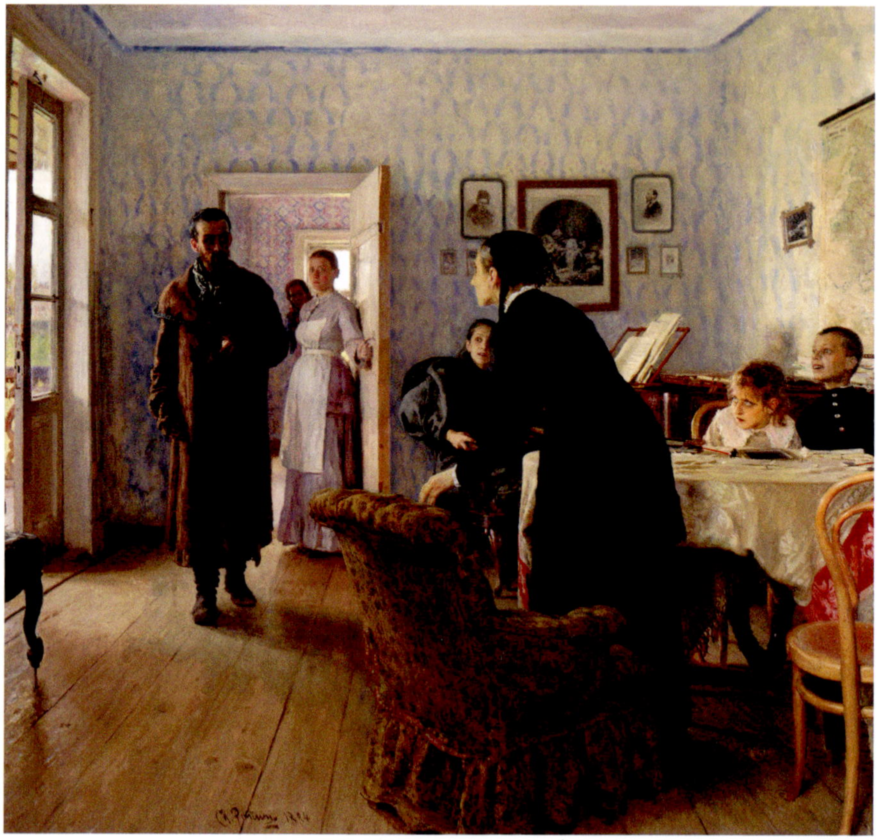

36
Ilya Repin
They Did Not Expect Him, 1884–8
Oil on canvas
160.5 x 167.5 cm (63 ¼ x 66 in)
Tretyakov Gallery, Moscow

achieved this end by abandoning all traces of subject matter and concentrating the meaning and impact of their work exclusively in the visual experience it afforded. For this reason the first impression given by many of their works is one of explosive suddenness and speed, shocking the senses into attention (plates 40, 41 and 43). Such works represent focal points of energy suspended in their own space. Like icons, they are centred and self-sufficient; they are bold and decisive in their sense of design. The dynamic in Malevich's Suprematist works, for instance, is achieved on account of the polarities set up between their motionless parts. Unlike Kandinsky's works of the same date, in which the sense of dynamic is largely established through the impression of a sequence of forms unfolding in time like music, Malevich's Suprematist work is charged with a kind of static electricity, complex and brittle like spillikins (plate 83). As with some types of narrative icon in which even the most dramatic scenes can seem to be frozen in time and space, the effect of these works depends on the unity and immediacy of their overall impact, not on any sense of temporal drama they may convey as abstract narratives.

Curiously, this instinct for the intense and dramatic within the static, or between static elements, is manifest in other areas of Russian art – particularly in the dramatic narratives of the Wanderers working in the 1870s and 1880s. In the Renaissance-derived tradition of the West, a sense of drama was frequently communicated through the use of gesture, particularly of the arms, which lead the eye through the painting, facilitating the impression of movement and sequence. Russian artist Anton Losenko (1731–73) had attempted to introduce this grand rhetorical manner to Russia in the 1760s, having studied academic history painting with neo-Classical masters in Paris and Rome. Initially, it was unsuccessful, receiving little attention at court, but it eventually came to epitomise the Classical ideal at the Academy of Arts until it was rejected by the critical realists in 1863. Significantly, in contrast to this rhetorical manner, many of the most tense and dramatic realist works of the second half of the nineteenth century, including the religious works discussed above, are entirely free of exaggerated gesture and movement. In several cases, such as Nikolai Ge's *Peter the Great Interrogating the Tsarevich Alexei* (1871), the artist does not represent the most dramatic moment in the chosen narrative (in this case, Peter accusing his son of treachery and awaiting a response); he represents the awful moment just after it, in which there is no outwardly dramatised speech or action but which is nonetheless highly charged. The tension is polarised between silent, static characters. The same is true of Ilya Repin's *They Did Not Expect Him* (1884–8, Plate 36), which shows an exile returning to his family. In this highly dramatic work, the tension is not discharged in the painting through a chain or network of active and reactive gestures. On the contrary, it is concentrated in, and between, the psychological states of the characters present, all of whom are sitting or standing still; it is simply held in place – highly charged but unresolved, undiffused, unguided. Malevich shared this feeling for the static structure of a work and it underpins his Suprematist compositions. He recognised it in his predecessors, commenting (as already quoted above) that 'they sensed the non-figurative, but they produced figurative work'.

Something of this feeling for the highly charged dynamic that exists between static, self-contained elements is present in avant-garde colour theory which was precedented, according to several contemporary writers and critics, in icon painting. The neo-primitivist painter Alexander Shevchenko, for instance, was particularly interested in the expressive potential of colour which he promoted as a painterly element with a value and impact of its own, rather than as a means to a non-painterly end, such as optical illusion. He also recognised this quality in icons, in which the effect of colour is achieved through the relationship *between* distinct colour-fields rather than through the transformation or grading of colours *within* colour-fields. In his essay *Neoprimitivism: Its Theory, Its Potential, Its Achievements* (1913), Shevchenko describes how it is the repetitive highlights on the coloured garments in icons, rather than any colour-grading or colour-change, that enable their colours to flow into the background:

> We advocate colour as such, and restore painting not to impressionistic luminism or to the local colours of the academy, but to paint, in all its lustre, in its self-sufficient meaning... We abolish reflection [which presupposes space], the academic bauble [naturalism], and advance a new principle, the principle of flowing colour. Flowing colour, methodically reiterating the same colour or its shade, indicates a movement of colour – and in movement is life.
>
> Flowing colour is encountered for the first time, as a quite definite painterly principle, in our icons, where it is expressed in the highlighting of the garments by colours flowing (passing) on into the background.[67]

At an artistic level, Shevchenko's fundamental intention was to liberate the expressive potential of the technique of art, particularly in relation to colour, from any secondary, non-painterly considerations. In 1912–13, he made scientific analyses of the nature and laws of colour, and in 1918–19 he set up a group, Colour Dynamics and Tectonic Primitivism, to develop his discoveries and reconcile them with observations on the effect of colours in *lubki* (popular prints, Plate 120) and icons. This group included the artist Alexei Grishchenko, who also regarded icons as a precedent and source for the regeneration of contemporary art – publishing books on the subject in 1913 and 1917,[68] and lecturing on the importance of iconic simplicity and directness as expressive forces ('How and why we should consider icon painting') in 1915. The group, which held a single exhibition in Moscow in 1919, sought to uphold the three principles of 'structure, knowledge of the laws of colour, and knowledge of the material with which we operate in creating the easel painting'.[69]

In his book, *The Russian Icon as the Art of Painting*, written in 1917, Grishchenko celebrates the aesthetic wisdom of icons. He praises Matisse for his appreciation of icons (and his rejection of the Wanderers), claiming that when he returned to Paris he was so dissatisfied with his use of colour that he cut up several of his works. During his own visit to Paris in 1911 (the same year as Matisse's visit to Russia) Grishchenko showed photographs of icons and works by the Wanderers to a number of young Cubist artists who praised the former highly and disparaged the latter. Grishchenko compared the new Russian interest in the formal properties of icons to French primitivism, stating that both Picasso and Matisse considered themselves to be direct beneficiaries of Giotto and the Italian primitives (as well as non-European cultures) and he credited the French for opening the eyes of Russian artists to the artistic intelligence of their own tradition.

Grishchenko was particularly interested in the artistic and formal properties of icons – the unique understanding and use of colour, and their architectonic compositions. He realised that layers of soot had obscured icons for centuries but also felt that to see beyond their 'physical brightness of the colours' (revealed by new cleaning techniques) into their 'unusual beauty' required a certain training and inclination which differed from a typical classically oriented education. While he appreciated the insights that Prince Trubetskoi brought to icons in a 1916 lecture on 'Contemplation in Colour' (in which a mystical and intellectual approach was taken), he rejected the supposition that 'psychologism, allegory and symbolism' were the key to understanding icons. He claimed that many icons, such as icons of saints, have no intellectual agenda at all, whereas icons of the late Moscow school, which are 'full of symbolism and intricate allegory', reflect the spirit of German *kunstkammers* (cabinets of curiosities), illustrated bibles and theological treatises; they are complex and arcane but not profound. He was especially critical of the sentimental and romanticised recycling of iconic imagery that he saw in the works of Stelletsky, Goncharova, Kuzma Petrov-Vodkin, Nicholas Roerich and Alexander Savinov, considering them to have jettisoned all trace of the artistic depth that underpinned the narrative dimension of icons (their colour, texture, composition etc) in favour of shallow mystique.

Shevchenko's interest in the artistic example of icons was partly due to the nationalistic associations that icons could bring to contemporary art. His theory of neo-primitivism combined a feeling for the moral superiority of 'truthfulness to the medium' – which mitigated against two-dimensional illusions of three-dimensional space and the manipulation of colour for illusionistic purposes – with a philosophy of history that located the source and destiny of 'true art' in the East (thus liberating Russia from any hint of long-term indebtedness to western Europe). In this way he conspired to make neo-primitivism – which he regarded as a 'profoundly national phenomenon'[70] (as well as the 'artist's religion')[71] – seem determined, and therefore morally sanctioned, by the logic of history.

The role of iconic colour in the regeneration of Russian art was also raised by the art critic, teacher and museum director Nikolai Punin (1888–1953), who was one of the most outspoken advocates of avant-garde art in Russia from 1913. In his article 'Directions in contemporary art and Russian icon-painting', published in *Apollo* in December 1913, Punin criticised the self-indulgence of contemporary practice and its alienation from the people, calling for a 'renewal of art by means of a return to forgotten traditions'. The article is particularly critical of western-style individualism and subjectivity which, Punin claimed, lead either to a world of obscure private fantasies or to 'formalistic' art – art that is excessively preoccupied with the aesthetic or physiological impact of its forms, selected by an artist for personal reasons that are frequently incomprehensible and irrelevant to the general public. At one point, Punin even dismisses excessive subtlety in the use of colour on the grounds that it will not be appreciated by most people and is therefore worthless to the point of being self-indulgent. In place of 'formalism', Punin demanded a type of art that is accessible to all people and which must therefore be based on an objective system or principle that can be understood widely, rather than on the personal psychology of a private individual. Icons, he maintained, provide a precedent for this type of art, based on an objective emotional and symbolic system that was accessible to the whole of society. He explained how line, colour and composition in icons were not used according to the personal preference of the painter or even (primarily) as representational tools; they were used according to an ancient system in which each feature communicates a depth of meaning and emotion that it has absorbed over the centuries.

Having expounded the virtues of icon painting as a form of art in which painters transcended personal self-expression in favour of a more objective and universal language of feeling-associations (as well as traditional symbols, which he underplayed), Punin turned to the question of the relevance of icons to contemporary art, arguing that if the ancient emotional resonance of colour is overlooked, painting becomes dry and formalistic, 'far from eternity, truth and art':

> These are the conclusions drawn from this examination of Russian icons. We believe that icons, in their magnificent and living beauty, will help contemporary art accomplish achievements which differ from those that have been influencing European art for the last few decades. We, who were deceived by the individualistic-symbolistic tendency of contemporary art on the one hand, and who feel alienated from a formalistic understanding of art on the other, are looking for other values, other [sources of] inspiration, another [kind of] art. There is reason to believe, or so it seems, that old Russian icon painting is a revelation for us and that it can feed a heart that is not only able to formulate witty sentences, but also to deeply and truly love [the processes of] creation – the true joy of our ambiguous existence – over many years.[72]

Several years later – in his 1921 monograph on Tatlin – Punin described the feeling for colours as self-sufficient forces as a typically Russian characteristic. He contrasted it with the 'arbitrary' and 'subjective' approach of the West where colours were selected from an unlimited range of chromatic tones and juxtaposed in gradations for no better reason than to achieve an illusion of modelling or describing forms. His earlier anticipation that the example of icons would facilitate the evolution of Russian art towards its natural disposition was borne out by Tatlin:

> Until the reign of Peter the Great, Russian painting had worked with pigment as a painting material, as the result of dye pigment. Although it used to gravitate towards a flat and even decorative colour structure, never – with some rare exceptions – was colour perceived by icon painters as the relationship within the chromatic scale. Hence the beautiful tradition of a powerful and healthy art was still preserved in the schools of icon painting and house-painters' workshops. The so-called body painting, conditioned by an old and firm technique, is to a certain extent a national characteristic of Russian painting. Tatlin unconsciously absorbed both that technique and that understanding of colour, subsequently preferring these to the French manner of painting.[73]

Malevich expressed a similar attitude towards the role of colour in the new art in a series of pedagogical charts which he produced in 1927 (although many of the ideas expressed in the charts date back to the first decade of the century). The purpose of the charts was to reveal universal laws underlying the artistic effects of the various technical components of painting – line, colour, form and structure – as manifest throughout the history of art. In the tenth chart, *The Assimilation of the Colour Stimuli in the Creative Process of the Artist* (Plate 37), Malevich assembles a series of images from various sources – including an icon to represent religion – in order to illustrate how 'waves of colour stimulus acquire a painterly structure independently, regardless of the subject matter to which they will be applied'.[74]

Malevich regarded the stylised use of colour in

37
Kazimir Malevich
The Assimilation of the Colour Stimuli in the Creative Process of the Artist, 1927
Stedelijk Museum, Amsterdam

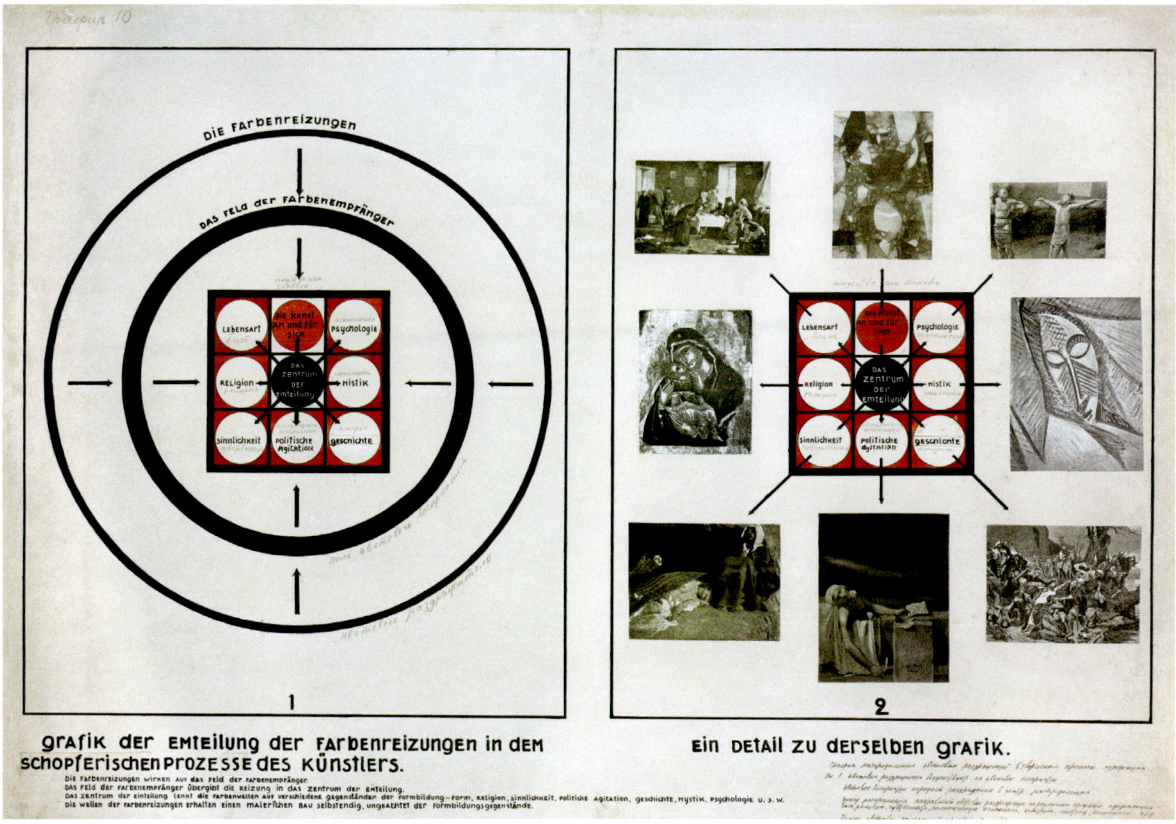

icons as a kind of primitive prototype for the pure colourism of Suprematism. In his eighth chart, he differentiates between painting that is primarily determined by structural principles (which he represents with works by Rembrandt, Paul Cézanne and Georges Braque) and painting that is primarily determined by principles of colour. To epitomise colour painting he selects an icon, together with paintings by Holbein and Matisse and a detail of a Matisse – placed on its side, so as to shake off its appearance of being representational.[75] Evidently, he would have shared Liubov Popova's view that 'the intrinsic value of colour is clear to us in the Novgorod icons of the fourteenth and fifteenth centuries'. The sculptor Vera Mukhina, who became internationally famous for her monumental sculpture of a *Worker and Collective Farm Worker*, designed for the Soviet pavilion at the International Exhibition in Paris in 1937, recalled how Popova 'taught me to look at colour and the colour relationships in Russian icons.'[76]

Malevich acknowledged that 'in many [historical] works, the tasks of visual representation, and the tasks of colour painting and "painting as such", are all being tackled simultaneously'.[77] Yet because the colours in such works – icons and other precedents – are not exclusively 'composed according to the independent laws of colour painting' but are also 'a means for expressing a desired content', he regarded them as imperfect forms of art. Nevertheless, as Dmitri Sarabianov has written, 'To a certain extent, Malevich's Suprematist canvases gravitated towards icons. They strove to be a contemplation of life, a contemplation in forms and colours. However, Malevich stressed an important distinction between his work and icon painting. Suprematist paintings do not depict anything or anyone, whereas in our visible world the icon always has the role of representing the deity.'[78]

Because icon and fresco painters were dependent on their own resources for their pigments, their palettes revolved around natural colours such as

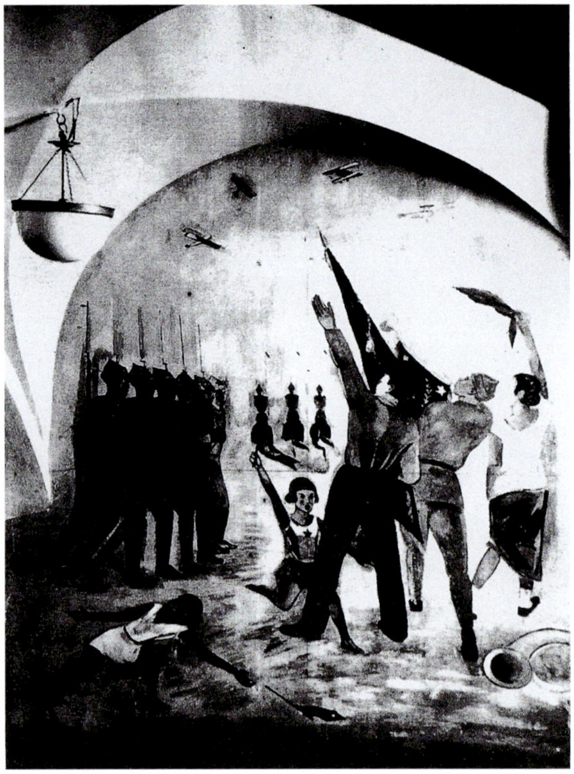

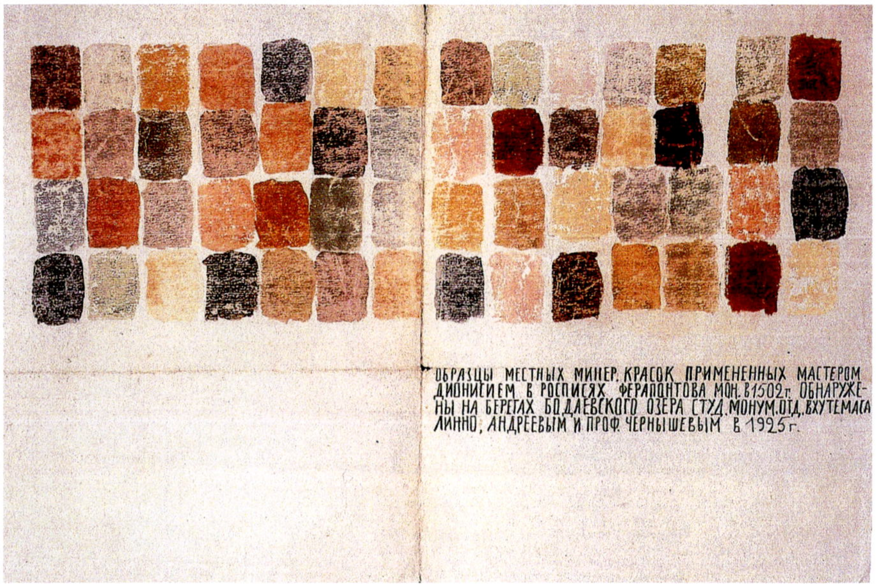

terra verte, vermilion, sienna, umber, ochre etc. The painters of the avant-garde, on the other hand, were not restricted by circumstance in this way. Nevertheless, despite their unprecedented audacity in other areas, their choice of colours remained surprisingly reserved (Plates 77, 83). Where they could so easily have amplified their revolutionary message by adopting the strident palette of the German Expressionists, they chose a rather musty palette – like that of icons and old Russian frescos – in which even the primary colours seem somewhat subdued. Rather than exploit synthetic reds, yellows and greens, readily available at the time, they used warmer earth colours which, though they function nominally as dull reds, yellows and greens, are often more closely related to the ruddy and sandy browns of icons. Cool blues and rich purples are, on the whole, used sparingly in both avant-garde art and icons; frequently they do not appear at all. In many cases – especially in Suprematist works – the concentrated content of the image is set against a white or ivory background.

Well into the Soviet period the study of Russian icons and frescos was advocated as a key to understanding colour. In the 1920s, students of monumental fresco painting at the VKhUTEMAS school were taken on visits to churches in Yaroslavl, Pskov, Novgorod, Vladimir and Rostov in order to 'study the works of the great masters and learn the secrets of their processes'. Their teacher, Nicolas Chernychev, the 'soul' of the department, was a passionate expert on the subject and was committed to applying ancient techniques to the development of a contemporary tradition of wall-painting. This interest is unmistakably present in the work of his pupils, some of which reflects the colour, design and even spirit of its ancient prototypes.[79] Having used the walls of the departmental studios for practice, students were put to work on ensembles of frescos in schools, barracks and workers' and peasants' clubs – for instance, the Djerzinski Barracks in Moscow in 1929 and the Proletariat Club in 1930. Of these two projects, only designs and photographs survive (Plate 38).[80] One of the students who

38
N. Korotkova

Victory, 1929
Fresco in the Djerzinski Barracks, Moscow (destroyed)

39

Samples of pigments collected from Ferapontov Monastery (1502) by students of Nicolas Chernychev at the VKhUTEMAS School of Design, 1925 worked on these projects, N. Korotkova, described their long stay, under the guidance of Chernychev, at Ferapontov Monastery in northern Russia where they copied the frescos of the famous fifteenth-century icon painter Dionysii: 'We gathered stones of finely nuanced colours and reduced them to powder in preparation for paintings. It was with these very same stones that Dionysius prepared his colours long ago'.[81] Technical studies made by the students using minerals found at the site still survive (Plate 39).[82]

Another aspect of much avant-garde art that finds a meaningful precedent in icons is the enjoyment of the pictorial potential of letters and words. The reason for including words in icons was purely practical – to identify festivals and saints depicted and to present the utterances of the saints and prophets on their scrolls. Larionov mimics this iconic feature in his portrait of Tatlin (1913)[83] and his *Self-portrait* of 1910–12 (Plate 21), where he bombastically identifies himself by means of a large white inscription reading 'self-portrait of Larionov'. Malevich imitated the same feature in his *Portrait of Matiushin* (1913) by writing the name of the sitter, subsequently over-painted, in the left-hand margin of the painting.[84] In both cases, the size and quirkiness of the letters de-sophisticates the image, taking attention away from any pretensions to psychological insight, which viewers conventionally seek in portraits, as if to reduce them to the level of illustrations in a child's learn-to-read picture book. At the same time, the letters interfere with the pictorial space of the images in an irreverent and anti-classical way. The script in icons was also influential as a compositional element. There are numerous examples of icons in which the forms of the letters have their own powerful visual and artistic impact, and make a significant contribution to the overall effect of the design (Plates 34, 122). Their visual impact must have been especially striking to illiterate people, the vast majority of the population of Russia until the nineteenth century. The script in such cases is often highly stylised and decorative and, particularly where the words are broken up or abbreviated, it can border on abstraction. Even to literate people unversed in Old Church Slavonic (including Larionov and Malevich), it can be incomprehensible, accidentally and ironically becoming a parody of meaning. In many avant-garde paintings and prints, words were partly dismantled and scattered in a similar way, subject to the same explosive force as the abstract forms amidst which they appear (plate 40). Often associated with punchy slogans and catchphrases, their function was to infect the viewer with a sense of their own conviction.

The avant-garde use of letters and words as pure forms was not determined exclusively by artistic considerations. The trend may have reflected an awareness of the need to reform Russian orthography, which had scarcely changed since the time of Peter the Great and which had been newly debated by the Academy of Sciences from 1903. The Russian alphabet had become archaic and inconsistent. Not only did the complexity of its forms obstruct efforts to promote literacy in Russia but it was also seen to be overloaded with ecclesiastical anachronisms. Several of its features (relating, for instance, to ancient differences in pronunciation that could no longer be detected) were redundant. In an attempt to rationalise and simplify the alphabet, individual letters and accents were abstracted from its sacrosanct fabric and evaluated independently. After several years of discussion, the Soviet of People's Commissars passed a decree in 1918 conflating the roles of some letters and abolishing others. Besides their practical value, these changes were clearly ideological. Rumour had it that the letter **ѣ** was absorbed into the letter **e**, because it looked like a church with a spire on it. Several anti-Bolshevik printers continued to use the old typefaces and in the 1920s delegates of armed sailors went round the printers in Petrograd (as St Petersburg was then called), confiscating the printing dies for obsolete letters.[85]

Artists' preoccupation with the forms of letters also had a deeper resonance with ideas currently being developed in the context of Orthodox Christian belief. Their impulse was to undermine the tendency of the mind to evaluate its perceptions in relation to a preconceived frame of reference, rather than in themselves. When words ceased to be seen purely as disposable carriers of meanings (determined by conventions underpinning the use of verbal language), they were elevated to the level of primary artistic realities – they became valuable as forms and sounds (and ultimately as mere 'beings') in themselves, not simply as signs. As with icons, their value came to lie in the truth-transmitting factuality of their physical reality rather than in their conditional 'references to meaning': they became sacramental transmitters of value rather than symbolic, or merely significative, ones. In more senses than one, the Word was made flesh.

The extent to which words actually incarnate and realise meaning (or value), as opposed to simply referring to it, was central to the literary debates of the Symbolist poets, especially Andrei Bely and Vyacheslav Ivanov. In his essay 'The Meaning of Words' of 1909, Bely formulates his understanding that value or meaning is only realised – made both *conscious* and *real* – to the extent that it is embodied in form. With this theory, which recalls aspects of medieval nominalism, he was not simply referring to the way in which an object or idea can be given a name with which to refer to it thereafter, regardless of time. On the contrary, he was proposing that unless such an object or idea is embodied in form, it is not fully realised and, more importantly, that it is only 'embodied in a form' to the extent that it is being presently apprehended as such. That is to say, the pure objectivity of being is only realised by the pure subjectivity of consciousness, because that is how it is sustained in form. Apart from its present realisation in this way, a value is undetermined as a thing in itself and therefore non-existent as such; (even to call it 'hypothetical' or 'potential' would be to offer it a form of a kind).[86] For Bely, therefore, forms, especially word-forms, were not merely crucial as agents of meaning but also as agents of existence, and, as such, they functioned sacramentally, as 'icons of meaning' (or 'icons of pure value'); they enabled meaning to be realised by being the forms in which meaning is realised.

Such a notion is not only entirely consistent with the religious philosophy of the Symbolists, whose imagery is pervaded by sacramental metaphors, it was also being hotly discussed by Orthodox theologians, just as Bely's and Ivanov's essays on the relationship between form and meaning – 'The Meaning of Words' and 'The Testaments of Symbolism' (1910) respectively – were being published. The Orthodox debate, which ran from 1907 to 1913, had been stimulated by a revival of interest, among Russian monks on Mount Athos, in the ancient tradition of hesychast prayer. In this tradition, the primary practice of monks was ceaseless, contemplative repetition of the name of Jesus until awareness of his presence became mystically transferred from the mind of the supplicant to the heart. In this instance, some monks (the *imiaslavtsy* – name-worshippers) identified the name of Jesus so closely with the grace of the name of Jesus (or the effects of the prayer) that they came to regard the name itself as God, resulting in what some believed was verbal idolatry.[87] Opinion among Moscow clergy was divided between those who sympathised with the name-worshippers, on the grounds that the name of Jesus was part of God's energy (rather than his essence – a key distinction controversially sanctioned in the fourteenth century), and those who considered the name of God to be a mere sign, with no inordinate sanctity of its own. Both positions had ancient precedents. The name-worshippers considered their view to be obedient to the Old Testament commandment against 'taking God's name in vain' and may have been influenced by Jewish beliefs about the magical power of names. Many Orthodox Jews continue to avoid writing the name of God, preferring 'G–d' to 'God' (albeit to avoid the possibility of damaging the visible name rather than because they believe the practice to be wrong in itself). On the other hand, the ancient Stoic orator and philosopher Dio Chrysostom (*c.*AD 40–120), widely accepted as having influenced the earliest Greek Christians' attitudes towards images, pointed out that even thoughts about God are images of a kind, in that they represent something other than themselves. In his defence of images against iconoclasts, he maintained that if visual images of God are to be banned, then thoughts of God should be banned too – which would of course be absurd to enforce as law.[88] Although the Church authorities eventually pronounced against the name-worshippers, partly in order to undermine the possibility of theological freedom as a matter of principle, the debate had a lasting impact on contemporary poetry, and it may also have contributed to the liberation of letter-forms from their burden of delivering meanings, ultimately enabling them to become no more than concentrated moments of visual and aural impact, with innate value rather than referential significance.

While the Symbolists conflated form and meaning, accommodating the notion of meaning only to the extent that it was embodied in form and thereby stripping it of any kind of 'abstract existence', the Futurist poets that succeeded them dispensed with the notion of meaning altogether. In this respect, they resembled the most extreme name-worshippers more than the Symbolists. They advocated that whatever value or energy was present in the world existed not for the sake of any implicit symbolic or sacramental significance but by virtue of the fact that it merely existed as a material being, with its own formal impact. The chief exponent of this tendency was Velimir Khlebnikov who had been associated with the Symbolists before developing the concept of the 'transrational', or *zaum*, in 1913. Whereas the Symbolists aimed to establish the necessary value of word-forms by developing a kind of sacramental theology of words, Khlebnikov intensified the appreciation of the formal impact of words by isolating them from the various contexts and conditions that gave them meaning. These included the conventions of grammar and vocabulary, and the pronounceability, audibility and general comprehensibility of vocal utterances. The fact that words were conventionally expected to convey intelligible meanings only served to intensify the impression they could give, in Khlebnikov's hands, of meaninglessness or 'trans-meaning'. In order to promote a state of pre-rational awareness and 'total' communication, Khlebnikov looked to the traditions of provincial religious sects in which ancient pagan rituals, including ecstatic 'speaking in tongues', were still being practised.[89] The simultaneous chanting of different parts of the same hymn, practised in some Orthodox services (in order to make the entire hymn singable in a shorter period of time!), may also have served as a stimulus. With regard to the graphic impact of word-forms, Khlebnikov's disruption of the layout and legibility of text on a page or other surface may well have been inspired by the extravagant dismembering and radical abbreviation of words (mainly the names of saints and feasts) that are commonly found on icons.

Part of the artistic appeal of letters lay in the fact that they are primarily flat; they do not create the illusion of depth and therefore did not offend the avant-garde's distinctive sense of the 'morality of aesthetics'. Particularly in a printed context, avant-garde letters tended not to have serifs – for serifs turn letters into decorative objects with a 'top' and a 'bottom', like candlesticks or pieces of furniture. On the contrary, they were deliberately designed to look mechanical and impersonal. The simultaneous 'stamping' of the printing technique – in contrast to the directional cursive flow of handwriting – is consistent with the sudden impulsive appearance and message of the communication.

Popova's linocut design for the cover of her *Six Prints* (1917–19, Plate 40) is a fine example of this 'graphic rhetoric' and is typical of her aim, in her most mature work, to develop a powerful energy between shapes and planes in two dimensions. Despite her background in Cubism, which she studied in Paris, 1912–13, and her experience in Tatlin's studio, where she worked in 1912–15, her interest in the dynamic potential of the picture surface was surely inspired by the powerful graphic effect of icons, which she studied from the outset of her career. Indeed, according to Sarabianov, one of the early lists of her works makes reference to a (now lost) nude painted in 1913, on the back of which was written 'copy of Cranach's Madonna' – presumably produced alongside Tatlin as he was working on his own *Composition-Analysis* of a Cranach (Plate 33).[90] In 1909, Popova had travelled to Kiev, where she was especially impressed by Vrubel's frescos in the St Cyril's Church (Plate 17), in which Vrubel adapted the style of Byzantine art (itself visible in the eleventh-century mosaics in the cathedral) to his own purposes. In the following year she travelled to Italy where she studied the Renaissance masters (especially Giotto), as well as

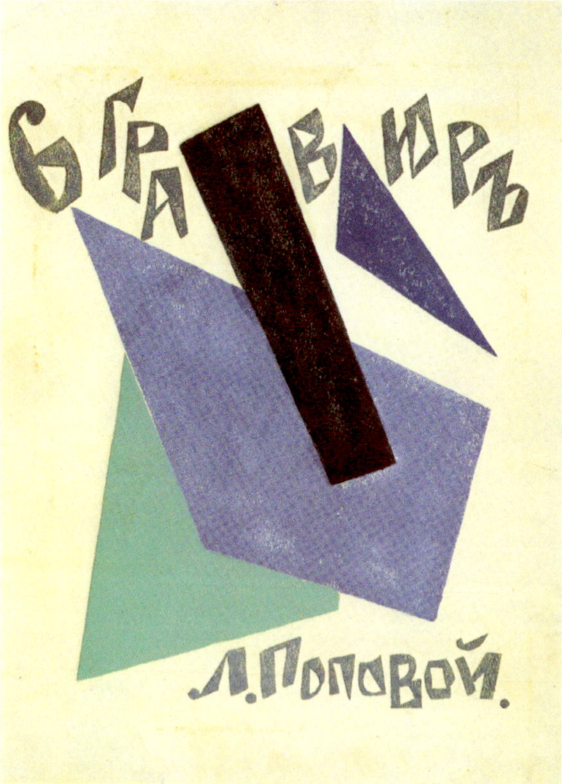

40
Liubov Popova

Design for the cover of *Six Prints*, 1917–19
Linocut on paper
41.7 x 29.9 cm (16 3/8 x 11 3/4 in)
Costakis Collection

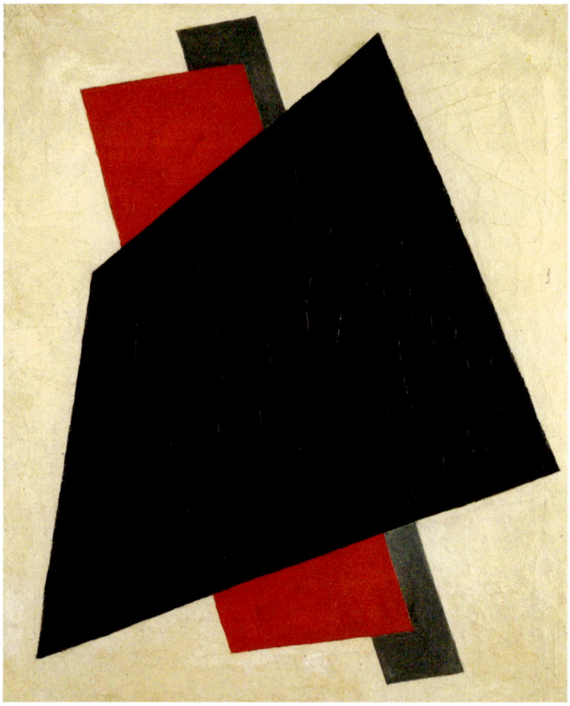

41
Liubov Popova

Pictorial Architectonics, 1916–17
Oil on canvas
89 x 71 cm (35 x 28 in)
Costakis Collection, Tretyakov Gallery, Moscow

making visits to the ancient centres of medieval icon painting in Russia – Novgorod, Pskov, Suzdal, Yaroslavl and Rostov the Great.[91] Her early enthusiasm for icons, however, 'was not manifested immediately in her compositions'; in the words of Sarabianov, it 'functioned rather as potential, reverberating later at the outset of the mature period of her artistic career'.[92]

In this respect Popova's development was characteristic of several neo-primitivist and Cubo-Futurist artist-colleagues, who awakened to the expressive potential of visual art – growing to identify with it and appropriate it – by learning to appreciate the visual language of icons. Olga Rozanova, for instance, who Popova met while studying art in Moscow from 1904, had been brought up in Vladimir, the ancient capital of Russia, where several medieval churches survived and where she made sketches of icons and frescos, some by Andrei Rublev, in the Cathedral of St Sophia.[93] It was not until 1911, when she moved to St Petersburg and became involved in various avant-garde groups, that her experience of icons began to affect her work, informing and facilitating the development of her characteristic neo-primitivist, Cubo-Futurist and Suprematist styles.

Popova's Cubo-Futurist works from 1913 show clear affinities to the fragmented forms of icons but such experiments were common among her contemporaries and, unlike the neo-primitivist and Rayist works of Larionov and Goncharova, there is little to suggest that these works were unduly influenced by icons. It was not until she began to relax her dependence on the language of Cubism that a truly iconic dimension begins to appear in her work – a sense of monumentality, grandeur and composure. Interestingly, it is already possible to see Popova's preoccupation with large-scale, abstract, unfragmented forms in her Cubo-Futurist work, though initially these forms emerge as a secondary effect of the juxtaposition of smaller scale fragments. They become increasingly prominent and authoritative in her work from around 1916 when the ambiguous honeycomb effect of her Cubism begins to disappear.

A juxtaposition of work from her *Pictorial Architectonics* series (Plate 41), dating from 1916–17, with traditional icons of Christ in Majesty (Plate 42) is strongly suggestive of the extent to which Popova was sensitive to the graphic power of icons and of its psychological effect. The Popova paintings in question consist of a number of variously shaped coloured planes superimposed over each other. The arrangement of planes is centred and static, usually contained within the picture space. The distinctive shape of each plane is always clearly defined, even when one plane is partially covered by another, and the planes appear parallel to the picture surface. The colour of each plane is bold and unmodulated. The frequent presence of the fiery combination of black and red, traditionally associated with passionate energy and occult power (and later to become the primary colours of the cult of Lenin), is particularly striking. The backgrounds are almost always buff-coloured, clearly resembling the gesso ground of all icons. By comparison, the traditional iconography of Christ in Majesty, faithfully reproduced in innumerable icons over the centuries, represents the triumphant Christ enthroned against a background of three large geometrical shapes: a red diamond, a blue-black oval and a red rectangle. Because the diamond and rectangle have concave sides, the forms give the impression of being stretched vertically from two squares (one turned at 45°) and a circle. A multitude of winged faces, representing the Cherubim (a mystical order of angels), are depicted in the blue oval, while anthropomorphic symbols of the four evangelists (man, lion, bull and eagle) can be seen in the four corners of the rectangle.

The image is the climactic centrepiece of the iconostasis (Plate 5) and represents a summary of the esteemed 'Celestial Hierarchy', a scale of divine agency, systematically formulated by a Syrian monk, Dionysius the Areopagite, in the fifth century. The text, originally believed to have been written by a follower of St Paul, was hugely important to both the Eastern and Western Churches. Dionysius' *Celestial Hierarchy* describes a spiritual ladder that leads from Christ down through nine orders of spiritual being towards the realm of humanity, which is served by the lowest order of spiritual beings, the Angels. Each of the shapes in the icon can be said to correspond to a different level of spiritual energy. The winged faces in the blue oval represent the Cherubim, the second order of spiritual beings. Christ's throne is suggestive of the Thrones, the third order; the fact that Christ's throne has 'wheels within wheels', taken from the vision of Ezekiel (chapter 10), corresponds to the fact that the order of Thrones was considered to be the 'chariot of God'. The level of Angels, ministering directly to human beings, is implicitly suggested by the anthropomorphic symbols of the evangelists which are always winged, like angels. The eighth order – the Archangels – is also present in the scheme by virtue of the fact that, on the iconostasis screen, icons of the Archangels Gabriel and Michael appear beside icons of the Mother of God and John the Forerunner, which are placed adjacent to the central icon of Christ in Majesty.

The significance of geometrical shapes in icons is not merely symbolic. It is ultimately rooted in an ancient tradition of understanding the complexity of the phenomenal world by seeing it in terms of the coherent numerical relationships that inform it. The ancient understanding, attributed to Pythagoras, was that the numerical relationships that inform the world are compatible and commensurate on the basis of their common subsistence in the number one, or unity – all numbers are multiples and modifications of the number one. For this reason, the unity of the world is traditionally expressed in the visual arts and architecture through the use of regular geometrical shapes and relationships. Just as all numbers were seen to subsist in the number one, so the infinitely divergent forms that numerical

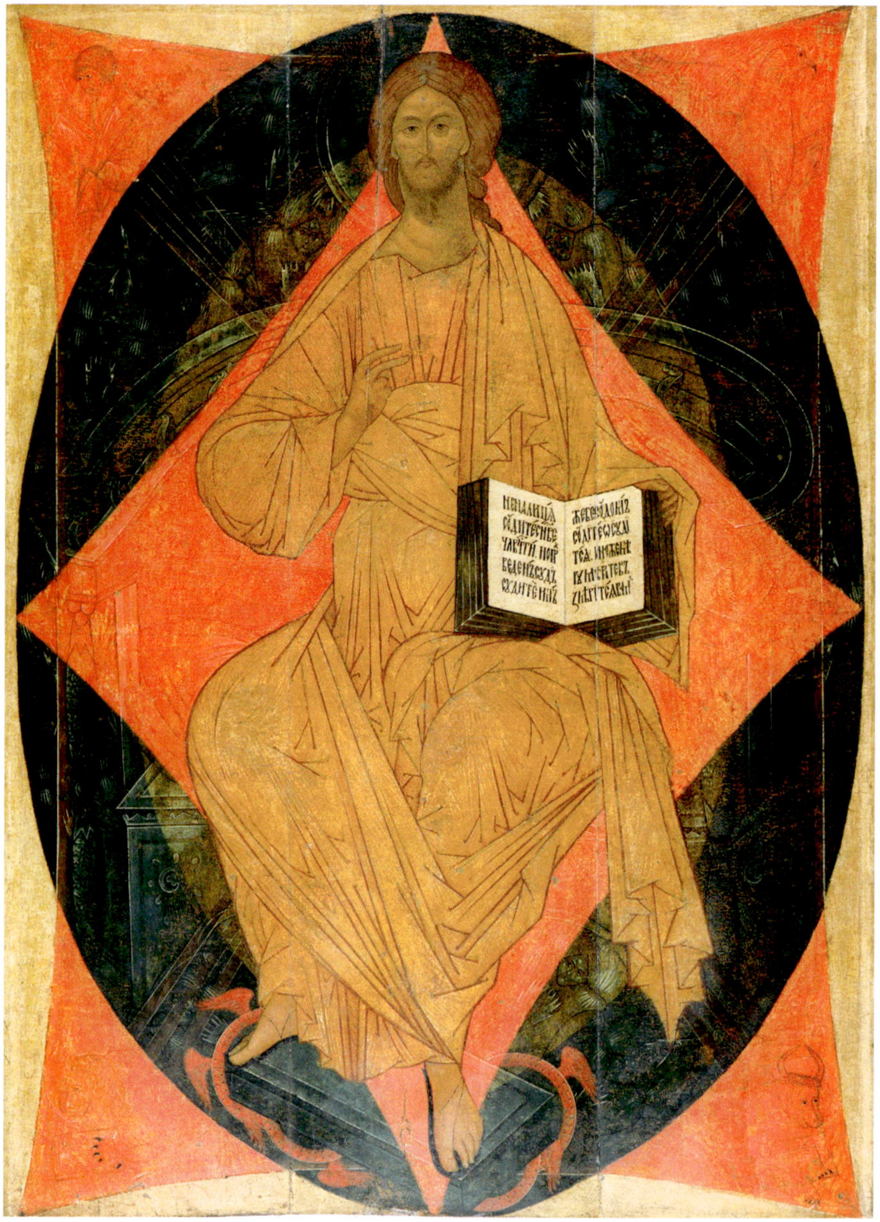

42

Christ in Majesty, Rostov the Great, *c.*1500
Tempera on wooden panel
145 x 113.3 cm (57 1/8 x 44 5/8 in)
Tretyakov Gallery, Moscow

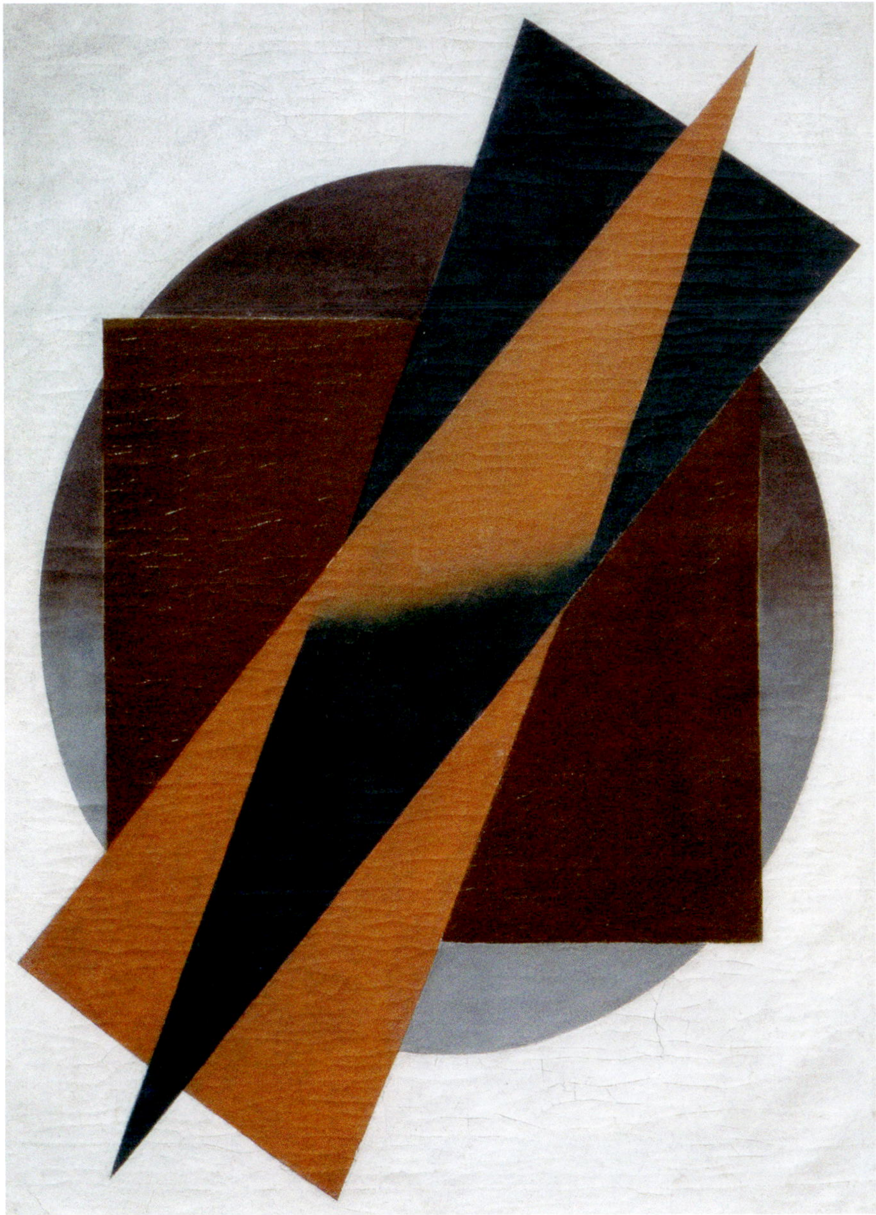

43
Kliment Redko

Suprematist Composition, 1921
Oil on canvas
75 x 50 cm (29 ½ x 19 ⅝ in)
Costakis Collection, Tretyakov Gallery, Moscow

relationships assume in the created world were seen to subsist in a unity of their own – the unity of existence. In icons of Christ in Majesty, this unity is stated largely through symbols; the manifest diversity of the universe is seen to subsist in the unity of the incarnate Christ. In Popova's *Pictorial Architectonics*, an equivalent meaning is conveyed in a comparable way: the diversity of energy is united in the coherence of its relationships and in the singularity of its aesthetic impact.

Icons of Christ in Majesty may also have left their mark on other artists. Black and red are the colours that dominate Malevich's most minimal works (for instance, his *Boy with Knapsack* of 1915, Plate 35) and his trilogy of *Black Square, Black Circle* and *Black Cross* may well have been conceived to correspond to the icon's background of rectangle, oval and diamond respectively.[94] The early Suprematist works of Kliment Redko (1897–1956), from 1921, have a unity of impact that relates closely to that of Popova's *Pictorial Architectonics*. In 1910, Redko enrolled at the school of icon painting at the Pechersky Monastery near Kiev, where he met Vasily Chekrygin.[95] Considering that he was only 13 years of age at the time, it is scarcely surprising that something of the artistic integrity of icons should have reappeared in his own work, albeit in a sublimated form. His *Suprematist Composition* of 1921 (Plate 43) consists of an overlapping oval, square and diamond (generated from two interacting triangles) in red, black and dark brown on an ivory ground, and thus resembles an icon of Christ in Majesty in all respects except for the representation of Christ in the form of a man. It is hard to believe that the Suprematist work of Ivan Kudriashev (1896–1972), who studied under Malevich at the State Free Art Workshops (SVOMAS) in Moscow, 1918–19, was not also informed by a similar appreciation of icons of Christ in Majesty. A series of Kudriashev's designs for the foyer of the First Soviet Theatre in Orenburg, where he set up a branch of the Suprematist school UNOVIS in 1919, is focused around a central configuration of geometrical forms, superimposed over each other – a circle (usually red) over a square (usually black, sometimes turned 45° to form a diamond) over a rectangle – as in such icons. Smaller geometrical fragments of colour are suspended around this dense centrepiece, sometimes overlapping with clusters of bolder, more stable forms, to the left and right of the central form, which anchor the design. The designs are simultaneously static and flat, and dynamic and spacious. On one hand the shapes are monochrome and rectilinear, and are disposed in a more or less symmetrical manner; on the other hand, a sense of depth and movement into and out of space is conveyed by the diminishing sizes of the shapes (some of them seeming to recede) and the orientation of some of the diagonals towards the centre of the image as if they were orthogonals in a perspectival space.

Several of these designs resemble triptychs (or tripartite designs such as the bottom half of Plate 1). One major design takes on the extended composition of an iconostasis as a whole (Plate 44), placing a central configuration of bold geometrical forms (in the place of a Christ in Majesty) between rows of strongly vertical configurations, resembling the icons of the Mother of God, John the Forerunner, the archangels and other important saints on the *deisis* row of the iconostasis. The continuation of these lateral configurations up into arched bands of clustered forms above the central arrangement (each one remaining distinct rather than flowing into its neighbour) strongly recalls the rows of icons of feasts, prophets and patriarchs that form the upper part of an iconostasis. Kudriashev appears to have adapted the internal dynamics of the screen – operative within its static component parts – to his own purposes, using the effect of perspective to duplicate the 'centripetal' effect of the gestures and gazes of the saints which all turn towards the central image of Christ.

As painting progressively liberated itself from the bondage of extraneous dependencies and references, more and more artists came to feel that an appreciation of the dynamics of the picture surface – as a kind of 'truthfulness to the medium' – was a characteristic of Russian art *per se*. In discussions about the content of a possible national Museum of Painterly Culture in 1919, Alexander Rodchenko (1891–1956), who worked in a Suprematist style before taking a key part in the development of Constructivism in the 1920s, maintained that whereas western painting was primarily concerned with the illusions of light, form and depth, Russian painting was more involved with the visual potential of the surface of a picture which, in reality, operates in only two dimensions – the vertical and the horizontal. He maintained that the source of this national affinity with the integrity of the two-dimensional surface lay in icons and, as a result, icons were to be amply represented in the prospective museum – selected on the basis of their professional and technical originality rather than their historical interest

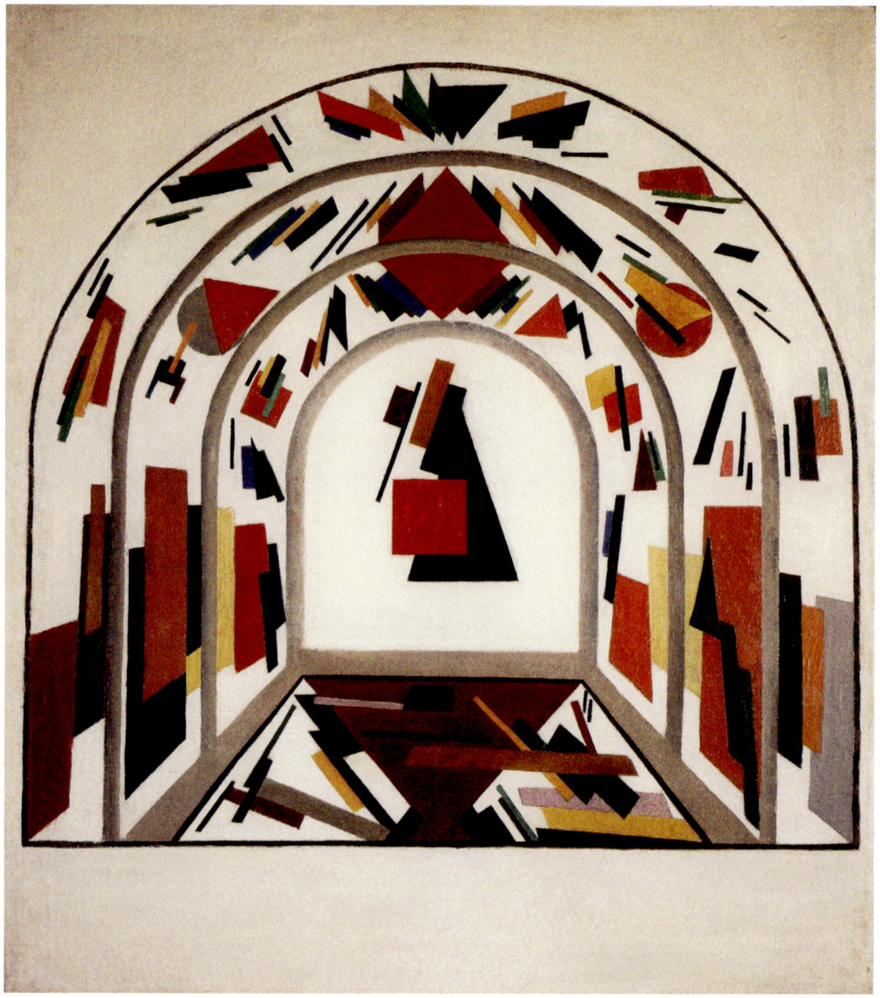

44
Ivan Kudriashev
Plan for the Interior Decoration of the First Soviet Theatre in Orenburg, 1920
Oil on canvas
103 x 89 cm (40 ½ x 35 in)
Costakis Collection, Tretyakov Gallery, Moscow

45
Attributed to (follower of?)
Alexander Rodchenko

Composition, 1918
Oil on wooden panel
93 x 51.5 cm (36 5/8 x 20 1/4 in)
Art Gallery of New South Wales, Sydney

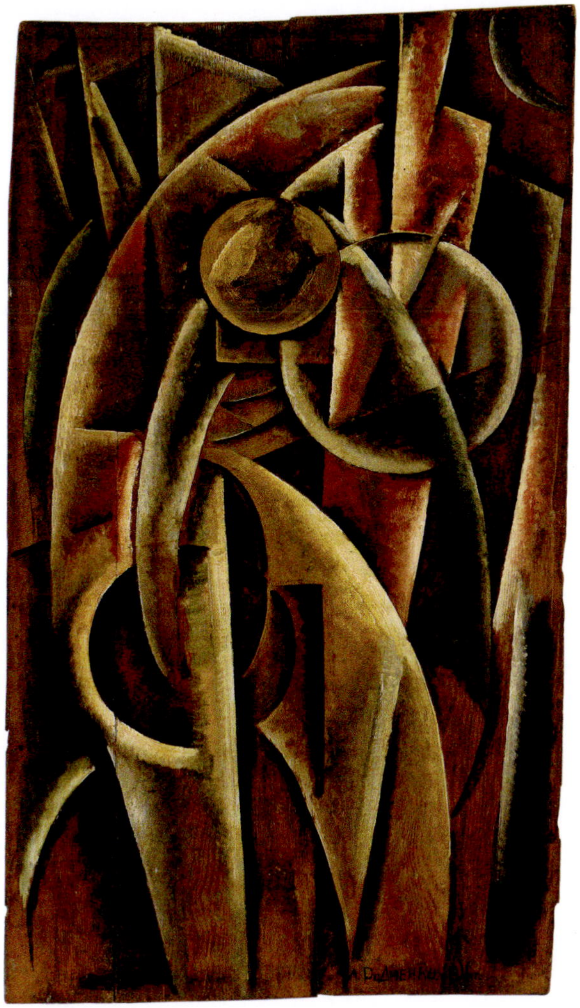

or aesthetic appeal, which he considered to be a western irrelevance. Having distinguished between the illusionistic and decorative (non-illusionistic) potential of the picture surface, he further differentiated between 'applied' ornament that merely embellishes a utilitarian form and 'decorative' or pure ornament that is determined by the surface itself, affecting the viewer on the basis of its own qualities: 'Russian painting's source is the icon – decorative adornment [pure ornament], that is, a value unto itself, unlike applied ornament which has no life of its own but exists only as an adjunct to an object. This great decorative colour-resplendent element is the prime mover of Russian painting, which we [currently corrupted by western influence] do not value, do not know'.[96]

Rodchenko's own preoccupation with surface dynamics is amply born out in his work from this period up to 1921, when he abandoned painting in favour of utilitarian design. His early semi-figurative paintings clearly reflect his interest in icons, in which the absence of perspective and modelling forces lines and planes to appear flattened up against the picture surface. His *Two Figures*,[97] for instance, of around 1916, appropriates the icon's reflective sensibility (the tilted heads), subdued earthy tonalities and construction from arcs in a manner that recalls the earlier abstracted iconic works of Vladimir Tatlin and Naum Gabo (Plates 32, 68). Another earthy *Composition* (Plate 45), in which the visual language of fragmented, translucent, back-lit rectangles and circles, sometimes eclipsing or inter-penetrating each other, is distinctly Rodchenko-esque, is very strongly suggestive of an icon of the Mother of God with Christ. Forms resembling the small halo of Christ and the fingers, long neck and stooping shoulders of the Virgin are all present in the work, alongside abstracted echoes and reverberations of those forms. The work is also painted on a wooden panel (with visible grain), constructed from several vertical planks in a typically iconic way. It may well be an example of a work produced by a student or associate of Rodchenko, applying the master's recommendation to analyse historical works from the point of view of their constructive and compositional principles, while also reflecting his purely formal interests.[98]

Despite his evident appreciation of icons at this date, Rodchenko made it clear that he had no interest in the past as such, and he made no attempt to attach significance to any similarities that might exist between his work and icons. Unlike Larionov and Malevich who did develop the symbolic and philosophical implications of their iconic works, any response that he may have had to icons was purely formal. Indeed, he was passionately keen not to be reduced to a consummation of, or comment on, the past, loudly proclaiming the areas in which he considered himself to be an innovator: 'In each work, I conduct a new experiment without the advantage of my past, and in each work I set a different task. If you survey my entire output over all this time, you will find one enormous and completely new work. If you want to tack the past on to it, get yourself to a museum and contemplate that.'[99]

Rodchenko's later non-objective works shrug off any manifest association with icons and iconography (Plate 50). However, the visual language of rigorous geometrical forms, painted in subdued colours and assembled in compositions of strong but delicate poise on a vertical panel (often of wood), remains distinctly iconic, reflecting the artist's profound awareness of the abstract compositional principles of numerous icons (e.g. Plates 47, 51). It also recalls the notion, already proposed by Vladimir Markov in his *The Principles of the New Art* in 1912, that the spontaneous and free creativity that contemporary artists were now seeking already existed, albeit disguised by iconography, in primitive religious art and that 'even the freest art is based on plagiarism ... because old, beloved forms instilled in the soul unconsciously repeat themselves'.[100] Interestingly, exactly the same vocabulary of overlapping circles and ellipses, receding planes and diagonals surfaces – reacquiring iconography in the process – in Rodchenko's classic photographs of the 1920s (Plate 49).

Despite Rodchenko's insistence on independence, his awareness of the purely compositional and constructive element in icons is not only suggested by his own work; it is also reflected in his educational work at the VKhUTEMAS where he taught from 1920. The programmes that he developed revolved around analysis of the basic elements of painting – colour, form, line, construction, *faktura* (painterly quality) and materials – and included 'observation of examples of the treatment of elements in works of art of different periods'.[101] By the end of 1921, students working along these lines were formally convened into an 'Objective Analysis Group'. This analytical, almost anatomical, attitude towards the educational potential of historical art was by no means unique to him. As we have seen, Tatlin was studying the geometrical structures of the Old Masters in 1913. The method was also being intensively developed in Germany by Johannes Itten who, both before and during his tenure as a teacher of painting at the Bauhaus from 1919, had been encouraging his students to analyse and sense works by Old Masters (ranging from Giotto to Grünewald to Rembrandt) in terms of their constituent geometrical elements – circles, triangles and rectangles. It was also advocated in relation to historic architecture by the Constructivist architect Ilia Golosov, who taught alongside Rodchenko at the VKhUTEMAS from 1920. While acknowledging the value of the western Classical tradition, Golosov stressed the unique importance to Russia of traditional churches which he cited as structures built 'according to eternally unchanging laws of the aesthetic structuring of masses in space':[102] 'The study of traditional architecture must undoubtedly enter into the programme of teaching on architecture but under no circumstances should it be taught on the level of its external appearances as style. It should aim to convey an understanding of its essence: of the principles for building up masses; of the placing of masses and of the ways of perceiving them; of the relationship of plans to elevations; and of the functional suitability of form.'[103]

The same approach to structural and compositional dynamics – in this case applied specifically to

46

Entry into Jerusalem, c.1450
Tempera on wooden panel
82 x 67.8 cm (32 ¼ x 26 ¾ in)
Tretyakov Gallery, Moscow

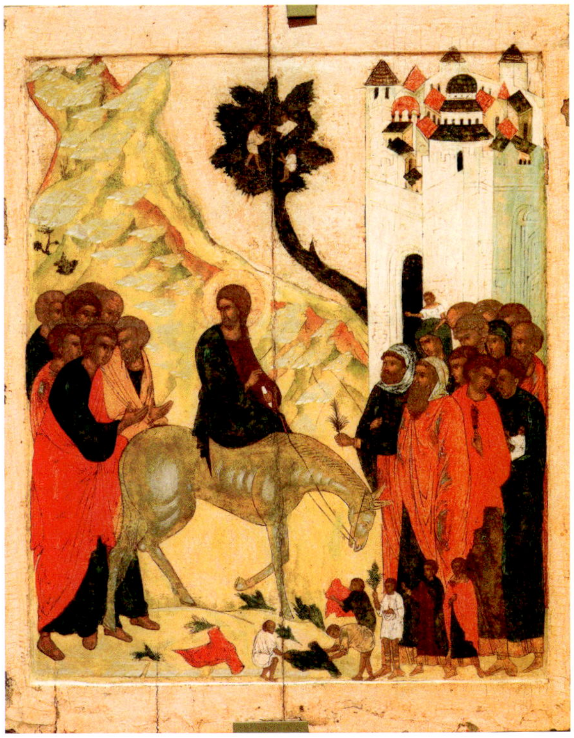

icons – was advocated by the art historian Nikolai Tarabukin, whose lecture 'The Last Painting has been Painted' (1921) and book *From the Easel to the Machine* (1923) were central to the development of the theory of production art in Russia. Several years before writing these works, Tarabukin began writing a book on *The Philosophy of Icons* (*Smysl Ikony*). Although it was not published until the 1980s, A.G. Dunaev (Tarabukin's closest relative at the time of its publication) states that the work was mostly conceived in 1916 and that he continued to work on it until the mid-1930s.

In *The Philosophy of Icons*, Tarabukin expounds the 'sanctity of utility' in contrast to the indulgent arbitrariness of aestheticism and he celebrates the compositional wisdom of several examples of icon painting. In a section dedicated to 'Rhythm and Composition in Old Russian Painting', he analyses the compositions of several fifteenth-century icons – an Entombment, an Entry into Jerusalem, a Deposition from the Cross, a Vladimirskaya Mother of God and Andrei Rublev's *Old Testament Trinity*. In each case, he stresses how the composition of the icon is based on an arrangement of fundamental geometrical shapes; the compositions are primarily tripartite and the relationship between their various elements is rhythmic, even musical – 'with three chords' or 'like a tripartite sonata' – though the 'melody of icons is silence'. The absence and inversion of perspective refers to the finitude of this world and to the higher dimensionality of the spirit. The dynamics of the compositions underpin the narrative direction of their design. Regarding a fifteenth-century icon of the Entry into Jerusalem (Plate 46), he wrote:

> The composition of the icon of Christ's Entry into Jerusalem is based on a ring ... a dynamic, but complete and resolved, form of compositional structure... The ring ... encompasses 1) the crowd escorting Christ, left, 2) the figure of Christ on the donkey, centre, and 3) the crowd greeting Christ, right ... but it also extends beyond the picture frame, as suggested by the eclipsed groups of figures to the left and right of the icon. ... A semicircle gathers the three parts of the composition into a single rhythmic and narrative whole. Each part is developed according to a particular rhythm and tempo. The first part (the figures escorting Christ) is developed vertically. In tempo it presents a muted 'andante' movement, flowing from left to right, as suggested by the varied positioning of the feet, the figures' slight inclination forward and the hands stretched out in the direction of movement. Compositionally the theme is shaped into an ellipsis, using the contour of the heads to unite the crowd. The second theme (Christ on the donkey, the tree, the figures in the foreground) takes the form of a spiral (emphasised by the twisted figure of Christ) and accelerates at an 'allegro' pace. ... The donkey, highlighted in white, attracts attention to

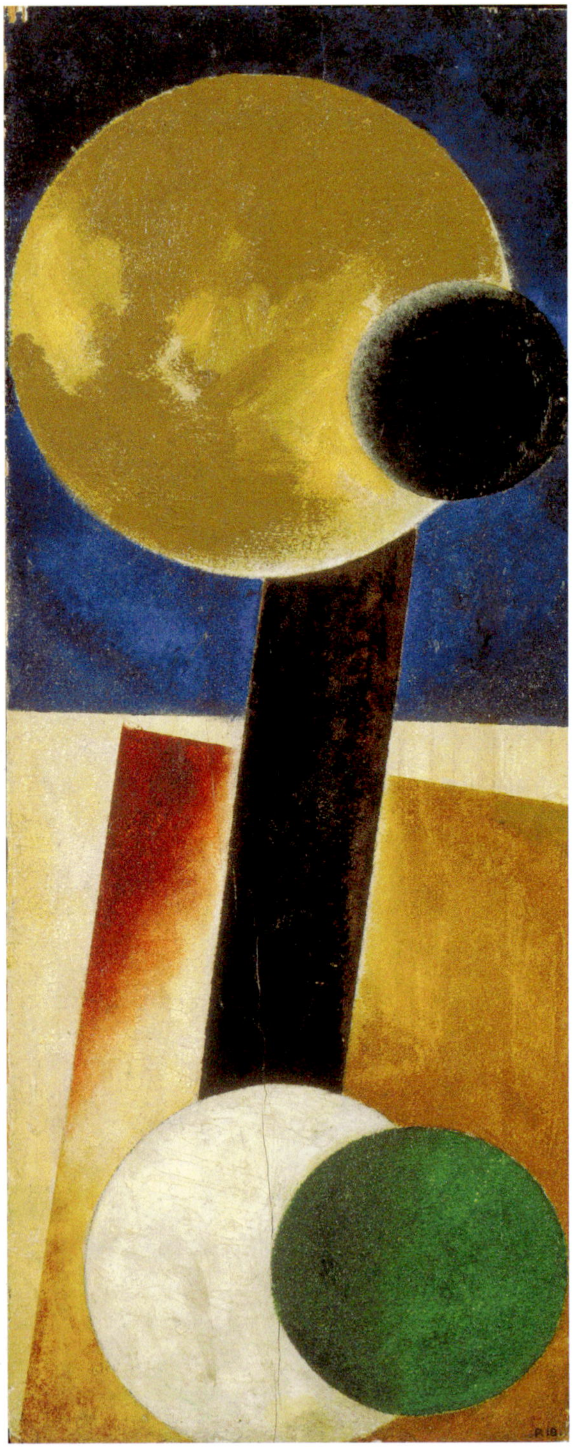

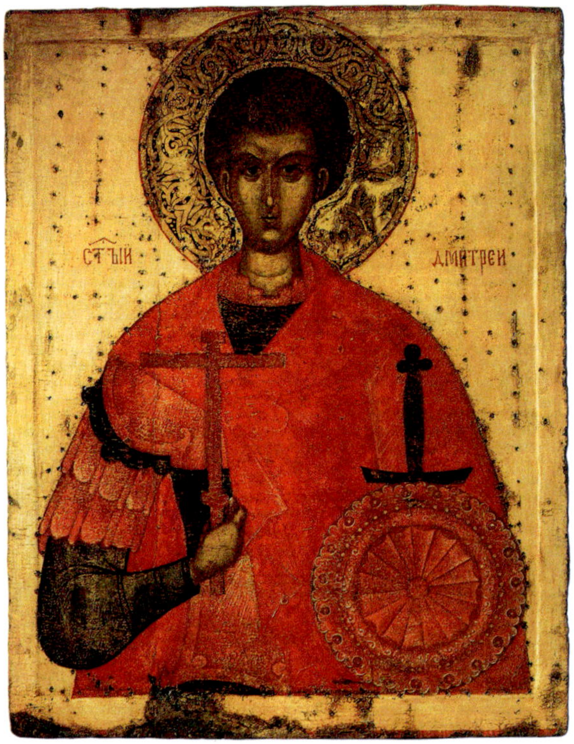

47
Alexander Rodchenko

Non-Objective Composition, 1918
Oil on wood
53 x 25 cm (20 7/8 x 9 7/8 in)
Russian Museum, St Petersburg

48

St Dmitri, Pskov, mid-15th century
Tempera on wooden panel
88 x 67 cm (34 5/8 x 26 3/8in)
Russian Museum, St Petersburg

> the centre of the icon and directs the movement horizontally from left to right, as the development of narrative demands. The third part of the composition introduces a new theme (the crowd greeting Christ). Outwardly, this theme is developed as a motionless vertical axis, though internally the crowd is permeated by the tension of expectation, expressed through ... the complex positioning of heads and the outstretched hands holding palm branches. Like the first theme, this theme is also elliptical, uniting the crowd into an inseparable whole.[104]

Numerous other icons lend themselves to the kind of compositional analysis that Tarabukin and Rodchenko were advocating. In many cases, the removal of a few recognisably figurative elements – such as the face (in icons of the saints) or the human figure (in feast icons) – can result in compositions of pure abstraction.

A fifteenth-century icon of *St Dmitri* in the Russian Museum, St Petersburg, is one of many examples of icons that border on geometrical abstraction (Plate 42). Its overall composition is curiously suggestive of the kind of exercise in 'graphic construction on a flat surface' that Rodchenko was devising for the syllabus at the VKhUTEMAS from 1920. Broadly speaking, the composition is extremely hieratic, comprising a triangle resting on its base (the overall figure), two circles (the halo and shield) and a rectangle, with 'virtual' sides (established by the cross and the sword hilt) that are parallel to the edges of the icon. Both circles are double – the halo contains the head of St Dmitri, and the rim of the shield is differentiated from its centre. The symmetry and stability of this astonishingly powerful arrangement of shapes is minutely qualified by the asymmetry of the forms within it. This internal dynamic is polarised between the circular shield and halo, and the two double cross forms (the cross and the sword-hilt) counterpoised to each other at 180°; the 'rhyming' of these shapes only serves to intensify the effect of their differences – size, colour, orientation, centrality and internal articulation. The overall stability of the central pyramidal form, for instance, is reinforced by the rectitude of the rigorous virtual rectangle that appears to be contained by the two crosses. At the same time, however, that stability is also subtly undermined – both by the asymmetrical position of the rectangle, and the fact that it is more contained by the dark sword-hilt to the right (strongly standing out against the red background) than the red cross on the left, which is only

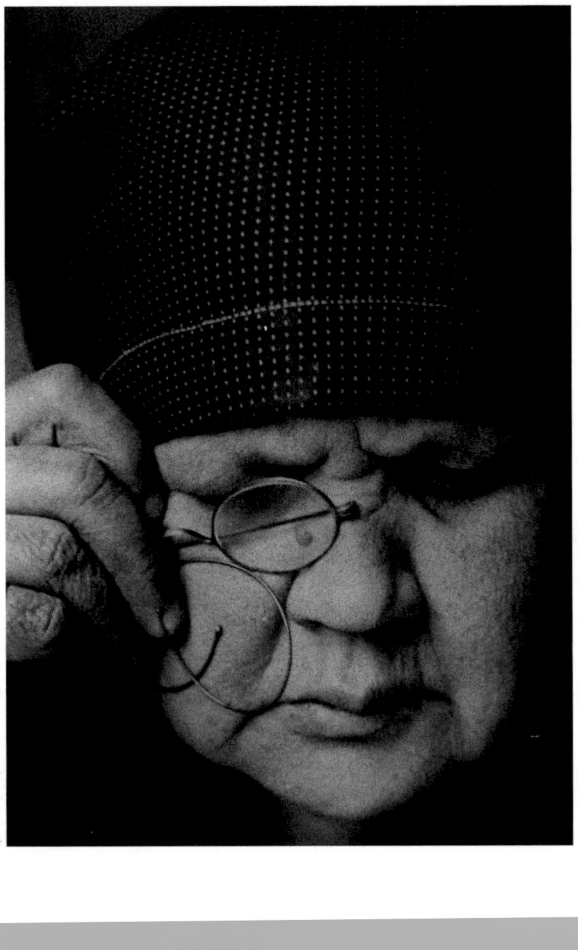

49
Alexander Rodchenko

Mother, 1924
Photograph
22.5 x 16.5 cm (8 7/8 x 6 1/2 in)
A. Rodchenko and V. Stepanova Archive, Moscow

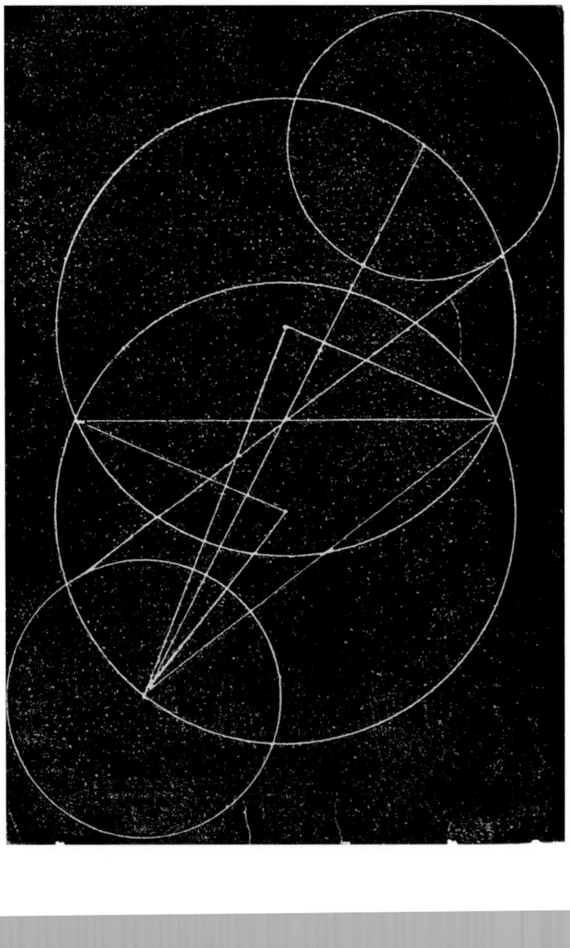

50
Alexander Rodchenko

Construction no. 60, 1921
Linocut
22.5 x 15 cm (8 7/8 x 5 7/8 in)
A. Rodchenko and V. Stepanova Archive, Moscow

slightly differentiated from its background. The fact that the rectangle only exists by implication, in contrast to the boldly stated presence of the pyramidal form of the saint, further qualifies their relationship. A similar constructive-destructive relationship exists between the circles (the halo and shield) which create a powerful stabilising alliance within the overall composition but, at the same time, qualify, undermine and animate the composition by means of their imbalance in size, colour-contrast, symmetricality etc. The inequality of the stark red-black colour contrast and the subtle monochrome articulation of the saint's garment (its patterns and folds) further intensify the purely visual interest of the image at the expense of its role as representation.

This elaboration of an asymmetrical dynamic between geometrical forms had been characteristic of Rodchenko's own non-objective compositions from 1918 (Plate 47). These works are largely concerned with circles as self-contained moments of force (conveyed by the impression of blurred-edge backlighting) and their interrelationships. Such relationships are often made explicit and further developed by the complex array of rectilinear shapes and lines, often spread out in fans, which link them. Some examples, especially the more mathematically conceived and less textured linocuts of 1921 (Plate 50), recall didactic icons, common from the sixteenth century onwards, in which a doctrine, insight or vision is communicated in a complex quasi-diagrammatic way, often accompanied with text (Plate 51). Even in their own time, many people including monks found these icons incomprehensible. Rodchenko turned this potential for confusion between form and content to advantage. In his own words: 'by placing organisation in the foreground, [line] strips the work of its value as an [aesthetic] end in itself, bringing to light the constructive principle in each construction'.[105]

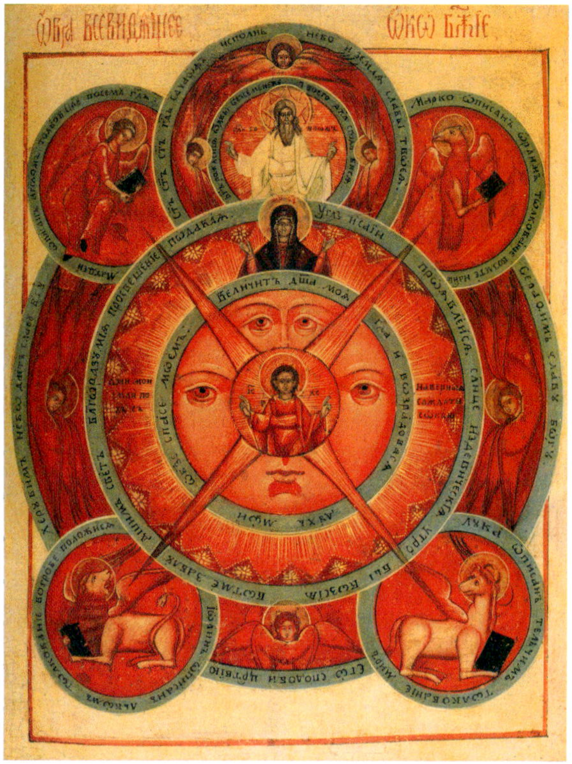

51

The All-Seeing Eye of God,
19th century
Tempera on wooden panel
45.2 x 34.5 cm (17 ¾ x 13 ⅝ in)
Temple Gallery, London

Rodchenko's interest in texture may also have been encouraged by icons. The regular formations of lines used in his *Line Constructions* from 1918 bear some resemblance, both in their form and aesthetic function, to the hatching patterns sometimes used in icons to decorate unmodulated expanses of fabric. Linear hatching in its most concentrated form appears in icons of the Hodigitria Mother of God where the garments of the Christ Child are sometimes completely covered with tightly knit webs of gold lines (known as *chrisography* – writing in gold) to convey, and transmit, his divine nature (Plate 14). Similar lines of force are used in icons of the Transfiguration (Plate 20) and Descent into Hell (Anastasis, Plate 2) – again, to transmit the blessings of Christ. These images, in which the resplendent figure of Christ is set against layers of geometrical forms, are particularly conducive to the kind of analysis that Rodchenko was both practising and advocating. Firstly, the use of clusters of straight spreading lines to represent emanations of spiritual energy is visually and conceptually compatible with Rodchenko's vision of lines as vehicles of pure dynamic force; and, secondly, the iconography of energies and worlds – represented as geometrical lines and forms – immediately draws attention to the schematic structures underlying the compositions. These forms, indicating the various levels of Christ's supernatural powers, consist of circles or vesicas (composed of sections of circles – common in Rodchenko's work), superimposed by diamonds, darts and stars (see also Plate 128).

If an awareness of icons is never explicitly reflected in Rodchenko's work, it certainly is in the work of the Hungarian artist, Bela Uitz (1887–1972), who met Rodchenko in Moscow in 1921 and whose *Iconanalyses* of the following year were very directly influenced by Rodchenko's compositional analyses. The idea of reducing icons to their compositional elements – which he also explored most abstractly in linocuts – may well have been stimulated by Rodchenko's teaching methods.

Uitz was one of the leading members of the Hungarian avant-garde. Having graduated from the Academy of Fine Arts in Budapest in 1914, he travelled to Florence and Rome where he was particularly inspired by the monumental rhetoric of Renaissance fresco painting. The sense of scale and human drama in Michelangelo's Sistine Chapel ceiling made a lasting impact on his work, underpinning his lifelong preoccupation with the dignity, drama and poetry of the human form; it is clearly reflected in the style of the political posters and murals that he produced up to the end of his career. Having returned to Hungary in 1915, Uitz became involved with various revolutionary groups and periodicals (including the Activists in 1915 and *Ma* from 1917), and worked in a quasi-expressionistic but structured style. During the brief period of Soviet communism in Hungary in 1919, Uitz directed the Proletariat Arts Workshop, actively promoting and producing communist propaganda. Following the fall of the communist regime in August 1919, he fled to Vienna, where the *Ma* group, banned in Hungary, continued to be active and was exposed to the latest artistic theories from Russia. In November 1920, the *Ma* group hosted a lecture on contemporary Russian art by Konstantin Umanskii. Umanskii had been sent to Germany and Austria-Hungary by the International Office of the Department of Fine Arts in Moscow to promote links between Russian and German artists in the name of world socialism. His lecture, based on his book *Neue Kunst in Russland 1914–1919*, which was one of the first assessments of Russian art to reach the West (published in Potsdam and Munich in 1920), included a slide presentation of work by various leading Russian artists including Malevich, Rodchenko and Tatlin. Uitz attended and it partly inspired him to visit Moscow the following year.[106]

In May 1921, Uitz visited Moscow to attend the Third International Congress of Communism. Through contacts he made at the Congress he visited the VKhUTEMAS workshops, where he was introduced to Rodchenko who was teaching painting and graphics there, and Malevich. Rodchenko's work, as well as the programme of studies that he was developing for the school, had a direct impact on Uitz, inspiring him to experiment with abstraction for the first time and – more importantly in the present context – with the compositional principles of Russian icons. The outcome of these experiments was a unique and concentrated series of analytical studies and major oil paintings that are more directly based on the compositions of icons than anything produced by his Russian contemporaries. Uitz subsequently abandoned this abstract and analytical approach to his work, though not without very explicitly and coherently integrating the design principles that he discovered from working in this way into some of his later figurative and narrative images; that is to say, he distilled a compositional logic from icons and directly reapplied it to subject matter that was meaningful to him.

Uitz's series of *Iconanalyses* and icon-related works, painted after he returned to Vienna in 1921, were not intended to be abstract versions of known icons but were built up from compositional principles derived from studies of icons; some, it appears, were more closely based on icons than others. The overall manner of *Iconanalysis I* (Plate 52) is clearly related to Rodchenko's recent work but its immediate source was an unidentified icon of *St George and the Dragon* (Plate 53). In Uitz's work, the saint, with a small round head, is shown on horseback (the large central concentric circles correspond to the horse's head), wearing a billowing red cloak (hanging down diagonally, centre left side) which is highly stilted and stylised as in icons. He plunges his spear into the dragon's head (the circle in the bottom right-hand corner of the image), which is represented against a jagged and dark form – the dragon's cave. Behind the saint, rhomboids resembling rooftops can be seen; these are based on schematic representations of the town which, according to legend, the dragon was terrorising before St George overcame it. Despite being clearly and closely based on an iconic prototype, Uitz has thoroughly abstracted his model, reducing it to the constituent static forms and the dynamics between them. He evidently felt that, regardless of its religiosity, which did not interest him, it was informed by an understanding of artistic and compositional principles.

Iconanalysis III (Plate 54), painted in tempera on paper, shares something of the diagonal dynamic of *Iconanalysis I* but is more hieratic, balanced and stable in its composition. The rectilinear roof-like structure in the top-left corner and the scaled, layered form in the top-right corner are clearly based on the architectural ensembles and rock formations that are universally represented in the corresponding positions in icons of the Old Testament Trinity and elsewhere (Plates 6, 27, 45, 53). The downwardly radiating isosceles triangle at the centre of the composition also echoes the effect of the steeply triangulated form of the central angel in icons of the Old Testament Trinity; the long straight lines that appear throughout the work may be related to the

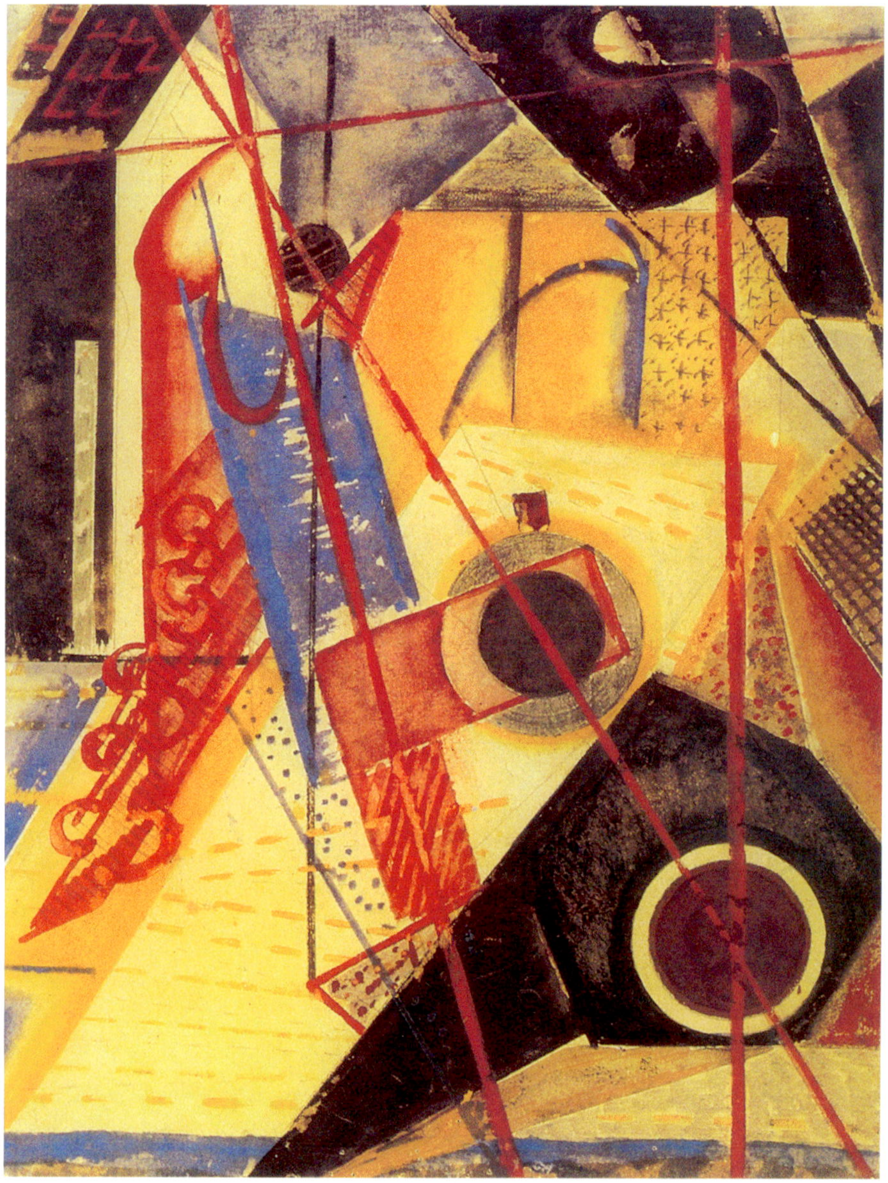

52
Bela Uitz

Iconanalysis I, 1921
Tempera on paper
39.7 x 30 cm (15 ⅝ x 11 ¾ in)
Pushkin Museum of Fine Arts, Moscow

53

St George and the Dragon, 16th century
Tempera on wooden panel
44 x 35 cm (17 ⅜ x 13 ¾ in)
Temple Gallery, London

54
Bela Uitz

Iconanalysis III, 1921
Tempera on paper
39.7 x 29.8 cm (15 ⅝ x 11 ¾ in)
Hungarian National Gallery, Budapest
© DACS 2007

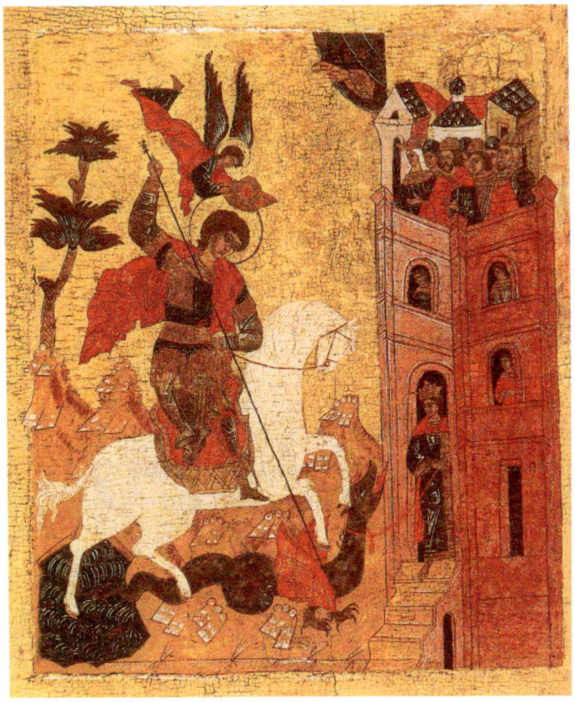

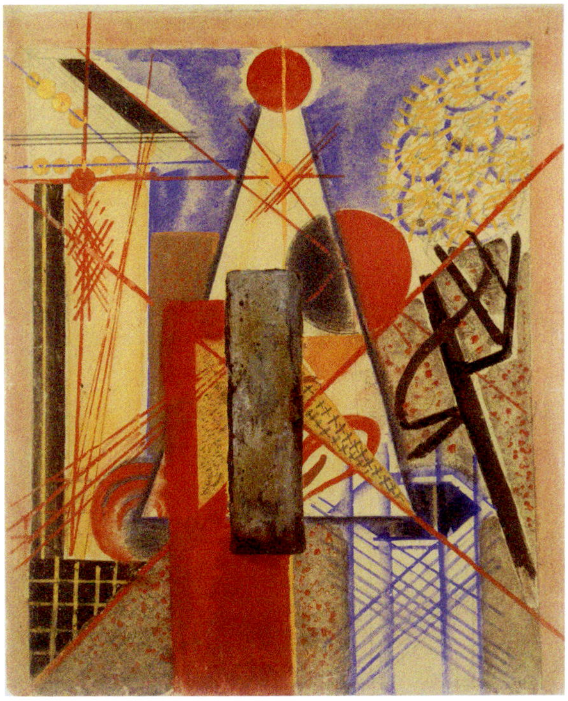

staffs that the angels hold in the icons; the roundels may relate, albeit in a much modified and displaced way, to the angels' halos. Similarities drawn from other icons could also be suggested, for instance, the resemblance between the polygonal form in the bottom right of the study and the washing wells in icons of the Nativity, always tilted up towards the picture plane (as in Plate 130), though it is not clear whether Uitz mixed his sources in this way.

Iconanalysis IV (Plate 55) repeats the firm hieratic structure of *Iconanalysis III* – the circle at the top centre of the composition with the triangular form radiating down from it – but it is less fractured and multilayered, and its connection to the figuration of a specific icon type, probably the Intercession of the Mother of God (Pokrov) (Plate 20), seems clearer. In icons of the Intercession, the Virgin hovers above the congregation of a church with her arms outstretched; angels hold her vermilion veil (not unlike the broad triangle, outlined in red, at the top of the image) over the saints who are gathered in two symmetrical groups below; the saints wear long red, blue and pink robes, their heads clustered together forming a sea of haloes – again, similar to the 'play of circles' that Uitz has developed here. The three circles at the top of the composition may again relate to the ever-popular Old Testament Trinity (Plate 6), where the haloes of the angels are disposed in exactly the same pyramidal manner.

In 1922, Uitz painted a number of large-scale oil paintings, based on his analytical studies of icons. Some of these are called 'abstractions' but all of them include abstracted rather than fully abstract forms. *Harc*, or *Struggle*, is clearly figurative but the overall composition cannot be related to any particular iconography.[107] The central figure is reminiscent of the Archangel Michael, as seen advancing towards the Mother of God in icons of

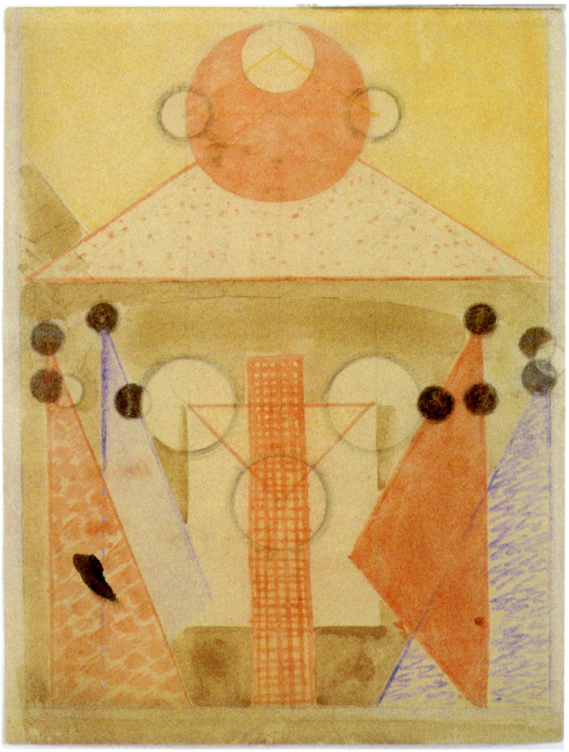

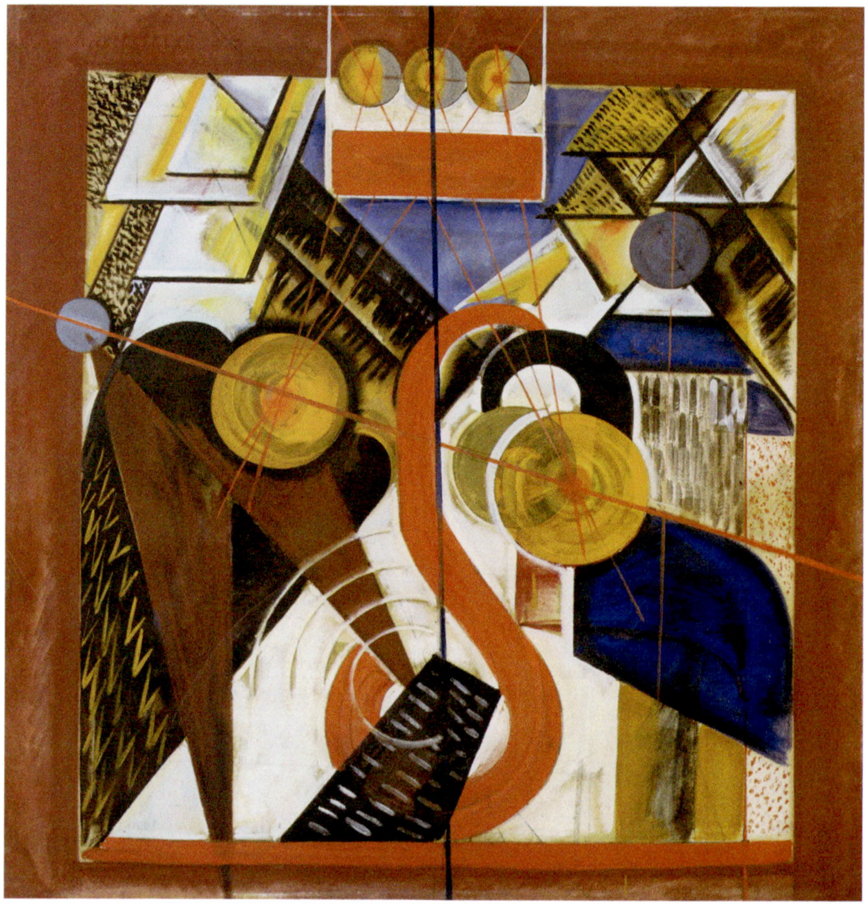

the Annunciation, and the small seated figure to the right may have been based on the left-hand angel in icons of the Old Testament Trinity. However, it is impossible (and unimportant, according to the artist) to be more precise than this. More important was the way the dynamics in the composition operated.

Iconanalysis with the Holy Trinity (Plate 56), also completed in 1922, is more abstract than *Struggle* but its model – an unidentified icon of the Annunciation – is more certain (Plate 57). This source is suggested by the impression of a winged and feathered figure to the left of the painting (the Archangel Michael) and a lower (seated?) figure in blue to the right (the Mother of God, often associated with blue). Both forms are 'stooping' and 'haloed', as they are in icons of the Annunciation. In the top left and right corners of the analysis, layers of flattened rhombus shapes mimic the stylised perspective and high viewpoint of iconic architecture typically found in these positions in Annunciation icons. The bold form of the vermilion veil that often hangs between buildings in icons (see plate 58) has been rotated 90° and is now placed vertically between the two figures; its typically stiff shape has been preserved. According to Orthodox belief, the Annunciation took place when the Virgin was making the veil of the temple. This apocryphal story was based on the Jewish tradition whereby a young virgin was selected each year, on the basis of auspicious signs, to make a new veil to cover the tabernacle in the synagogue (in this respect, the veil also anticipates the iconostasis). Apocryphal accounts of the early life of the Virgin relate how Mary was chosen for the auspicious signs she showed and, in icons, she is always represented as such, holding a vermilion spindle and thread (in contrast to the western tradition where she is usually reading a Book of Hours, reflecting the more

55
Bela Uitz

Iconanalysis IV, 1921
Watercolour on paper
40 x 30 cm (15 ¾ x 11 ¾ in)
Hungarian National Gallery, Budapest
©DACS 2007

56
Bela Uitz

Iconanalysis with the Holy Trinity, 1921–2
Oil on canvas
156 x 143 cm (61 ⅜ x 56 ¼ in)
Hungarian National Gallery, Budapest
©DACS 2007

57

Annunciation, Novgorod, *c.*1500
Tempera on wooden panel
33.3 x 27.5 cm (13 ⅛ x 10 ⅞ in)
Temple Gallery, London

58

The Mother of God appearing to St Sergius of Radonezh, Trinity-St Sergei Monastery, early 16th century
Tempera on carved wood
27.8 x 19.8 cm (11 x 7 ¾ in)
Russian Museum, St Petersburg

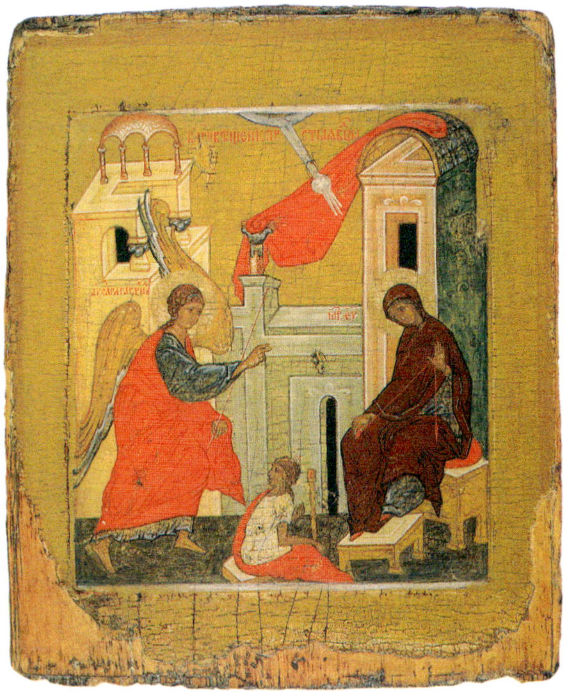

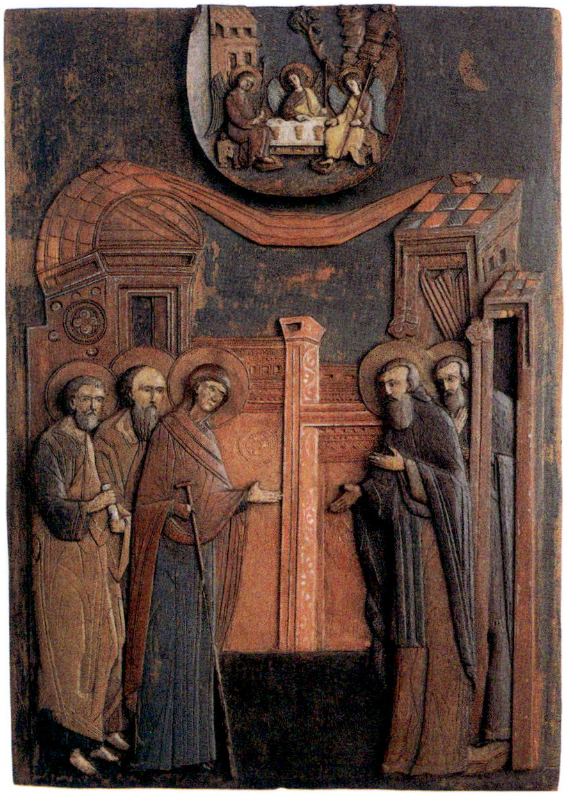

evocative genre orientation of the West). It is this piece of fabric that is seen mystically hanging between buildings in icons and which appears in Uitz's *Iconanalysis with the Holy Trinity* exactly where the act of making it is usually represented. The trinitarian name of the painting comes from the three circles, boxed at the top centre of the composition; diminutive representations of the Old Testament Trinity – three haloed angels sitting around a table – are commonly represented in this position in many different icons (Plate 58). In the example shown here, which represents the Mother of God blessing St Sergius's founding of the Trinity Monastery at Sergeev Posad, the veil is shown in exactly the stylised shape in which it appears in Uitz's work, albeit rotated by 90°. The division of God's emanations into three trinitarian rays, which is also seen at the top of many different icons (Plates 57, 130), is echoed in Uitz's linear connection of each of the three smaller 'haloes' with both of the larger ones, as if each of the three persons of the Trinity is blessing the two lower figures. The Archangel's communication with the Virgin is similarly made explicit by means of a red shaft that runs through the centres of their haloes, recalling the long thin staffs that angels hold in icons of the Annunciation, Old Testament Trinity and elsewhere.

While abstracting the compositional principles of icons and reconfiguring them in his own way, Uitz also produced a series of 37 linocuts, called *Analyses*, that evolved from his *Iconanalyses* but which were not directly based on them (Plate 59). These were clearly inspired by Rodchenko's linocuts of 1919 (reflecting their compositions but also their interest in texture) but tended to be more symmetrical, either through direct reflection across a central axis or through 180° rotation around a central point (see plate 50). Although these works

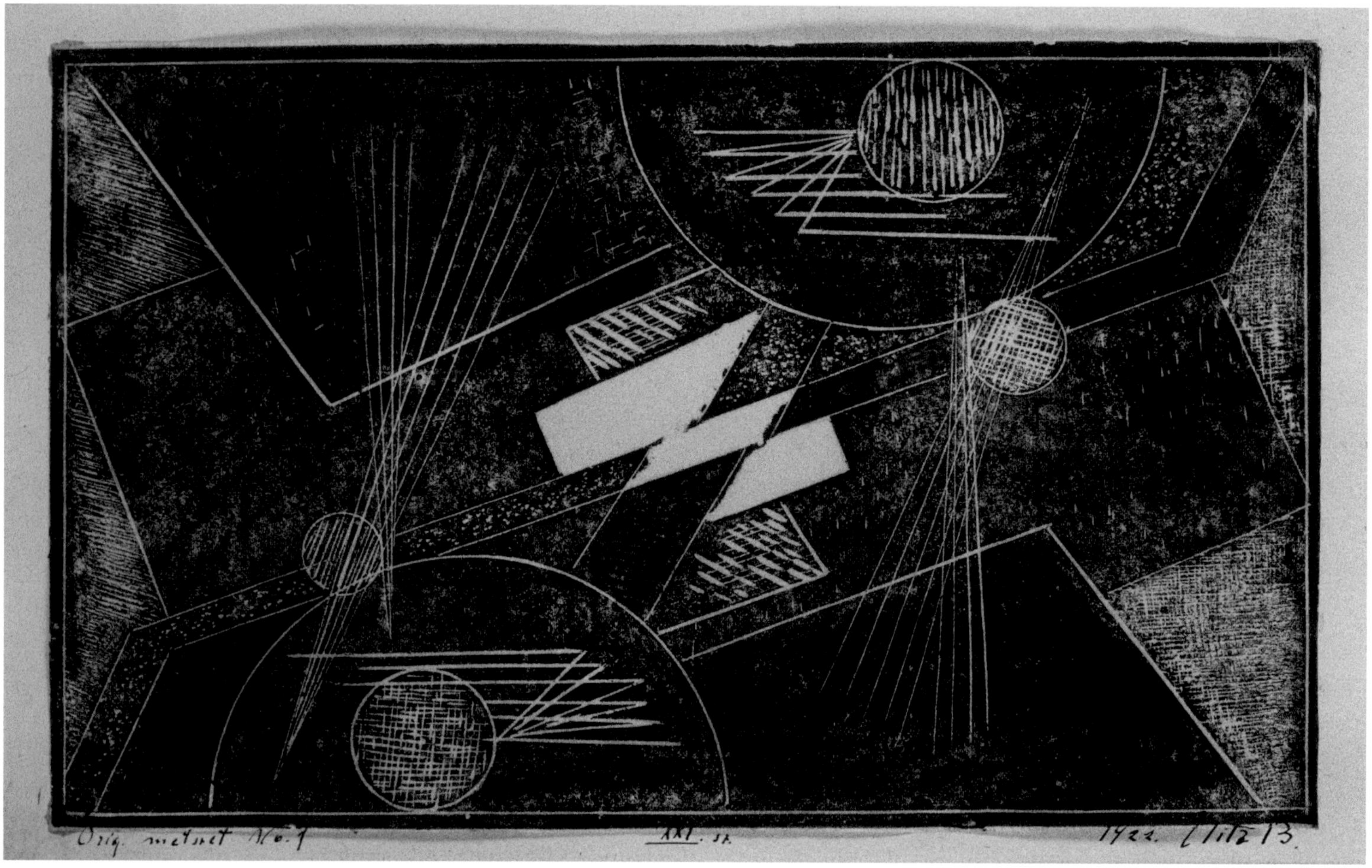

59
Bela Uitz

Analysis no.25, 1921–2
Linocut
32.3 x 20 cm (12 ¾ x 7 ⅞ in)
Hungarian National Gallery, Budapest
©DACS 2007

are not manifestly iconic, it is immediately clear that some of the features Uitz abstracted from icons and reworked in the *Iconanalyses* have been sublimated here – particularly the sense of compositional unity and the singularity of impact that icon painters achieved by establishing dynamic lines of force between static forms.

It is also conceivable that Uitz may have been influenced, if only remotely in this instance, by the symbolic nature of icons – if not their specific symbolic meanings. In 1923, he published an article 'An Experiment in Ideological Form' in the journal *Ek* (*The Wedge*), in which he theorised that geometrical forms are symbolically invested with ideological significance and that the evolution of mankind towards a classless society has accordingly been reflected in the historical evolution of architectural forms – especially the circle, triangle and square. The hierarchical society of the ancient Egyptians, for instance, was associated with an equilateral triangle – most of the mass of society was tightly concentrated at the bottom of the structure, fittingly reflected in the pyramids. Medieval feudalism was represented by an isosceles triangle; the structure was still hierarchical, but there was greater upward aspiration from below, reflected in the soaring Gothic cathedrals, and the social (and architectural) structure was correspondingly less stable. He linked the square and the circle with centralised and therefore hierarchical structures but did not give examples. These forms had also been long understood in the West to symbolise the heavenly, divine and terrestrial realms (as transmitted from the Classical world) and they were used as such in Orthodox iconography. The circle, for instance, represents the unity and infinity of God, with no beginning or end;

like the universe itself, it can move without causing displacement – by rotating. It has no base but rests in the element of air, as manifest in the central dome of most Orthodox churches (always reserved for an image of Christ Pantocrator). The triangle represents the Trinity and appears in icons and elsewhere as the omniscient eye of God; it is a dynamic form, rising up like a flame, and is therefore associated with the element of fire. The square represents the four 'corners' of the earth; it is associated with the four evangelists, who brought the gospels 'down' to the world and who are depicted in the pendentives that support the domes in Orthodox churches and in the corners of icons of Christ in Majesty (see plates 5, 42). (The icon is a flattened version of the Pantocrator image in domes which are supported above and between the pendentives.)

Uitz's belief in the evolutionary significance of geometrical forms also finds an intriguing parallel in the Orthodox tradition – the original plan for the Church of Christ the Redeemer, one of the most prominent neo-Classical churches in Moscow – though it remains unclear as to how or whether he may have known about it. The present Church of the Holy Redeemer, reproducing the Russo-Byzantine design realised by Konstantin Ton in 1832 and destroyed by Stalin in 1931, was erected in 1995. The original plan for the Cathedral, which was produced by Alexander Vitberg, an artist of Swedish extraction but born and bred in Russia, did not develop beyond its foundation before being discontinued.[108]

60
Alexander Vitberg

Design for Church of the Holy Redeemer, early 19th century
Engraving

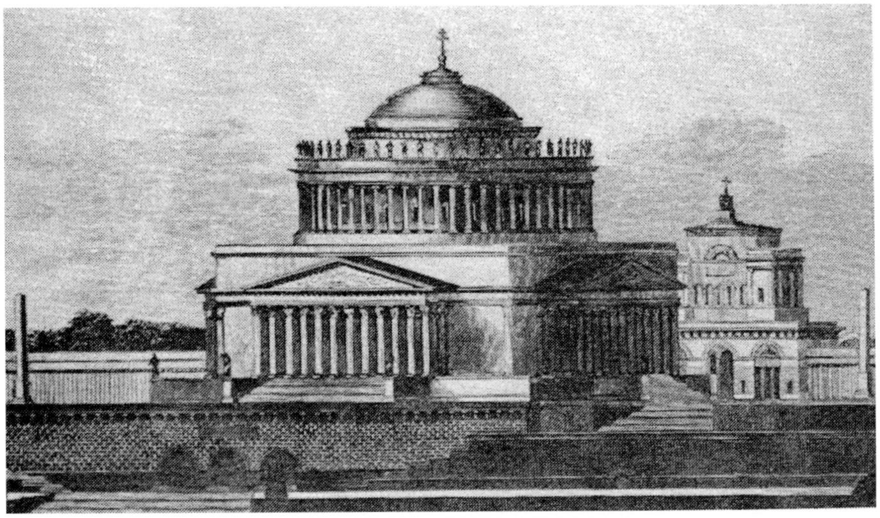

The building project was initiated by Tsar Alexander I who devised a competition to design a cathedral to commemorate the soldiers lost in the Russian victory against Napoleon in 1812. Vitberg was trained as a painter but he was so inspired by the project that he submitted a design and, against the odds, won. His projected building, conceived on the most monumental and impressive scale, was to consist of three churches, one above the other (Plate 60). Each level was loaded with symbolic meaning. The first church, beneath ground level, was to be square/rectilinear in imitation of a sarcophagus, symbolising death of the human body, and was to be dedicated to Russian war heroes whose remains were to be kept there; it was to be consecrated to the Nativity of Christ. The second church, at ground level, was to be in the form of a cross, symbolising human suffering and redemption through the suffering of Christ; it was to be decorated with frescos of Christ's Passion and was to be consecrated to the Transfiguration. The third Church, based on a circle, was to consist of a vast dome – far broader than a traditional Orthodox dome – and was to be free of imagery, just as the ideal neo-Classical mind is free of thought when contemplating the Divine Idea; it was to be consecrated to the Resurrection of Christ. The overall design was based on an evolutionary principle that linked the three levels (from the foundation upwards) with a sense of logical necessity and invested them with transcendental visionary significance: from body to soul to spirit; from Nativity to Transfiguration to Resurrection;

from death to life to eternity; from square to cross to circle. (Parallels with Malevich's iconic *Black Square, Black Cross* and *Black Circle*, to be discussed later, are also highly suggestive here; see page 142 and plate 85.) Although the Christian frame of reference would clearly not have appealed to Uitz, the sense of evolutionary progression and, above all, the symbolic and deterministic way of thinking come remarkably close to the way he approached geometrical forms in his experiment.

When Uitz returned to Vienna from Moscow in 1921, he took his 'experiment in ideological form' a step further. The process had begun in his *Iconanalyses*, in which he abstracted the compositional elements of icons from their original context in order to analyse them, partly detaching them from the distractions of narrative. He then worked on them in a fully abstracted condition – in his series of linocut *Analyses*, the only fully abstract works that he produced – exploring what he considered to be the innate properties and effects of geometrical forms. Finally he returned these forms to the context of narrative art with a better understanding of what they signified and how they functioned, allowing them to exercise their pure ideological potential before 'dressing' them with subject matter. In some ways, this process reflected Rodchenko's instruction to undertake analyses 'in order to bring to light their fundamental and secondary elements and the laws of their organisation'; that is, initially, their 'construction' and 'rhythm' and, secondarily, their 'emotion' and 'configuration'.[109] The work in which Uitz attempted most completely to realise this reconciliation of compositional and narrative potential was the series of 14 etchings, based on the theme of General Ludd, which he produced in 1923.

General Ludd was the quasi-legendary British representative and leader of a community of handloom weavers who rose up against the introduction of machine-power looms in Nottingham during the Industrial Revolution. Fearing for their livelihoods, from 1811 the weavers began breaking into factories and private houses in order to destroy the new machines, which produced much more fabric than they could and at much greater speeds. The machines enabled mill owners to increase dramatically their output and profits, often using young children for cheap labour, without improving the lot of the workers. The workers' loss of earnings was so drastic in some cases that they were pushed to the brink of starvation. Even so, extreme parliamentary reactivity led to the execution, exile and imprisonment of numerous Luddites.

Uitz regarded General Ludd as an archetypal leader of the proletariat, inspiring his followers to rise up against the establishment, and as a precedent for the Hungarian uprising of 1919.[110] His cycle of aggressively pro-communist images includes women and children working under appalling conditions in a factory; a secret meeting of Luddites in the hills; Luddites swearing an oath; General Ludd and his followers smashing machines; the long march of the Blanketeers; the Peterloo Massacre; Jones, a participant, in prison; and a scene of execution. The mood of the images, which were initially conceived as a series of frescos, is extremely dramatic and expressive, and draws directly on Japanese representations of grimacing warlords – massively exaggerated and overbearing – as well as Michelangelesque muscularity and the majestic fresco style of Fernand Hodler, whose work was widely known after the First World War through journals.[111]

Despite the variety of external influences on its highly dramatised and impassioned figural style, the composition of the *Ludd* series was based on a minutely worked out geometrical system, the language of which had been developed in the earlier

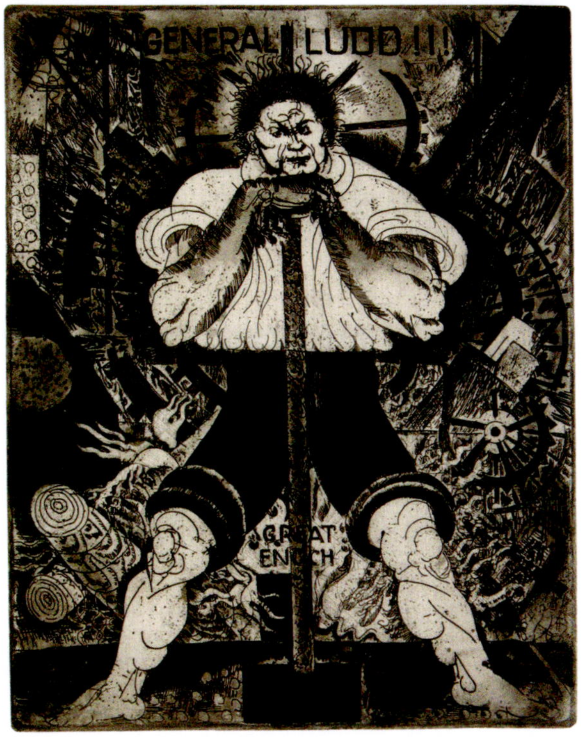

61
Bela Uitz

Great Enoch, 1923
Etching
42.5 x 33.1 cm (16 ¾ x 13 in)
Hungarian National Gallery, Budapest
©DACS 2007

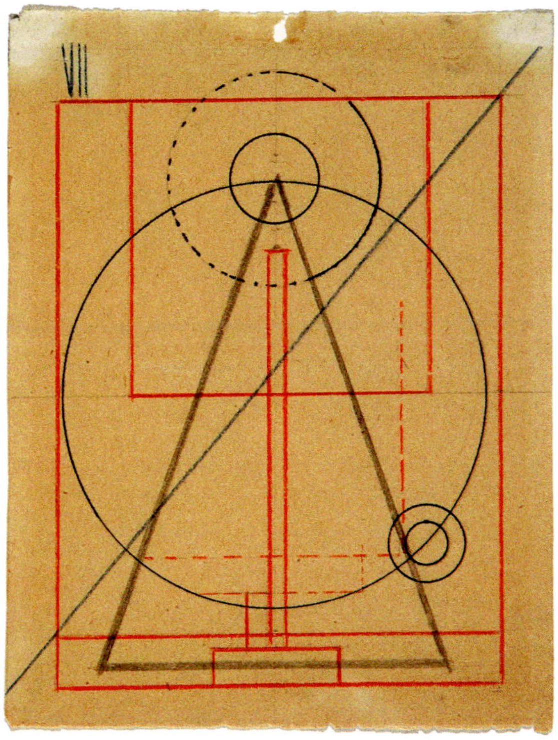

62

Bela Uitz

Design for *Great Enoch*, 1923
Coloured pencil on paper
19.4 x 14.9 cm (7 ⅝ x 5 ⅞ in)
Hungarian National Gallery, Budapest
©DACS 2007

series of *Analyses*. As Uitz wrote of the series:

> The compositions did not get that way by chance... Each composition is built up of three rudimentary elements, like a skeleton, viz. the circle, the triangle and the square. For the body: the ball, the cube and the cone. I built these elements up consciously. Often, when the composition did not turn out right, I went back to the abstract and re-drew the three elements. With such a method I managed quite strong compositions — their form was the same; their content, the birth of the proletariat.[112]

Uitz's designs for the series still exist, some of them in several versions, reflecting precisely how he worked on the compositions. *Great Enoch* (Plate 61), for instance, was based on three independent compositions, each of which developed the underlying composition of the design in terms of distinct types of geometrical form: circles, triangles and rectilinear forms. In the conflated design (Plate 62), the independence of the three designs is maintained by drawing each type of shape in a different colour – black, blue and red – though not always in the same colours throughout the series (thereby undermining any suggestion of colour symbolism). It is not only the major elements of the designs that were based on geometrical calculations; in *Great Enoch* (and several of the other etchings), even relatively discrete features, such as the cogs of the machines and the rectangular hammer-heads used to destroy them, were conceived as structural elements in the composition before being clothed with narrative identity, and hatched and textured with markings that recall passages from the *Iconanalyses*.

It is ironic that Uitz should have chosen an anti-technology movement (whose name is still used to describe people who resist change brought about by new technology) to symbolise contemporary socialism, which wholeheartedly embraced mechanisation as an agent of social change. In Soviet Russia, machines were invested with the power to raise the country to the level of other industrial nations, to retrieve creative culture from the clutches of an exclusive and subjective elite, and to mass-produce goods at low prices for the benefit of all society; destroyers of machines, called 'wreckers', were considered to be counter-revolutionary and were often very severely punished, exiled or killed. It is also ironic that, despite the aggression and atheism of their message, the design concept of Uitz's *Ludd* series was based on the compositional logic of icons. Operating both as independent designs, each one cohering around its own internal principle, and as incomplete moments in an iconographic and ideological whole, the images can be compared to a series of narrative festival icons. Although the impassioned mood of the images appears to be at odds with the highly calculated manner of Uitz's compositional technique, the artist evidently considered the two facets of his art to be mutually enhancing at the most minute level.

As we have seen, several painters of the avant-garde were intent in realising the potential of the two-dimensional picture surface without escaping into pictorial illusionism, which they considered to be a denial of two-dimensionality and therefore a falsification of the language of art. Some artists – the Suprematists, for instance – who were interested in the idea of 'higher dimensions' (both of space and of human awareness) – considered the notion of eliminating the illusion of the third dimension (spatial depth) to be analogous to the transcendence of the three-dimensional world.[113] Others felt the very opposite – that, by confining themselves to two dimensions, they were in fact imposing a limit on the ability of art to capture a reality of more than two dimensions: flat, non-illusionistic art may be 'true' to the medium of painting, but was painting 'true' to the nature of reality? The artists who grew up around Tatlin, eventually giving rise to Constructivism, thought not and aimed to achieve the same harmony of form and content that 'easel painters' sought to achieve in two dimensions, at a higher level – in three dimensions. By working in this way, they considered themselves to be engaging directly with the space in which the 'real' physical world exists, and not merely theoretically and symbolically in an artificial space, as they believed the Suprematists were doing.

It could be said that while Malevich and the Suprematists adapted their content to the two-dimensional nature of painting, the Constructivists adapted the nature of their medium to the three-dimensional content of reality. Rather than flatten the third dimension into a two-dimensional surface (with no visual reference to illusory space), the Constructivists evolved painting, via collage, into a three-dimensional medium. In relation to constructed objects, the metaphor of pictorial illusionism (which the Suprematists had associated with philosophical and moral illusion) did not arise as it did in flat image-making, because a constructed object is indeed as three-dimensional as it appears to be. And whereas the Suprematists had to develop a pictorial language that was true to the limited and artificial world of two-dimensions, the Constructivists were subject to no such limitations. On the contrary: suddenly all the possibilities of three-dimensional reality became available to them. As an early celebration of this new freedom real materials, such as wood, glass and iron, began to appear in their work. Even air, which occupies spaces that are unoccupied by other materials, was engaged as a constructive substance.

While making a significant contribution to the two-dimensional work of the avant-garde, icons were also instrumental in the evolution of Constructivism, especially setting a precedent for the notion of art as 'object' rather than as 'image'. Contrary to the impression given by the world of reproductions, an icon is not simply a picture painted on a flat surface; it is a fully three-dimensional structure. Not

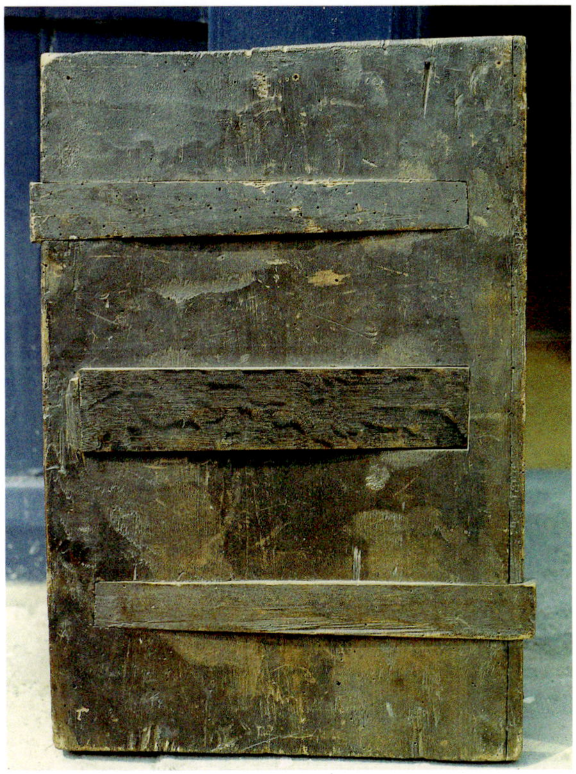

63

The back of an icon,
16th century
Temple Gallery, London

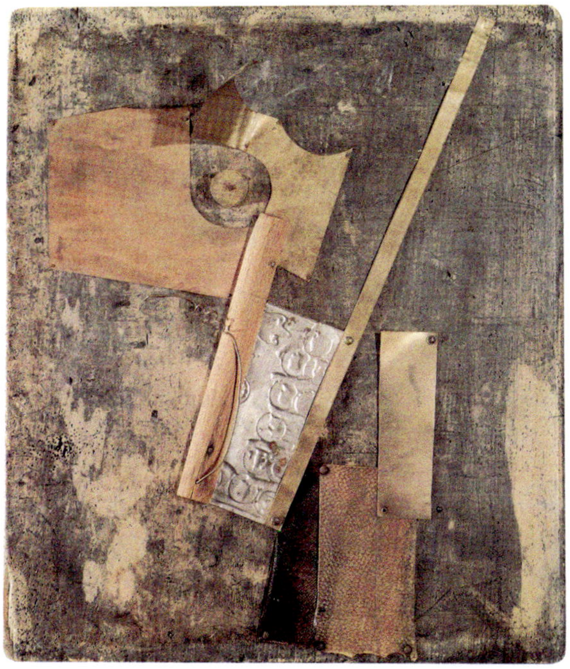

64
Vladimir Tatlin

Painterly Relief, 1913–14
Wood, oil, metal sheet
63 x 53 cm (24¾ x 20⅞ in)
Tretyakov Gallery, Moscow

only are icons engaged as objects – to be touched and kissed, and not merely to be looked at – they are *made* as objects, bringing together a multitude of materials and technical processes. The image itself is painted on to a thick wooden panel, or several joined together in the case of large icons. As a result of the natural tensions in the tree from which the wood is hewn, the panel settles into a slightly bowed shape as it seasons (clearly visible in Plates 20 and 57). In order to stabilise the wood in this bowed position, and to prevent it cracking, deep horizontal grooves are incised into the back of the panel from the sides, and wedge-shaped batons (*shponki*) are inserted into the grooves (Plate 63). The *shponki* often taper in order to ensure a tight fit without requiring nails; occasionally, their projecting ends can be seen from the front. As a result of its construction, a panel can seem inordinately thick in relation to its height, especially in the case of small icons which can have the proportions of a thick book.

On the front of the icon, the central area of the panel (*polya*), reserved for the image, is slightly recessed in such a way that the remaining raised area serves as a frame (*kovcheg*) (e.g. Plates 29, 57). Before painting begins the panel is scored and primed with several layers of gesso, bonded over a thin sheet of muslin; in worn icons, the muslin can often be seen through holes in the gesso or at the edges of the panel (Plate 57). The nature of an icon as a structure is increased by the presence of raised metal halos, or a *riza* – a decorative silver-gilt casing (originally hand-beaten), sometimes adorned with jewels, that covers many icons (Plate 14). In some icons, every part of the surface is covered by metal except for the flesh parts – the faces and hands of the figures. It is often the case with ancient examples that *rizas* are attached to the icon in a rough and ready way, vigorously nailed to the panel with adjacent strips of metal often only crudely matching and fitting together. The overall impression is often rugged and elemental. In 1914, as the first Russian artists were beginning to raise the two-dimensional image into the third dimension, the artist Vladimir Markov, who also wrote about the sculptural art of the Easter Islands, Inuits and African-Americans, wrote:

> Let us remember the icons; they are embellished with metal halos, metal casings on the shoulders, fringes and incrustations; the painting itself is decorated with precious stones and metals, etc. All of this destroys our contemporary conception of painting... Through the resonance of the colours, the sound of the materials, the assemblage of textures, we call the people to beauty, to religion, to God... The real world is introduced into [the icon's] creation only through the assemblage and incrustation of real, tangible objects. And this seems to produce a combat between two worlds, the inner ... and outer.[114]

It was precisely the tactile, elemental quality in icons – assemblages of wood, metal and textile – that awakened Tatlin, hitherto a painter of illusionistic pictures (albeit with highly structured compositions) to the expressive potential of a more tactile three-dimensional art. Berthold Lubetkin, who studied under Tatlin, remembered him saying: 'If it wasn't for the icons, I would have remained preoccupied with water-drips, sponges, rags and aquarelles'.[115] Along with many other artists of his time, Tatlin was profoundly impressed by Larionov's ground-breaking exhibition of icons in Moscow in 1913. Lubetkin recalled 'how, inspired by the icons, Tatlin started to drill his boards, mounting rings, screws and bells on them, marking and screwing the background, gluing abacus beads, mirrors, tinsels and arriving at a shimmering, dangling and sonorous composition'.[116]

We have seen how Tatlin's passage from fully representational work to a more abstracted form of figuration was underpinned by his awareness of the compositional principles of icon painting. His movement from image-making to object-making was an integral part of this process, as the example of icons, initially as structured compositions but subsequently as fully constructed objects, continued to exert its influence on him. Indeed it was as a result of his constructive rather than merely compositional interests that the critic Nikolai Punin commented that 'the influence of the Russian icon on Tatlin is undoubtedly greater than the influence upon him of Cézanne or Picasso'.[117]

Strongly evocative of an icon is a relief by Tatlin from around 1915, consisting of a thick wooden panel crudely encrusted with metal sheets, one of which is embossed with undecipherable ornament, suggestive of text (Plate 64). The positioning of, and relationship between, the circular form and arc at the top centre of the image recall Tatlin's analytical sketch of 1913 after a Virgin and Child by Cranach (Plate 33). His *Corner Counter-Reliefs* (1915, such as Plate 65), which are like sculptures with backs rather than bases, were not only constructed from iconic materials – rough wooden panels and batons, resembling *shponki*, and sheets of hammered metal, resembling *rizas* – but they were also designed to be displayed in corners. Although he does not refer to the fact that, in traditional Russian

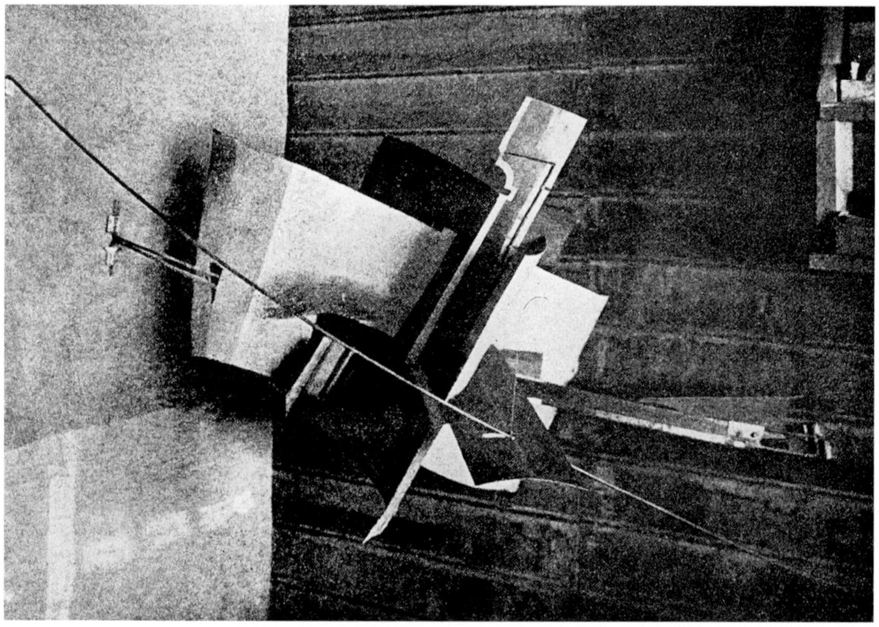

65
Vladimir Tatlin

Corner Counter-Relief, 1915
Medium and dimensions unknown
Location unknown
Reproduced in *Das Kunstblatt*, no.11, 1922, p.496

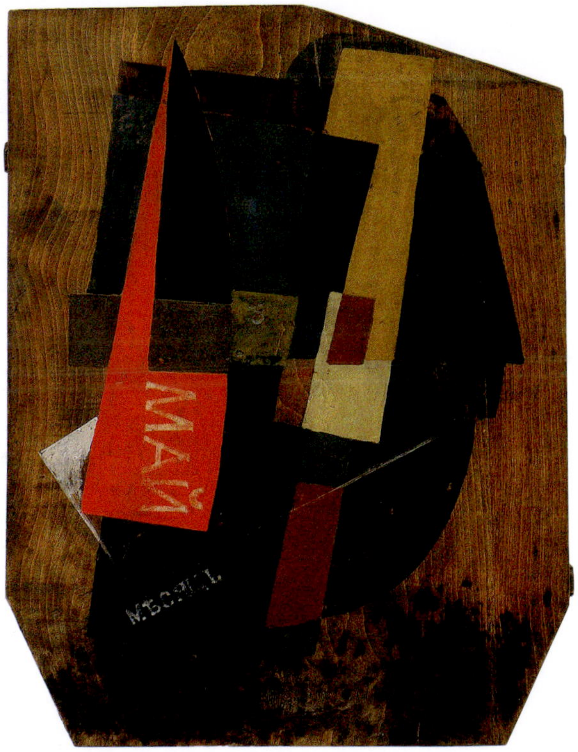

66
Vladimir Tatlin

The Month of May, 1916
Tempera on wood
52 x 39 cm (20 ½ x 15 ⅖ in)
Staatliche Museen zu Berlin, Preussischer Kulturbesitz

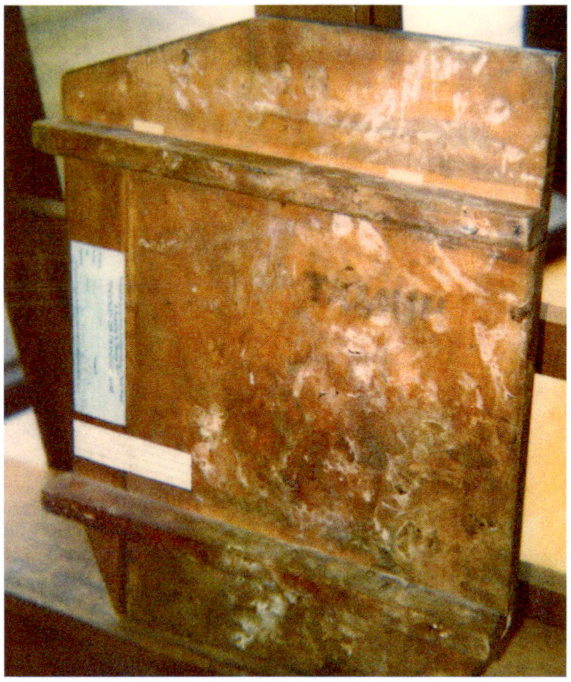

67
Vladimir Tatlin

The back of *The Month of May*, 1916
Staatliche Museen zu Berlin, Preussischer Kulturbesitz

homes, icons are always hung over the corners of rooms, it is inconceivable that Tatlin could have created these works without full awareness of their iconic associations. Tatlin's composition, *The Month of May* (1916, Plate 66) is not only iconic in its technique (paint on wood panel) and in the hieratic organisation of the painted forms, but also – even more strikingly in this context – in the construction of the panel which is clearly held together on the back by *shponki* (Plate 67). It is highly unlikely that he would have made this gesture – one that is unnecessary from a purely structural point of view – without wanting its iconic resemblance to be communicated.

Tatlin's lasting interest in icons is reflected in numerous works – or photographs of works, now lost or destroyed – from his pre-revolutionary years. Although he made no attempt to account for the iconicity of his own work, it is no less palpable than the iconicity of Suprematism. Its emphasis, however, is quite different. Tatlin's response to icons is, like his work as a whole, elemental and rooted in the physical world, and is not conducive to metaphysical elaboration. The essence of his constructed works resides in their manifestation of spatial dynamics, not because such dynamics are symbolic or meaningful in some way (as they were for Larionov, for instance) but simply for their own sake. In this respect, his approach resonates with the sacramentality of icons. Not only do icons represent sacred subjects but, more importantly, they are believed by Orthodox Christians to participate substantially, or materially, in what they represent. The prevalence of this belief is borne out by the fact – evident in Orthodox churches all over the world – that many Orthodox believers do not engage with the iconography or appearance of icons. They engage with them physically, touching them or crossing themselves before them (often without even looking at them), enabling their blessing power to be transmitted mystically within the form of that physical process. Indeed, because their power resides in their physical actuality rather than their religious meaning or aesthetic impact, blind people and even dead people are believed to be able to benefit from icons by touching or being touched by them (as shown in Sergei Ivanov's *Death of a Migrant* (1889), Plate 99).

The influence of icons on Tatlin shifted from the iconographic and stylistic to the compositional and constructive. A combination of these influences can also be detected in the series of assemblages constructed by Naum Gabo (1890–1977) from sheets of wood and metal between 1915 and 1918: *Constructed Heads Nos 1 & 2, Head of a Woman* and *Constructed Torso*. Gabo's training was as a scientist and engineer (his father was a metallurgist) and it is significant that his approach to Constructivism emerged as much from an interest in the structural technicalities of materials as from the expressive potential of Cubism. One of the most striking features in Gabo's *Heads* is the way they combine the contemplative mood of iconography with the high stylisation of iconic design and the physicality of iconic construction. In *Head of a Woman* (1917–20, Plate 68), for instance, the characteristically tilted head and inscrutable averted gaze clearly associate the woman with icons of the melancholy Tichvin Mother of God with Christ ('Hodigitria') (Plate 4). The woman's long, narrow nose and small mouth are typical of such icons, and add further to the impression of iconic silence and dignity. The deliberate iconicity of the work was underlined by the fact that it was designed to be displayed in a corner – like Tatlin's *Counter-Reliefs* – and was mounted this way at the exhibition of Russian art held at the Van Diemen Gallery in Berlin in 1922, as Malevich's *Black Square* had been in Moscow in 1915 (Plates 69, 86).

The pensive expression of Gabo's *Heads* is strongly enhanced by the purely compositional effect, which also shows signs of iconic influence. Although they are clearly three-dimensional objects, the fact that they are constructed from planes, such that their component parts are differentiated by lines rather than by the relationship of masses, reflects an essentially graphic dimension in Gabo's approach to sculptural form at this stage in his career. This impression is reinforced by the fact that Gabo made considerable use of drawings in the working out of key aspects of his sculptural ideas. The graphic manner of Gabo's early assembled works resonates closely with the highly stylised graphic design of icons in which the description of forms was also based on a dynamic interaction of arcs and planes, sometimes with the stiffness and angularity of metal. In some respects, the *Heads* seem to open out the flattened folds of iconic form-description into three-dimensions. Gabo's awareness of the 'constructive' dimension of iconic graphics may have been awakened in him by Cubism which he

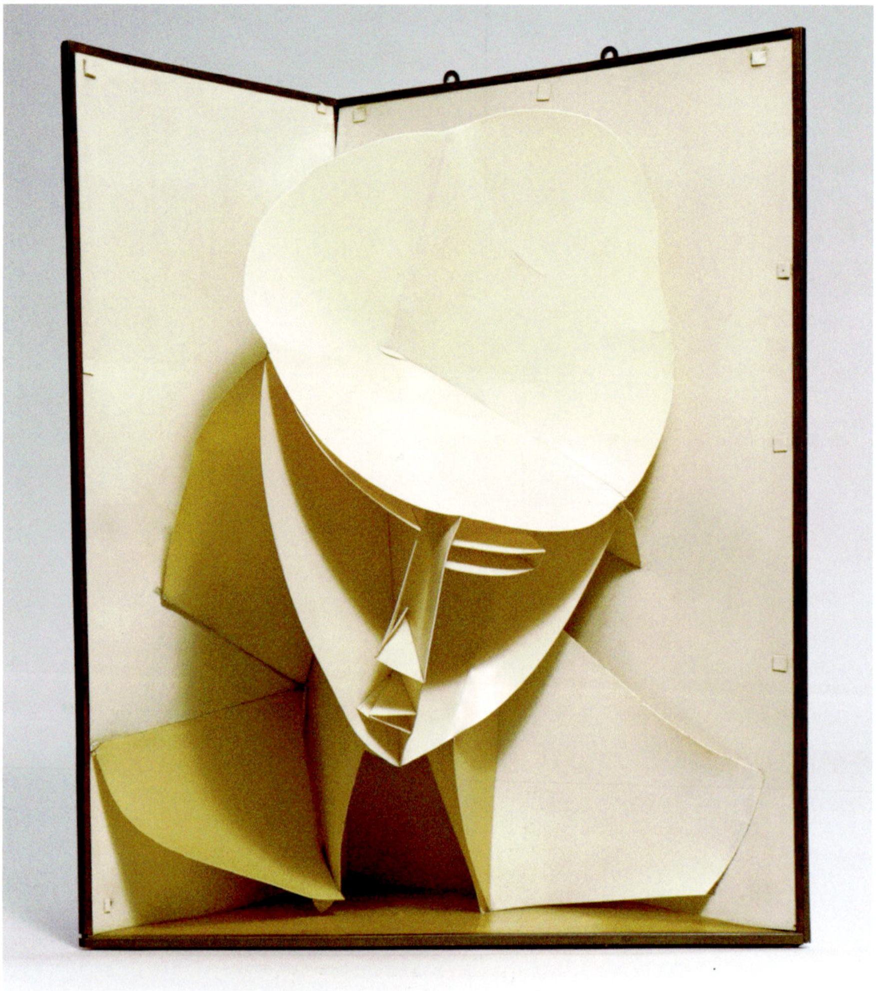

68
Naum Gabo
Head of a Woman, 1917–20
Celluloid and metal on wood
61 x 48.5 x 34.5 cm
(24 x 19 ⅛ x 13 ⅝ in)
Museum of Modern Art, New York

69

Photograph of the exhibition at the Van Diemen Gallery, Berlin, 1922, showing Gabo's ***Head of a Woman*** exhibited in the corner
David King Collection, London

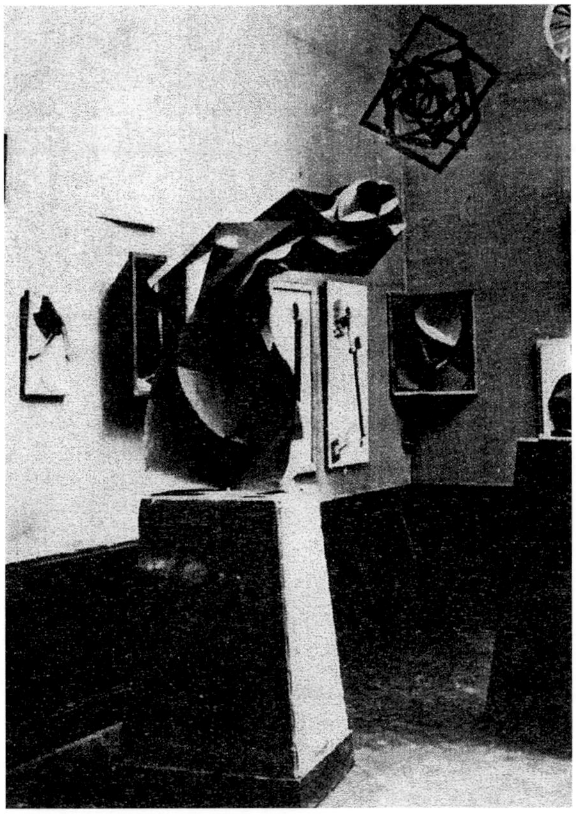

encountered in Paris in 1914, while visiting his brother, Antoine Pevsner.[118]

Whether inspired by Cubism or not, Gabo acknowledged that 'as a young man I was influenced by Russian Byzantine art'.[119] It was through his nanny, Praskova, that he first became aware of icons: 'In our nursery, on the wall opposite me, hung an icon and a lamp that was always lit ... we went to bed and slept at night and woke up in the morning with its image'.[120] In an interview, recorded in 1972, he recalled how icons 'certainly made the most decisive impression on me. I still think and feel that in the icons there were the beginnings of my education in painting'.[121] Gabo recognised that the impact of icons, and Russian art in general, had been widespread among his contemporaries, stating that 'the whole history of Russian art had a greater influence on our generation than [Cubism, Futurism and all the rest of western ideologies] taken together'.[122]

Gabo attributed the continuity in Russian art to the prevalence of unique values that unify it and differentiate it from western art at a most fundamental level. In his essay 'The Concepts of Russian Art', written in 1942, he outlined the definitive and abiding characteristics of Russian art. In contrast to the western priorities of self-expression and representation, Gabo described Russian art as being: 'first, purely idealistic in its content; second, utilitarian and collectivistic in its social function; and third, abstract in its formal expression'.[123] With the exception of the elite classicism of the eighteenth and nineteenth centuries, which Gabo regarded as a temporary impingement of western values on Russian culture, the content of Russian art is essentially 'not of this world'. In view of the fact that the basic iconographic and compositional parameters of icons were fixed by the Church, the typical icon painter, like the non-objective artists of his own day:

> did not need to look for inspiration or imitation of the surrounding material nature. He looked for it in the inner world of his spiritual or aesthetic impulses. Every line in the ikon or fresco, every coloured shape, is transformed from a detail into a theme. The rhythmic movements of the lines, the harmonious relationships of the colours and shapes to each other and the whole were the only expressions of his emotions. And this, contrasted with European painting, is basically an abstract conception of art.[124]

Gabo recognised that the intellectual agenda of icons, manifest through their iconography and composition, was strictly prescribed by the Church as a matter of immutable doctrine – as unalterable as the liturgy itself – and that the potential for artists to excel was concentrated in their pictorial skills, based on 'innate intuition'. This facility for understanding the picture surface constituted the tradition of craftsmanship that was passed on from one generation to the next, only emerging, free of extraneous parameters, in the modern age: 'It was only natural, therefore, that an ecclesiastic painting constituted for the Russian artist an abstract scheme in which he had to fit his own pictorial ideas. This being so, the painter was restricted to the basic elements of painting – lines, shapes, colours – and in that, the Russian iconography displays a miraculous variety of individual compositions. These elements in fact alone constitute its whole splendour.'[125]

It was precisely this instinct for line, shape and colour – developed over a period of several centuries – that Gabo witnessed resurfacing in the work of his contemporaries. One such artist was Gabo's own brother, Antoine Pevsner, whose work from this period explored the possibility of realising a sense of spatial dynamics within the static flatness of illusory pictorial space. Pevsner acknowledged that his interest in this subject was stimulated by icons. He was particularly struck by the use of inverted and inconsistent perspective in icons, in which the outlines of rectilinear forms that should – according to the laws of conventional optical perspective – recede to a single vanishing point, are seen to project towards various different points, both in the foreground and in the background, thereby creating an ambiguous and unstable impression of space. Even when the direction of the convergence is consistent, the lines rarely converge on to a single point. To further intensify the confusion, buildings seen from above are frequently juxtaposed with buildings of the same height seen from below. The resultant clashes seemed, to Pevsner, to create a kind of kinetic impression in the eye, stimulating his interest in the way space could be perceived and represented, though whether he was right to imagine that icon painters had a sophisticated agenda regarding the effects of perspective on the viewer is debatable. Icon painters were certainly not trying to create a comprehensive and consistent illusion of depth. On the contrary, they had no interest in merely reproducing the known world, which they considered to be corrupted by the fall of Adam; instead, they aimed to reveal a higher invisible world – which they believed in fact to be uniquely revealed through icons. Although they represented objects in a highly stylised manner that seems to imply numerous different and inconsistent spatial frames of reference, there is no evidence to suggest that icon painters had a more self-conscious purpose than to realise their vision of the other world (and to be faithful to their models).

Whatever the case, Pevsner was fascinated by the way the use of lines could have such a powerful effect on a viewer's perception of space. In an interview in 1957, he recalled an icon of Christ holding the Bible (probably a Christ in Majesty, as in Plate 42) that he had seen on a visit to a monastery near Novgorod in 1910, 'I looked at this image for a long time and was struck by the eyes which seemed to look straight into mine; then I observed the hands in the icon and noticed how it was impossible to tell which way the Bible was leaning. I looked again at the eyes and noticed to my terror that instead of being fixed on me, they were now closed. According to my position, the eyes seemed to open or close, the Bible also.'[126]

This experience convinced Pevsner that the impression of space was not so much associated with a sense of mass and substance as with the articulation of voids, as evoked by artful distribution of lines and planes. According to Pevsner's biographer, Guy Massat, this 'discontinuity, separation and division between the open and the closed, due to a clever use of inverted perspective on a concave surface, was Pevsner's first experience of the void as a generator of sensory expressions' and Pevsner himself said: 'these forms which seemed sometimes open, sometimes closed, were to become an essential aspect of my work'.[127]

Gabo and Pevsner firmly believed in the autonomy of art as a language with its own expressive value, but they also fully subscribed to the growing socialist ideal of functionalism in art. In fact, they considered it to be a fundamental characteristic of Russian art. The functionalist ideal was based on the notion that aesthetic experience for its own sake is a bourgeois indulgence, superfluous to the necessary realities of life, and that all creative energy should be subsumed in the design of utilitarian objects. The ideal was seen to be reflected in icons, which served a spiritual and social purpose for all people rather than a subjective aesthetic or emotive one for an elite, and again in the realist painting of the nineteenth century which was explicitly informed with social responsibilities at the expense of personal self-expression. Icons were a truly popular art and, as such, they prepared the way for a communist 'theology' of art. Above all, they did not generate and sustain values that supported a system of class differentiation and discrimination. On the contrary, where the efficacy of western art was seen to depend on, and subtly sustain, the exclusive luxuries of education, leisure time and wealth, icons were considered to be equally accessible to all classes of society, and to be direct embodiments of the beliefs, values and interests of the people. The fact that so much eighteenth-century Russian art was both elitist and highly westernised in style was made to suggest that western art is inherently aligned with social inequality, serving further to underline the inherent association of traditional national art with a sense of social responsibility. Gabo regarded the re-emergence of this ideal at the time of the Revolution as the revival of traditionally Russian concern, 'an organic continuation of an innate Russian aesthetic concept'.[128] This ideology, he later recalled, 'laid special stress again on the absolute values of the basic elements of art and their intrinsic power to influence human psychology, and so mould the spiritual life of society; it also laid stress on bringing art again into the everyday life of the masses by incorporating it into the design of everyday things'.[129]

However, unlike most of his Constructivist contemporaries, who demanded that all creative activity should be rigorously channelled into the design and production of utilitarian objects, Gabo's understanding of 'function' involved a far broader non-materialist vision of public service. Like his nineteenth-century precursors, who insisted that art and literature should serve the regenerative social function that ordinary citizens were forbidden to engage in directly through politics, he also believed that art should aim to meet the spiritual needs of individuals and create environments conducive to harmonious living. In this respect, his ideal came significantly closer to the icon, whose function is spiritual healing – 'a ritual object, a thing for worship, and to that extent a utilitarian phenomenon'[130] – than to the ideals of his materialist contemporaries. At the same time, he distanced himself from Malevich's transcendentalism, which he considered to be aloof from the practical needs of this world: 'Life does not know rationally abstracted truths as a measure of cognisance, deed is the highest and surest of truths.'[131] Considering his highly individual response to the Russian tradition – one that was neither abstracted like the Suprematists, nor materialistically utilitarian like the Constructivists – it is scarcely surprising that Gabo should have felt attracted to the more liberal cultural atmosphere of western Europe. Like Kandinsky, Chagall and El Lissitsky, he emigrated from Russia in 1922, to be followed by Pevsner a year later.

Despite its great diversity, Russian avant-garde artists were united both in their rejection of pure aestheticism and in their demand for a more purposeful and inclusive role for art. Ironically, Alexander Benois, who contributed so much to the *fin-de-siècle* aestheticism of the World of Art, anticipated this turn of events as early as 1902, envisioning the call to functionalism as part of the destiny and mission of Russian art as a whole: 'Historical necessity, historical sequence requires that an age that would absorb man's individuality in the name of public benefit or of a higher religious idea would come again to replace the refined epicureanism of our time, the extreme refinement of man's individuality, his effeminacy, morbidity and solitude.'[132]

The Constructivist approach to the legitimate utility of art differed radically from that of the Suprematists, though it could claim with equal conviction to be the rightful heir to the national tradition. Malevich's commitment to the higher purpose of art resulted in a kind of transcendental existentialism in which the existence of reality was seen to be capable of its own self-expression, without the mediation of art; like Christ for icon venerators, reality became a self-evident truth for him and, as a result, pure 'art' gradually refined itself out of existence. The Constructivists moved in the opposite direction, attempting to create an art that was not based on the flight from illusion but which embraced the immediate appearance of reality, without any recourse to a metaphysical agenda; that is to say, it plunged itself into the functions of life; it claimed no legitimacy where it was not fully fused

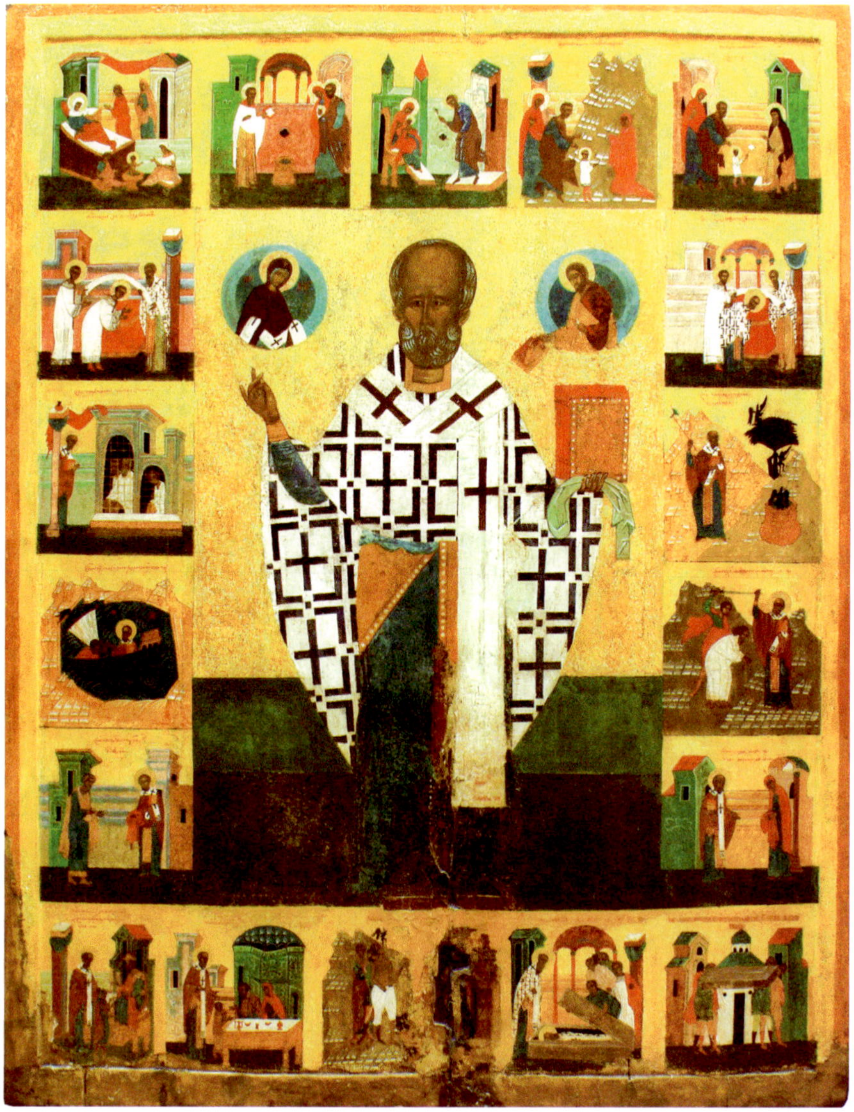

and integrated into the actions of life. They came to regard the old model of art appreciation as no more than a complacent and outdated social convention that simply gave an air of respectability to the falsehoods and injustices that it concealed. The Constructivists' rejection of aestheticism, epitomised by painting – which they disdainfully referred to as 'easel painting' – ultimately led them to insist on

70 *(opposite)*

St Nicholas of Mozhaisk with scenes from his life, Suzdal, 16th century
Tempera on wooden panel
124 x 93.2 cm (48 7/8 x 36 3/4 in)
Temple Gallery, London

71 *(this page, left)*
Alexander Rodchenko

Photograph of Varvara Stepanova wearing her 'Optical' design, 1924
A. Rodchenko and V. Stepanova Archive, Moscow

72 *(this page, right)*
Varvara Stepanova

'Optical' design for fabric, 1924
A. Rodchenko and V. Stepanova Archive, Moscow

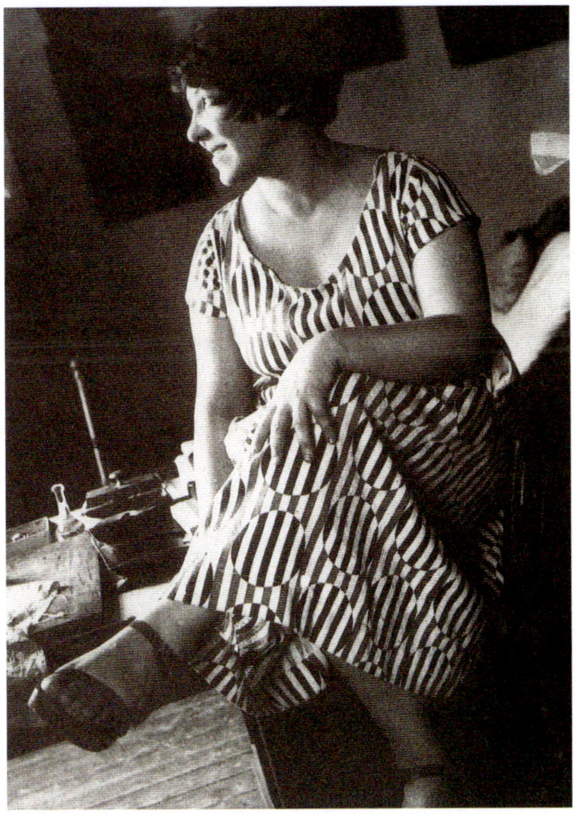

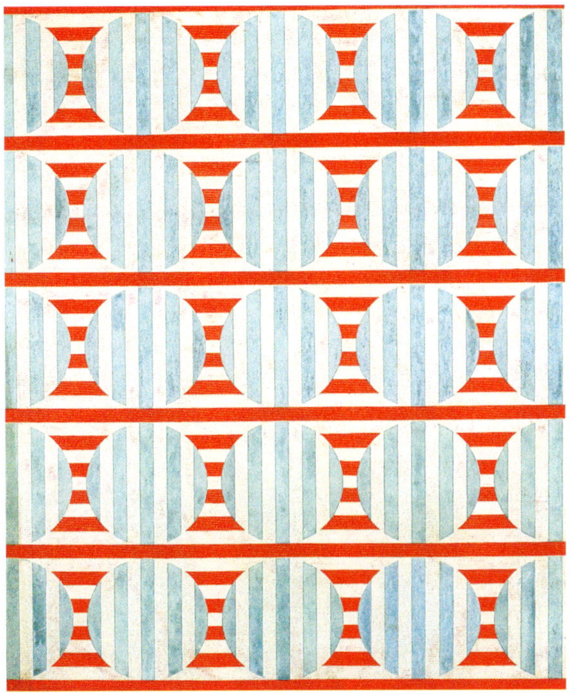

the utilitarian application of all creative endeavour. Just as icons were not traditionally regarded as works of art in their own right but had a down-to-earth practical function in the social and spiritual life of the community, so the Constructivists increasingly came to reject the idea of art as a sophisticated form of entertainment for an elite class and began to engage it as a vital agent of social change. To this end, they submitted their personal creative ambitions to the anonymous and communal production of popular utilitarian objects on a massive scale. In keeping with this view, they demanded that the consumption and use of such objects be determined not by vanity and status anxiety as in the self-conscious 'art' world, but by purely practical, economic and material considerations. They advocated that objects should cease to function as abstracted indices of self-image, wealth and taste, but become dynamically integrated, through use, into the overall cycle of a way of life given over to the realisation and practice of communist ideals.

The prioritisation of function over aesthetics is reflected in designs that Liubov Popova and Varvara Stepanova produced for the clothing industry from 1922, when issues around the legitimacy of fine art were coming to a head. They abandoned the general aestheticist orientation of 'fashion' in favour of a range of ultra-practical uniforms, specifically designed for particular activities and professions (pilots, surgeons, sportsmen etc). Where clothing had previously expressed the self-image of the individual (the subjectivity of the ego), it was now required to reflect the function of the individual – the way in which he or she served society. Both artists were keenly aware of the traditions of Russian folk costume, and it is inconceivable that they could have been unaware of the precedents for their own designs set by the function-specific vestments of Orthodox bishops and metropolitans, especially as represented in medieval icons. In this instance, there is also an uncanny resemblance between Stepanova's flattened schematised designs (Plates

72, 71) and the repeating patterns of crosses (called *polystavron* – 'many crosses' in Greek) that decorate the garments of the clergy in early icons (Plates 70, 103). The *polystavron*, which show no regard whatsoever for the folds of the fabric that they adorn, are clearly in keeping with Christian symbolism, forming a visual counterpart to the Orthodox monastic practice of perpetual prayer (hesychasm), in which monks invoke the name of Christ without ceasing and thereby sublimate themselves in him. In exactly the same way, Stepanova's repetitive designs evoke a sense of the faceless mechanistic ideals of Soviet communism according to which the individual sacrifices him- or herself to the operation of the state.

The parallels between this thoroughly recontextualised attitude towards objects and the role of icons in Orthodox Church ritual was articulated by the philosopher-priest Pavel Florensky who was teaching at the VKhUTEMAS school precisely when the Constructivist re-evaluation of art was taking place there. Between 1918 and 1920, he had worked for the Commission for the Preservation of Monuments and Antiquities of the Lavra of Trinity monastery at Sergeev Posad, which was committed to protecting the monastery and all it stood for against the staunchly anti-religious Bolshevik regime. During this period he wrote several essays on the significance of icons, including *Iconostasis*, mentioned above and *On Reverse Perspective*. In 1918, Florensky wrote an essay on 'Church Ritual as a Synthesis of the Arts', in which he insisted that an icon's significance and value depends on its symbiotic relationship to its context – the rituals of the Church – and that it should not be abstracted and made to stand as a self-sufficient autonomous object, in a museum or a salon. He argued that its impact is fundamentally interwoven with that of the chanting, candlelight, incense, architecture and movements of the officiating clergy etc, in the midst of which the viewer experiences it. By extension, he claimed that religious art represented the highest synthesis of artistic activities, advocating that a 'total complex of research and teaching institutions' should be attached to the Trinity Monastery as a perfect response to the artistic needs of the time: 'This would be a model institution as well as a truly miraculous and historic attempt to bring into being that ultimate synthesis of the arts for which our modern aestheticians yearn'.[133]

Florensky's vision of a radical reorientation of art education towards a total synthesis of the arts in the service of a higher integrated ideal was realised – though not as he had envisaged it – at the VKhUTEMAS workshops which flourished from 1920–30 and where he taught 'Analysis of Space' from 1921.

Although the Constructivists' egalitarian attitude towards art was adopted largely on the basis of revolutionary idealism, it was anticipated by the painters of icons to the extent that icons were also produced by workshops in large quantities as functional objects. Icon painters did not value originality for its own sake. Because they understood the Orthodox canon of iconography to be uniquely sanctioned by tradition, they were content to reproduce the same images over and over again. Access to the value of art was accomplished by submitting to the living tradition through which it was transmitted. Self-expression played no part in a painter's agenda – he only had his illusions to express; hence the comparative lack of variety in the compositions and subject matter of icons. In contrast to the western tradition in which originality has always been deliberately sought – to glorify the artist and owner, and to stimulate the viewer – the orientation of icon painters was to surrender their own preferences to the purposes of God. Thus, in a way that was consistent with the Constructivist ideal of communality, icons had an objective function apart from the simple gratification of artist and viewer: just as the function of Constructivist art was either utilitarian (at a physical level) or social (in the case of political propaganda), so the function of an icon was exclusively to facilitate and magnify the revelation and realisation of God in the world. The consistency with which later icon painters adhered to the tradition of iconography and the lack of self-consciousness with which they 'serviced' worn or damaged icons, regardless of their age, is a testimony to the extent to which they regarded icons as functional rather than aesthetic objects.[134] Just like the Constructivists, traditional icon painters never signed their work. Until western influence reached Russia in the sixteenth and seventeenth centuries, it had never occurred to them to do so. Not only would it have been inappropriate for an individual to take credit for this sacred work (aimed at self-transcendence) but, just as the Constructivists dispersed the production process throughout a factory workforce, so the production of an icon was often divided between a number of artisans, each one trained to execute a different aspect of the work: carpentry, preparation of the gesso, drawing, under-painting, flesh painting, gilding and varnishing.

One of the most outspoken advocates of the most extreme form of Constructivism – advocating industrial mass production over 'applied art' or craft – was the critic Nikolai Tarabukin, who declared in a lecture at INKhUK (State Institute of Artistic Culture) in Moscow in 1921 that 'the Last Painting has been Painted'. In his book *From the Easel to the Machine* (1923), in which he consolidated his ideas on this subject, Tarabukin describes not only how fine art ('easel painting') has completed its evolution towards its own dissolution, especially since Édouard Manet and the Impressionists, but that the making of useful objects has also been superseded by the higher transpersonal principle of industrial mass production. Although he demanded that all man-made objects be rigorously functional, he discriminated against the application of Constructivist design to handmade utensils, as if such design was a kind of bourgeois ornament in the old-fashioned manner, advocating that legitimate creativity be invested in the mechanised production process rather than in objects themselves. In effect, he developed an idiosyncratic theory of non-objectivity in that the value of objects was not seen to reside in the objects themselves but in the production-consumption process of which they formed a part; the object itself was not valuable and scarcely had its own identity. By implication, the same could be said of the objects' producers and consumers – their subjects; these too are subsumed in the process of production-consumption. These details would not be significant in the present context if it was not for the fact that many of Tarabukin's Constructivist theories are deeply resonant with his understanding of icons, as expressed in his *The Philosophy of Icons*, conceived in around 1916. In the light of this text, there is a strong case for suggesting that Tarabukin's ideas about legitimate production were influenced by, and perhaps even precipitated by, his understanding of icons.

This case rests not so much on what Tarabukin says that icons are, but on what he says they are not. Although he does not refer to himself as a believer, his attitude towards icons is fundamentally Orthodox and is entirely accepting of their religious validity. It also reflects the influence of mystically inclined writers such as Evgenii Trubetskoi, Florensky and Aleksei Losev, which he acknowledges. Regarding the religious status of icons, he maintains that they need to be blessed in church in order to rise above primitive totems, that they are miracle-working, linking man with God, and that they transcend time. As we have already seen, he also described and celebrated the ingenuity and abstraction of their compositions in great detail. In order to help him articulate a sense of the iconic, which is essentially ineffable, he is frequently required to compare icons to conventional fine art and, in so doing, he uses the ideal of icon painting as a foil against which to develop his notion of the illegitimacy and immorality of conventional art. Icons, for instance, are not art as such, with an aesthetic agenda; they are functional sacred objects. Unlike works of fine art, they are not signed; likewise, they are not merely personal and emotional, they are objective, meaningful and ideological; nor need they be 'original', expressing a new idea; their appearance is not arbitrary and subjective, it is determined by an internal principle.

While celebrating traditional aspects of the Orthodox Church, Tarabukin considered the Church in his own day to have become commoditised in keeping with the lifestyle of the bourgeosie.[135] Although it would theoretically be possible to create new icons, since they are not restrained by time, the twentieth century did not provide an atmosphere that was conducive to creating sacred objects of this kind.[136] Ironically, the Bolshevik regime did provide a circumstance in which the cultish, utilitarian and programmatic aspects of icon painting could have been revived though, of course, after the Revolution sacred art ceased to form part of the discourse of the arts. Despite Tarabukin's evidently passionate and profound belief in the significance of icons, it is perhaps not surprising that he neither mentioned icons in his later published works nor published his early writings about them. However, his argument against conventional art, which was clearly articulated in relation to icons, remained intact and was highly visible and influential. Significantly, it served as a counterfoil for his new ideology which, like a new casting from an old mould, retained some of the characteristics of its predecessor: functional, transpersonal, objective, ideological.

Throughout the period leading up to the Russian Revolution, icons provided a meaningful and legitimising precedent for almost every aspect of the new avant-garde art: its stylised visual languages, its sense of national identity, its universal social application, its physical materiality, its functionality and the irrelevance of self-expression. However, their potential was by no means exhausted in these ways for, insofar as the avant-garde movement was concerned with the artistic and social aspects of icons, it was not relating to them at the level of their true identity. On the contrary, it was relating to them for the sake of their secondary and incidental attributes, adapting them to its own ends without reflecting the profound insights and satisfying the spiritual longing that originally gave rise to them.

The multilayered significance of icons for the avant-garde movement was perceptively described by Benois in an article, 'Letters on Art: Icons and the New Art', that he wrote for the newspaper *Rec'* in April 1913. By this time, Benois was just beginning to appreciate how the avant-garde dismantling of naturalism, which he had hitherto considered to be a wanton act of cultural vandalism, could indeed become a form of entry into a dimension of life that has no equivalent in the outside world, an insight into that which is 'hidden in the soul'.[137] In the article, he makes the point that contemporary artists were responding to the artistic dimension of icons, but not to their spirituality; in so doing, they were demonstrating that they had not yet penetrated the surface and reached the depth of their own art. He indicated that the purely aesthetic interest of avant-garde artists in icons reflected a superficial attitude towards their own potential while the prospect of a deeper understanding of icons seemed also to offer a deeper understanding of themselves. The article, which has not been published in translation before, is presented here almost in its entirety:

> Some coincidences in the life of the arts give the impression of a kind of intervention of fate. Today we have before us one of these fateful 'pre-ordained' coincidences. For many years a narrowly specialist group of people have been studying and collecting antique icons – not so much out of interest in their artistic merits as out of veneration for their antiquity and holiness. In an entirely different domain – the domain of purely painterly creativity – work has been progressing on simplification and on liberation from academic traditions. ... And now, we are witnessing a strange and highly significant meeting – the two paths have crossed, have merged. Even the most ardent and daring innovators see a valuable sign for themselves in something which up until now had appeared to have died away hopelessly. Russian Futurists of all doctrines, already prepared to set light to the museums of ancient art, have been so struck by the treasures of antiquity which appear to them so close in spirit, that with regard to them they have already replaced anger with mercy and do not hide their wish to learn from these 'old men'.
>
> Behind this miracle are the purely outward advances made in restoration. ... It is about seven or eight years since the technique of cleaning icons of the grey-brown patina of time and of the over-painting of different centuries reached a new stage of development... This is resulting in a kind of 'icon Pompeii'; restorers are currently conducting further excavations with a growing passion and discovering new treasures.
>
> Yet, however happy the extraordinary revival of ancient beauty has been, this renaissance of Byzantium could not have played the role of a kind of rejuvenator of contemporary art if the path of the latter had not itself come to a kind of historical crossroads at exactly this moment. Only ten years ago, the 'icon Pompeii' would not have produced any impression on the art world. It would have enticed art lovers towards renewed impressions and, in particular, it would have delighted refined people with their beauty. But no-one would have thought of *learning* from icons, of considering them as a saving lesson in the general confusion. Now the affair presents itself completely differently and it seems that one would have to be blind not to believe in the salutariness of the icon's artistic effect, in their huge capacity to affect contemporary art and in their unexpected closeness to our times. Not only does any 14th century *Nicholas the Miracle Worker* or *Nativity of the Mother of God* help us understand Matisse, Picasso, Le Fauconnier or Goncharova; but through Matisse, Picasso, Le Fauconnier and Goncharova, we feel the great beauty of these Byzantine pictures much better, the fact that they have youth, power and animation.
>
> ...Two characteristics are common to both arts – one of these is a reluctance to settle with what we call 'realism', resulting in stylisation; the other is a certain sensuous relationship with colour which leads to a search for musicality... On the one hand, stylisation leads away from the objective representation of living phenomena; every worldly sense, everything which is 'reasonable' disappears in these enquiries into pure line and formal fusion. On the other hand, the use of colour lifts the art above the prosaic, away from feelings linked to everyday

experience, towards the world of the fairy tale, into a realm belonging to another world. In the works of the Cubists, just as in icons, the 'advice of good sense' ends, while a mad dream begins – the logic of the irreal – and art returns in full to its mystic meaning.

...In order for these two forceful currents to form one powerful abundant river, even for a short time, it is necessary for artists of our time not only to appreciate the 'new' beauty of the ancient (though strangely familiar) art of icons aesthetically, but also to rise to it with all their soul and become spiritually revived thanks to this contact. The byzantine faith, as it appears to us in these pictures, is not simply an external conformation of art to the Church but the frame in which those former artists were constrained to create, by the very sense of their life, the sincere sustenance of their souls. Only thanks to that belief could their creative work take on the character of a mystical recovery of sight and the sense of conviction which comprises the basic strength of their work.

I am not speaking of a full renaissance of byzantine faith, about which stubborn fanatical antiquarians are dreaming and which is so unthinkable by its very essence that even to say it is 'unwanted' is comic. ... But one should remember that what we admire in icons today is not simply their bright colours, their wonderful graphic sense, their incomparable technique but the depth of the spiritual life depicted in them.

...Superficially, one can copy their manner ... trace the drawing in a firm and assured, quick and accurate hand, borrow their range of colours, capture all the particularities in the looks of the figures – their deportment, stature and movement, in the background and clothing... It is likewise perfectly possible to modify many of their manners and oddities. But for contemporary art to develop for itself an essence like that of icons, a spiritual metamorphosis would be necessary, and not only of individuals but of artistic creation as a whole. Then, perhaps we will be able to leave behind that naive and hopeless imitation into which Vasnetsov and Nesterov have already fallen, to protect ourselves from that vulgar charlatanism and to find the sincere artistic word of our times. Vrubel, that prophetic and mystic nature, was close to that, but he was too alone. The worst thing is that some people call his painting 'untalented daubing' without reproof and that, generally speaking, the leaders of the youth appear not even to be talented comedians but simply rough, tasteless, irritating 'provincial' buffoons.

For the rest, all is not in vain. If one already accepts that the afore-mentioned 'meeting' happened not accidentally, that there is some kind of lawfulness in it, then one must allow that the same sense may appear in what lies ahead. In these situations, to think only of the present day is thoughtless and even sinful. ... The fact that a kind of Babylonian uproar has happened should not be cause for alarm. ... It should soon bore the noise-makers themselves, the most vociferous must get hoarse, and the riotous must tire. ... When the smoke of passion passes, when the youthful desire to play the buffoon cools, when they are all taught and learn reality, then the real artists among today's youth will wish to look into the deep mysterious eyes of life; then they will despise all the so-called scientific theories which now amuse them, and turn to art itself.

Only from this moment could one count on Russian icons ... to become comprehensible and

> salutary in the fullest sense. From that moment artists will remember their real calling. ... Then it will appear that ancient icons are not simply a kind of artistic work of church etiquette, but an original and individual liberated word of life, found and expressed with sincere inspiration. ... It is precisely because of this that the art is so powerful and captivating; it is precisely for this reason that the strength of its effect has not weakened even up until now.[138]

Benois' point here is clearly not about the visual or technical impact of icons on contemporary art. While he certainly recognised the liberating effect that the aesthetic impact icons could have on artists, he also saw how easily the transformation of visual references, whether simple or extreme, could become an end in itself. His point is about engaging with art as a medium for living at the deepest level. Icons served as an example of this kind of relationship to life through art. Benois sensed that the contemporary renewal of interest in icons was leading to an appreciation of their spiritual depth and that this was a sign that a similar capacity for spiritual depth and artistic integrity was developing in contemporary culture. The renewal of interest in icons was both a cause and an effect of this development. On one hand, icons could function as a catalyst for artists and viewers alike, reflecting their own depth to them; on the other hand, their re-evaluation was itself a sign that contemporary culture was becoming sensitised to them and, above all, to the depth from which they arose. Benois considered it to be significant – 'lawful' – that the sacredness of icons was being revealed at this time. It was as if the sacredness that was transmitted to the faith-based world through icons in the Middle Ages had been withdrawn from history in the intervening years, as society turned its attention to more secular concerns, only to be re-revealed in the present time in a manner that was consistent with the forms of contemporary culture.

However, Benois' vision did not extend to Malevich. Although he was able, albeit after a considerable struggle with himself, to appreciate the value of Goncharova, he could not fathom Malevich. He could find a historical logic in Goncharova's work, eventually coming to accept the suffering, which he experienced in seeing her most strident and disjointed paintings, as redemptive.[139] But Malevich's work eluded him, partly because he felt alienated by its anarchic elements and partly because he could not relate to non-objectivity – total non-representation. He also reacted strongly against the hanging of the *Black Square* over a corner of the room, in the manner of an icon when it was first exhibited, at the 0,10 exhibition in St Petersburg in 1915, regarding it as blasphemous (Plate 86). With the benefit of hindsight, it was not so much his perceptions – that the *Black Square* was both self-referential and iconic – that distanced Benois so profoundly from Malevich (for it *is* self-referential and iconic), it was the value judgements he brought to them – that their self-reference was indulgent and arbitrary, and that their iconicity was blasphemous. Malevich of course rejected these interpretations as narrow-minded and conventional. He wrote several texts promoting the historicity of his work, framing its qualities of iconic self-reference as absolute sacred autonomy – a consummation and transcendence of historical time. How he achieved this is the subject of the next chapter.

NOTES

1. Grabar, I., *Repin*, vol.I, Moscow, 1963, pp 136–7, cited in Abel, pp 141–62. Also see Repin, I. & Stasov V., *Perepiska*, vol.I, Moscow, 1948, p.84, cited in the same article, and Valkenier (1989), p.117. See also Jackson (1998), pp 394–409.
2. 'Osnovy khudozhestvennoi ocenki' ('The Foundations of Artistic Evaluation') in *Mir Iskusstva* (*World of Art*), 1899, vol.I, p.5. See Smolik, p.19.
3. Gray, p.48.
4. Goncharova, N., preface to the catalogue to her second one-person exhibition in Moscow, Vystavka Kartin Natalii Sergeievny Goncharovoi 1900–1913 (Exhibition of Pictures of N.S.G. 1900–1913) in 1913. English translation in Bowlt (1988), p.55.
5. Parton, p.42.
6. Preface to the catalogue of her one-person exhibition (1913) in Yablonskaya, pp 63–4.
7. Vrubel in a letter to his sister, Alexandra (Asya), in 1890. Yaremich, S., *Mikhail Alexandrovich Vrubel, Zhizn i tvorchestvo* (*M.A. Vrubel, His Life and Work*), Moscow, 1911, translated by Gray, p.32.
8. 'Zavety vrubelya' ('The Testament of Vrubel') in *Apollon*, 1913, no.5, pp 15, 18, cited in Isdebsky-Pritchard, p.89.
9. Sarabianov & Adaskina, p.14.
10. Letter from Ilya Oustroukhov to Aleksandra Botkina, 25 October 1911, Tretyakov Gallery Archive 48/672, sheet 1–2, translated in Rusakov (1975), p.285. For Matisse in Moscow, see Hilton (1969–70) and Gritz, T. & Kardzhiev, N.
11. From an interview reported in 'U Matiss' ('With Matisse') in *Rannee utro* (*Early Morning*), 26 October 1911. Translated in Rusakov (1975), note 6, p.287.
12. Reported in the Petersburg weekly newspaper, *Protiv techeniya* (*Against the Current*), in October 1911. Translated in Rusakov (1975).
13. 20 March 1910. *Chroniques d'Art 1902–1918*, Gallimard, Paris, 1960, pp 79–80.
14. Apollinaire, G. See also Marcadé, V., p.180.
15. *Alexander Archipenko*, catalogue for an exhibition at the UCLA Art Galleries, with foreword by K. Kuh, 1967, p.18, cited in Isdebsky-Pritchard, p.88.
16. *Prayer* is reproduced in Michaelsen, K.J., *Archipenko: A Study of the Early Works 1908–1920*, Garland Publishing, New York & London, 1977, S1.
17. *Parizhskiy Vestnik* (*The Parisian Messenger*), no.14, 1911. See Marcadé, V., p.180.
18. Boris Anrep (1883–1969) later settled in Britain, where he became known for the mosaics he produced for the Tate Gallery (1923) and the National Gallery (main vestibules) from 1926. The mosaics, which introduced an element of Russian exoticism to the general revival of Byzantine culture in Britain at the beginning of the twentieth century, are Byzantine in their medium, their monumentality and their schematisation of the figure (though not in their overall style). See Bullen, pp 665–75, and Oliver.
19. Shevchenko, A., *Neo-primitivizm. Ego teoriya. Ego vozmozhnosti. Ego dostizheniya* (*Neoprimitivism: Its Theory, Its Potential, Its Achievements*), Moscow, 1913. See Bowlt (1988), p.48. Examples of Stelletsky's work made with paints using medieval recipes survive in the Art Museum in Tula. See Benois (1911).
20. Larionov's 'Predislovie. Vystavka ikonopisnykh podlinnikov i lubkov' ('Introduction to an exhibition of genuine icons and lubki') and a list of exhibits are published (in French) in Gayraud, pp 41, 107. 1913 saw a second exhibition of icons, including examples from the collections of Ilya Ostroukhov and Stepan Riabushinsky at the Institute of Archaeology in Moscow, and an All-Russian Folk Exhibition in St Petersburg.
21. From an unpublished lecture, 'The Origins of Constructivism', given at Cambridge University School of Architecture in May 1966 and later at the Royal College of Art, London; communicated personally to John Allan, who quotes it in Allan, pp 24–5. See also Lodder (1987), n.32, p.269.
22. Larionov, M., 'Les Icones' (*c*.1920) in *Une Avant-Garde Explosive. Textes traduits, réunis, et annotés par Michel Hoog et Solina de Vigneral*, Lausanne, 1978, pp 132–3, quoted in Parton, p.89.
23. Larionov, p.132.
24. Ibid pp 132–3.
25. See Valkenier (1986), p.55. Excerpts of contemporary reports are given in 'Russkaia khudozhestvennaia letopis', *Apollon*, no.2 (1913), p.61, and Voloshin, M., *O Repine*, Knigoizdatel'stvo Ole-Lukoe, Moscow, 1913.
26. Larionov, M. & Goncharova, N., *Luchisty i budushchniki. Manifest* (*Rayonists and Futurists: A Manifesto*), Moscow, 1913, translated in Bowlt (1988), p.89.
27. Parton, pp 137, 232, notes 30, 31.
28. From an added final chapter in the second edition of *The Fourth Dimension* (1914). Cited in Henderson (1975–6), p.103.
29. Larionov, *Rayonist Painting*, in Bowlt (1988), p.98.
30. *Gregory Palamas*, p.72.
31. Florensky (1922), p.69.
32. Illustrated, respectively, in Milner (2007). p.62, and Parton, plate 15.
33. Florensky (1922), p.126.
34. For biographical details see Misler, pp 13–28.
35. Ibid p.19.
36. Parton, p.137ff.
37. Florensky (1996), p.127.
38. Ibid p.128.
39. Ibid p.118.
40. Ibid pp 119–20.
41. From Malevich, 'Avtobiographicheski zametki 1923–1925' ('Autobiographical Notes 1923–1925') in *Kazimir Malevich* (1988), p.102.
42. Turowski, p.71.
43. In a personal conversation with Professor Horbachev in Kiev.
44. Malevich, K., *Glav iz avtobiographii khudozhnika* (*Chapters from an Artist's Autobiography*), 1933, partly translated into French in Marcadé, J.-C. (1978), pp 157–9.
45. From Malevich, *Glav iz avtobiographii khudozhnika* (*Chapters from an Artist's Autobiography*), translated in *Kazimir Malevich* (1988), p.110.
46. Ibid p.111.
47. Ibid.
48. Nakov (2002), cat.nos F–202 (pencil drawing) and F–203 (gouache), p.100. Of the pencil drawing, Nakov writes: '*Le peintre a donné ses propres traits au personnage central*'.
49. Birnholz (Jan 1977), p.10.
50. Lunacharsky, A., 'Russian Artists in Berlin' from *Ogonek* (*Little Flame*), 1927, in Zhadova (1982), p.327.
51. Inverted perspective is directly associated with Byzantine art in Shlovsky.
52. Misler (2002), p.223.
53. See Florensky (1983).
54. Zhadova (1988), p.16.
55. Recorded in a personal memoir by D. Danin in *Uletavl, Druzhba narodov* (*Flown Away, Friendship of the People*), no.2, 1979, pp 220–36, cited in Lodder (1987), p.11, n.29; see also Zhadova (1988), p.16.
56. Zhadova (1988), p.53.
57. Ibid pp 56, 63–6.
58. V. Khodasevich quoting Tatlin, cited in Zhadova (1988), p.56.
59. Zhegin, L., 'Remembering Vasilii Chekrygin' in Petrova (2002), p.196 and n.848.
60. 'Khramovoe deistvo kak sintez iskusstv' referenced in Bartlett (1998).
61. From an unpublished manuscript, 'From Materials for a Speech on Style', 1921, translated in Sarabianov & Adaskina, p.357.
62. Malevich includes this painting in his chart, *Protsess tvorcheskoi pererabotki tsvetovikh stimulov khudozhnikom* (*The Assimilation of the Colour Stimuli in the Creative Process of the Artist*), reproduced in *Kazimir Malevich* (1988), no.10, p.216.
63. From Malevich, K., *Glav iz avtobiographii khudozhnika* (*Chapters from an Artist's Autobiography*), translated in Marcadé, J.-C. (1978), p.168. Parts of the Russian text in English translation can also be found

in *Kazimir Malevich* (1988), p.109.
64. Blank, pp 67–80.
65. Ibid p.70.
66. Andersen (1976), vol.III, p.10.
67. Shevchenko, A., *Neo-primitivizm. Ego teoriya. Ego vozmozhnosti. Ego dostizheniya* (*Neoprimitivism: Its Theory, Its Potential, Its Achievements*), Moscow, 1913. See Bowlt (1988), p.51.
68. *O sviaziakh russkoi zhivopisi s Vizantiei i Zapadom* (*On the Links of Russian Painting with Byzantium and the West*), Moscow, 1913, and *Russkaia ikona kak iskusstvo zhivopisi* (*The Russian Icon as the Art of Painting*), Moscow, 1917. The quality and condition of the icons illustrated here, and their tentative attribution to Andrei Rublev, reflect a naivety in the aesthetic appreciation of, and academic knowledge about, icons at this date.
69. Matsa, I.L., *Sovetskoe iskusstvo za 15 let* (*Soviet Art of the Last 15 Years*), Moscow & Leningrad, 1933, quoted in Bowlt (1988), p.43.
70. Shevchenko, A., *Neo-primitivizm. Ego teoriya. Ego vozmozhnosti. Ego dostizheniya* (*Neoprimitivism: Its Theory, Its Potential, Its Achievements*), Moscow, 1913. See Bowlt (1988), p.48.
71. Ibid p.44.
72. Ibid p.258.
73. Punin, N. (1921) in Zhadova (1988), p.390.
74. Malevich's teaching diagrams are reproduced in *Kazimir Malevich* (1988) and in *Malevich* (1989).
75. Noemi Smolik suggests that Malevich may have been confirmed in his selection of colours for Suprematism by Andrei Bely's description in *Mir Iskusstva* of the seven colours used in icon painting. *Malewitsch* (1995), p.22.
76. Translated in Sarabianov & Adaskina, p.357. Also Yablonskaya, p.221.
77. Diagram 14 in *Malevich* (1989), p.41.
78. Sarabianov, D., 'Kazimir Malevich and His Art, 1900–1930' in *Kazimir Malevich* (1988), p.71.
79. Khan-Magomedov (1990), vol.2, p.823.
80. Ibid pp 813, 846–7.
81. Ibid p.828.
82. Ibid p.822. Caption: 'Examples of mineral colours used by Dionysius in his frescos at Ferapontov Monastery in 1502. They were found in Bodaevskoye Lake by students from the Department of Monumental Art at Vkutemas, Linno, Andreyev and Professor Chernychev in 1925'.
83. *Nathalie Gontcharova/Michel Larionov*, cat.59.
84. Compton (1976), p.581. Cf also Bojko, pp 14–15.
85. Comrie & Stone, p.212.
86. For Bely's notion of 'value', see Cassedy, S., 'Bely's Theory of Symbolism as a Formal Iconics of Meaning' in Malmstad, pp 296–312.
87. Hughes & Paperno, p.290; Evtuhov, p.210.
88. 'If Phidias is to be condemned for carving his image, you must condemn Homer too'. Bevan, p.73.
89. Douglas (1986), p.187.
90. Sarabianov, D., 'Tatlin's Painting' in Zhadova (1988), p.56.
91. Dabrowski (1991), p.11.
92. Sarabianov & Adaskina, p.14.
93. Gurianova, p.19.
94. Smolik, pp 27–8.
95. Rudenstine (1981), p.440.
96. Recorded by Stepanova in a diary entry for 27 Mar 1919, Rodchenko and Stepanova Archive, Moscow; translated in Dzhafarova, S., 'The Creation of the Museum of Painterly Culture' in *The Great Utopia*, pp 478–9.
97. In the Rodchenko and Stepanova Archive, Moscow. Reproduced in Dabrowski, Dickerman & Galassi, plate 1, p.145.
98. The *Composition* was in the collection of Alexander Archipenko, a relative of the sculptor, in the late 1970s.
99. Rodchenko in *Vse-opyty*, 1921, from the Rodchenko and Stepanova Archive, Moscow, published in Noever, P. (ed.), pp 130–2.
100. Cited in Howard, p.123.
101. See Rodchenko's 'Organizational programme of the workshop for the study of painting in State Art Colleges' (1920) from *Khudozhestvenno – konstructorskoe obrazovanie*, no.4, Vniite, Moscow, 1973, in Khan-Magomedov (1986, *Rodchenko*), p.291.
102. 'New Paths in Architecture' in Cooke & Ageros, p.29.
103. Ibid p.28.
104. Tarabukin, p.166. My thanks to Ariadne Arendt for translating this passage.
105. Rodchenko, A., *Liniia* (*The Line*), INKhUK Archive, Moscow, 1921, translated in Khan-Magomedov (1986, *Rodchenko*), p.294.
106. Bajkay (2005), pp 157–65.
107. Reproduced in Passuth, p.111. See also Bajkay (1987), cat.429, plate 40, and Mansbach, cat.165, reproduced on p.224.
108. Brumfield (1993), pp 396–7.
109. Khan-Magomedov (1986, *Rodchenko*), pp 75, 287.
110. Unsourced notes at the Museum of Modern Art in Edinburgh indicate that George Grosz had reason to claim that Uitz's choice of the subject must have been influenced by a play on the same subject – *Die Maschinen-Sturmer (The Machine-Wreckers)* – written by a former political prisoner Ernst Toller in 1922. Uitz, however, always denied that there was a connection. In 1924, Uitz set out to paint a series of murals on the subject in Britain but hearing of the defeat of the Labour Party, decided to go to Paris, where he stayed until 1926.
111. For instance, Hodler's *Battle at Marignano* and *The Rising of the Students at Jena*, from *c.*1899, in the National Museum in Zurich. Eva Bajkay suggests that the *Ludd* series may also have been influenced by frescos by Karl Volker for the Verlagsgebaude of the *Klassenkampf Zeitung* in Halle, 1921, now destroyed.
112. Unpublished translation by Eva Bajkay for the Scottish National Gallery of Modern Art, Edinburgh.
113. Henderson (1975–6), pp 97–108. Also Henderson (1983), p.238ff.
114. Markov, V., translated in Lodder (1987), p.13.
115. Lubetkin, B., 'The Origins of Constructivism', lecture given to Cambridge University School of Architecture, 1 May 1969, cited in Lodder (1987), p.12.
116. Ibid.
117. Punin, N., 'Obzor techenii v iskusstve Peterburga' ('A Survey of Artistic Trends in St Petersburg') in *Russkoe iskusstvo*, no.1, 1923, p.18, quoted in Lodder (1987), p.11.
118. Cubism catalysed several Russian artists towards an awareness of the abstraction within their own tradition. Exposure to Cubist sculpture in Paris may have induced the sculptor Vera Mukhina, who studied in Paris in 1912–14, to introduce explicitly iconic elements into her work. In her *Pieta* of 1916, now destroyed but known from a photograph, the regular stacked folds in the garment of the mournful subject of the work almost exactly duplicate the stiffly triangulated drapery of the central angel in Rublev's *Old Testament Trinity*. In Paris, Mukhina met Popova, who is known to have drawn her attention to icons.
119. *Gabo*, p.156.
120. Lodder & Hammer (2000, *Gabo on Gabo*), p.168.
121. Lodder & Hammer (2000, *Constructing Modernity*), p.3.
122. *Gabo*, p.165.
123. Gabo (1942), p.49.
124. Ibid p.51.
125. Ibid.
126. From an interview with Rosamond Bernier, 'Propos d'un sculpteur', in *L'Oeil*, 1956, no.23, cited in Massat G. p.189.
127. Ibid.
128. Gabo (1942), p.53.
129. Ibid.
130. Ibid p.51.
131. Gabo, N., & Pevsner, A., *Realisticheskii manifest* (*The Realistic Manifesto*), Moscow, 1920, in Bowlt (1988), p.212.
132. Benois, A., *Istoriya russkoi zhivopisi v XIX veke* (*The History of Russian Painting in the 19th Century*), St Petersburg, 1902, translated in Bowlt (1988), p.5.
133. Misler, p.101.
134. Ouspensky (1992), vol. 2, p.336.
135. Tarabukin, p.105.
136. Ibid p.118.
137. Benois, A, 'Dnevnik Khudozhnika' in *Rec'*, 21 October 1913, p.4, quoted in Sharp, J., 'The Critical Reception of the 0,10 Exhibition: Malevich and Benua' in *The Great Utopia*, p.42.
138. Benois (1913). My thanks to Rosanna Kelly for this translation.
139. Sharp, J., 'The Critical Reception of the 0,10 Exhibition: Malevich and Benua', in *The Great Utopia*, p.42.

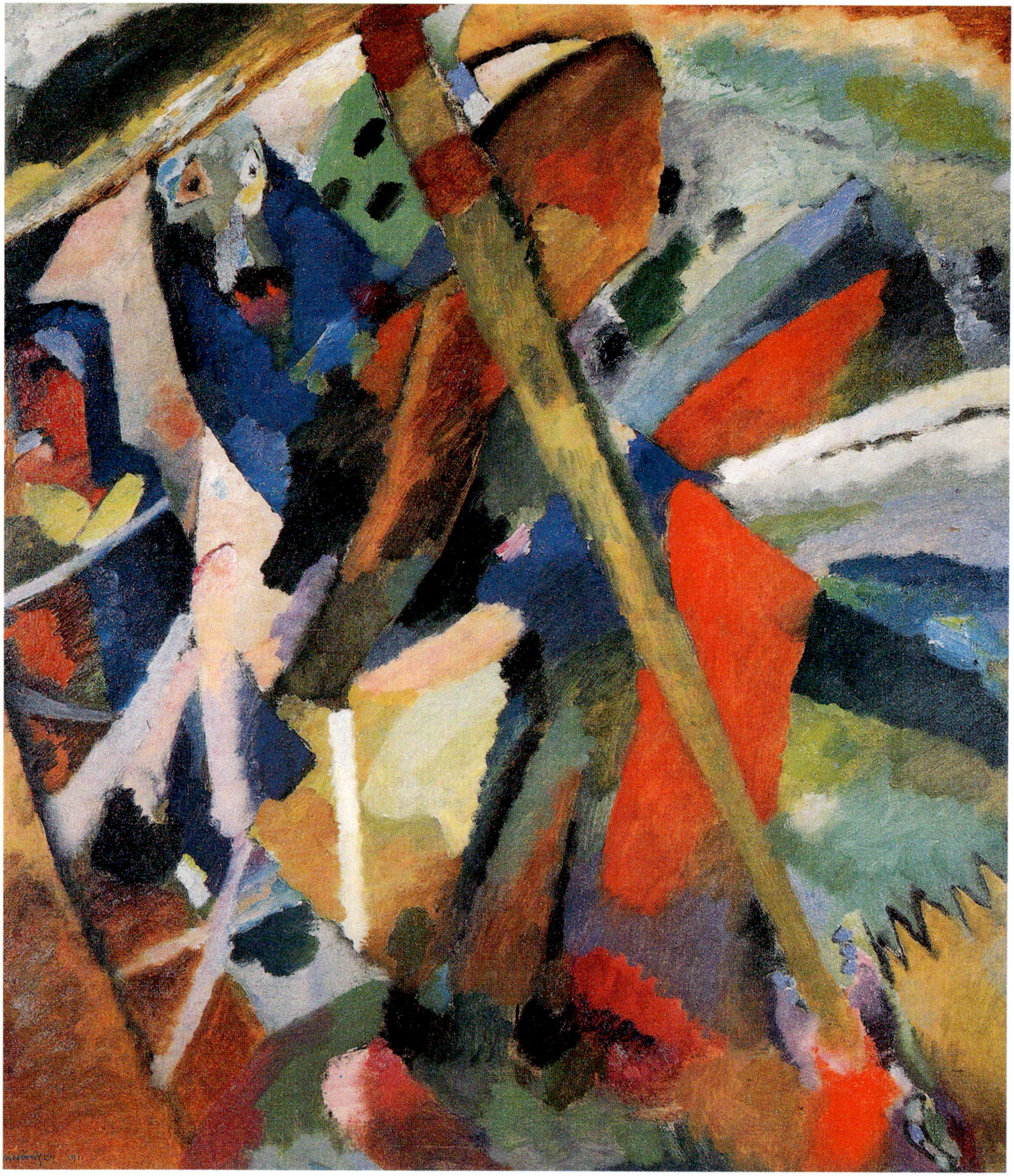

4

Imagery, Iconography and Self-Transcendence

If there was one aspect of Russian icons that the avant-garde movement wholeheartedly rejected, it was the attitude of religious belief that underpinned them. The avant-garde movement prided itself on being scientific and objective, and it eschewed the emotionally manipulative potential of illusionism and all tendencies towards arbitrary subjectivity. The Christian Church was an obvious target for criticism, firstly because it claimed to monopolise access to the truth in an autocratic and unscientific way and, secondly, because – at least prior to the Revolution – the central state transformed the emotional advantage derived from this monopoly into political power.

Since the one characteristic of icons that is exclusively Christian is their iconography (in the tautological sense that it is impossible to use Christian iconography without making reference to Christianity), it is scarcely surprising that the one aspect of icons that rarely surfaces in avant-garde art is their iconography. In the comparatively few instances in Russian modernist painting where there are explicit iconographical references to icons, the images in question are mostly isolated from their original Christian settings and their use, therefore, is not iconic in the fullest sense of the word.[1]

The most prominent artists to have absorbed elements of Christian iconography into their own artistic languages are Wassily Kandinsky and – despite being Jewish – Marc Chagall. Significantly, both artists developed highly personal styles, eventually emigrating to the West in the 1920s where their manifest subjectivity and spirituality were more acceptable than they were in Russia. The visionary and idiosyncratic dimension of their work was evident long before the Revolution stigmatised these qualities and it is reflected in their response to the poetics of Christian iconography, regardless of its Christian significance.

As Chagall was Jewish, it was clearly not the Christianity of iconography that appealed to him. However, his early encounter with the visionary iconography of icons (as well as their naive but expressive graphic styles) awakened him to the potential of art to go beyond the merely descriptive, and to create and enter into a sacred and weightless world. For instance, the x-ray vision of his *Pregnant Woman* (1913), in which the unborn child can be seen in the womb of the mother, may be indebted to icons of the Virgin of the Sign in which the Christ child is represented in a medallion over the Virgin's breast. Though the poetics of visionary insight may

73
Wassily Kandinsky

St George, 1911
Oil on canvas
107 x 95 cm (42⅛ x 37⅜ in)
Russian Museum,
St Petersburg

have been appropriated from the icon, there is nothing to suggest that its doctrinal or even Christian associations have been adopted too.

The same can be said of *The Flying Carriage* (also 1913), in which a rider and carriage rise up away from a (burning?) wooden house into a flaming red and orange sky, leaving a man carrying a bucket and a woman with upraised arms behind them (Plate 74). This evocative and inscrutable image is clearly based on an icon, *The Fiery Ascent of the Prophet Elijah*, an Old Testament scene that was incorporated into the Orthodox canon of iconography partly to enable pagan venerators of Perun, a pre-Christian god of thunder and lightning, to identify with Christianity (Plate 75). The figure of Elisha, shown receiving the falling mantle of Elijah as a sign of his legitimate succession as prophet, clearly inspired Chagall's bucket-carrier who gestures towards the carriage from behind it. When asked in 1974 about a possible connection between the two images, Chagall is said to have responded 'most positively'.[2] Even so, despite the Old Testament origins of the scene, which presumably made the icon more meaningful to the artist, there is no religious agenda in the work. Its inheritance from the icon is purely poetic license, and it probably relates more to Chagall's knowledge that his home town, Vitebsk, was burning at the time of his birth than to any religious concept.

By helping him to form his own attitude towards art, icons also made Chagall aware of the extent to which the tradition of visionary art had died in Russia. While he clearly felt that to return to icon painting would be anachronistic, he also felt a deep sympathy for the role that icons once played in Russian cultural life. After seeing the icons at the Alexander III Museum in St Petersburg (now the Russian Museum) in 1910, he wrote:

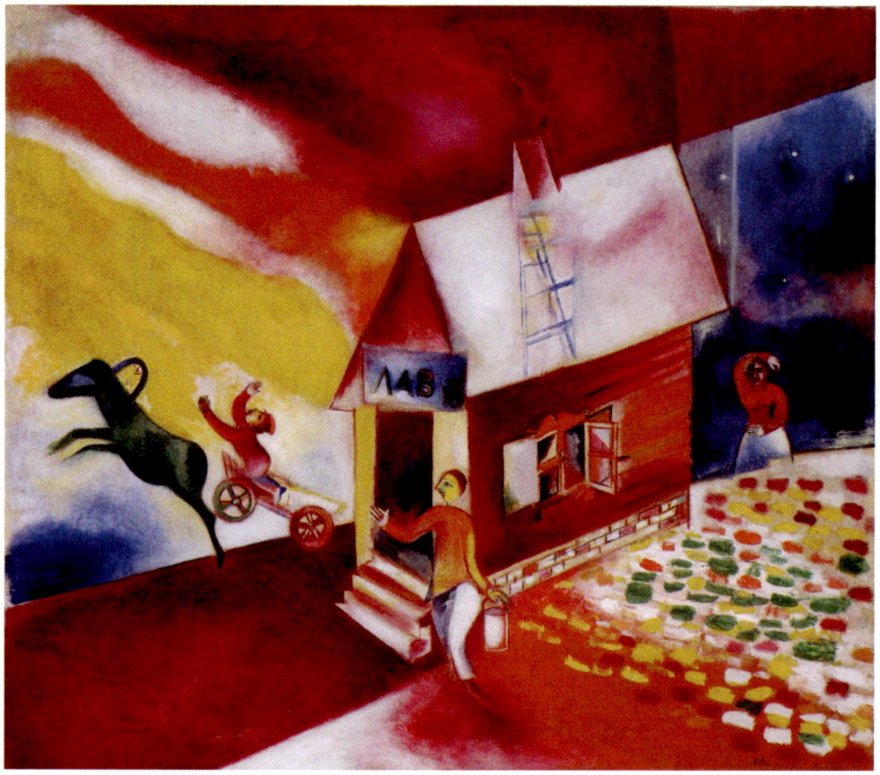

74
Marc Chagall
The Flying Carriage (La Calèche Volante), 1913
Oil on canvas
106.7 x 120.1 cm (42 x 47¼ in)
Solomon R. Guggenheim Museum, New York
Photograph by David Heald, ©The Solomon R. Guggenheim Foundation, New York 49.1212
©ADAGP, Paris and DACS, London 2007

> My heart was rested by the icons. I remember the shock I felt when I saw the icons of Rublev, our Cimabue, in the shadows, with the surface of an encaustic image, as at Pompeii or Fayoum, and a true linear purity. With him, I was born to the mystical and religious, but after him I no longer knew what to look at and he was not what I was looking for. I wondered: Why is there no Russian art? Why has Russia had no substantial art since the art of icons?[3]

Despite borrowing liberally from icons throughout his life, Chagall did not use iconic motifs in order to develop an iconic dimension in his own work. On the contrary, his debt to icons was as a source – one among many – of pictorial and poetic ideas, regardless of the significance that those ideas may have had in their original iconic contexts. In strict contrast to the Orthodox attitude towards iconography, Chagall's images are dreamy and undidactic, frequently indifferent to any attempt to convey specific meanings. It is not inconsistent therefore that, regarding his *Golgotha* of 1912, he later claimed to have deviated from the conventional iconography by painting the crucified Christ as a child, specifically in order to 'get away from the tradition of Russian ikons'.[4]

Like Chagall, Wassily Kandinsky was attracted to a non-Christian dimension of icons. However, whereas Chagall moved in a continuous indeterminate world of reverie – to which his paintings give momentary and fragmentary access – Kandinsky was more interested in the particularity of individual images along with the psycho-physical effects of sensation.

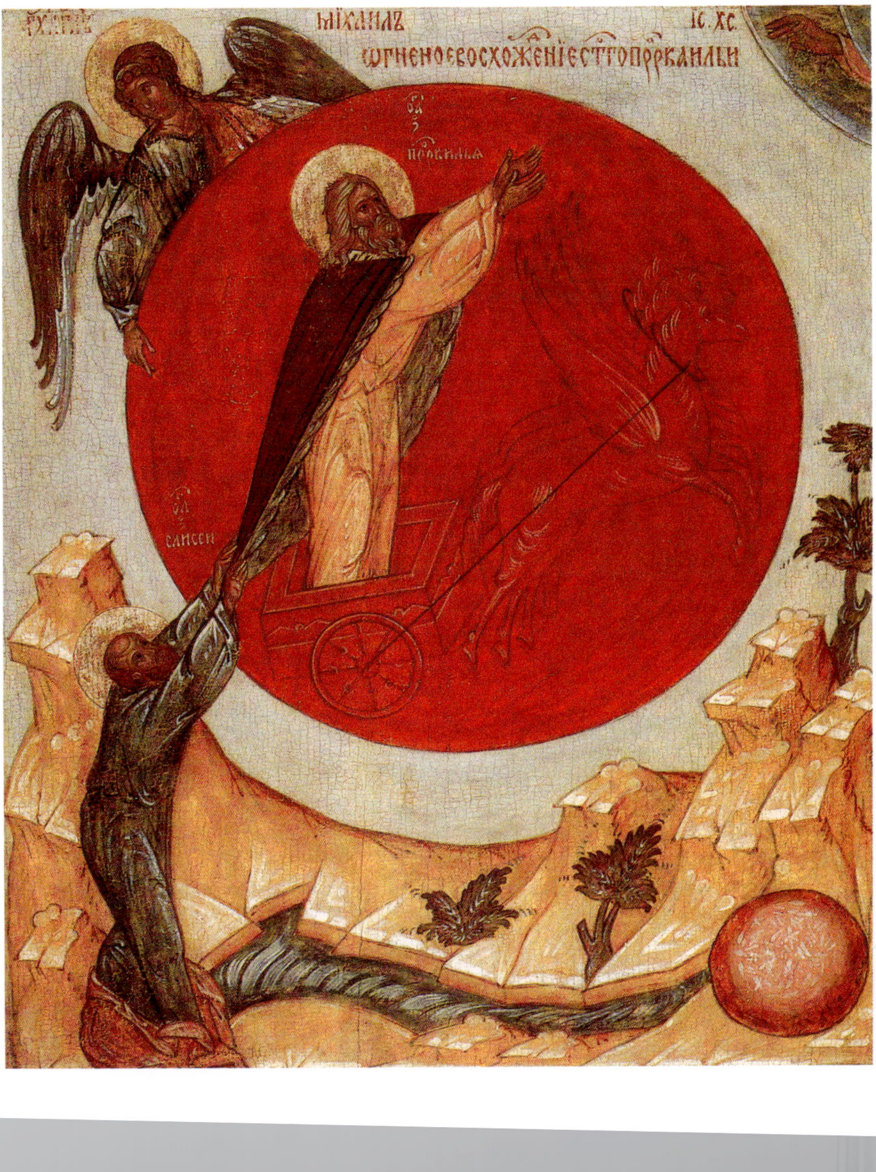

75

The Fiery Ascent of the Prophet Elijah, Novgorod, 15th century
Tempera on wooden panel
55 x 46 cm (21 $\frac{7}{10}$ x 18 $\frac{1}{10}$ in)
Temple Gallery, London

According to his friends, Kandinsky was a practising member of the Russian Orthodox Church and certainly the array of Christian images that can be seen in the background of photographs of his home in Murnau – two small brass icons, a Crucifixion and a small, dimly visible metal-clad icon of the Mother of God with Christ – suggest more than a purely artistic interest.[5] However, although the iconography of icons is obviously Christian, Kandinsky tended to read some Orthodox imagery as superficially Christianised representations of a far deeper psychic and preconceptual dynamic that was rooted in the shamanistic cultures of northern Russia and Siberia. Indeed he is known to have resented the way in which the Church had attempted to disempower and control these cultures by converting them to Christianity. Nevertheless, despite the quasi-political implications of some icons (for instance, *The Fiery Ascent of the Prophet Elijah*, mentioned above), Kandinsky was interested in icons to the extent that they were absorbed into the lives of ethnic cultures. As early as 1889, when he was still a full-time student of ethnography and law, he recorded some aspects of their use on a research expedition to the northern province of Vologda in 1889. Thirty years later, the impressions made by this early experience of a peasant household were still vivid in his imagination: 'I remember so well how I stopped on the threshold struck by an unexpected scene... The "sacred corner" was covered with painted and printed icons, in front of which was a red icon lamp gleaming like a modest and proud star, aware of something special and living its own life, whispering quietly and mysteriously'.[6]

However, it was not until he had seen the work of the French Impressionists that Kandinsky was able to appreciate the compositional interest of icons. Following an exhibition of Impressionism that he saw in Moscow in 1895, he wrote: 'From that moment on, I looked at the art of icons with different eyes; I had acquired an eye for the abstract in art'.[7] His new 'acquisition' was reflected over 15 years later in a series of works entitled *St George*, painted by the artist while he was living in Russia in 1911.

Icons of St George and the Dragon are fundamental to Orthodox iconography (Plate 53) and Kandinsky is known to have had an icon of the subject in his own collection (plate 76).[8] Although it was the ambiguous shamanistic and folkloric implications that originally attracted him to the saint (traditionally associated with the mythical figure of the Sun-god/World-Watching-Man), it was the appearance of the saint as depicted in icons – in mounted combat – that most informed the aesthetic dimension of his art. Such icons often exemplified the state of dynamic equilibrium – between dark and light, positive and negative, active and passive, masculine and feminine – that the artist was seeking in his own work. In almost all examples of the icon, the force of good is represented in the top-right corner of the panel by the hand of God, which appears from within a section of a circle symbolising the heavens (the section of town buildings on the right in Plate 53 is a rare additional detail; the fact that it is considered to be 'extra' is reflected in the unresolved re-location of the quadrant). At the opposite pole, in the bottom left-hand corner of the icon, the realm of evil is represented in the form of a dark cave. The force of good is conducted down, through the spear of St George, into the dragon, whose emergence from the cave corresponds archetypally to the emergence of basest passions from the depths of the subconscious mind. Cutting across the downward diagonal thrust of the spear, the saint's horse leaps diagonally upwards. In many cases, the horse turns its head back towards the centre of the image, thus further elaborating the dynamics of the composition. The curvaceous silhouette of the rearing horse is reflected in the sinuous form of the dragon which typically lies supine beneath it. In the current example, the powerful movement of the horse is also counteracted by the tapering flourish of the saint's cloak which unfolds above it, along a parallel axis but in the opposite direction. Above all, the design succeeded in combining a powerful system of internal dynamics with an equally powerful coherence and unity of overall impact. It generated a sense of polarisation between opposites while at the same time maintaining a consistent and continuous circuit of energy that also enabled the image to function on a higher plane as a single organic structure.

Although Kandinsky's images of St George and the Dragon eventually border on total abstraction, it is the prerogatives of the iconic narrative – man, horse, spear, dragon – that underpin their composition. In one example (Plate 73), in which the image of the saint and the dragon fill the entire canvas, the component parts of the narrative are still decipherable (a blue horse, lozenge-shaped shield, tapering spear, bright red cloak, dragon's serrated wing and blood red wound), but it is the coherent interaction of dynamic thrusts, to which Kandinsky found this particular nexus of relationships so conducive, that creates the overall impact of the image. In this respect, the image is comparable to the *Iconanalysis I* of Bela Uitz (Plate 52), also abstracted from an icon of St George and the Dragon, though it stands in contrast with Uitz's later 'Ludd' etchings in which the geometrical concept of the composition was established

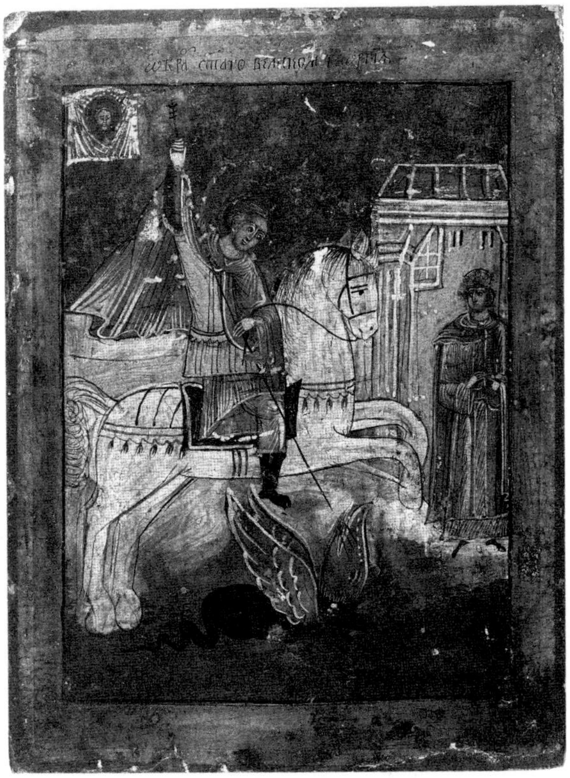

76.
Icon of St George and the Dragon,
late 19th century
Medium and dimensions unknown
Formerly in Kandinsky's personal collection
Musée National d'Art Moderne, Centre Georges Pompidou, Paris

before the narrative, rather than the other way round.

Natalia Goncharova (1881–1962) was rare among her contemporaries in that she produced avant-garde paintings with Christian references throughout her career. Despite the outspoken nationalism of her most avant-garde primitivist years, during which she dissociated from artists whom she considered to be over-westernised, she eventually moved to the West herself. She initially left Russia in 1915 because Diaghilev invited her to design sets and costumes for the Ballets Russes. She settled in Paris in 1919, became a French citizen in 1938 and died there in 1962. The sources that influenced her were many, including peasant, Scythian, oriental and Spanish art, but were always subject to an impression of decoration, immediacy and exuberance in her work. Many of her early paintings, especially until she settled in Paris, were influenced by icons, adapting their characteristics to the artist's own ends; other examples actually copied icons. It is significant that the most important of these works were painted in 1909–11 when the comfortable Fauvist element in her style, based on observation, was being gradually transformed into a more edgy and angular primitivism, with an increasing quota of mythical iconography. This transformation was greatly facilitated by the inclusion of works of art – especially non-western works such as Japanese prints, Taoist figurines and Scythian *stelae* – in her still-lives. This practice not only reflects her avowed intention to identify with the non-European sources of the Russian tradition (including that of icons which the foreword to the catalogue of her 1913 exhibition ascribes to 'Arab and Indian images')[9] but it also enabled her, even within the conventions of naturalism, to introduce oriental styles into her own work. The Cubistic tone of the background in *Pillars of Salt* (1910), for instance, is set up by the figurines, based on early Slavic idols, many of which are in reality as faceted and angular as they look in the painting.[10]

The movement away from naturalism towards greater stylisation enabled Goncharova to introduce a more mythical element into her work. This is clearly reflected during this period in her use of Christian iconography. Best known among her Christian works is the series of four paintings of *The Four Evangelists* (1910–11), exhibited at The Donkey's Tail exhibition in 1912 (Plate 23). These works were clearly based on the icons of standing saints that are traditionally assembled in rows at either side of the main icon of Christ at the centre of an iconostasis (Plates 3, 90, 122) – the screen of icons that separates the sanctuary from the congregational area of an Orthodox church. The proportions of the panels, the tilted heads and sorrow-laden stoops of the figures, their large feet and expressive hand gestures are all typical of such icons. Goncharova did, however, adapt her iconic sources to her own ends. Standing saints in icons, for instance, are usually represented without

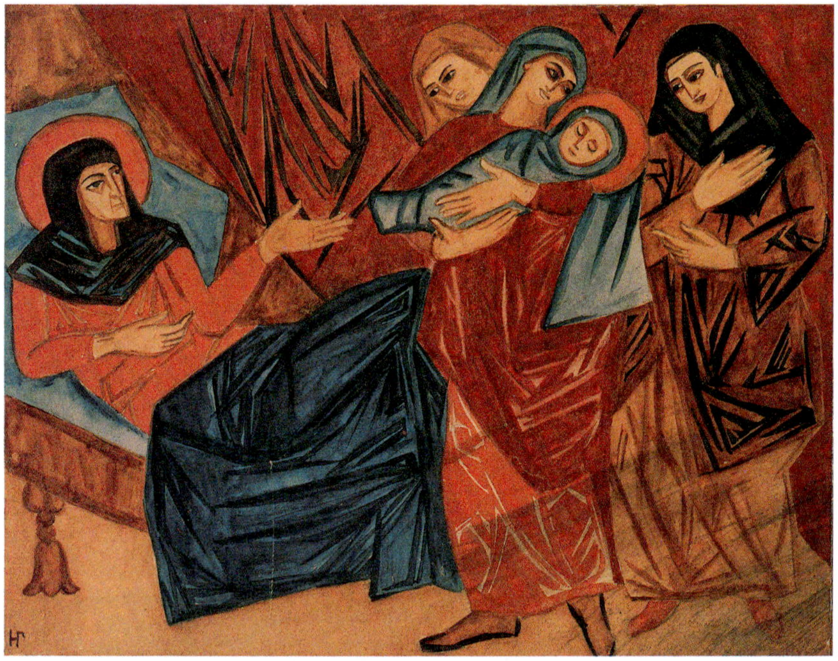

77
Natalia Goncharova

Nativity, 1910
Watercolour on paper
23.9 x 29.8 cm (9⅜ x 11¾ in)
Private collection

unfurling scrolls (Plate 122); scrolls are held by prophets, usually shown half-length. Furthermore, the evangelists are never represented in icons as standing saints – they usually appear, writing their gospels, on the Royal Doors of an iconostasis.

Similar comments could be made about several other works with Christian subject matter that Goncharova produced at the same time. Her *Nativity* (1910, Plate 77), for instance, is clearly related to icons of the Nativity of the Mother of God (Plate 29) in which the Virgin's mother, St Anne, reclines on a tilted and diagonally receding couch where she is greeted by three maid-servants. As in iconic representations of St Anne, Goncharova's Mother of God wears a vermilion gown with a deep blue overmantle. Besides its typically iconic range of earthy colours, three-quarters of the painting is taken up with the characteristically flattened and angular forms of iconic drapery folds.

This 'primitivist' appropriation of the monumental simplicity of icons appeared in the work of a number of artists at this time, amounting to something of a 'genre'. It became the characteristic type of figuration in the early work of Pavel Filonov, albeit fragmented like shattered glass, as well as that of Maria Siniakova. Both artists placed miniature figures and scenes in the perimeters of their work in imitation of icons of saints, in which scenes from the life of the saint are placed in a demarcated border around the central figure (Plate 70).[11] In contrast to the iconic simplicity of Malevich's neo-primitivist work, in which simplicity is used for expressive impact, the monumental figures in the work of these artists make a conscious reference to the Christian piety and peasant naivety of icons. A rather more refined response to the simple poetry of iconic figuration is present in the work of the painter, Kuzma Petrov-Vodkin (1878–1937), who was inspired by the entire tradition of Christian art in Russia, absorbing influences both from its source in Russian icons and frescos and from its regeneration at the hands of Vasnetsov, Nesterov and Vrubel. Petrov-Vodkin also painted icons and became involved in church decoration projects on a number of occasions.[12] He freely acknowledged the iconic inspiration behind many of his practical artistic solutions – his luminous but deliberately limited palette, the translucence of his paint surfaces, the static monumentality of his figures, his inconsistent viewpoints – and in 1920 he gave lectures on 'the Artistic Significance of Icons' in Novgorod.[13] By means of an erratic and intoxicated sense of perspective, he aimed to induce a feeling for the rotundity of the whole earth, an experience that was powerfully sensory but which also served as a living metaphor for visionary and iconic insight into the deepest nature of things. In his *Mother* of 1915, in which a mother and child (clearly referencing a Hodigitria icon, for example Plate 4) are depicted directly in front of an empty icon case, traditionally mounted across a corner, the iconisation of his figures is made explicit (Plate 78).

The most direct and comprehensive attempt to translate the iconographic world of icons into

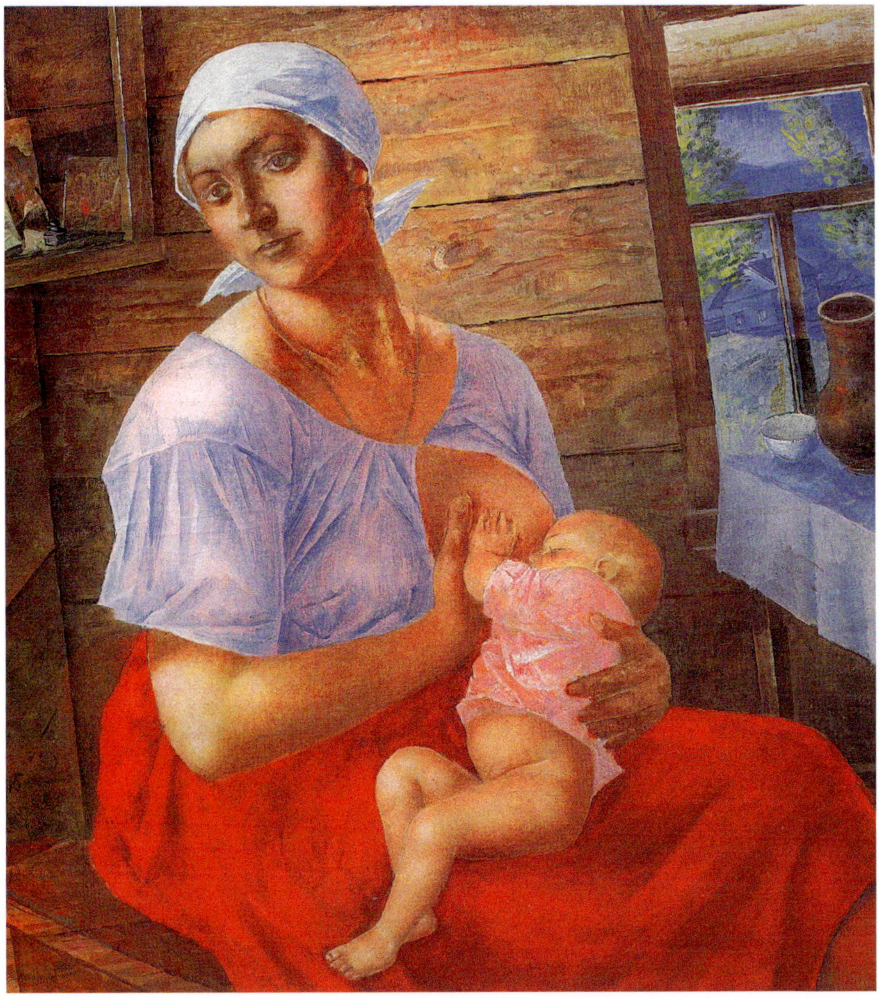

78
Kuzma Petrov-Vodkin

Mother, 1915
Oil on canvas
107 x 98.5 cm (42 1/8 x 38 3/4 in)
Russian Museum,
St Petersburg

avant-garde art was Diaghilev's plan in 1914 to stage a Byzantinesque ballet, *Liturgie*, inspired by Byzantine mosaics and Cimabue, and based on the Orthodox Mass. The project was intended to present the Orthodox liturgy as a total aesthetic work of art, co-ordinating sound, sight and movement. It may have been stimulated by, or in reaction to, a very different kind of project – a 'mystery play' called *The King of the Jews*, written in 1913 by Grand Duke Konstantin, the uncle of the tsar, and first performed in January 1914 to incidental music commissioned from Alexander Glazunov, director of the St Petersburg Conservatory.[14] As the representation of biblical figures on stage was prohibited by the Church, this royal drama was performed in private to invited audiences in the Winter Palace, though it was also covered by the press. Even the imperial family, however, was not exempt from religious censorship and, consequently the figure of Christ was never to be seen on stage (though Glazunov did give him a theme tune, from which the whole score was said to have evolved) – he was only to be seen by the other actors. Diaghilev's project suffered from some of the same resistance and was never realised.

With the benefit of hindsight, *Liturgie* resonated with Florensky's vision of the Orthodox liturgy as a synthesis of the arts although, in Florensky's case, the synthesis was conceived to result in a spiritual rather than an aesthetic experience. Diaghilev developed the plan when he was travelling around Italy with his new protégé, Leonide Massine, who he entrusted with the choreography of the piece. According to the novelist and poet Ivan Bunin, Dmitri Stelletsky was Diaghilev's first choice as costume designer but Stelletsky turned the offer down, considering it inappropriate – in keeping with the church censors – to treat the sacred liturgy as theatre.[15] The commission was then given to Goncharova who left Russia in order to undertake it. Larionov worked with her on the stage sets. Goncharova had already been working for Diaghilev (on *Le Coq d'Or* in 1914, based on folk themes) and had considerable experience of working with Orthodox imagery. Stravinsky was to produce a score, for unaccompanied voices, with the help of Mestrovic, a scholar in liturgical music. The project was never realised, partly due to lack of funds but partly due to problems involving the music. Firstly, like Stelletsky, Stravinsky refused to write a score on the grounds that it was inappropriate to present the Orthodox liturgy as 'art'.[16] Efforts to develop a rhythm from the sounds of the dancers' footsteps on the floorboards and to adapt ancient chants from Kiev also failed. In 1915, Massine

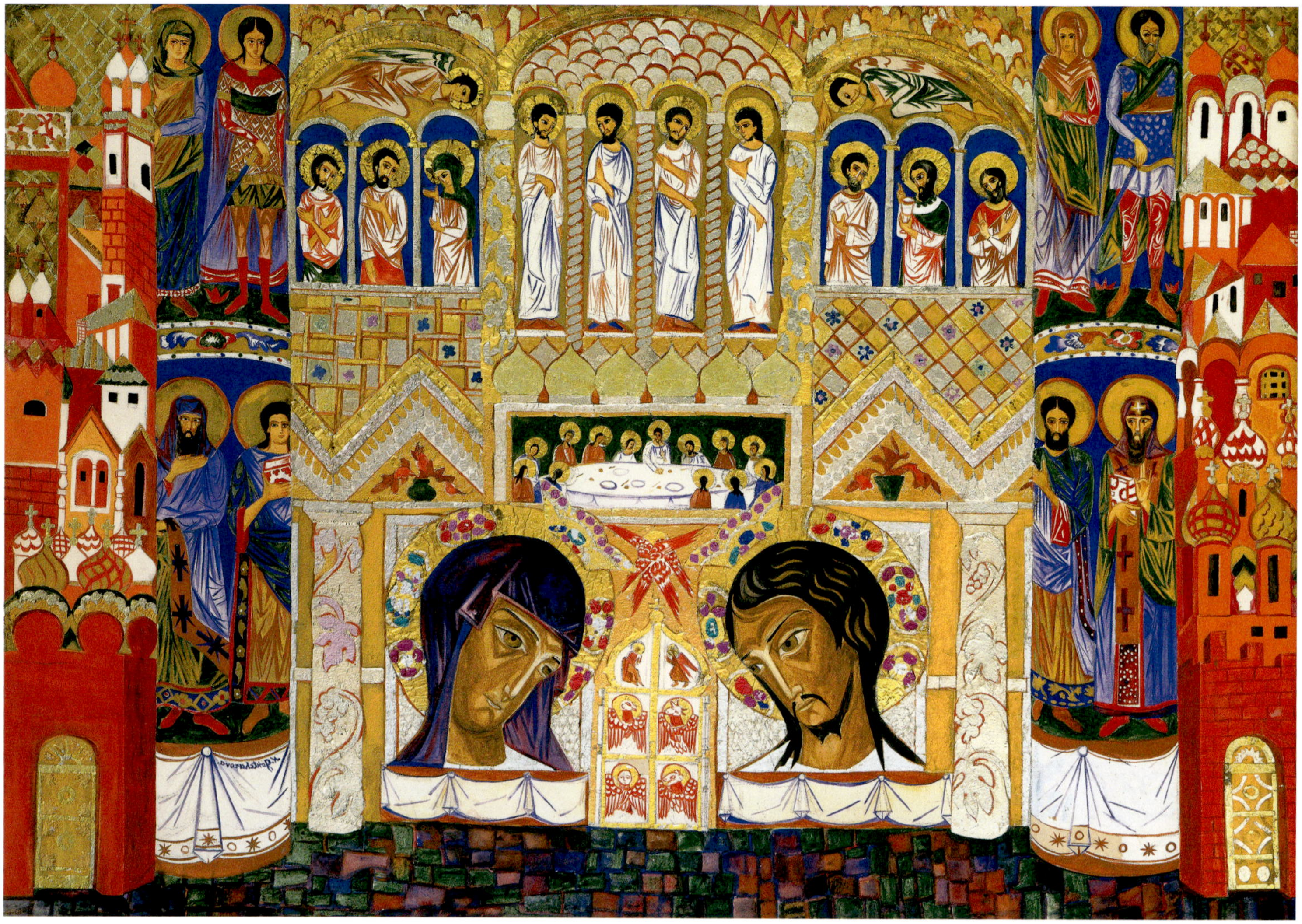

attempted to choreograph the ballet without music but, after 22 rehearsals, Diaghilev wrote to Stravinsky, despairing that 'absolute silence is death' and resolving to use sounds instead of music to 'fill the ears with harmonies' – at one time considering using Filippo Marinetti's Futurist Orchestra – but that venture also came to nothing.

The ballet was initially inspired by the Byzantine mosaics and early Italian 'primitivist' paintings that Diaghilev and Massine had seen in Ravenna, Florence and Rome. It was to consist of 'a stage performance of the Mass in six or seven short scenes; period, High Byzantine'.[17] The 'scenes' corresponded to feasts of the Orthodox Church rather than the parts of the Mass itself, and were to be enacted in front of a backdrop based on an iconostasis, designed by Goncharova. A surviving design for the scheme liberally adapts features from an Orthodox Church interior, including the columns adorned with tiers of Orthodox saints, to create a rich and exotic impression (Plate 79).[18] The Royal Doors, representing the four evangelists beneath an 'Annunciation', with a 'Last Supper' above, are the only truly authentic features of an iconostasis to be included. The other details, including a quaternity of saints resembling Goncharova's earlier canvases of *The Four Evangelists* and flanking panoramas of a city of Orthodox domes, are purely atmospheric.

79
Natalia Goncharova
Design for the stage set for *Liturgie*, 1915
Watercolour, pencil, cut and pasted paper and foil on cardboard
55.2 x 74.6 cm (21 ¾ x 29 ⅜ in)
Metropolitan Museum of Art, New York

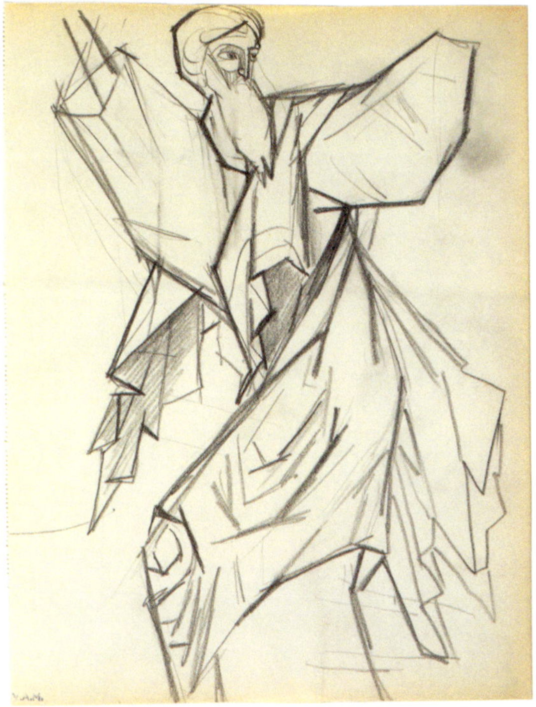

80
Natalia Goncharova

Drawing of apostle for ***Liturgie***, 1915
Pencil on paper
Dimensions unknown
Victoria and Albert Museum, London
©ADAGP, Paris and DACS, London 2007

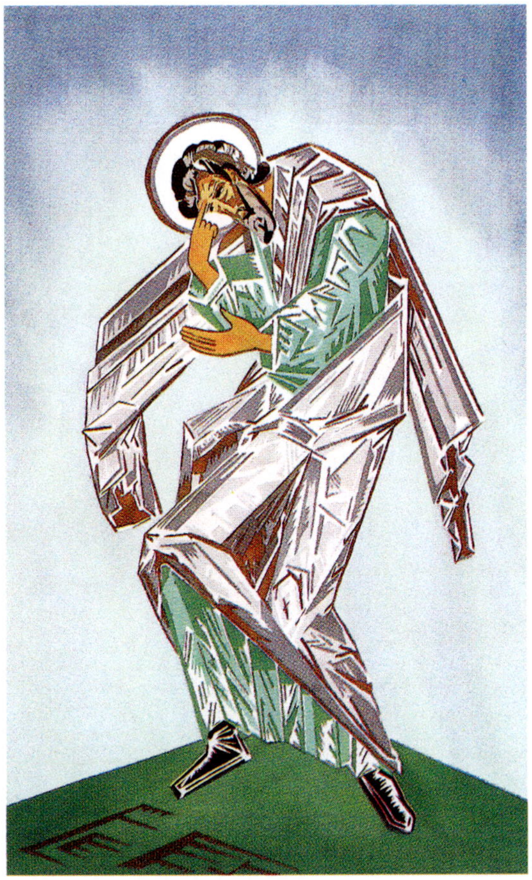

81
Natalia Goncharova

St Matthew from a portfolio of 'pochoirs' of costume designs for ***Liturgie***, 1915
Stencil on paper
57.2 x 34.5 cm (22½ x 13⅝ in)
Collection of Nina Lobanov-Rostovsky

Despite the cancellation of the production, some drawings survive and a portfolio-edition of her designs was published in Lausanne in 1915 and in Paris in 1927 (Plates 80, 81). These designs, which were clearly based on icons, include a shepherd and king for an 'Annunciation', seraphim and cherubim for an 'Ascension', a Mother of God in repose, as represented in icons, for a 'Nativity', a Christ, a St Anne, a Judas, a soldier and various saints. The deferential postures of the figures, their long robes, long hair and beards and haloes were required by the theme of the ballet.

More significant is the way Goncharova has attempted to adapt the mode of icon painting, which is essentially flat and static, to simulate a sense of balletic movement. In place of the solemn procession of figures towards Christ, as depicted on an iconostasis, the *Liturgie* figures are contorted and flattened into positions of exaggerated gesticulation. In many cases, one foot is positioned far in advance of the other (a disturbance that is unprecedented in icons), creating a spread of stretched drapery that is pervaded by dynamic faceting; the figures' haunches are mostly thrown back and their arms thrust forwards in token gestures of deference, opening up equivalent areas of dramatic contrast in the top half of the figure. Apart from the backgrounds, which are largely monochromatic, as in icons, most of the surface of each design is occupied by swathes of highly agitated drapery built up from linearised and fragmented folds, with occasional passages of flat ornamentation. Were it not for the figures' heads and hands, these images would number among the most abstract and dramatic works of Goncharova's entire oeuvre.

Massine had harboured the idea of choreographing scenes from the life of Christ since childhood. According to his memoirs of 1968, *Liturgie* had been 'not only a technical challenge, but even

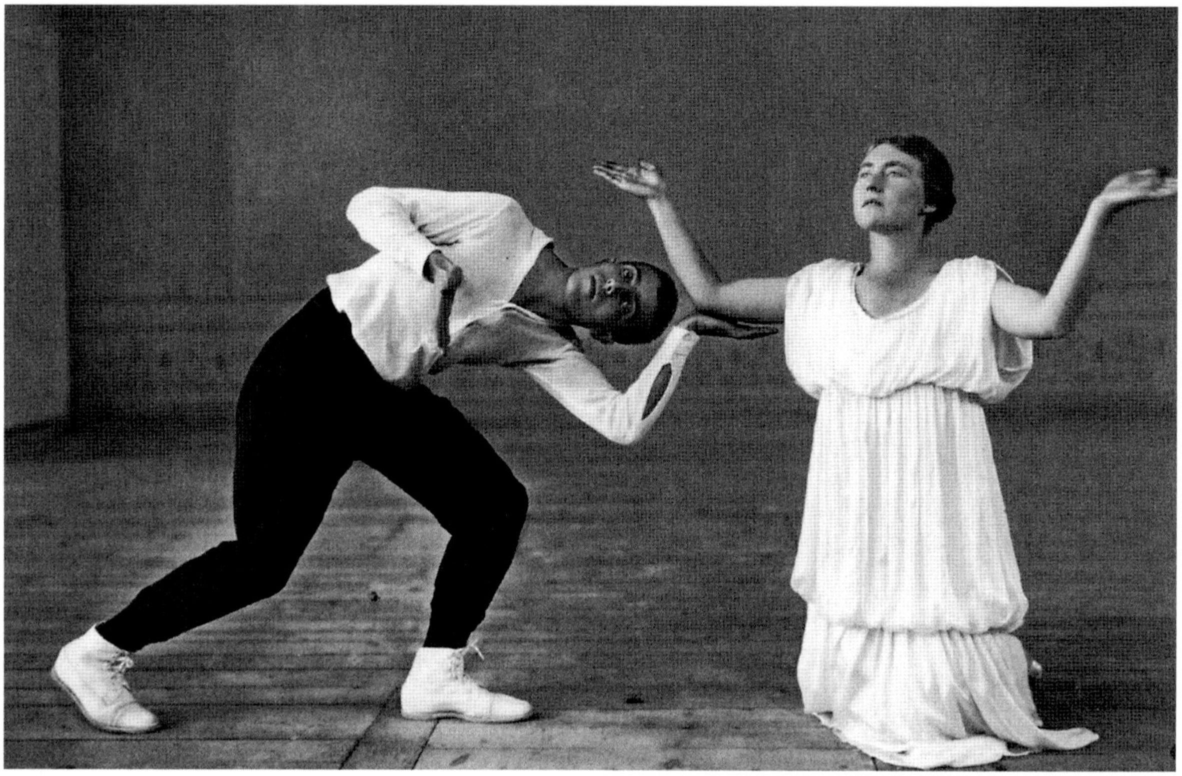

82

Massine and Sokolova in rehearsal for the Annunciation, *Liturgie*, 1915

more the first artistic realisation of a theme which had taken deep root in my subconscious when I was a child. I found it profoundly satisfying to interpret the scenes of the life of Christ in ballet form.'[19] In keeping with Goncharova's designs, his choreography, which was supervised by Larionov, was to include movements that evoked the stiffness of figures in icons, sometimes compressed into a single picture plane and to be seen frontally, at other times incorporated into an abstract group, expressive of a higher idea. According to Lydia Sokolova, who was to take on the role of the Virgin in the ballet, the figures were to give the impression that every movement and gesture was directed from above; all the dancers, whether soloists or not, were to count silently to co-ordinated rhythms.[20] This impression is indeed conveyed by photographs of rehearsals, taken in 1915. In the Annunciation scene (Plate 82), for instance, the figures of the Angel Gabriel, played by Massine, and the Virgin are realised as static gestures, whether simply juxtaposed and turned towards the viewer, or more directly engaging with each other. In one photograph Sokolova's raised hands give the impression of winding up thread, as in icons of the scene. As in Simone Martini's *Annunciation* which inspired the scene and which Massine had seen in the Uffizi Gallery in Florence in 1914, the figures represent an idea rather than enact a drama. Something of this impression of picture-making, rather than drama-making, is also present in the Ascension, in which the forms of the bodies are stylised to such a degree that they lose their own figuration and spill over into the ecstasy of abstraction.

It is highly likely that Massine was influenced by the pioneering work of the theatre director Vsevolod Meyerhold, whose development of acting as an art form in its own right – and not merely as a medium for communicating the prescribed idea of a writer – was revolutionising theatrical practice in Russia at this time. Meyerhold's development of a vocabulary of stylised movement and gesture for the sake of its expressive potential – over and above the demands of realistic representation – involved a thorough investigation of non-realist traditions of acting, such as Chinese theatre and the *commedia dell'arte*. His movement away from conventional stage-auditorium and actor-audience dualities recalls the ritual re-enactment of the Last Supper and Passion of Christ in the Orthodox liturgy, in which the congregation clearly participates, albeit passively. Meyerhold also referred to Old Master paintings as examples of intensely communicative and poetic gesture and is known to have shown reproductions of paintings by Hans Memling and Botticelli to the actors preparing for his staging of Maurice Maeterlinck's *Sister Beatrice* in 1905 for this reason. In a later production of the play, actors were placed in static monumental groupings against a shallow and flattened stage set, like a bas-relief, and were instructed to chant rather than speak their words. The actor Alexander Mgebrov described how the performers 'did not so much act as conduct a religious service'.[21] Regarding the study of paintings, Meyerhold explained in a lecture he gave not long before his execution in 1939: 'In the pictures of the great artists you will find interesting compositions, interesting rhythmical solutions. Then when you have to find a compositional solution for a scene in a production, your imagination, trained on works by great artists, will indicate the correct way to you'.[22]

Whether Meyerhold saw icons in this way must remain a matter for speculation. What is clear is that, like Massine, he was using ancient pictorial traditions as sources of expressive posture. The vocabulary of gestures and sequences that he conceived – later to be developed into his celebrated technique of ' biomechanics' – was distilled into a series of *études* and principles, rather like technical exercises for musicians. These *études* were introduced in order to minimise the random and arbitrary manifestation of subjective feeling on the part of the actor; on the contrary, they were predesigned to activate and facilitate a range of specific internal emotional dynamics in both the actor and the viewer alike. They were usually adapted for the stage but Meyerhold also used them in their raw state in his productions. Massine may have seen them at Meyerhold's open rehearsal sessions but he may also have known them from the public demonstrations that Meyerhold organised in Moscow in February and March 1915.

Evidently, the seeds sown in Massine's mind by *Liturgie* made a deep impression on him for he was to revisit the idea of sacred ballet in later years. In 1938, he choreographed a ballet – *Nobilissima Visione* – at the invitation of Paul Hindemith, who had been inspired by Giotto's frescos of St Francis in Santa Croce in Florence and by early French music, especially that of the fourteenth-century composer Guillaume de Machaut. The décor was provided by Paul Tchelichev. In some respects, *Nobilissima Visione* appears to have made use of some of Massine's ideas for *Liturgie*: '*Nobilissima Visione* was not really a ballet at all. It was a dramatic and choreographic interpretation of the life of St Francis in which Hindemith, Tchelichev and I tried to create and sustain throughout a mood of mystic exaltation'.[23] This is explicitly the case in relation to a still later work, *Laudes Evangelii*, 'based on the attitudes depicted in Byzantine mosaics and the paintings of the primitive Lucca and Pisa schools' and produced in 1952. Referring to the text on which it was based – a thirteenth-century Italian version of a Latin liturgical drama about the passion of Christ – Massine reflected:

> I was much moved by the simplicity and sincerity of the dialogue, and began to wonder whether in using it as the basis for a ballet I might not at last accomplish what I had set out

to do so many years before in *Liturgie*. Here, surely, was a genuinely primitive treatment of the subject which lent itself admirably to the kind of simplified choreography I had been trying to evolve then with Larionov... It seemed strange, after so long, to be working on something so similar to *Liturgie*. Everything – text, music [orchestrations of thirteenth-century Umbrian chants], the possibility of production – had fallen into place so easily that it seemed almost as if Diaghilev himself were giving me back my lost opportunity.[24]

Despite Goncharova's deep sympathy for icons, her Christian works cannot be regarded as iconic in the traditional sense of the word for, although they were based on the appearance of icons in a most direct way – clearly demonstrating the common ground between her neo-primitivist work and icons – they lack the sacramental context and function of Orthodox sacred art. Moreover, where the exaggerated stylisation of icons is natural and incidental – an icon painter's duty was simply to copy a traditional model without questioning its authority – Goncharova's neo-primitivist style was largely developed for expressive purposes. As Benois acknowledged in his appreciative reflections on Goncharova's 1913 exhibition, these works were:

not imitations ... but works full of freedom and bright inspiration. Although I would not go so far as to call them *profound*, there is no longer any possibility to create a new religious painting distinguished by that same sort of profundity that distinguished Byzantine painting from the Gothic. This would require not only the efforts of individuals but also vast waves of religious *élan* and culture. Goncharova's approach to religious subjects is clearly aesthetic; right now, it cannot be anything else. Yet of all of the various aesthetic approaches to religious themes to appear in recent years, Goncharova's is probably the freest and most captivating.[25]

It should also be pointed out that, although aspects of Goncharova's style – particularly the disposition of her figure-types and the angular flattening of her drapery – are consistently indebted to traditional medieval icons, much of her Christian iconography is related to later Catholicised icons that had themselves departed from the Byzantine tradition. These became increasingly commonplace in Russia in the seventeenth and eighteenth centuries, partly due to the general influx of western ideals under Peter the Great but particularly following exposure to the Catholicised culture of the Ukraine and White Russia which were reclaimed from Catholic Poland, after a period of 300 years, in the seventeenth century. Goncharova was interested in icons as the fruits of popular religious life – not as high imperial or ecclesiastical culture. It was therefore inevitable that she should have been drawn to the elements of Catholic piety and sentimentality – images of the Virgin and Christ crowned[26] and the Virgin holding a rosary[27] – that had crept in to make them more personable, despite the fact that such images were foreign to the ancient Russian tradition.

It is hardly surprising that avant-garde artists were rarely influenced by Christian iconography *per se*, for it is precisely in their attitudes towards Christianity and religious psychology that the two arts were most mutually exclusive. Whether it was rejected on the basis of its illogicality or the religious sensibility of the artist, the unscientific principle of belief in a supernatural deity was clearly at odds with the materialistic pragmatism of most exponents of the avant-garde. It is equally unsurprising that on those rare occasions when Christianity was actually incorporated within the avant-garde world view, it was met with fierce controversy. At the first Union of Youth exhibition in 1910, a painting of the *Torture of the Saviour* by Vladimir Markov was withdrawn. Goncharova's Christian paintings were also regarded as sacrilegious outside her own circle. In 1912, the Public Censor had considered it blasphemous to include her paintings of *The Four Evangelists* (Plate 23) at such an irreverently named exhibition as The Donkey's Tail and ordered the police to confiscate them.[28] Two years later, the paintings were exhibited again and, along with 18 other religious works by the same artist, they were challenged due to their supposed blasphemous distortion of their sacred precedents. Goncharova upheld the sincerity of these works, justifying the idiosyncrasy of their style by drawing attention to the fact that every period of icon painting – Russian, Byzantine, Ukrainian, Georgian, post-Peter the Great – has its own 'physiognomy' and its own particular style. She even defended them on the grounds of her religious belief: 'Others argue – and argue with me – that I have no right to paint icons. I believe in the Lord firmly enough. Who knows who believes and how?'[29] The number of religious works in the exhibition is itself a testimony to her concentrated attraction at this time to icons as a source of creative energy for her own work; there is nothing satirical or patronising about them.

Of all the explicit references to Christian imagery in the art of the Russian avant-garde, surely the most radical and profound was the Suprematist work of Kazimir Malevich. As we have seen, he had already absorbed figurative and aesthetic aspects of icon painting into his Symbolist and primitivist works which are, broadly speaking, comparable in orientation to Goncharova's primitivist works. However, he was soon to pass beyond a mere similarity to icons towards a total identification with them. Malevich's experiments with Cubism and Futurism enabled him to move so far beyond the expressionistic use of line and colour that the rational and pictorial coherence of subject matter was eventually abandoned altogether. Having dispensed with all pictorial reference to the outside world, his early Suprematist works of 1914–15 concentrate the attention of the viewer in an experience of pure abstraction. The paintings represent nothing more than simple relationships between shapes in space (Plate 83). He retains, however, the aesthetic sensibility of icons, resonating profoundly with their sense of colour, architectonics and graphic design (Plate 84). Significantly, as we shall see, most of these configurations involve crosses, either explicitly or implicitly. Although these shapes and forms are static and inert in themselves, they are arranged in such a way that a powerful charge is created between them, evoking in the viewer a state of dynamic equilibrium. They are delicately impossible to move; like leaves drifting on the surface of a pond, they are held together by a fragile but binding surface tension.

In these early Suprematist works, Malevich created a visual language which was inherently expressive, a language that was expressive of meaning on account of its own forms; that is to say, the ability of early Suprematism to convey meaning did not depend on a frame of reference beyond the image itself. Despite their great advances, however, Malevich soon perceived a shortcoming in these works. Although their abstraction liberated them from dependency on exterior frames of reference for meaning, it also removed them from reality as a whole, establishing them as independent, isolated worlds. Thus, although the language of early Suprematism was inherently expressive, it was limited in that it was expressive only of its

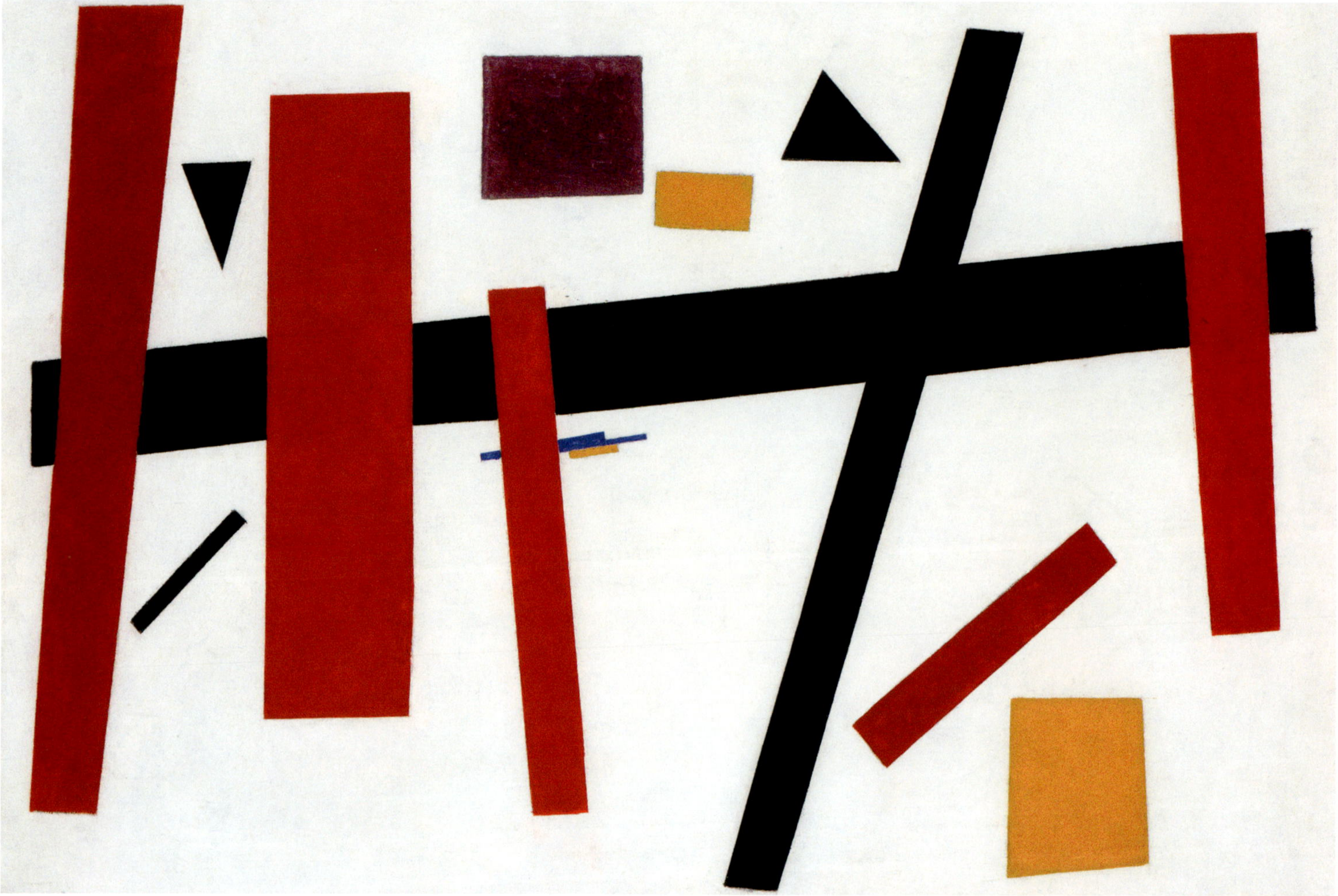

own reality. Malevich's early Suprematist works represented reality; they related to reality remotely, through correspondence or equivalence, rather than participating directly in reality. Malevich attempted to go beyond this limitation by dispensing with the multifarious contents of these compositions and creating a series of paintings of single forms whose interior spaces appeared to be infinite and undifferentiated – chiefly, the square, the cross and the circle. These forms were seen to be confluent with the infinity of reality rather than distinctively abstracted within it or merely representative of it. It is in this sense that they resemble and – from the artist's point of view – ultimately become icons.

The classic image in this series was the *Black Square* of 1915 (Plate 85). With this work Malevich conceived a form in which the total absence of interior differentiation intimated the infinite, undifferentiated nature of reality as a whole. Because the image had no object apart from itself, Malevich referred to it as 'non-objective': 'this was no empty square which I had exhibited but rather the feeling of non-objectivity'.[30] The meditation behind the *Black Square* was that as it had no content, there was nothing in it by which it could be identified as being separate from the infinity of reality; it was indistinguishable from reality. It did not merely represent reality, therefore; it *was* reality. Malevich himself stressed that Suprematist forms 'will not be copies of living things in life, but will themselves be a living thing'.[31] As such, despite its

83
Kazimir Malevich

Suprematism no.50, 1915
Oil on canvas
97 x 66 cm (38 ¼ x 26 in)
Stedelijk Museum, Amsterdam

84

Old Testament Trinity,
Novgorod, mid-16th century
Tempera on wooden panel
147.2 x 113.3 cm (58 x 44 ⅝ in)
Russian Museum,
St Petersburg

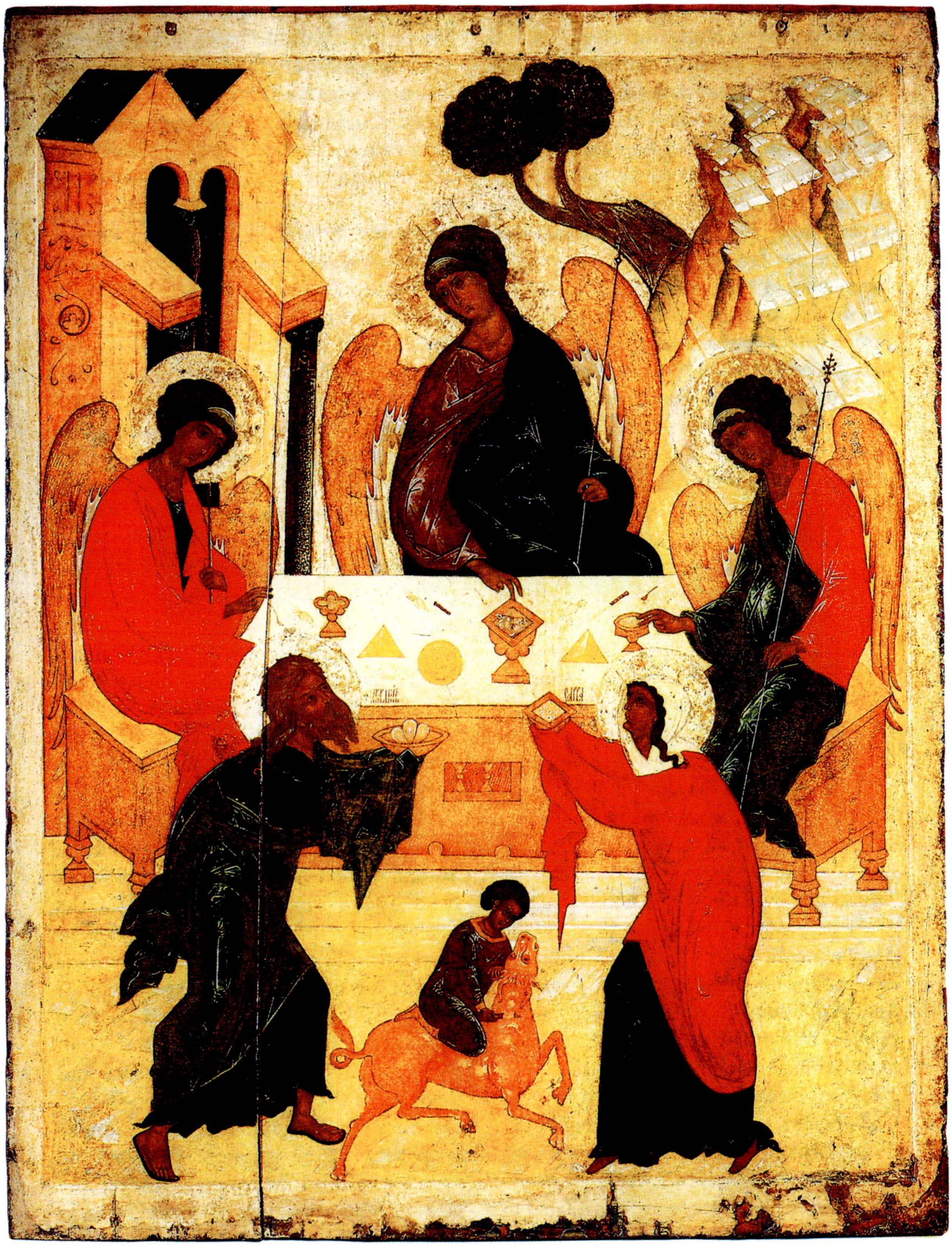

apparent differences, the *Black Square* comes closer to the ultimate significance of icons than any other work of the period. For like the *Black Square*, icons are not simply illustrative, narrative, emotive or decorative. On the contrary, they are believed to participate substantially in, and transmit, what they portray: as extensions of the incarnate Christ, they are seen as sacramental objects – consubstantial with the reality of God, not merely representative or symbolic of it. Indeed, icons are painted, as an active form of prayer, in order to celebrate and perpetuate the incarnation of sacred reality in material pictorial representation. As a result, Orthodox Christians engage in icon veneration as a form of direct communion with Christ and the saints. At a purely material level, believers are known to have eaten flakes of icons and frescos as a source of blessings, or to have placed the eucharistic bread on the surface of an icon with a view to receiving it directly from the hand of a saint.[32]

Malevich considered his *Black Square* to be an icon. When he said that 'an icon in a museum collection is an object in which the religious fiction has been dropped while the non-objective art and reality have remained in it', he could have been talking about this work.[33] He emphatically proclaimed its iconic status by hanging it across the corner of the room at the first Suprematist exhibition, 0,10, in St Petersburg (then called Petrograd) in 1915 (Plate 86). This corner position was traditionally reserved in Russian homes for icons and so, by hanging the work in this way, he was presenting it as an icon, stripped of all superfluous religious and artistic characteristics or 'accidents' (Plate 87). In a highly critical review of the exhibition, published in 1916, Alexander Benois accused Malevich of blasphemy. Benois' criticism, however, only served to confirm Malevich's success in presenting the *Black Square* as an icon: 'Without a number but high up in a corner just below the ceiling in the holy place, is hung a "production" without doubt by the same Malevich, representing a black square against a white background. There can be no doubt that this is an "icon"'.[34]

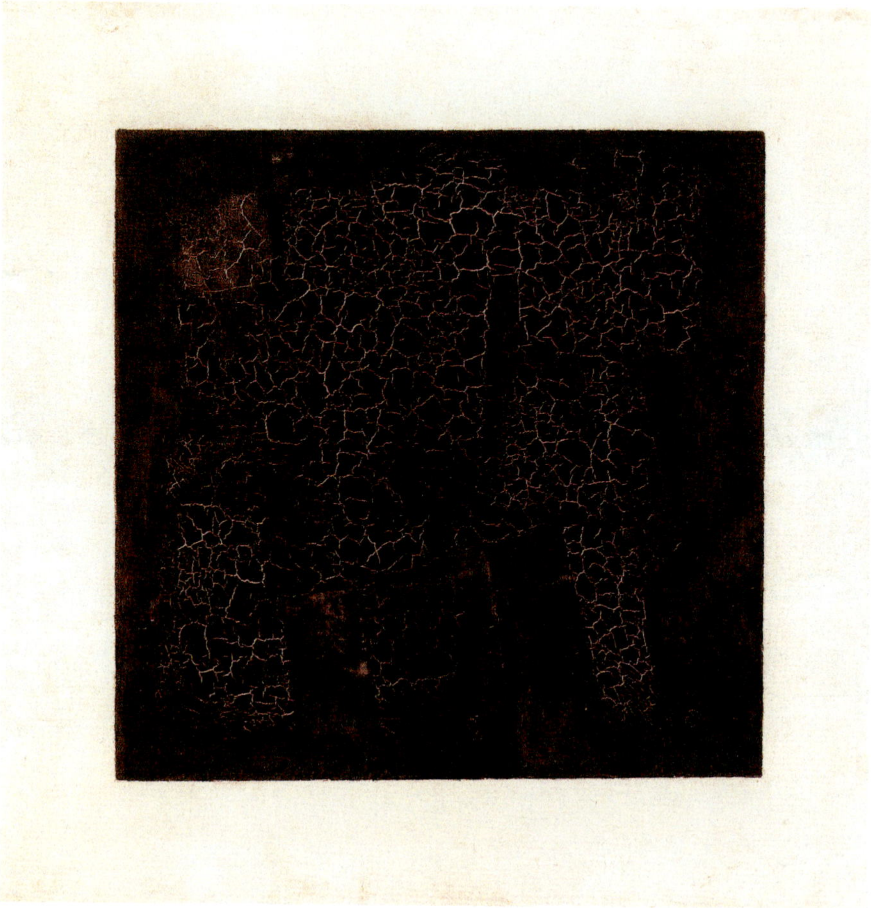

85
Kazimir Malevich
Black Square, 1915
Oil on canvas
79.5 x 79.5 cm (31¼ x 31¼ in)
Tretyakov Gallery, Moscow

The origins of the tradition of placing icons over the corner of a room are obscure. The time-honoured practice is popularly seen as a way of setting the holy image apart from the conventional decoration and use of a room; corner icons (often more than one) are typically 'scarved' with a cloth and illuminated by candles. The tradition may derive from the sixth-century legend of the mandylion, in which the ailing King Abgar of Edessa is healed by a towel (the mandylion) on which Christ had wiped his face (Plate 1).[35] Because the mandylion, which had miraculously received an impression of Christ's

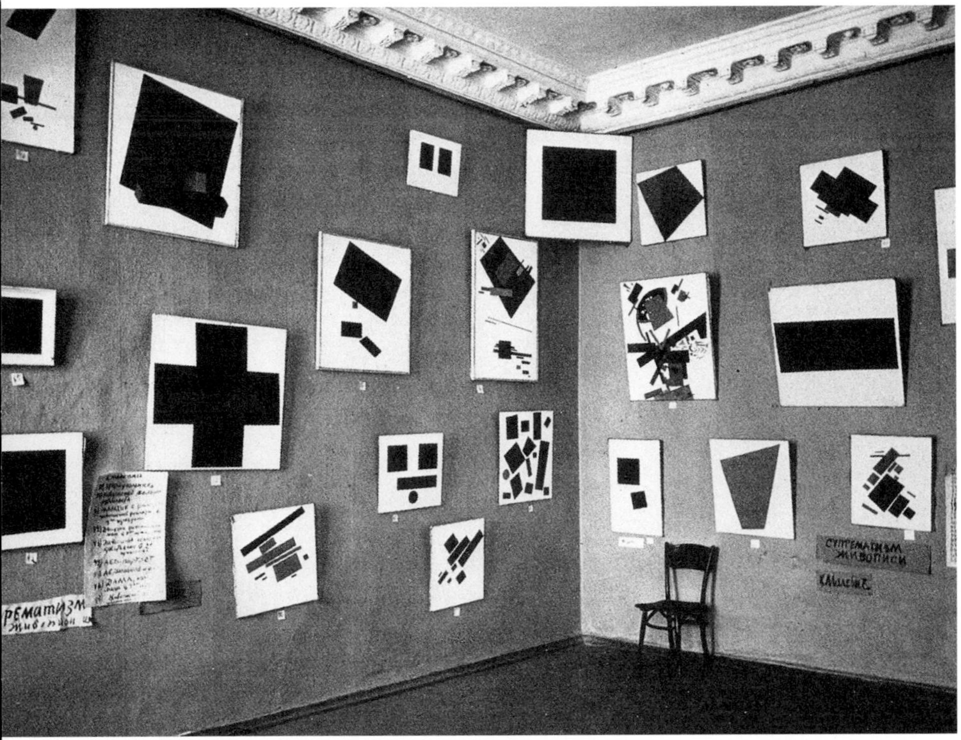

86

The Last Futurist Exhibition, 0,10, Petrograd, 1915
David King Collection, London

face, was believed to be an 'an image of Christ not made by human hands', it was considered not only to give divine sanction to the practice of icon painting, but also to provide an archetypal representation of the Divine. Following his miraculous recovery, King Abgar is said to have hung the mandylion in a corner of the city walls, previously occupied by images of pagan idols. When the city later reverted to paganism, the bishop attempted to preserve the mandylion by walling it into its corner; when it was later recovered, the lamp that the bishop had placed in front of it was still burning.[36] Just as the miraculous creation of the mandylion set a precedent for the icon-painting tradition as a whole, so it is not inconceivable that the legend of its miraculous survival in a protected corner may have led to the tradition of 'sacred corners' in Russian homes. If this were to be the case, it is not difficult to see how Malevich may have wanted to place the *Black Square* in the corner of the room in order to intensify its association with the God-created mandylion which it parallels in that it also reveals the fullness and sufficiency of reality, unmodified by human hands. However, seeing that the mandylion was taken from Edessa to Constantinople in 944 and that the custom of a 'sacred corner' did not take root in Byzantium, it is difficult to accept that it could have percolated through to Russia from this source.

It is more likely that the custom derived from a popular tradition, probably associated with Russian paganism, and was adapted as cultural labels changed.[37] For instance, considering the popular conception of Christ as 'Tsar of the Heavens', it may be linked with the location of the seat of honour in the Tsars' Throne Hall, in the Faceted Palace of the Kremlin, towards the corner of the room, a tradition that dates back to the seventeenth century at the latest.[38] This off-centre position was presumably necessitated by the fact that the central areas of the walls (and the corners) were occupied by the exceptionally low springing of the vaults. Drawings from the early seventeenth century record how icons were displayed above the throne, a tradition that may well have acquired its own autonomous significance (Plate 88). Engravings of the wedding of Peter the Great and Catherine I in 1712 show icons over two of the corners in the room at Peter's Winter Palace – in contrast to earlier representations of ceremonial occasions.[39] An image of Peter lying in state after his death in 1725 includes two cartouches, presumably made of silver, hanging in the same positions, though on this occasion they contain secular crests. The 'corner' custom may also be related to the way in which the 'hand of God', commonly seen blessing saints in icons, is placed in a quadrant in the corner of the icon

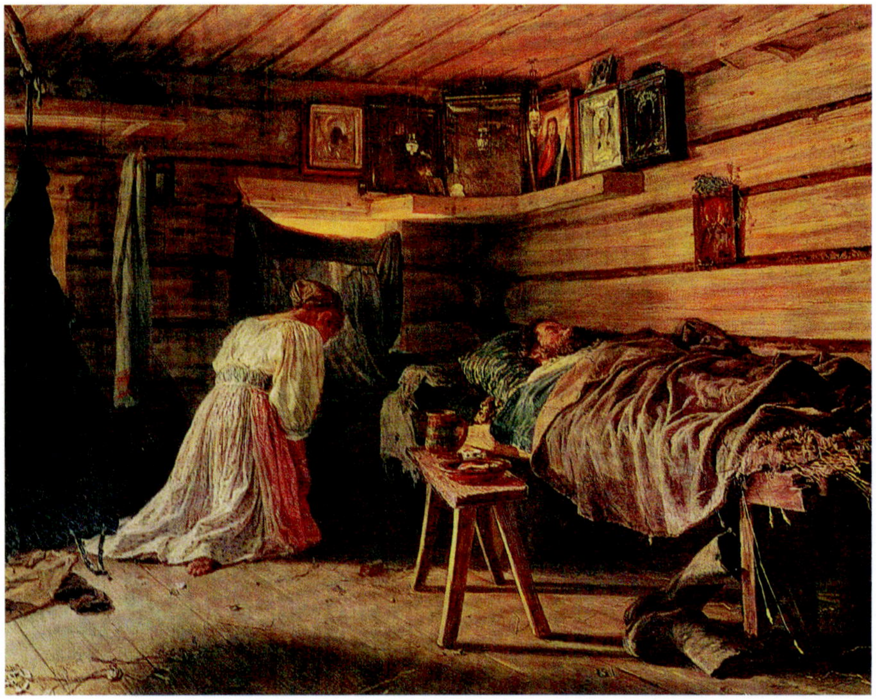

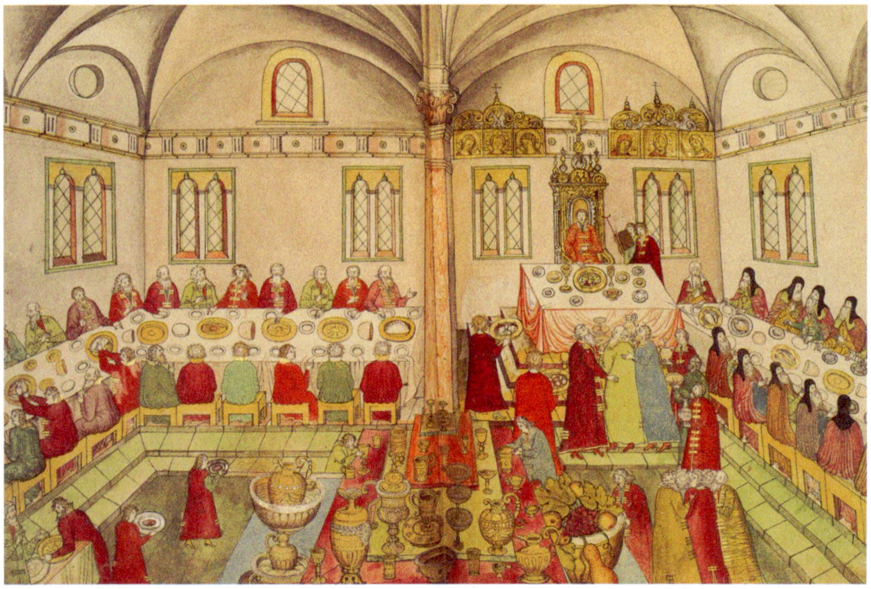

87
Vasily Maximov

The Sick Husband, 1881
Oil on canvas
70.8 x 88.6 cm (27 ⅞ x 34 ⅞ in)
Tretyakov Gallery, Moscow

88
Ivan Vereshchagin

A Banquet in Palace of Facets, 1672–3
Watercolour on paper
Dimensions unknown
Historical-Cultural Museum, Moscow

(Plate 75). Whatever its actual source, Malevich capitalised on the fact that, since time immemorial, popular tradition in Russia associated the corner of a room with the sacred image. He re-interpreted the custom in the light of his own understanding:

> The image is the final path, the image is something which bars the exit, by means of the image the further path is interrupted, everything which has paths converges towards the image, all paths lead to the image, particularly if it is holy, hence I see the justification and true significance of the Orthodox corner in which the image stands, the holy image, as opposed to all other images and representations of sinners. The holiest occupies the centre of the corner, the less holy occupy the walls on the sides. The corner symbolises that there is no other path to perfection except for the path into the corner. This is the final point of movement. All paths, whichever path you were to choose and tread, if you are going towards perfection, will converge into the corner; whether you were to walk in the heights (the ceiling), down below (the floor), on the sides (the wall), the result of your path will be the cube, as the cubic is the fullness of your comprehension and is perfection.[40]

By placing his *Black Square* over the corner of the gallery, Malevich was underlining his understanding of the work as a consummate totality that operated on a number of different levels. On one hand, it was total as a painting, heralding the consummation – and thus the end – of his art and of all art as such. On the other hand, he regarded it as an inevitable totality in the broader context of human life. It represented both the consummation of the tradition of art and, in relation to human mortality, the unique and inescapable point of

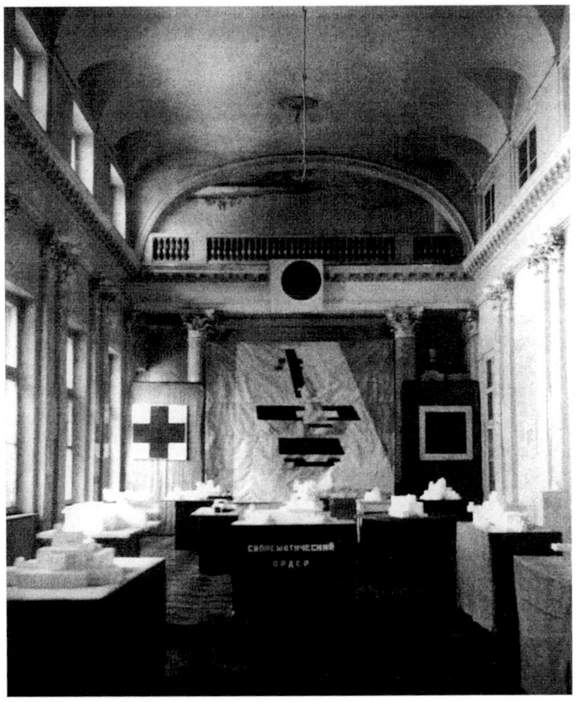

89
Nikolai Punin

Photograph of an exhibition of the work of the Institute of Artistic Culture (INKhUK) in Leningrad (St Petersburg), 1926
Private collection

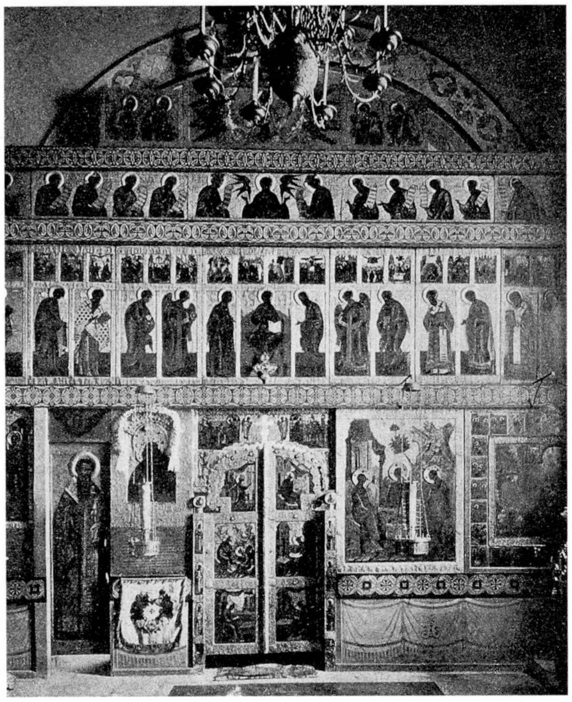

90

Iconostasis in the side chapel of St Sophia, Novgorod, 16th century

'exit' – self-transcendence and death. Like a death and resurrection, it is equally a moment of exit and a point of entry into a new perception of reality.

Malevich's original display of the *Black Square* across the corner of a room was only the most famous occasion on which he adopted the display contexts of icons in order to sacralise his own work. In 1926, his display of work by artists and designers associated with INKhUK (State Institute of Artistic Culture in Leningrad), where he had been teaching 'Formal and Theoretical Systems' since 1923, closely resembles the interior of an orthodox church, fitted with an iconostasis (Plates 5, 89, 90). At one end of the room a minstrels' gallery, surmounted by a balustrade and supported by two classical columns, projected into the display area. The columns divided the gallery into three sections – two narrow spaces at the sides and a wider opening in the centre. Each of the spaces at the sides (between the columns and the walls of the room) was sealed off by a panel on which Malevich's *Black Cross* and *Black Square* were hung. Above the central space (against the balustrade) hung his *Black Circle*. The transformation of the gallery into a closed area concealed by a tripartite screen not only suggested an iconostasis, complete with deacons' doors to left and right of the central Royal Doors, but also contributed to the elevation of the entire display area into a highly charged and unified space, sustained by the effect of all the exhibited works together, rather than a neutral room in which a sequence of works are hung on the walls to be seen as independent and complete objects.

The artist took a comparable approach to the exhibition of his work at the Polish Art Club in the Polonia Hotel in Warsaw in 1927. The paintings, which covered his entire career, were grouped by style, but a photograph taken at the opening of the exhibition clearly shows that the Suprematist works in particular were closely ranged beside each other, giving an overall impression of a screen of work (all unframed, and with no labels), as opposed to an array of individual pieces. In this case, four small detailed Suprematist compositions were surmounted by three larger, more spacious and numinous paintings, including two *White on White* works, which were themselves flanked by two medium-sized works. The effect is suggestive of a typical iconostasis screen, in which a row of small detailed festival icons is tightly ranged above a row of larger, simpler and graver icons of standing saints. The presence of double doors beside the paintings, resembling the Royal Doors at the centre of the iconostasis, only serves to intensify this impression.[41]

In their own ways, both icons and the *Black Square* are to be engaged as forms of sacred art; both were conceived as agents of self-surrender, in contemplative identification with which the viewers could be drawn beyond themselves into the higher identity of a divine or absolute reality. However, because the selfless, non-objective nature of reality could not be realised until the presumption of a subject/object distinction had been released, Malevich realised that it would ultimately be erroneous to regard icons or the *Black Square* as sacred objects *per se* – for to do so would be to regard them as discrete objects, thereby sustaining a discrete subject, the viewer, by implication. As a result, in order to transcend the subjective mind, the art object itself must be dissolved, released, annihilated. This is precisely what takes place in his *White Square* (1918), which is consequently one of the most significant paintings to have been painted in the twentieth century. In this work, the form of the *Black Square* is so absorbed into the context in which it arises that it almost entirely ceases to be differentiated. 'The familiar recedes ever further and further into the background... The contours of the objective world fade more and more and so it goes, step by step, until finally the world ... becomes lost to sight. No more likenesses of reality, no idealistic images – nothing but a desert! But this desert is filled with the spirit of non-objective sensation which pervades everything.'[42]

In other works from the *White on White* series, the depicted forms are seen to be half sinking into their surrounding spaces (Plate 91). While in Malevich's earlier Suprematist works, shapes are clearly distinguished from each other and are represented above their background and parallel to the picture surface, in these works half the forms are already resubmerged in infinity. This is the point beyond which the separate observer cannot go. By pursuing the forms of these works, the attention of the viewer is drawn with them into the void where it too is dissolved.

Malevich's *White on White* series took him to – and beyond – the very limits of art as an expressive medium. While engaged on these works, Malevich began to see that not only the forms of art but even the very concept of art imposed a limitation on his realisation of the formless infinity of reality. He understood that just as an abstract visual form is separated from infinity on account of its distinctiveness, so the concept of art is also a distinctive form, a thought-form, which separates itself from the infinite field of consciousness in the same

91
Kazimir Malevich

Suprematism, 1918
Oil on canvas
97 x 70 cm (38 ¼ x 27 ½ in)
Stedelijk Museum, Amsterdam

way. For this reason, Malevich expressed his desire to go 'beyond whiteness'; that is to say, to go beyond the forms of art – even the most minimal of which polarise experience into separate object and subject – but also to go beyond conceptual forms into the undifferentiated state of consciousness that precedes the mind. When this sublime level of peace has been achieved, Malevich imagined, 'there will be no more need for reason, hearing, sight or sense of touch, for there will be nothing to overcome, there will be no existence to oppose me and direct my consciousness away from itself and towards the conquering of existence itself. And then it will no longer matter whether my own single reality/non-objectivity exists in the cube or not'.[43]

It was, paradoxically, through his involvement in art as a means of transcending art that Malevich came closest to creating an 'avant-garde icon'. Just as the identity of an icon is perpetually deferred from itself on to Christ, so the significance of late Suprematism lies in its selfless transparency to the infinity of reality. Through this gesture of release, Malevich acknowledged that reality and truth are already inherently manifest in, and as, the world on account of the fact that they are already inherently real and true. He realised that they do not need to be expressed through art, because they are already inherently expressive of themselves. This is a simple realisation but it is also profound for, by intuiting the truth, it mitigates the need to search for the truth as if the truth were not already present. In exactly the same way, an icon has no identity of its own, but is only a part of the whole. An icon is only a manifestation of the incarnate Christ; it is nothing else. Except for its perceived participation in the material substance of God, an icon is essentially 'meaningless'. Icons were not created as aids in the search for spiritual realisation (thus subtly presuming that the truth is not already realised); they were conceived as practical objects to magnify, articulate and celebrate – in the liturgical sense – an intuited religious truth (that the truth is already realised in the world via Christ). Nor were they originally conceived as works of art with a view to creating aesthetic impressions; to evaluate them on this basis is to overlook their true significance. In surrendering the motive and concept of art, therefore, Malevich realised the essential meaning and significance of icons in a contemporary form. Regarding the dissolution of the sense of a separate self into the sense of reality as a whole, Malevich's intuition comes extremely close to that of the Orthodox monastic practice. A similar condition of thoughtlessness was described by St Gregory Palamas in the fourteenth century: 'Contemplation ... is a union and a divinisation which occurs mystically and ineffably by the grace of God, after the stripping away of everything from here below which imprints itself on the mind, or rather after the cessation of all intellectual activity; it is something that goes beyond abstraction (which is only the outward mark of the cessation)'.[44]

The same paradoxical need to 'sacrifice God as an object of mind or thought' was expressed by Florensky in his *Iconostasis*, in which he identifies the icon screen as the membrane between the visible and the invisible worlds, mindful and mindless consciousness, 'to present one's body as sacrifice means to attain the spiritual sensitivity of knowing God's will as "good, and acceptable, and perfect". But such sanctity is, as it were, the thesis to which is opposed the antithesis wherein our yearning to so know God's will initiates in us a desire to philosophize about it, thereby replacing a true contact with heaven with our own abstract reasonings.'[45]

Florensky could also be commentating on the significance of Malevich's *White on White* works when he describes the paradoxical situation whereby the sacred essence of an image is only revealed to the extent that the image transcends itself or is transcended:

> it is not you, O iconpainter, who has created these images; it is not you who has shown to our joyous eyes these vividly alive ideas; no, they themselves have appeared within our contemplation, and you have simply taken away the obstacle that hid their light from us, for you have helped strip away the scales that covered our spiritual sight. And because you have helped us, we now see – no longer your masterpiece – but the wholly real images themselves.[46]
>
> When this happens, the material iconostasis will self-destruct in that vast obliteration which will destroy the whole image of this world ... and then we will contemplate, in pure love, the immortal glory of God, i.e. immediately, or unmediated.[47]

In direct parallel with Florensky, Malevich was seeking to realise that state of consciousness in which the truth about reality is expressive of itself, not requiring the prisms of art and the mind to mediate on its behalf. In the context of the Orthodox tradition, St Gregory Palamas also acknowledged that knowledge of the Divine is not attained through manipulation of self or circumstance but that it arises gracefully beyond the mind, as a function of reality: 'If all intellectual activity has stopped, how could angels and angelic men see God except by the power of the Spirit?'[48]

Malevich described a similar experience of being drawn beyond himself by a power other than himself. Significantly, he refers to the 'place' of spiritual intuition as a 'desert'. This image had been central to the Orthodox imagination ever since the Desert Fathers established the first hermitages in the Egyptian desert in the third and fourth centuries and barren, rocky caves are abundantly depicted in icons as a symbol of spiritual retreat and withdrawal (Plates 6, 9, 26, 53) – even though the location of Russian Orthodox hermitages was dense forest rather than rocky desert: 'I was grabbed by a kind of timidity bordering on fear when it came to leaving the "world of will and idea" in which I had lived and worked and in the reality of which I had believed. But *a blissful sense of liberating non-objectivity drew me forth into the desert,* where nothing is real except feeling ... and so feeling became the substance of my life.'[49]

Malevich's artistic development was the vehicle through which a deeper and more intangible spiritual evolution was made possible for him. It was through the development of his art, itself determined by its own inner logic, that he came to realise the truth about art and about himself. He was led by the inner momentum of that logic to realise that the perfection of art in absolute non-objectivity presupposes non-subjectivity or self-sacrifice – not in the conventional negative sense of pain or killing but in the entirely positive sense of 'making-holy' (*sacrum facere*) or surrendering the sense of a separate identity into the formless force-field of consciousness. At the same time, he observed how humanity tends to separate itself, by virtue of its object-based thinking, from the transrational field of divine being in 'God is Not Cast Down':

> Admitting the perfection of the universe, [Man] admitted [that] God ... does not think; only he [Man] thinks, for God – as the absolute of the perfection of nature – can no longer think. By such an admission [Man] has singled himself out as a thinking being and extracted himself from the perfection of God's creation... He alone

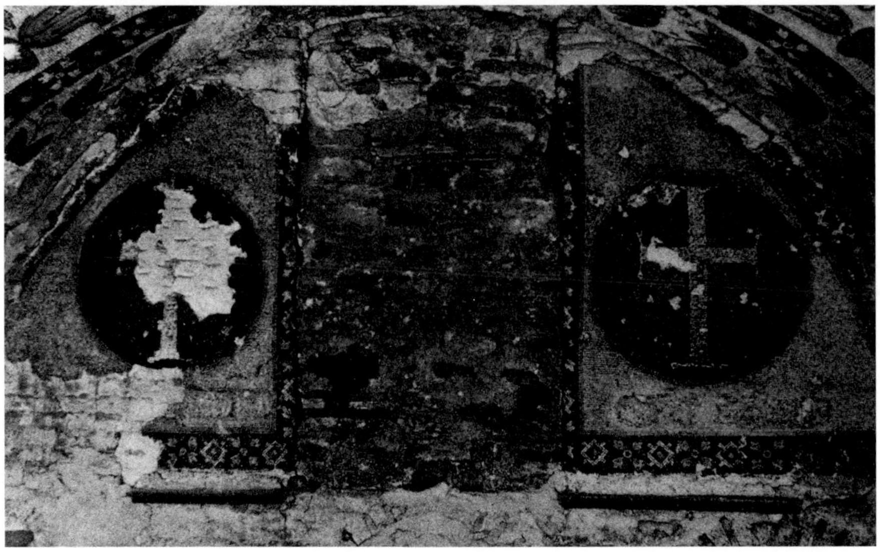

92

An iconoclastic alteration (8th century) of earlier figurative mosaics in the Patriarchal Palace, Istanbul

> began to strive for an understanding of nature, of God as perfection; having left the state of non-thinking, which was absolute perfection, he again strives through his perfect objects to embody himself in the perfection of absolute non-thinking action, as if some piece of carelessness had occurred and he had slipped and fallen overboard from the absolute.[50]

Malevich realised that by pursuing his Suprematist vocation towards non-objectivity, he was creating not only the form of the death of his art but also the form of his own death as a separate subjective identity. While working on the transcendence of art, he also worked on the sacrifice of self. This is reflected in the fact that, while eschewing all outwards signs of reference to external phenomena, with a view to arriving at total abstraction, a significant proportion of his works revolve around the quintessentially Christian form of the cross. Indeed, acknowledging the pervasive recurrence of the form of the cross in his Suprematist work, he conceded: 'the cross is my Cross'.[51] Unlike icon painters, for whom the cross was of course a narrative sign and a religious symbol, Malevich did not understand the cross in relation to a preconceived frame of reference. On the contrary, it was a non-objective sign for him – replacing the inertia and banality of subject matter. It existed in his works as an archetypal form, arising spontaneously as a result of his compositional technique, and it took on many forms. Interestingly, just as he used the cross as a form that transcends art, so the iconoclasts of the eighth and ninth centuries insisted that mosaic images of Christ and the saints should be cut out of their original settings and replaced by simple crosses. An example survives in the Patriarchal Palace in Constantinople (Istanbul) (Plate 92), in which the blank areas that once bore inscriptions identifying the saints in the roundels above them can also be seen. Like Malevich – albeit in a radically different context – the iconoclasts believed that the unknowable divinity of Christ is inherently incompatible with the finite limitations of this world and that it is compromised through representation. Consequently, they maintained, it is idolatrous and disregardful of his true nature to attempt to represent him in figurative form. However, they approved the form of the cross on the grounds that it is a sign of Christ, indicating his presence, like the footprint of a passer-by, whereas a symbol has an additional meaning and an image is a deceptive representation. Both in this context and in Malevich's Suprematist work, the form of the cross functions as an iconoclastic icon.

In a few key examples, Malevich made use of the four-armed Greek cross (Plate 93). Although the form is thoroughly abstract, in that it has no meaning or reference beyond itself, it is highly distinctive and is instantly recognisable throughout the Orthodox Church. The most striking and intensely abstract use of the form – one that closely parallels Malevich's version of it and shares something of its immediacy and hypnotic effect – appears in the stark representations of *polystavron* or 'many crosses' that were used to decorate the vestments of clerical saints, paying no heed to the

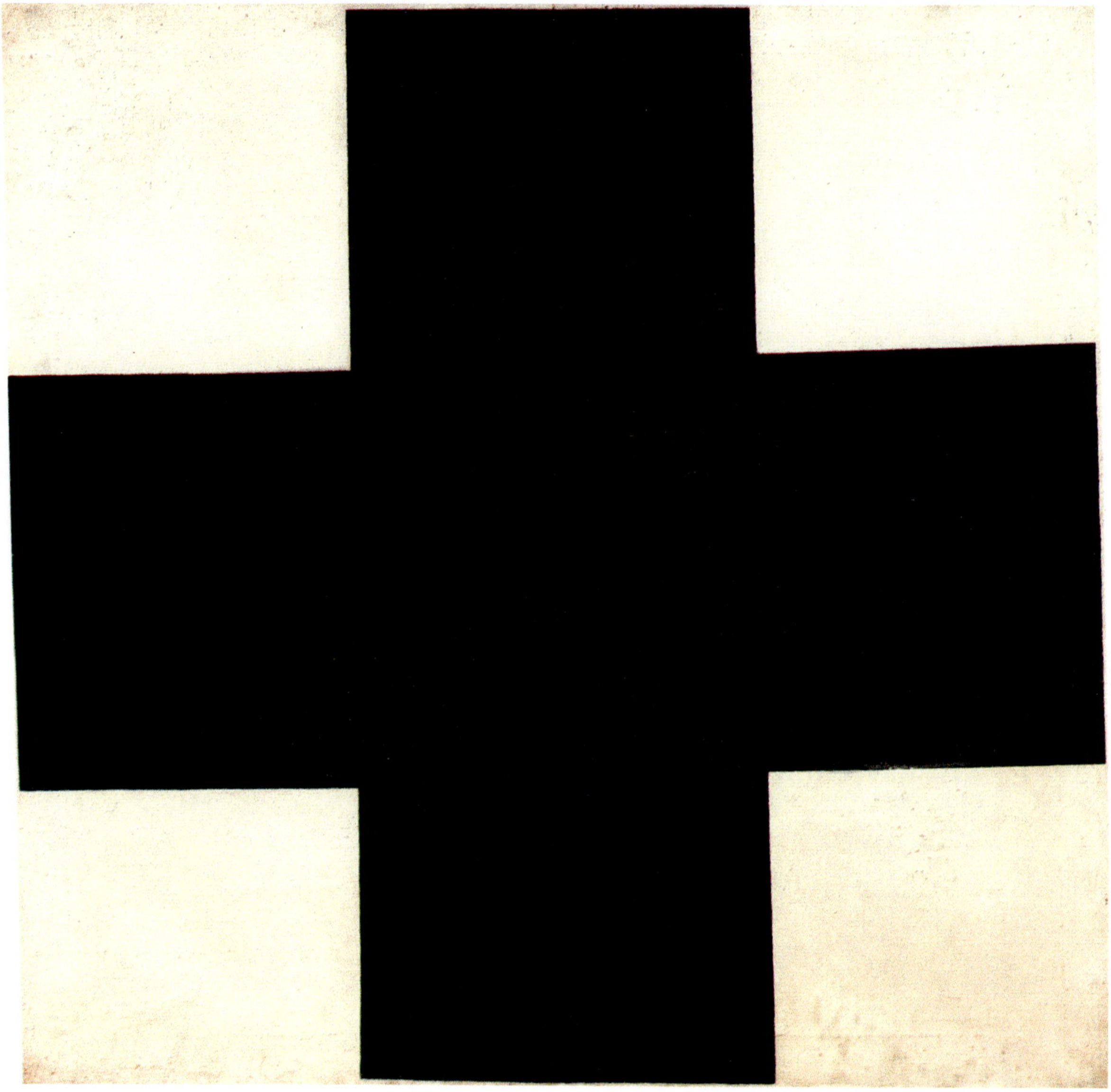

93
Kazimir Malevich

Black Cross, late 1920s
(duplicating 1915)
Oil on canvas
106 x 106 cm (41¾ x 41¾ in)
Russian Museum,
St Petersburg

folds of the garments (Plates 70, 103). Most of the crosses in Malevich's Suprematist work are far more ambiguous and suggestive. Broadly speaking, these more elusive crosses involve an axis (or axes) and quantities of shorter bars crossing it, often at slightly varying angles (Plates 83, 91). In some cases, in which the vertical and horizontal shafts do not actually meet, the dynamic between them is only implicitly that of a cross – they meet by extension. Even when the individual bars are broadened out into planes, the same compositional principle, anchoring all forms around a master axis, subtly prevails. Despite their variety, the basic configuration of the crosses – long shafts loosely crossed by a varying number of shorter shafts – is remarkably similar to that of the traditional eight-pointed Russian Orthodox cross which is composed of a vertical shaft crossed by two horizontal shafts (the horizontal beam of the cross and the panel on which was written INRI) and one tilting shaft (the foot-rest of Christ, Plate 94). The resemblance between the two types of cross is unmistakable, becoming more explicit in some of Malevich's later works, and it seems highly likely, despite his

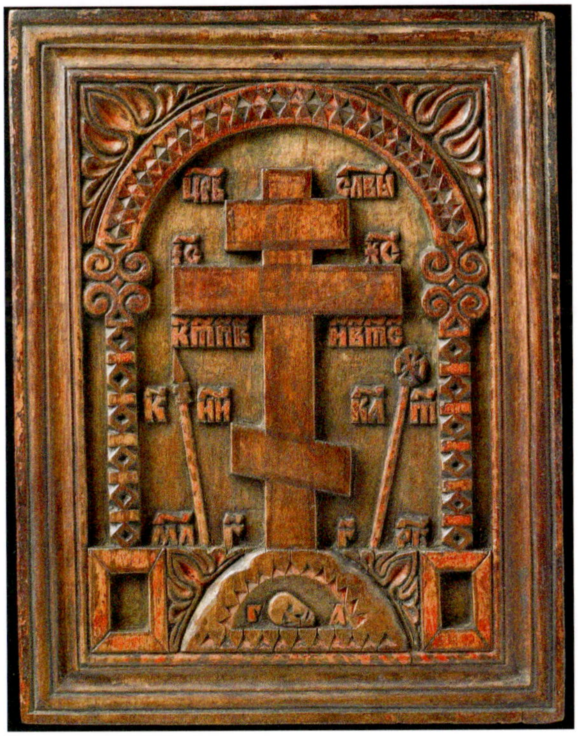

94

An Orthodox cross,
18th century
Wooden relief
Temple Gallery, London

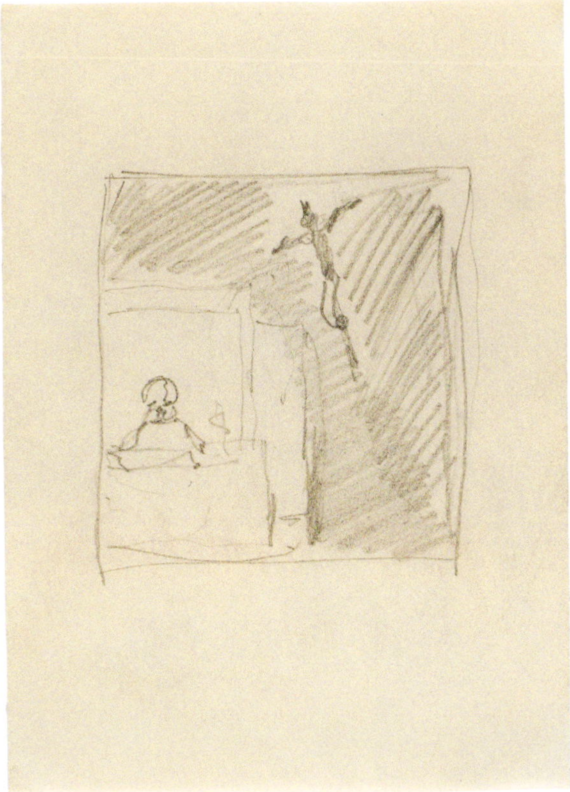

95
Kazimir Malevich

Interior with Figure and Crucifix,
1918
Pencil on paper
7.9 x 7 cm (3 ⅛ x 2 ¾ in)
Stedelijk Museum, Amsterdam

aspiration towards non-objectivity, that the artist was making surreptitious use of the sacrificial-redemptive associations of the form. For the Orthodox Church, the eight-pointed cross both recalled the Crucifixion story at a narrative level and had regenerative symbolic meaning. Apart from representing Christ's foot-rest, the sloping bar at the base of the cross is traditionally associated with the destinies of the good and unrepentant thieves at the Crucifixion. As the Orthodox liturgy makes clear: 'Between the two thieves Thy Cross was found to be a righteous measure, for the one was taken down to Hell by the weight of his blaspheming, while the other was lightened of his transgressions unto the knowledge of theology'.[52]

In the same way, the number eight is traditionally associated with the beginning of a new cycle in nature (as, for instance, in the seven-day week and the seven-note musical scale). Thus, the eight-pointed cross demonstrates the continuum of meaning in Orthodox theology between the historical, narrative dimension of Christianity (the death of Christ) and its symbolic significance (the Resurrection). In this way, the eight-pointed cross – and by extension the cross *per se* – perfectly demonstrates the equivalence of death of personal self and rebirth in God. One of Malevich's *White on White* Suprematist works in the Stedelijk Museum in Amsterdam, in which a tilted shaft is faintly crossed by three arcs, brilliantly conflates the consummate obliteration of art with the self-sacrificial but regenerative symbolism of the Orthodox cross (Plate 91). Only the last traces of these forms remain, as they recede into formlessness; both the form (fading) and the content (the cross) are images of self-sacrifice.

A series of sketches of crucifixions produced by Malevich for the opera *Voyna* (*War*) in 1918 makes the relationship for him between the form of the

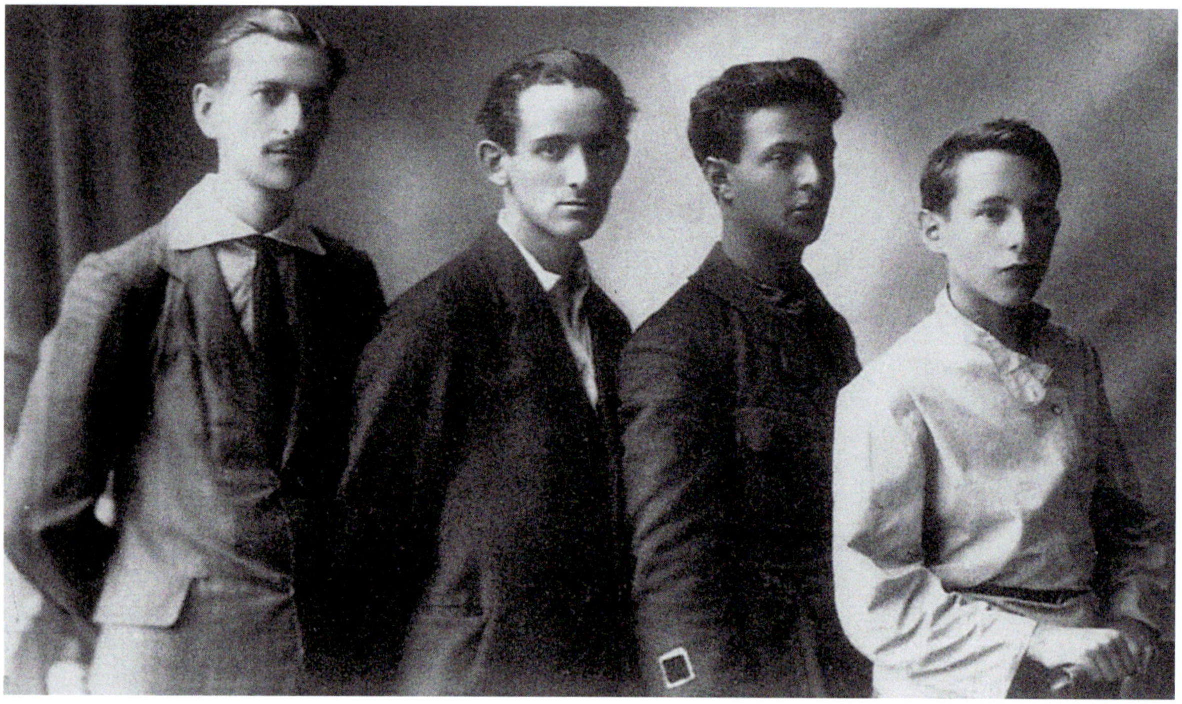

96

Members of UNOVIS, including Ilya Chashnik with a black square on his cuff, Vitebsk, 1922
David King Collection, London

cross and self-sacrifice explicit.[53] The fact that these crosses are floating in the air and are tilted slightly forwards distinguishes them from the historical event of the Crucifixion, strongly associating them with images of the Stigmatisation of St Francis which were popular in western art, especially in Italy, from the thirteenth century onwards (Plate 95). The Stigmatisation of St Francis depicts the moment at which St Francis, while praying in a remote hermitage, had a vision of Christ Crucified in the sky and received the wounds on Christ's hands, feet and side in his own body. The figure of the Crucified tends to hover steeply above the saint and lines of transmission can often be seen linking their wounds. The message of the event, which has countless equivalents in contemporary devotional writing, is that intense contemplation of Christ leads to identification with him (the ultimate state of grace), but that identification with him involves identification with his suffering. Stigmatisation is a particularly graphic and literal expression of this equation. In a more Malevichian context, meditation on the absolute to the point of identification with it is an act of self-sacrifice, for it is impossible

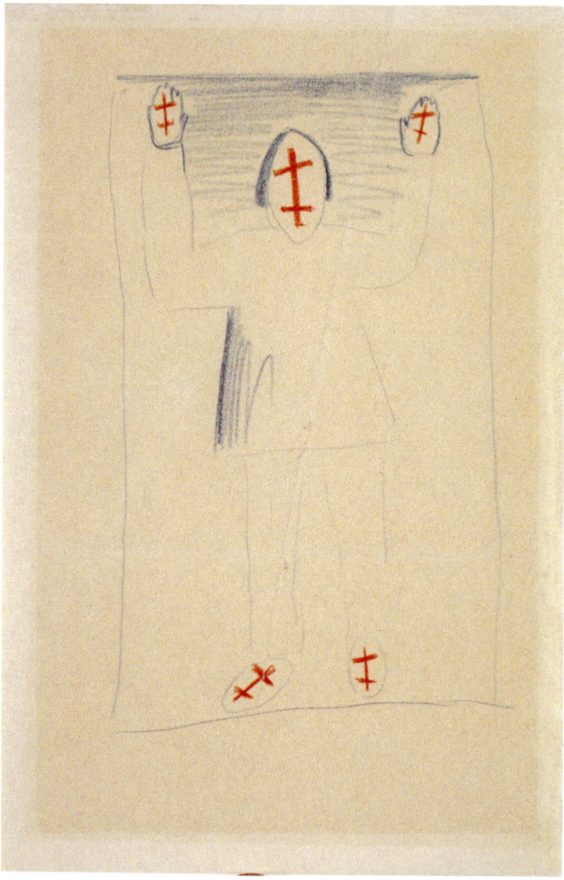

97
Kazimir Malevich

Standing Figure, *c.*1927
Coloured pencil on paper
35.5 x 22.5 cm (14 x 8 ⅞ in)
Stedelijk Museum, Amsterdam

to enter into the realm of the selfless Divine without sacrificing the sense of a separate self.

It can only be supposed that Malevich was appropriating some of these associations when he designed his floating crucifixes, one of which hovers above an unidentified figure exactly as in a trecento panel of the Stigmatisation of St Francis. The suggestion is supported by the fact that some members of Malevich's Suprematist group, UNOVIS (Affirmers of the New Art), were moved to ritualise their selfless commitment to their cause in a quasi-stigmatic way: just as the sign of the cross was often printed or sewn on to the garments of Christians in the Middle Ages as a talisman against demonic powers,[54] so UNOVIS members, including Malevich, sewed a black square on to their cuffs as a sign of their commitment to the establishment of a new world order (Plate 96). As the part of their clothing nearest to the palms of their hands, this gesture had an almost stigmatic significance, corresponding to UNOVIS's Suprematist motto of 1921: 'The overturning of the old world of arts will be etched across your palms.'[55]

Several years after his Suprematist adventure, Malevich made clear reference to stigmatisation in a number of drawings that are unusually explicit in their reflection on the religious implications of Suprematist iconography. An enigmatic drawing from the late 1920s, representing a standing figure stigmatised by crosses on his hands, feet and face, combines the Suprematist imagery of crosses with the iconography of the Crucifixion, resulting in an image of a Suprematist 'passion of man' (Plate 97). In a second drawing, of a head from 1930, the facial features are simultaneously obliterated and represented by a cross whose long cross-beam (in place of the eyes) and shorter tilted foot-rest (in place of the mouth) make it explicitly Orthodox; in this drawing, the very identity of man is transfigured. Two further drawings strongly suggest that this sense of the sacrificial destiny of man is implicit in the cruciform structure of the human body. The stiffness and strict horizontality of the arms in *Figure with Outstretched Arms* closely associate the image with the Crucifixion; in conjunction with this image, and with the image of a stigmatised face, a further drawing of a black oval in a horizontal rectangle above an Orthodox cross in a vertical rectangle is clearly anthropomorphic, eliciting sacrificial connotations from even the most abstract of Suprematist forms.

In retrospect, Malevich's stigmatised and cruciform-man drawings indicate that, by taking his art to a point of mega- and meta-abstraction, he was sacrificing his alter ego; by sacrificing his art for the sake of its own transcendental perfection, he transformed himself into the 'zero of form'.[56] In *The World as Non-Objectivity*, he makes a direct analogy between self-transcendence and death: 'Extreme old age is the threshold of a "world" outside the technology of space and time, nothing irritates hearing or sight, and reflections fade in the eye, the brain changes nothing, all conceptions pass into non-existence, into the non-relative world of consciousness, everything becomes reality, tranquillity descends. Everything has run, striven, and everything has disappeared in this single non-objective reality.'[57]

It is also significant in this context that, at the time of his own death in 1935, Malevich had the *Black Square* hung above his death-bed like an icon, as if it were both a qualification of his conditional life and a gateway into the beyond (Plate 98). A copy of the painting was also placed on his coffin which he designed for himself (as was the custom among peasants in rural Russia) and at his grave. His obvious belief that its material presence at his death-bed would serve as a blessing over the process of his dying corresponds exactly to the Orthodox belief in the graceful effect of icons in the same circumstances. In a traditional Russian household, the body of a dead person would be laid out with the head pointing towards the holy corner and the feet pointing towards the door (Plate 87)[58] A painting by Sergei Ivanov – *Death of a Migrant* (1889) – depicts a peasant, who has died while travelling, laid out on the ground with an icon on his chest. Significantly the icon is laid faced down – for the sake of the deceased, whom it blesses with its gaze, rather than the mourners – though it is laid on a cloth in order not to be contaminated by him (Plate 99).[59]

An illuminating parallel exists here between the *Black Square* and the music of the composer Alexander Scriabin (1872–1915) whose conception of his own late work as agency for the spiritual transformation of mankind resonates powerfully with the transformative vision of Malevich. Just as Malevich regarded the consummate apprehension of his *Black Square* as being dependent on the viewer's transcendence of all forms of objectivity and subjectivity, so Scriabin considered the act of listening to his work to be an active and fundamental part of its realisation, resulting in the self-transcendence of the audience, and ultimately the transformation of the world. Scriabin's use of the 'harmonic series' as the basis for his harmonic system resonates with the traditional reverence felt in Russia for that which is 'not created by human hands', in that the system consists of a series of overtones that are naturally generated from any fundamental tone. Moreover, as the 'harmonic series' rises in pitch, at ever-decreasing intervals, the ability of each note to function harmonically within the overall soundscape of the piece decreases, and the autonomy of each chord or cluster of notes – now juxtaposed, rather than related in a harmonic or narrative manner – increases. Such sounds, and the music composed around such sounds, become incommensurate with the conventional world of mutually dependent meanings, just as icons are incommensurate with the social, psychological and aesthetic agenda of fine art. It becomes quasi-liturgical in the sense that it involves repeated statements – celebrations or revelations – of a natural truth. Although this natural truth is conceptualised as the 'harmonic series', it is not merely significant or symbolic, it is psycho-physiological: at the premier

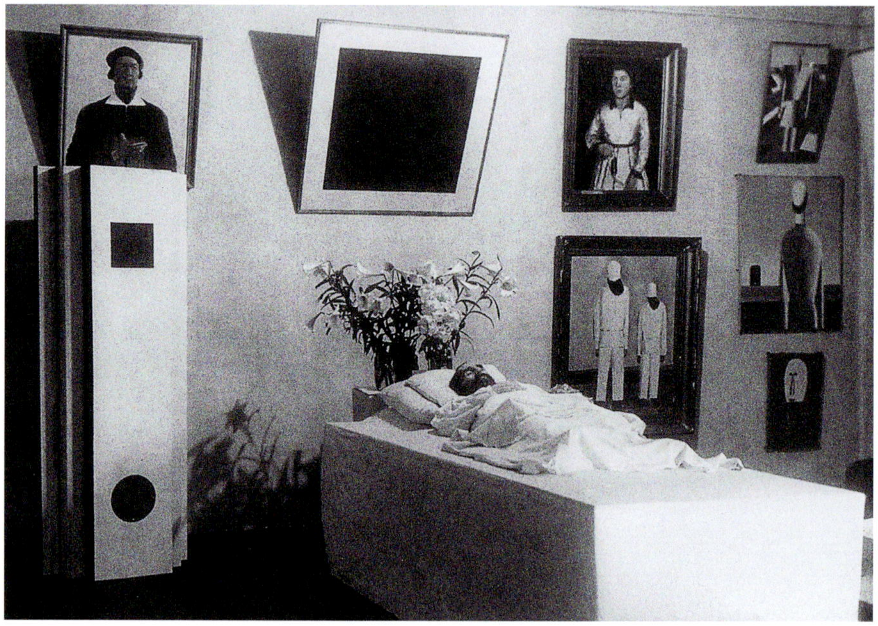

98

Kazimir Malevich on his death-bed, 1935
David King Collection, London

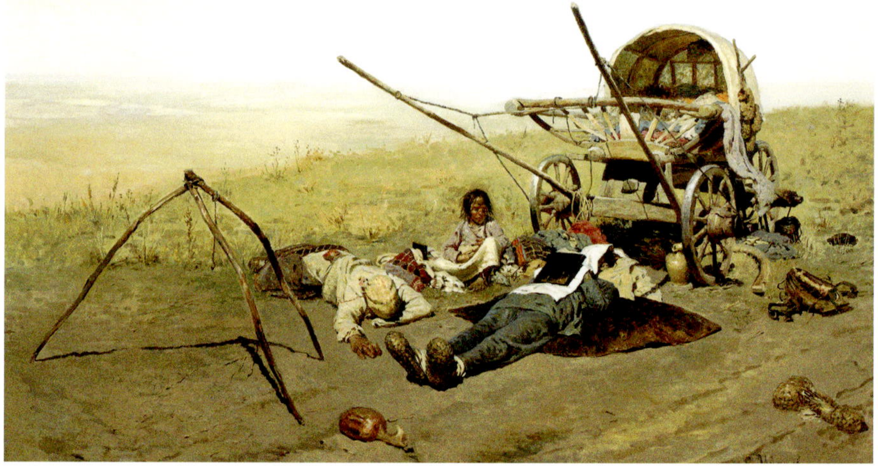

99
Sergei Ivanov

Death of a Migrant, 1889
Oil on canvas
71 x 122 cm (28 x 48 in)
Tretyakov Gallery, Moscow

of Scriabin's symphonic poem *Prometheus*, which was written in this manner in 1911, six people are said to have fainted on hearing the first chord.

Malevich's *Black Square* particularly recalls Scriabin's Ninth Sonata (op.68), which was written three years before, in 1912. To underline the sacramental character of the sonata, one critic described it as a 'Black Mass', evoking the 'necessary evil at the gates of knowledge' – a title that Scriabin accepted. Moreover, the sonata has been more recently described as having 'unusual squareness' on account of the stark, evenly spaced four-fold motif which opens and underpins it.[60] The two works share blackness, quaternity (even squareness) and the sacrificial aspiration (whether expressed as a 'mass' or as an 'icon') to transform darkness and death into whiteness and life. In several other cases, the most advanced works of both artists consistently share a way of concentrating intense energy in a highly charged array of expanding and contracting clusters of floating forms. There is no reason to believe that Malevich was directly influenced by Scriabin, whom he describes (using the terms of late Romanticism rather than the avant-garde) as 'an amazing but effeminate composer passing through us smoothly and evenly, even agreeably'.[61] However, the coincidence and depth of the similarities that can be found between them does usefully serve to highlight the late Romantic ancestry of Malevich's idealism as well as to reflect the intensely felt need for spiritual clarity that existed in Russia during the uncertain years leading up to the Revolution.

Parallels with Malevich's iconic abstraction also exist in the compositions of one of Scriabin's enigmatic followers, Nikolay Obukhov (1892–1954), whose entire oeuvre was underpinned by his fascination with the form of the cross. Obukhov was a fervent Christian and he approached his work more as a religious act than as art. But although his use of the cross has an overt symbolic agenda which his emigration from St Petersburg to Paris in 1918 enabled him to develop, he was also clearly interested in the cross as an abstract sign with its own spiritual impact. It is in all these capacities – the sacramental, the symbolic and the archetypal – that he provides a telling parallel, though not an actual link, to Malevich.

Although Obukhov spent most of his life in Paris, the foundations of his later work were laid in his homeland.[62] Most importantly, his development of a new system of notation, independently of Arnold Schoenberg, and his invention of a form of electronic musical instrument took place in the feverish atmosphere of pre-revolutionary Russia. The sacred purpose to which he put these means was rooted in the Orthodox tradition, various aspects of which pervade his thoughts and work. Above all, Obukhov regarded a work of art, especially music, as a medium for living communion with the divine. He believed that true art was not representational, in the sense that it stimulates the memory or imagination; on the contrary, like Scriabin and Malevich, he considered it to be a primary act, a reality in its own right. According to his way of seeing, the so-called 'composer' did not create the work as such; he was merely a facilitator, akin to a prophet or psychic medium.

This position resonated not only with the 'self-evident truth' of the Suprematist ideal but also with the notion of the icon 'not made by human hands' – a principle of non-subjectivity that underpins so much of the most intense Russian culture and thought, manifesting itself in innumerable different contexts. Indeed, one of Obukhov's earliest known pieces, a three-part meditation for piano on contemplation, grief and repose, was called *Icon* (1915).[63] Because the piece, which is unpublished and unrecorded, is called *Icon* in the singular (it is inscribed *Ikona*, in Russian, and *Icone*, in French, on the manuscript), it seems likely that it was conceived as a triptych rather than as three distinct 'icons'. Each of the three pieces (which last for approximately three and a half minutes when played together) consists of a series of brief but intense strings and clusters of notes placed in a stark, symmetrical arrangement (ABA), with an opening phrase, repeated in a modified form, followed by a more monumental figure (itself also restated), completed by a return to a slightly varied form of the opening figure. The notes are simply juxtaposed, rather than assembled in a fluent and flowing sequence; as a result, they bear more than a passing resemblance to a number of Malevich's Suprematist works. They reach their point of greatest intensity, not at the culmination of a progression, but simply at the middle of the piece, as if they were structured on the basis of a visual/spatial logic, rather than an aural/temporal one. As we shall see, the spatial organisation of Obukhov's scores became a matter of the highest importance to the composer in later years.

Whether these particular pieces came to be called 'iconic' for a specific or general reason is unknown. Bearing in mind the fact that *Icon* is named in the singular, it may well be that it – as well as the individual pieces – was intended to reproduce the simple symmetry of an iconostasis, in which a moment of ultimate intensity and depth is framed by simple, stark and solemn figures, for this is precisely how it is structured. Indeed, a concentrated triptych form of the iconostasis exists in the commonly grouped triad of icons of the Mother of God, Christ and John the Forerunner. This triadic grouping is a summary of the *Tchin* (prayer) row of the iconostasis screen, in which standing figures of Orthodox saints and archangels are seen to converge on the image of Christ, enthroned in Majesty between the Mother of God and John the Forerunner. The smallest examples of these triads of icons are sometimes hinged together. Seen in this light, it is not inconceivable that Obukhov's grouping of contemplation, grief and repose were intended to correspond to the Mother of God, Christ and John the Forerunner respectively, although Christ is typically represented in a majestic rather than suffering mode in this part of the iconostasis. Alternatively, the three pieces may have been intended to represent the three persons of the Trinity, as represented in icons of the Old Testament Trinity (Plate 6, 84). In this case, contemplation, grief and repose could be associated with God the Father, the Son and the Holy Spirit respectively, although interpretations of the image in which the central angel, traditionally represented against a tree, is associated with Christ were deemed over-manifest and heretical, as their implication that the left-hand angel specifically represented God the Father contravened the law against representing him. Whatever Obukhov's reason for associating the piece with icons, it was presumably this aspect of the work – ponderous, concentrated, luminous – that led his audience to find it too static.

Obukhov's belief in the peculiar power of the cross is evinced by his insistent use of the form in his work despite the fact that it could not always be perceived in the music itself. It is abundantly present in the scoring of his work, the choreography of its performance and the electronic instrument he invented, the *croix sonore*. The visual impact of his scores, often organised around the form of the cross, was a fundamental part of their significance, despite the fact that they were largely unseen by the public. In his development of a new system of notation, which dated back to 1914, he replaced sharp and flat notes with notes that were supposed to be

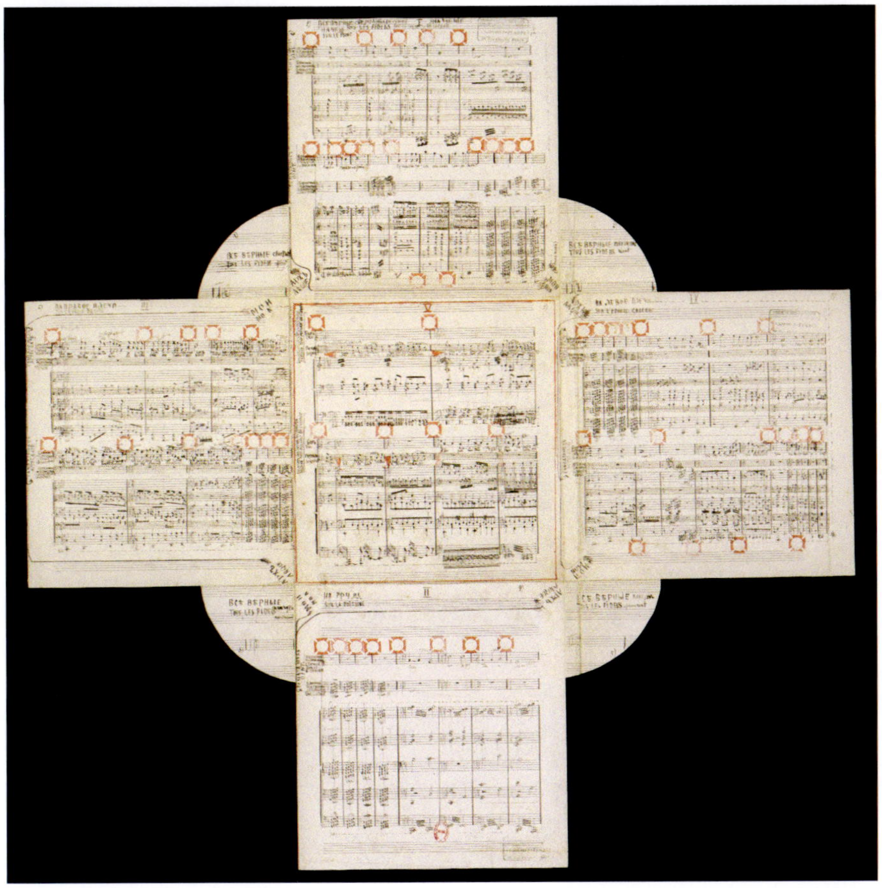

100
Nikolai Obukhov

A page from *The Book of Life*, 1918–*c.*1925
Mixed media on board
80 x 80 cm (31 ½ x 31 ½ in)
Bibliotheque Nationale de France, Paris

identified on their own terms, rather than as an alteration of another note. These notes were marked as crosses, somewhat in the manner of his contemporary, Yefim Golishev. They may have evolved from the crosses used in conventional notation to indicate double-sharps. However, the fact that Obukhov also stamped his bar divisions with large Maltese crosses and crosses with pointed ends suggests that, unlike Golishev, he may also have seen a broader Christian significance in them. In his more visually expressive pieces, many elements are written in red, adding to the overall impression of a sacrificial agenda in the work, though the suggestion that he used his own blood is surely apocryphal.[64]

Significantly, Obukhov's modernity arises more out of his extreme Romanticism than of any reactive anti-Romanticism. He clearly placed himself in the theocratic tradition of Russian Orthodoxy to the extent that, following the Revolution, he intended his music to play a part in the restoration to the throne of Tsar Nicholas II, whom he still believed to be alive and in hiding in the 1920s. In this respect, he was deeply conservative (not to say delusional, like so many Late Romantic visionaries). Of course, he was also radically at odds with contemporary revolutionary composers. Golishev, for instance, developed a serial technique at the same time as Obukhov, giving equal value to each of the 12 notes in a scale, but he considered it to have evolved as part and parcel of the evolution of communism and promoted it as an egalitarian alternative to what he considered to be the hierarchical and autocratic system of the classical tonic-dominant system of harmony.

Despite the fact that Obukhov was politically conservative, his music was ahead of its time; indeed, the fact that it was politically disengaged makes it all the more remarkable and original, if no less strange. His preoccupation with the *croix sonore*, devised in 1929 on the basis of experiments he had made in Russia before the Revolution, is a case in point. While still in Russia, Obukhov began work on an electronic instrument – one of the earliest instruments of its kind, a precursor to the theremin – that was 'played' by interfering with the electrical field around it. The field was regulated by an oscillator, and could be interrupted by moving the hands closer to or further away from an aerial, eliciting a sinuous haunting, wailing sound. Obukhov redesigned this experimental instrument in the form of his *croix sonore*, in which a large brass cross with a star at its centre was mounted on an orb (not dissimilar to the orbs, symbolic of the world, held by archangels in icons) in which the oscillator was concealed. As a result of this design, the activation of the instrument, affected by the player waving his or her hands in front of it, looked

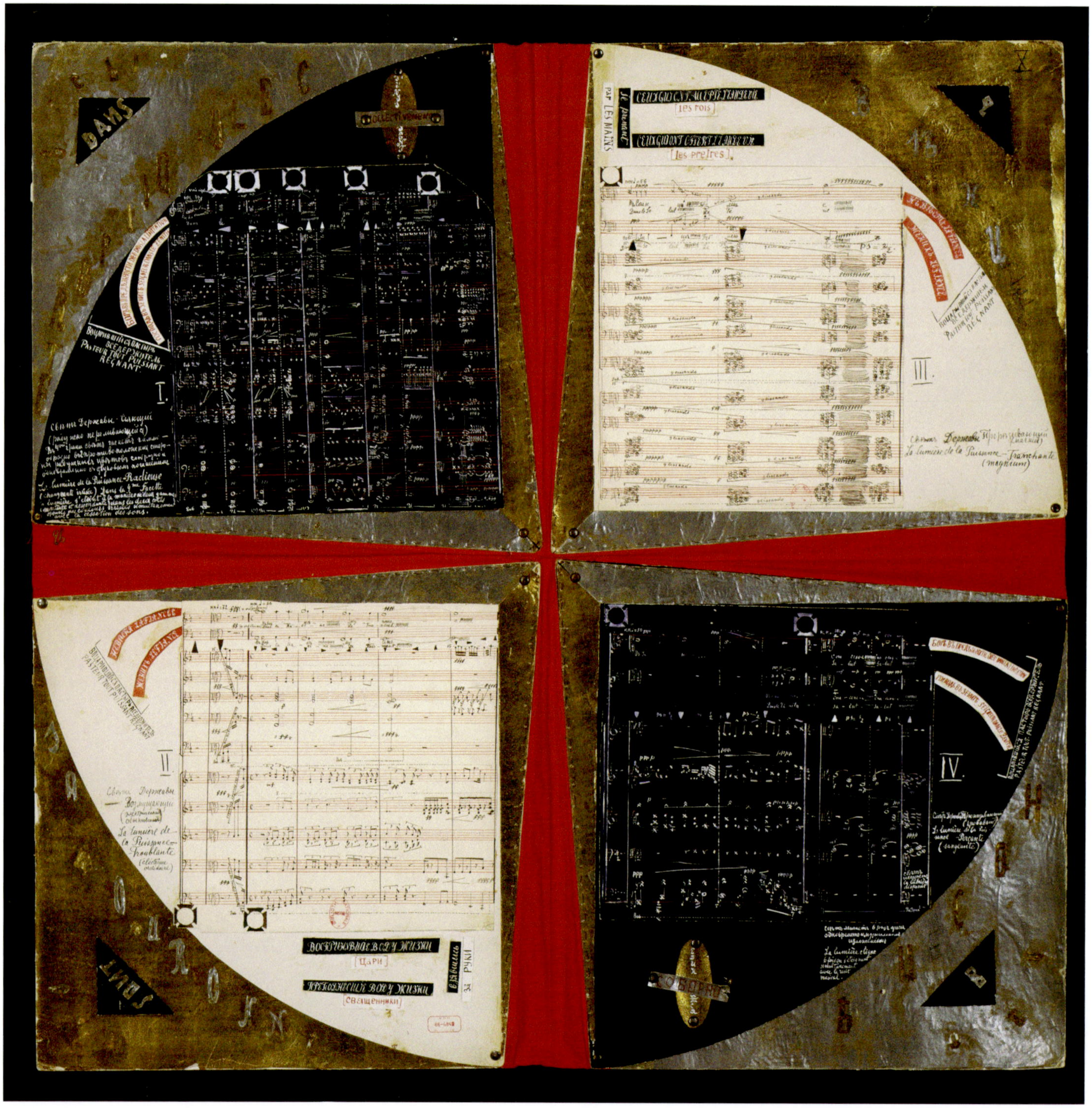

101
Nikolai Obukhov

A page from *The Book of Life*, 1918–*c.*1925
Mixed media on board
75 x 75 cm (29 ½ x 29 ½ in)
Bibliotheque Nationale de Paris

more like praying than playing. Observers of concerts in Obukhov's flat in Paris described the hallowed atmosphere in which women players knelt like pre-Raphaelite angels in silent veneration of the cross, generating a sound that seemed, significantly, not to be 'made by human hands'.

Obukhov's response to the visible form of the cross is impressively reflected in the most visually artistic of his musical projects – his masterwork, *The Book of Life (La livre de vie)*, an epic and programmatic piece for orchestra and choir, written between 1918 and the mid-1920s. The piece, which consists of seven chapters corresponding to the six days of creation and one day of rest, was conceived to be played in a circular purpose-built temple which was, according to one source, to be decorated from designs by Goncharova.[65] Three principal sections of the score consist of collages of different coloured papers, assembled in the form of crosses. One section, which unfolds into the form of a Greek cross, was to be read in such a way that the eyes of the reader are made to move as if genuflecting – from the top arm of the cross to the bottom, to the left, to the right (Plate 100). The faithful listeners were also required to participate in the ritual realisation of the work by whistling, murmuring, laughing and crying, and by making the sign of the cross, thereby undermining the status of the work as a discrete 'object' being consumed by a discrete listening 'subject'.[66]

The other two sections that are conceived as visual images are assembled from four boards linked to each other with fabric that allows them to be folded up and unfolded (Plate 101). Due to their centrality, colour, cruciformity and iconography (communicated verbally in these examples), both pieces share remarkable resemblances to icons of Christ Pantocrator. One piece consists of four near-squares (two red, two white) riveted into quadrants (covered with gold and silver paper respectively) which are joined together by black fabric to form a square in a circle, around the form of a cross.[67] Obukhov's music is written on the squares – white ink on the red squares, red ink on the white ones. The sections of the quadrants that are not covered by these shapes are ornamented with words assembled from individually attached letters (silver on the gold ground, gold on the silver ground) and plaques, the latter encrusted with texts in red, white, black, gold and silver; many of the letters are now missing. Other texts are applied elsewhere on the page, wherever space permits. The overall composition is arranged through rotational symmetry; the colours, the shapes of the plaques and the duplication of the texts in French and Russian, map on to each when rotated 180°.

The impression of an icon is immediately striking. Among the most obvious similarities are the hieratic frontality of the image, and its metallic cladding. Regarding composition, complex four-part icons, loaded with doctrine and ritual, also come to mind. The crude rivets which attach the squares to the quadrants are particularly reminiscent of the earliest metal-clad icons (to which metal protection was applied in small sheets), such as Plate 14, and enhance the Constructivist aspect of the piece. In general, the gold and silver plaques closely resemble the metal frames (*rizas*), identificatory name-plaques and detachable haloes that adorn innumerable icons. In this case the plaques are especially evocative of icons of Christ in Majesty, as their location – at top and bottom, left and right – resembles that of the anthropomorphic symbols of the evangelists in such pieces. The arcane range of colours and the superimposition of geometrical shapes are also suggestive of this icon-type, as indeed is the iconography of the collage which specifically celebrates the all-powerful majesty of

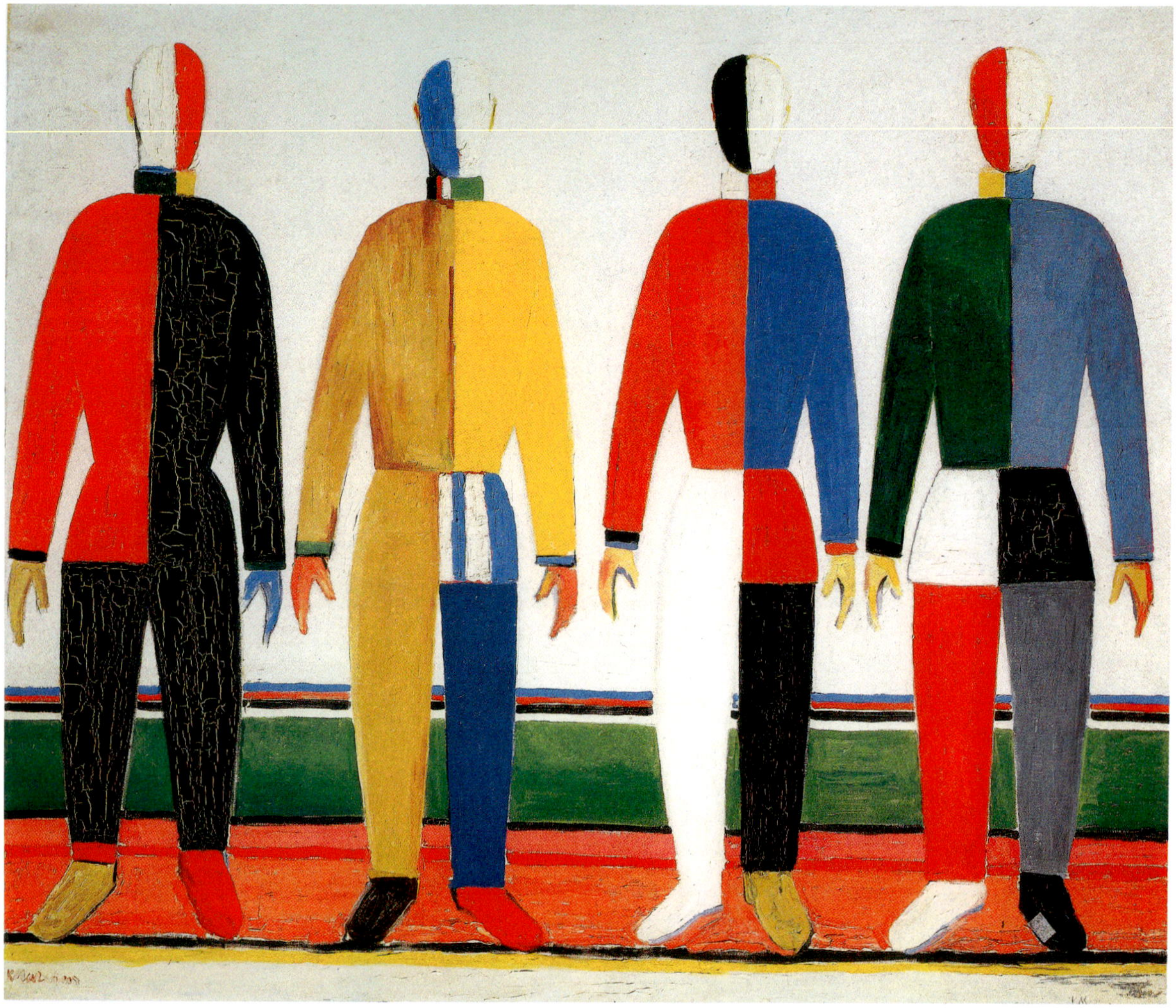

102
Kazimir Malevich

Standing Figures, *c.*1930
Oil on canvas
142 x 164 cm (55 7/8 x 64 5/8 in)
Russian Museum,
St Petersburg

God and the blessings he transmits – from 'the one who wears the crown' to 'those who are offered the water of life' – as kisses on their foreheads, both cheeks and lips. The index of the piece, which is also encrusted with metal plaques and introduced with the highly formalised elongated letters of the Old Slavonic style, divides the score into the mantle, sceptre, throne and crown of the All-powerful, recalling icons of Sophia in Majesty in which Wisdom is represented enthroned with crown and sceptre. Even the rotational composition of the collage serves an iconic purpose, encoding the potential of the piece to operate as a dynamic effective force (akin to visual music) and not merely as a detached and static text or image. As one of the texts (in the lower left square) explains: *'La couronne dans sa rotation atteint un tel degré de vitesse qu'elle obtient l'aspect d'une enveloppe spherique lumineuse changeante tout embrassant'* ('In its rotation, the crown reaches such a degree of speed that it takes on the form of a changing all-embracing spherical envelope of light').

The third of the three cross-pieces[68] differs from the example just described in that the quadrants and the squares within them are black and white, with white and black script respectively, all on red staves; the fabric that links the four panels is red, forming a large and dramatic red cross at the centre of the whole (Plate 101). Unlike the collage described above, the circle, which the

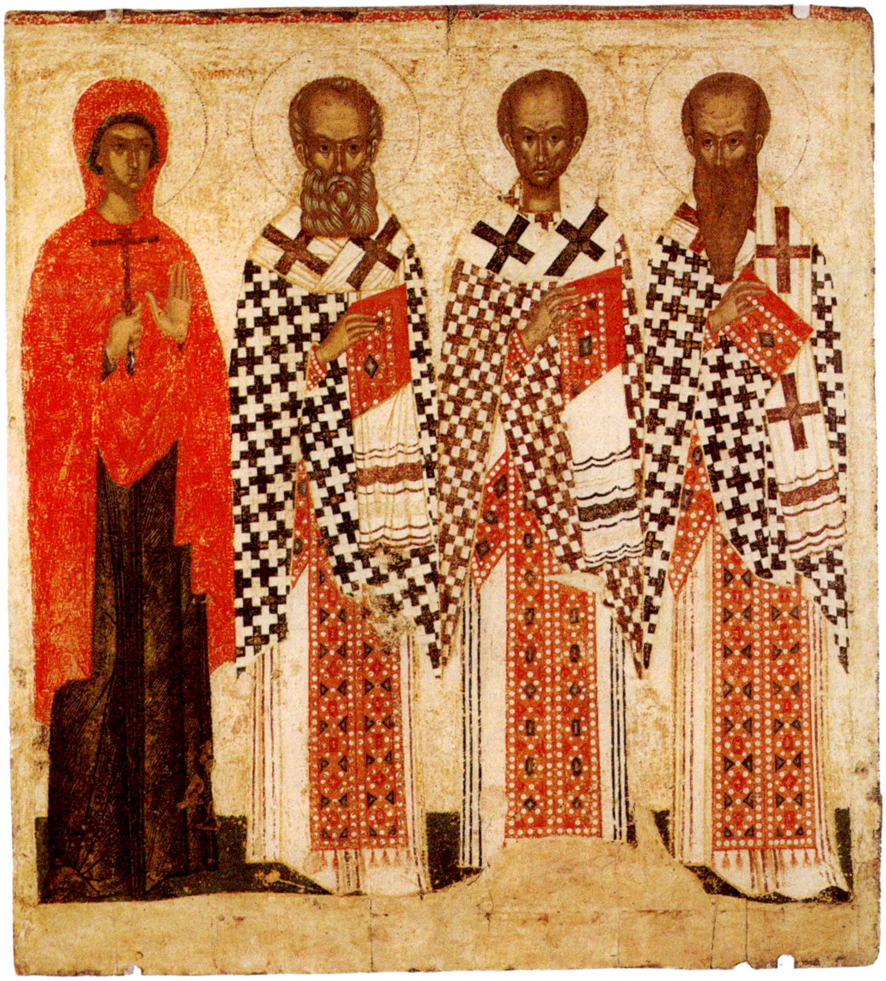

103
St Parascevi, and the Three Holy Hierarchs, Pskov, early 15th century
Tempera on wooden panel
147 x 134 cm (57 9/10 x 52 4/5 in)
Tretyakov Gallery, Moscow

quadrants come together to form, is set within a square, with gold and silver corners (and silver and gold words). In this case the composition of 'square, over circle, over square' comes even closer to the design of icons of Christ in Majesty (diamond, over oval, over diamond) than the previous example. Notwithstanding these details, the overall impression of both collages is one of simultaneous impact, as if the visual impression of the score enables the sound of the music, otherwise extended over time, to be concentrated in one almighty co-ordinated, theophanic and *iconic* blast. Obukhov's conception of the manuscript of *The Book of Life* as an icon – as well as the music – is reflected in the fact that he kept it in a 'sacred corner' in his home, among icons and candles.

Besides their iconic intensity, directness and immediacy, these pages suggest an obvious but uncanny relationship to Malevich's *Black Square*, *Black Cross* and *Black Circle* (Plates 85, 89, 93). However, the fact that there is no evidence to suggest that Malevich and Obukhov knew each other, or even knew of each other, highlights the significance of the cross not only as an image with widespread symbolic potential, but also as a form with archetypal resonances. Both artists identified strongly with the cross, using it in very different ways to translate the essence of what they believed to be an ancient – or rather eternal – tradition into an artistic language of the utmost modernity. The parallel is striking in view of the fact that Obukhov spent most of his working life in France and that most of his work post-dates Malevich's Suprematism by several years. This anachronism may be due to the fact that his work continued to feed directly on resources developed during his years in Russia, sometimes to the exclusion of more recent local impressions, and as a result of which he was never fully understood and accepted in his adopted homeland.

Following his consummation of the Suprematist ideal in his *White on White* paintings, Malevich's commitment to the process of object-transcendence was made manifest in a most tangible and practical way. He was not prepared simply to indulge his fascination with the paradoxical concept of a 'non-objective art object'. Recognising that this is a contradiction in terms, and that by definition the apprehension of an 'art object' precludes the realisation of 'non-objectivity', he sacrificed his identification with art and gave up painting, releasing his creative energy into his life and consciousness as a whole. For eight or nine years he did not paint at all, increasingly dedicating himself to realising his Suprematist aim through teaching and writing.

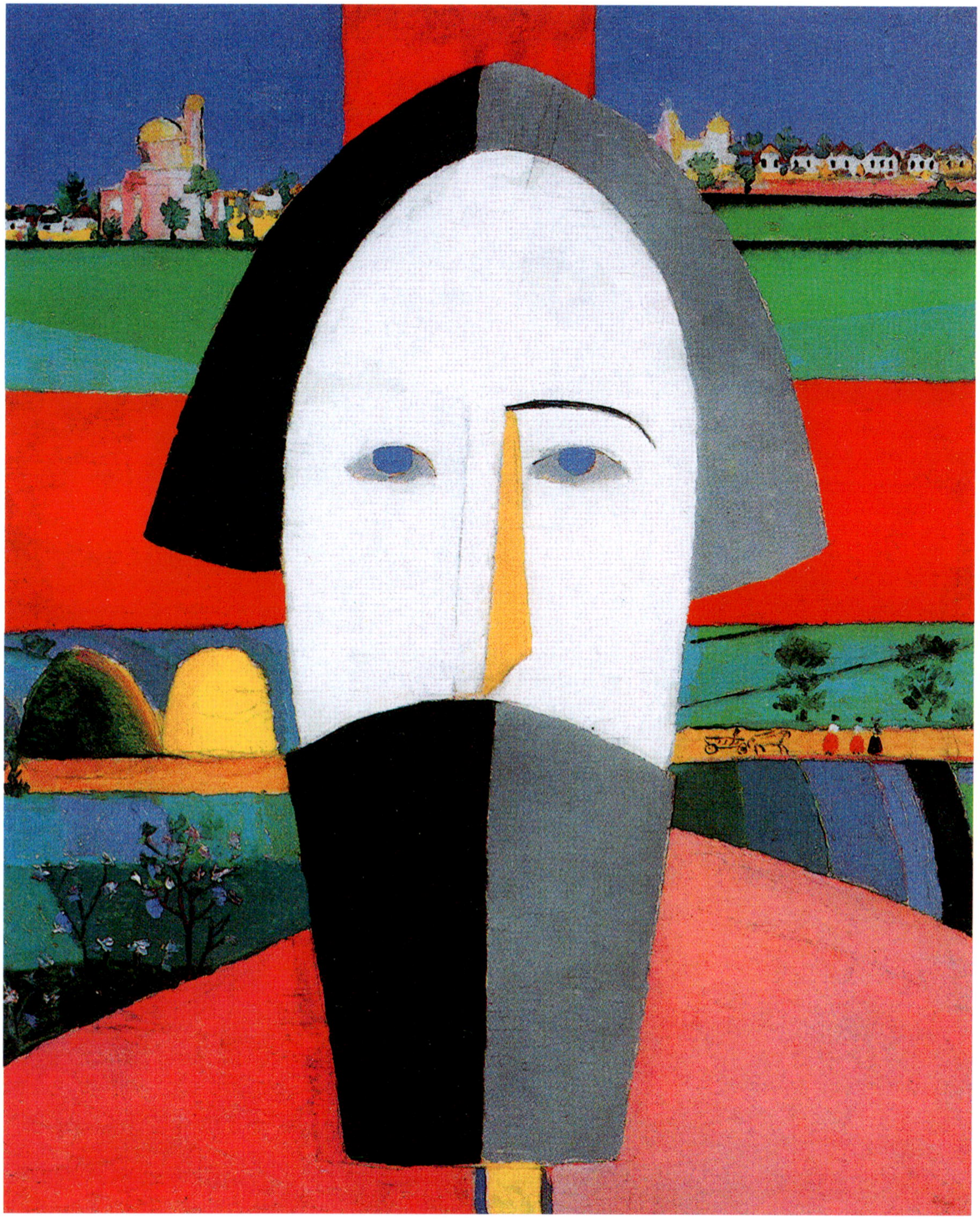

104
Kazimir Malevich

Head of a Peasant,
1928–9 version
Oil on plywood
69 x 55 cm (27 ⅛ x 21 ⅝ in)
Russian Museum,
St Petersburg

105
Kazimir Malevich

Self-portrait, 1933
Oil on canvas
73 x 66 cm (28 ¾ x 26 in)
Russian Museum,
St Petersburg

106
Kazimir Malevich

Madonna/Maternity, 1930–2
Pencil on paper
9.2 x 8.5 cm (3 ⅝ x 3 ⅜ in)
Museum Ludwig, Cologne

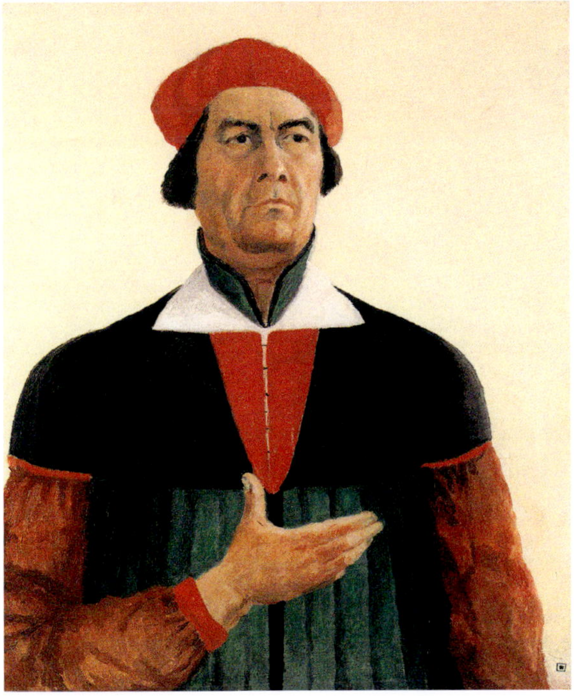

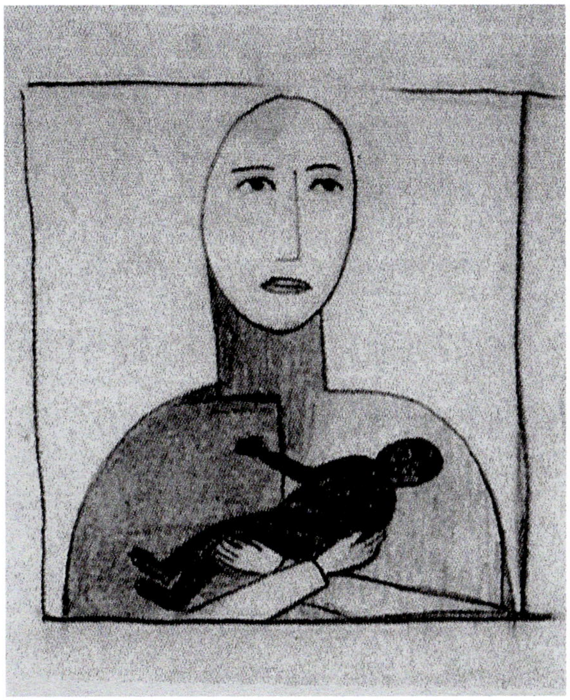

When he did eventually resume painting at the end of the 1920s, his works were either duplicates of his earlier work (painted to replace missing sections of his oeuvre), or else they are of decidedly inferior artistic value.

Both on their own terms and in their historical context, Malevich's late works have none of the universal significance attributable to his Suprematist development and, in many cases, the actual quality of the painting – never Malevich's primary concern – is very ordinary. His mannequin figures of 1928–32 are certainly of interest in the context of the life of a great philosopher-painter, and have some decorative appeal on account of their simple composition and fresh colours. However, there is a stiffness and monotony about them that is curiously out of keeping with the investigative spirit and sense of threshold that so characterises all his earlier work (Plate 102). At the same time, although these figures can be related generically to Constructivist costume designs, including his own (and to icons of the Holy Hierarchs, Plate 103), they share none of the Constructivists' vision of a new society united through action. Unlike Popova's costume designs, in which uniformity becomes a sign of strength and commitment to a collective ideal, Malevich's asthmatic figures seem uncomfortably restricted by their quasi-Suprematist body-tight uniforms. They are curiously dull and unmotivated, posing awkwardly for the painter. Their facelessness and expressionlessness are frequently more indicative of vacancy than of universality. His Renaissance-style portraits of the 1930s are no less devoid of energy and enthusiasm. The figures – representing specific individuals this time – stand impassive and wan, their hands half-heartedly gesticulating (plate 105).

To be fair, the works show all the signs of being an expedient compromise. While they certainly reflect Malevich's disillusionment at the Revolution's failure to realise his Suprematist dreams, and surely anticipate the Soviet state's mission to suppress the liberating power of individual creativity, they may also reflect his personal conviction that any attempt to realise the feeling of non-objectivity in an art 'object' is self-contradictory and ultimately futile. Malevich initially demonstrated his commitment to this conviction by renouncing art as a metaphysical medium. His continued commitment to it is demonstrated by the fact that each of his very last works – the Renaissance-style portraits – is qualified by the presence of a minute black square in one of its corners, suggesting that the truth about art continued to lie for him in the infinity of the *Black Square* (plate 105).

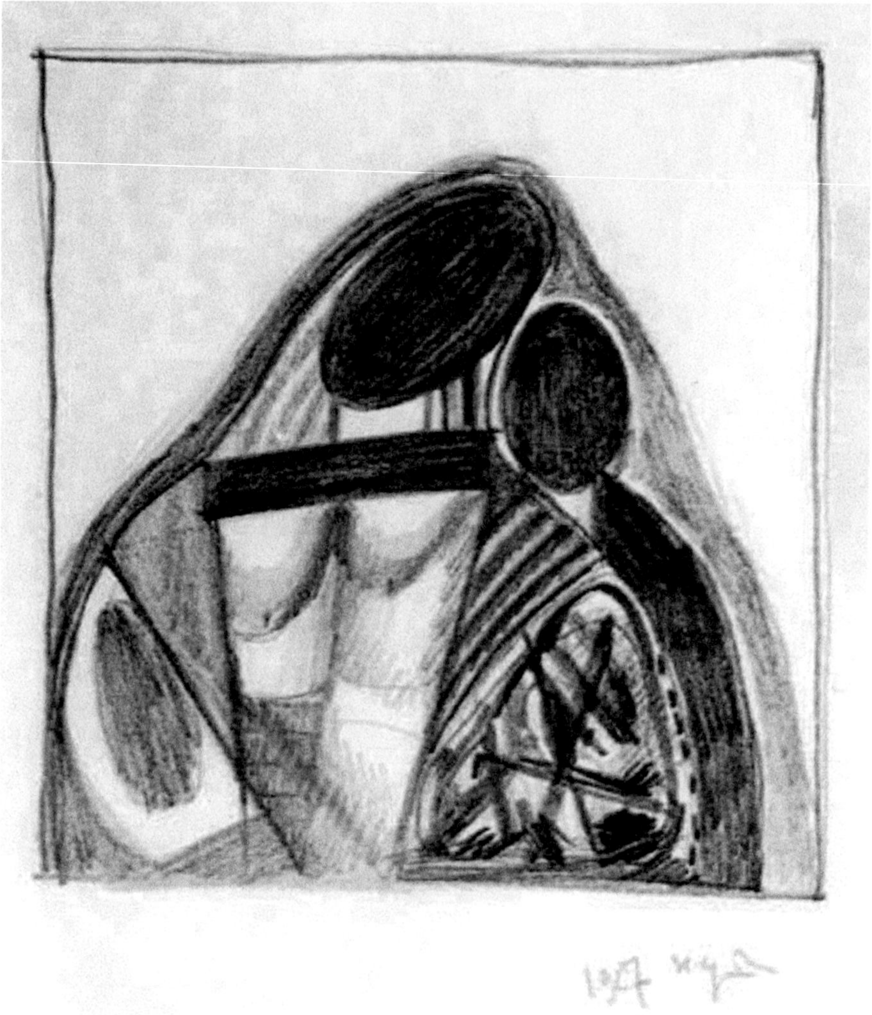

Where the influence of icons is still present in Malevich's late work, it is no longer recreated as a universal spiritual aesthetic – as was the case in Suprematism. On the whole, it is more overtly religious – regressively copying the appearance of an icon rather than translating its essence into a contemporary idiom. His *Head of a Peasant* of 1927–9, for instance, directly duplicates the intimate scale and frontality of many icons of the head of Christ (Plates 1, 104). The cross behind the peasant's head makes a direct reference to the cruciform halo of Christ in icons, thereby beatifying the lot of the peasantry in keeping with the agricultural idealism of the communists. The peasant's neat central parting, the long Byzantinesque nose, the ridged 'paper-fold' eye-brows, the intense heavy-lidded eyes, the long beard and the de-emphasised mouth are all typically iconic features. Moreover, unlike most of Malevich's paintings from this period – but like icons – *Head of a Peasant* is painted on a wooden panel.

A number of late works by Malevich can be directly associated with icons of the Hodigitria Mother of God. The *Self-portrait* of 1933, for instance, is chiefly comparable to icons of the Hodigitria on account of the artist's posture (Plates 4, 105). Although there are certainly similarities between the hieratic monumentality and gestures of the figures, their simulated frames and plain ivory backgrounds, the suggestion that Malevich was, by association, attempting to appropriate the Virgin's role as 'Pointer of the Way' (Hodigitria) – in his case, towards the greater reality of nothingness – seems excessive, especially if one bears in mind that these features are also present in portraits of other sitters. Two drawings of *Maternity* (Plate 106), from around 1930, are more convincingly associated with the image of the Hodigitria,

107
Nikolai Suetin

Drawing of a Mother and Child, 1927
Pencil on paper
22 x 17.7 cm (8 5/8 x 7 in)
Private collection

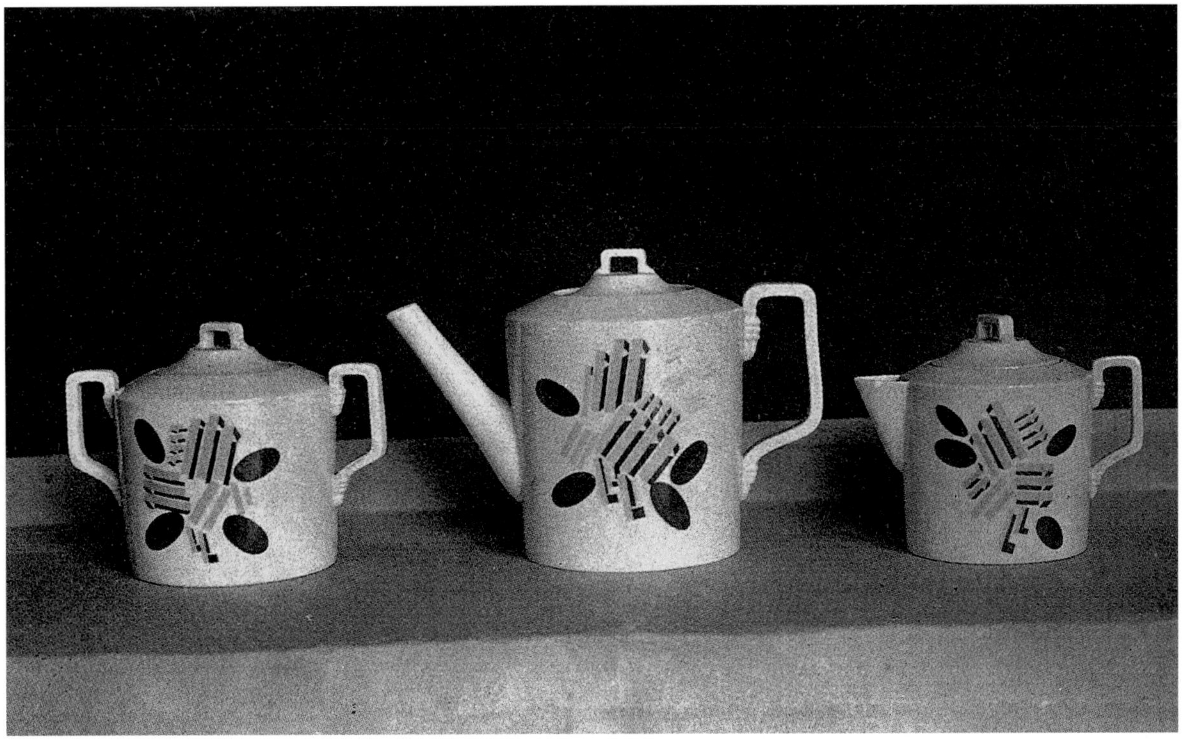

108
Nikolai Suetin

Pieces from the porcelain 'Brusnichka' tea service, 1929
David King Collection, London

which they clearly translate into mannequin form. The works strike a balance between compositional impact and iconographic implications, though the latter are clearly more dominant, reflecting the artist's current interest in the body as an anonymous unit of identity. As with *Head of a Peasant*, the images depersonalise their subject, reducing the Virgin and Christ to mere embodiments of humanity, though they also allow the simplicity of human motherhood to be associated with the sanctity of the Virgin.[69]

One of Malevich's most devoted protégés, Nikolai Suetin (1897–1954), also based designs on images of the Mother of God in the late 1920s, though Suetin developed the Suprematist potential of his models more thoroughly and explicitly than Malevich. At a time when Malevich was no longer exploring Suprematism, Suetin's interest in the image of the Hodigitria appears to have derived from his wish to infuse the metaphysical truths of Suprematism with emotional depth. He had been familiar with icons since his childhood, but intimated that it was only after the development of abstraction in European art that the visual language of icons, in which their emotional depth was encoded, could be understood and even used.[70] Suetin had been one of Malevich's students at UNOVIS, the Suprematist school that Malevich directed in Vitebsk from 1919–20. When Malevich moved to Petrograd in 1922, Suetin accompanied him and began working at the Petrograd State Porcelain Factory (renamed the Lomonosov State Porcelain Factory in 1925), which he directed between 1932 and 1954. The factory had been developed from the Imperial Porcelain Factory in 1917 and it quickly adapted itself to the prerequisite mass-production of utilitarian wares, mostly decorated with propagandist imagery and slogans.

In 1927, Suetin produced a number of drawings of single women, with featureless faces, in which the oval faces and bold overall silhouette of the shrouded figures are clearly associated with icons of the Hodigitria (Plates 4, 107). As in Malevich's paintings of faceless androids, begun in the same year, the figures are highly abstracted, partially reduced to an assembly of simple shapes. However, they differ from Malevich's hieratic and impersonal figures in that they have a distinctly melancholy disposition, chiefly communicated by their slightly tilted heads and delicate hands, which are also reduced to mute ovals. In contrast to their iconic prototypes, the shoulders of the women have been developed into bold horizontal bars (very slightly tilted off the horizontal axis) which form a fundamental part of the compositions. Visually, this feature, which is typically Suprematist, resembles the horizontal bar of the cross in the Crucifixion, further heightening the reflective mood of the images. One of the images, in which the folds of the Virgin's garments are exaggerated in order to function independently as compositional features, incorporates the form of the Christ Child into the design. In several cases, the hair of the Mother of God and the lining of her garment are represented as areas of parallel stripes, highlighted in such a way that they resemble the reflective tubular forms of the work of the French painter, Fernand Léger (and which also feature in Malevich's early paintings of peasants).

In 1929, Suetin developed these designs into decoration for a porcelain tea service, 'Brusnichka' (Plate 108), in which the clusters of ovals and parallel two-tone bars are simplified to such an extent that their source in the image of the Hodigitria is no longer recognisable, though its existence is abundantly clear from the intermediary designs produced two years earlier. Remarkably, the designs are not only iconic by virtue of the metaphysical agenda of their Suprematism, which runs parallel to the sacramental theology of icons; they indicate an explicit formal link between icons and Suprematism, in which the visual language of the former is seen to be organically abstracted, purified and reduced to its essence – both in its form and its content – in the latter.

Malevich's realisation of the absolute work of art was not only consummate for Russia; it was also consummate for the European art tradition as a whole. In his hands, the language of art, through which the depths of consciousness had, for several centuries, been mediated into human experience, had become progressively refined to the point at which it was no longer necessary. It was now possible, thanks to Malevich's instrumentality, for the depth of consciousness to be realised in itself, unlimited to personal experience and unmediated by art. Acknowledging the significance of his work, one contemporary critic called his *Black Circle* (visible in Plate 89) the 'full stop in the history of art'. In the West, this consummation led to the total crisis of twentieth-century art, in which (also precipitated by the evolution of psychoanalysis) art as such suddenly threatened to seem superfluous. The conventions of art survived, of course, developing their own new rationales. In the East, Malevich's contemporaries – the Constructivists and others – called for an end to fine art, but by the end of the 1930s, his own vision was also being overlooked. The communist regime insisted on the reintegration of the artist into the utilitarian fabric of society. One of the new purposes to which artists were put was to produce political propaganda which, as we shall see in the next chapter, had its own precedents in the icon-painting tradition.

NOTES

1. Some Romanian artists of the period were also influenced by the Christian iconography of Romanian Orthodox art. Constantin Brancusi's *Heads* are surely influenced by the heads of saints, which often appear to be isolated from their bodies by their large and brightly gilded haloes; the arching continuation of the profile of the nose into the eyebrow is particularly Byzantine. The parallel is especially convincing in relation to the large number of severed heads of martyrs which appear (retaining their haloes – and often horizontal) in sixteenth-century cycles of narrative frescos in churches throughout Moldavia. Significantly, some of Brancusi's surviving heads were also severed from full figures. The artist destroyed the bodies of the sculptures, keeping their heads, because he considered them to be too obviously subject to external influence – in this case, from African sources. See Rubin, W. (ed.), *Primitivism in 20th Century Art*, Museum of Modern Art, New York, 1984, pp 346–51. Dmitri Paciurea's life-size bronze of the reclining Virgin (1912, National Museum of Art of Romania, Bucharest), taken directly from an icon of the Dormition of the Virgin, is a unique attempt to adapt a time-honoured convention of icon painting to a completely new medium. *The Gallery of Romanian Modern Art*, Bucharest, 2001, no.74, p.131.
2. Rudenstine (1976), p.62. See also Friedman (1984), p.111.
3. Lassaigne, p.20. See also Venturi, pp 10–13.
4. Compton (1985), p.19.
5. Zweite, p.43, plate 4.27.
6. Povelikhina & Kovtun, p.70.
7. Vezin, p.37.
8. The style of the icon suggests that it was painted in the province of Vologda, where Kandinsky travelled as an ethnography student in 1889. Weiss, p.2, 3.
9. *Natalia Goncharova*, p.292.
10. Ibid cat.no.102.
11. See Filonov's *Peasant Family* (1914) and *The Mother* (1916); *Filonov* (1990), cat.nos 32, 46. Siniakova's *Eve* (1916) is reproduced in Marcadé, J.-C. (1989), p.33.
12. Betz, pp 38–45.
13. Rusakov (1986), p.110.
14. Translated into English in 1914 in Marsden. The Grand Duke used the pseudonym KR for Konstantin (Konstantinovich) Romanov.
15. Bowlt (1982), p.152.
16. 'I refused to do the ballet both because I disapproved of the idea of presenting the Mass as a ballet spectacle and because Diaghilev wanted me to compose it and *Les Noces* for the same price.' Craft & Stravinsky, p.48, n.1.
17. *Nathalie Gontcharova/Michel Larionov*, p.98; Kochno, p.101.
18. *Nathalie Gontcharova/Michel Larionov*, p.98.
19. Massine, p.74.
20. *Natalia Goncharova*, p.261; Sokolova, p.69.
21. This description is from Geldern, p.50.
22. Law & Gordon, p.97.
23. Massine, p.209.
24. Ibid p.239. The ballet was televised in the UK in 1961 and in the USA in 1962. The review in the *New York Times* read: '...at times the presentation almost seemed to be a succession of religious tableaux coming to life out of a stained glass window. The delicacy and inventiveness of the choreography ... imparted a mood of sustained awe... In the Ascension scene there was a grandeur of pictorial composition and a majesty of dimension rarely seen. The scene of the Crucifixion was unforgettable, a visual *tour de force* of Christ towering in agony above the boisterous soldiers fighting over his garments'.
25. *Natalia Goncharova*, p.294.
26. Ibid cat.no.106.
27. Ibid cat.no.83.
28. Chamot (1979), p.12.
29. From an album in the Khardzhiev Archive, published in Petrova (2002), p.215.
30. Chipp, p.342.
31. Malevich, *Essays*, vol.1, p.33, in Bowlt (Dec 1973), p.22.
32. 'Miracula SS. Cosmae et Damiani, miracle 15' in Mango, p.139. Practices of this kind are also mentioned in a letter from the Byzantine Emperor Michael II 'the stammerer' to Louis the Pious in AD 824. See Bevan, p.145.
33. Andersen (1976), p.297.
34. Milner (1984), p.240, n.12. Benois' very negative review was printed in the periodical *Rec'* in January, 1916. Cf also Sharp, J., 'The Critical Reception of the 0,10 Exhibition: Malevich and Benua' in *The Great Utopia*, p.42. For the word translated here as 'background', Benois used the word *oklad*, a technical term that refers specifically to the frame of an icon.
35. See p.currently p.17
36. Simmons (1981), p.236.
37. Significantly, some peasant homes in Bavaria have a comparable domestic corner shrine – the *herrgottswinkel* – in which sacred paintings on glass are displayed. See Lepowitz, pp 100–3.
38. Stanley, pp 363, 371.
39. The *Wedding feast of Peter the Great*, engraved by Alexei Zubov in 1712, is reproduced in Brikner, A.G., *Illiustrirovaniiaia istoria Petra Velikago*, St Petersburg, 1882, vol.I, after p.144.
40. Andersen (1976), p.354.
41. Turowski, pp 172–3.
42. Chipp, p.342.
43. Andersen (1976), p.289.
44. *Gregory Palamas*, p.34.
45. Florensky (1996), p.58.
46. Ibid pp 68–9.
47. Ibid p.63.
48. *Gregory Palamas*, p.35.
49. Chipp, p.342; see also Crowther, p.54.
50. Malevich, 'God is Not Cast Down' in Andersen (1971), pp 196–7.
51. Malevich said these words to Antoine Pevsner in 1919. Gray, p.240.
52. Kontakion for the ninth hour in the Liturgy of the Presanctified Gifts. See Ouspensky & Lossky, p.181. I am grateful to Tatiana Wolff for the quotation.
53. *Kazimir Malevich* (1997), cat.nos 46, 47. See also no.48.
54. *Oxford Dictionary of Byzantium*, Oxford University Press, 1991, vol.1, p.550.
55. *The Great Utopia*, pp 60, 63. See also Nakov (1986), p.69.
56. Bowlt (1988), p.118.
57. Andersen (1976), p.276.
58. Matissian, M., 'The Peasant Way of Life' in Vucinich, W. (ed.), *The Peasant in Nineteenth Century Russia*, Stanford, 1968, p.29. Cited in Hilton (1995), p.25.
59. Ironically, it looks rather like the *Black Square*!
60. Macdonald, H., sleeve notes to Scriabin's Complete Piano Sonatas (Ashkenazy), Decca, 1989, p.7.
61. Written in a letter to his composer-friend Mikhail Matiushin in November 1916; Andersen (1978), p.209.
62. For comments on the history of icon painting by Russian émigrés in Paris after 1917, see Struve; Aslanov, pp 71–4.
63. Bibliotheque National de France, Paris, MS.15303. See 'Obouhow', *New Grove Dictionary of Music*, Macmillan, London.
64. Sitsky, p.259.
65. Lebeau, p.68; Sitsky, p.257.
66. Bibliotheque National de France, Paris, MS.15226, 7e, II.
67. Bibliotheque National de France, Paris, MS.15226, 7e, I. Reproduced in Shaw-Miller (2002), p.74.
68. Bibliotheque National de France, Paris, MS.15226, 7e, III.
69. Malevich has also been credited (by his daughter) with painting a unique *Suprematist Madonna* which represents a standing Virgin and Child composed of purely Suprematist forms (Kirichenko, p.272, plate 300). Many aspects of the painting cast serious doubt on its attribution to Malevich.
70. Rakitin (1998), pp 135–8.

Владимир Ильич УЛЬЯНОВ (ЛЕНИН).

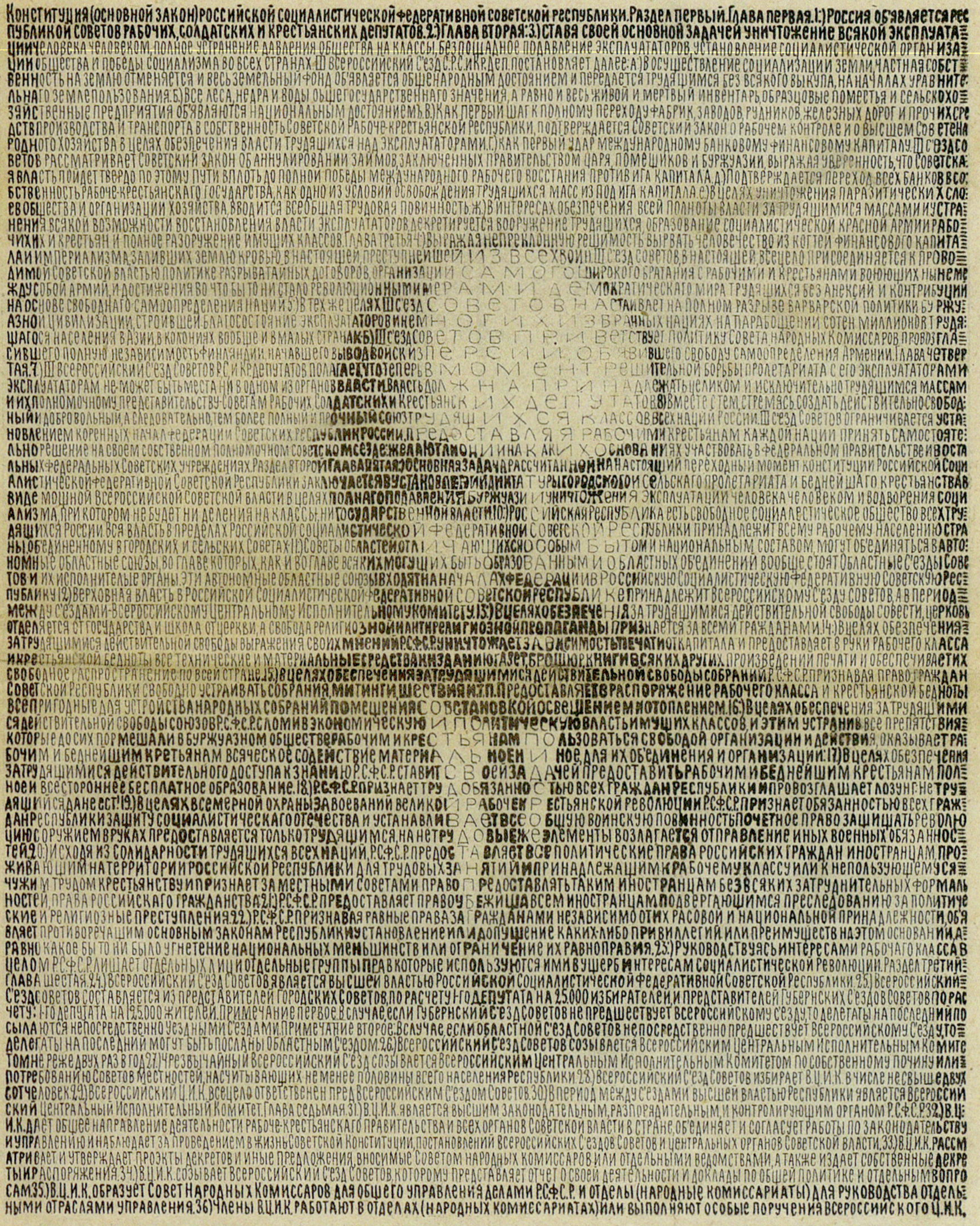

Портрет, выступающий на фоне текста первых 6 глав Конституции РСФСР.

Работа акад. Смоликова).

5

Icons and Propaganda

THE COMMUNIST REGIME was, of course, profoundly unsympathetic towards Christianity and the Church. Some radicals would have been glad to eradicate all traces of it, as well as all signs of aristocratic art and culture. Others were more practical – resolved to make use of the remains of the old culture, ostentatiously trivialising it in the process in many cases (Plate 110) – and others still, including artists, attempted to integrate it more subtly into a more organic vision of the future.

Although icons continued to influence avant-garde art in the early Soviet period, their influence as sacred art – that is to say, at a level that required that they be acknowledged for what they are – came to a head with the October Revolution of 1917. Prior to this time, prophetic intuition of radical change in the near future seemed to give every idealistic cause an air of inevitability. The phenomenon of 'God-building' – the attempt to liberate the human and spiritual essence of religion from its conventional and suppressive encrustations and reconcile it with new ideals of political justice – reached its peak at this time. The leading 'God-builders', Alexander Bogdanov and Anatolii Lunacharsky, believed that radical communism was too dry and theoretical to be widely appealing and that a more subtle and sympathetic contextualisation was necessary if the people were to accept it. The internal structural dynamics of religion, for instance, which were already operative in society, could be adapted to the communist cause. Indeed, they maintained that early Christianity had espoused the cause of the oppressed in a selfless and communally-minded way that was consistent with communism, but that in subsequent centuries the ideal had been distorted and corrupted by the institutional Church. In his pre-revolutionary *Religion and Socialism* (1908–11),

109
Smolnikov

Lenin, a page from ***Red October***, celebrating the 5th Anniversary of the October Revolution, using text from Lenin's constitution, 1922
David King Collection, London.

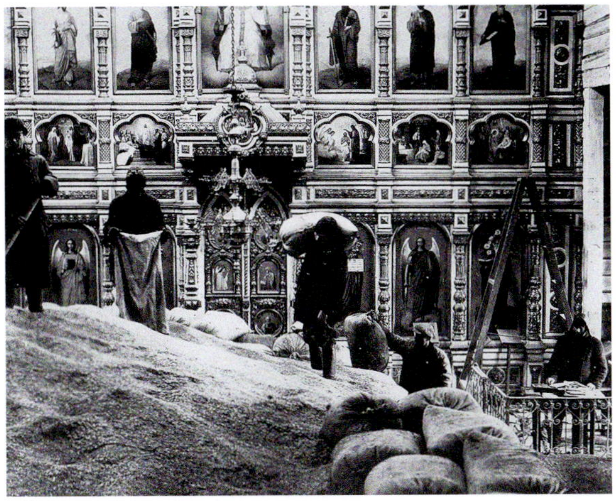

110 *(right)*

Church used as a grainstore, 1920s
David King Collection, London

Lunacharsky highlighted the parallels between Christianity and socialism by comparing 'production', 'the people' and 'scientific intelligence' with the three persons of the Holy Trinity – God the Father, who created the world, the Son in whom humanity is realised and the invisible Spirit.[1]

The God-builders also believed in an integral role for the arts in the accomplishment of the new order.[2] Several artists conflated the revival of traditional Russian art (including icons), the perfectibility of contemporary art and the promise of political change into one momentous ideal. The most ambitious cause, explicitly espoused by Malevich, was the total spiritual regeneration of mankind. In Malevich's case, the seed of this regeneration was prefigured in the icon which set a precedent for the perfection of art on its own terms. Following the Revolution, when he abandoned art for its own sake, Malevich found a way to reconcile the inner meaning of icons with the needs of Bolshevism. It was not until several years after the Revolution, when the dream of spiritual change was utterly shattered, that the peculiar logic that bound avant-garde art to icons was lost and the connections between them became more cynical, opportunist and arbitrary.

In his Suprematist years, Malevich considered his art to be unconditionally absolute and transcendental. It was entirely self-sufficient; it superseded everything that went before it. His achievement and expression of this absoluteness was greatly helped by his overt association with icons. He specifically adopted aspects of icon veneration – most obviously by displaying the *Black Square* in a holy 'icon corner' – in order to appropriate the metaphysical significance associated with them. But as religious objects or as historical works of art, icons held no interest for him; nor was he interested in other types of historical object for their own sakes. On the contrary, all art, of whatever origin, was to be subject to the social, political and spiritual needs of the present time. Despite being personally influenced by icons, he maintained that historic art *per se* was no longer alive as contemporary culture, and he dissociated himself from it vociferously and without sentimentality. He was not interested in history or religion; he regarded both disciplines as irrelevant conceptualisations of the world, manipulated by conservative power-holders that were keen to perpetuate the value and respect accorded to certain carefully chosen historical phenomena in order to maintain the social structures associated with them. He discarded the past like old clothes; when they were worn out, he threw them away. This was not to imply that they had always been useless; it was simply to say that they had now become useless, and therefore there was no point in keeping them. 'Nostalgia', and even 'interest' in history, were merely veiled forms of self-indulgence, concealing fear of change and the refusal to face present reality as the immediate content of consciousness. To historicise experience was a 'sophisticated' way of avoiding facing up to the reality of the present moment and to the political changes it demanded because they were threatening and uncomfortable.

In 'The Question of Imitative Art', Malevich argued that icons were obviously no longer operative as religious objects after the Revolution because the parameters of religion had been blown apart. Even when looked at as pure 'art' – managing, with the help of neo-primitivist or Suprematist eyes, to seem modern and 'non-religious' – they did not really have a role to play, for they only seemed to be modern; they were not actually modern: 'The icon can no longer be the same meaning, goal and means that it was formerly: it has already passed on into the museum where it can be preserved under the new meaning, not of a religious conception but of art. But as we go deeper into new creative meaning, it loses even that significance and nothing can be invested in it, for it will be the soul-less mannequin of a past spiritual and utilitarian life.'[3]

The logical conclusion that Malevich came to, from his exploration of non-objectivity, was that all art was superfluous to the extent that it brought a conceptual frame of reference to matter, including the material world, thereby creating duality (matter and image of matter), rather than simply allowing matter to exist as itself, in its manifest and unmediated state. In the early 1920s, this rejection of a conceptual frame of reference led him to a kind of existential materialism. This was not an atheistic denial of spirit: it was simply an expression of total dissociation from fantasised conceptualism and idealism. It was a rigorous kind of realism, in which all things already have sufficient existence as part of the material reality of the world and are subject only to their own laws; they should be allowed to act and evolve in accordance with those laws, whatever they may be, without being interpreted or filtered by an abstracted human mentality. Malevich was objecting to the notion of a dissociated transcendental absolute that was implicitly superior to the world, and that subtly legitimised a non-committal attitude to the world. Like his Suprematist paintings, the material world – by which he meant the already real and unmediated world – did not have any added 'religious meaning', 'symbolic significance' or 'hidden purpose'; it simply exists, operating without representing anything (in the way that figurative paintings 'represent' objects). From this point of view, the world itself is 'non-objective', signifying nothing beyond its radical, mere and absolute existence. It merely *is*.

The downside of Malevich's highly theoretical formulation was that society was currently incapable of realising non-objectivity as living experience because, as we have seen in the context of personal metaphysics (Chapter 4), non-objectivity implies non-subjectivity, and non-subjectivity involves a threat to personal identity that most people find intolerable and terrifying. He also argued that what was true of the personal psyche was true on a communal scale. He claimed that, like the identities of individuals, the various political identities of the period – capitalists and communists, as well as Christians – needed an objective world or frame of reference through which to articulate and propagate themselves. Without such an objective frame of reference to act as a mirror, or agent, of self-affirmation, their identities and power were unsupported and they therefore felt challenged.[4] Significantly, it was clear that, despite the systematic undermining of Christianity that followed the Russian Revolution, people continued to manifest their religiosity, contextualising the world of objects in new ways that enabled them to identify and locate themselves. As Malevich explained:

> One cannot say that art and religion are weak, they have enormous power over state materialism, always lowering it to the third level of importance [after religion and art]. Material thought or awareness [the 'existential materialism' referred to above] is still so weak in man that, at the moment of death, his materialistic attitude to the world takes a religious and artistic turn, and if he has not had time to approach God while alive, when he is dead, he will be turned [in]to an image within which his disciples wish to save themselves or wish to save him...
>
> This is why art in its imitative form is indispensable and necessary wherever there is a need for images and relics, until a new materialistic relationship to events is established, which will have no need for it,

> where even propaganda will not make use of the icon or the deification of the earth dweller for its simple purpose.[5]

As an alternative to Orthodox Christianity, the religious instinct of the people adopted the iconography of the new Orthodoxy – Bolshevism – through which to exercise itself, though many of the underlying thought-structures and patterns of practice remained unchanged. In his 'God is Not Cast Down', written in 1920, Malevich hypothesised that the logical conclusion of the new ideology was that the factory system of machines would eventually be so perfected, by virtue of rational human endeavour, that human labour would become superfluous and that human beings would thereby become free from the constraints of bodily work. He suggested that bodily actions would ultimately become automatic, directly subject to the laws of nature rather than human decision-making, and that the attention and thoughts of human beings would be liberated from concern with the material world. As such, the process shared many characteristics with traditional religion:

> Thinking of achievements [towards perfection, Man] built himself two paths: the religious technical school and the state or industrial one – the church and the factory... The two technical schools make for the same object, both strive to perfect technical questions, by means of which to achieve or resolve their aim. They are the same in both the deep and the superficial sense: ritual, pious attitude, worship, faith, hope for the future. Just as the church has its leaders, the discoverers of perfect religious systems, so also the industrial technical school has its own which it venerates and honours like the other. Likewise the walls of both are hung with images and portraits, martyrs and heroes in order of worth and rank, and in both cases their names are entered in calendars.[6]... The first notion sees life in the spirit as comprehension and service of God; it built itself a temple or church in which life passes in service, and for this it organises the production of the means necessary for service. The second notion sees life as self-perfection and built the factory where service is carried on in the creation of purely technical means. The former creates spiritual, the latter bodily perfection.[7]

Malevich also hypothesised how the parallels that exist between his theological and theo-industrial speculations could be extended to the cult practices of the two systems. This is nowhere better reflected than in his *Book on Non-Objectivity*, which gives a passionate account of a) how religious psychology is not 'non-objective consciousness' but is entirely object-related and dualistic, and b) how it was currently being transferred, in keeping with the social and political circumstances of the time, from Orthodox Christianity to the more politically motivated cult of Leninism. The text was first drafted four days after the death of Lenin, on 21 February 1924. Malevich frequently shows how far removed the popular cult of Leninism was from the kind of realism that he believed Lenin actually sought to realise, but he also attempts to reconcile his own theories about absolute art with the Lenin cult, however misguided it may have seemed to him. Above all, his experimental declamations reflect his belief that the political transformation of Russia and the Suprematist 'perfection of art' were aspects of the same higher transformation of mankind.

First of all, Malevich describes how the death of Lenin is the most significant event since the death of Christ; but in both cases, he continues, people have abstracted the events from their material contexts, investing them with extraneous significances of their own imagining, thereby inventing the superfluous and distracting world of religion and art. Both men were elevated from 'he', ordinary human beings, albeit of great stature,[8] to 'He' (with an upper case 'H'), abstracted personifications of ideas whose apparently divine source gives them authority of immense significance, shrewdly designed to be inherited by living political leaders. Malevich maintained that for reality to exist and function in its natural state, this invented and cultish realm of ideas – superfluous images and representations of the world – must be annihilated (as it had been in his own career as an artist).

Malevich recognised many similarities between orthodox Christian veneration and the cult of Leninism. To some extent, he was looking for signs of evolutionary necessity in the Revolution and he found them in resemblances to the very epitome of sacred culture in Russia – Orthodox Christianity. Christianity could be read as a prophetic rehearsal or ante-type of Leninism, just as medieval theologians had regarded the Old Testament to be a 'typological' prefiguration and justification of the New Testament. As one unidentified nineteenth-century mystic wrote that 'Socrates was orthodox in the structure of his soul', so Malevich claimed that 'the victory of the orthodox spirit has come in a renewed form'.[9] Equivalent portraits, music and buildings were created to furnish the two cults:

> The artists created a reality of Christ which did not exist [a fantasised conceptualisation and visualisation of Christ]. They will also create a portrait of Lenin in the future... In the image he has been transposed from material existence into sanctity, he has emerged from materialistic communism into spiritual religious communism, he rises above the materialistic plan of the action; like God he orders matter to take on a new order of relationships in his name.[10] ... Factory hooters have started to carry out the functions of bells and organs, the materialistic world has started to run along a religious path and therefore all machines, factory hooters, workmen and orators have begun to fulfil functions which conform to the circumstance of a new materialistic cult... All production must serve the new church, for everything that is born now is born in Leninism, every step is born on the path of Lenin, Lenin is in everything, no step can be taken without Lenin, just as no goal can be reached without God.[11]

Malevich regarded the factory as a place of authentic human engagement with material reality, committed to utilitarian service and unadulterated by idealism and religious fantasy. As a sign of the extent to which artistic culture had been subsumed in labour culture and made available to the masses, concerts for factory sirens and steam whistles, conducted with flags from the rooftops of the tallest buildings, were performed in Petrograd and Moscow at this time. However, much to Malevich's dismay, the factory too was soon romanticised and conceptualised. Following the Revolution, many churches were transformed into factory workshops. A series of diagrams from the early 1920s by the architect, Vladimir Krinski, shows how the towers of churches could be transformed into radio antennae, transmitting signals to aircraft, and their interiors into factory spaces. Despite their exaggerated and mechanised stylisation, these drawings were not satirical. One closely resembles Alexander and Viktor Vesnin's unrealised designs, of 1922–3, for the Palace of Labour in Moscow. Alexander Vesnin's sensitivity to this similarity is clearly anticipated in a drawing of an Orthodox chapel, surmounted by eight slender, closely ranged Orthodox crosses in a pyramidal formation, that he produced for a diploma project in 1911–12.[12] Another drawing shows a church interior functioning as an engineering workshop (Plate 111). The heads of the evangelists, traditionally placed in the pendentives of a church, supporting the dome, are obscured by wheels. These are connected by cables to massive machines on the ground. One of these machines stands in front of the iconostasis, exactly where the Royal Doors and the icon of Christ in Majesty would be (Plates 5, 90). A heavy-duty hook on a pulley is superimposed over the chandelier, with both hanging from the dome. A congregation of machine-workers is assembled in the foreground, ready to participate in this mechanical liturgy. Ironically, the dynamics of the machines follow the dynamics of the iconostasis, animated from Christ in the centre – rather as described by Malevich in relation to Lenin in the quotation above. Far from annihilating the Church, the image reframes its functions as the functions of a factory. It reduces the doctrines of the Church to the level of mechanical strategy but elevates machine-working to the level of a religious cult.

Although Malevich celebrated factory work, he rejected the highly romanticised agenda that was imposed upon it:

> Today, having torn itself away from religion, art communes with the factory, as though expecting the factory to change into a church, which will require icons, standards, banners and various kinds of relics and amulets...[13] The factory has ceased to be a factory, the workshop has ceased to be a workshop, the proletariat club has stopped being a club, everything has stopped being a thing, electric light has become the light of Lenin. The clubs have become purely places of prayer or audience in every-day existence. The factory has become a parish church.[14]

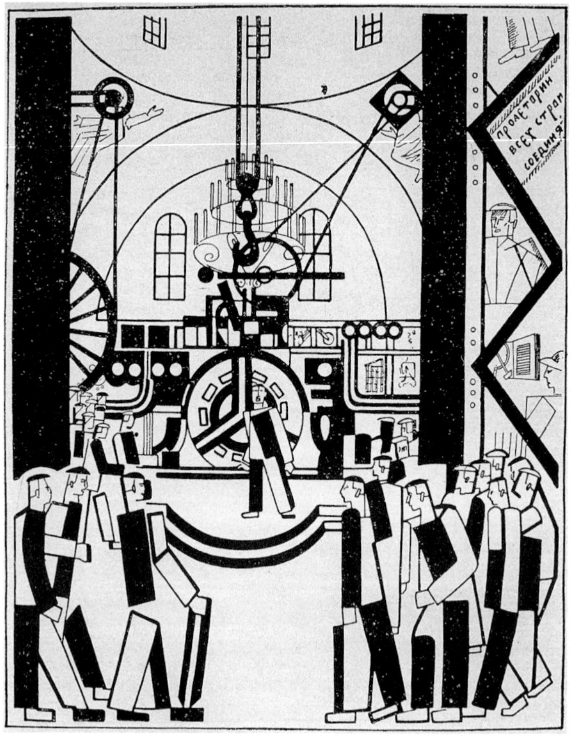

111
Vladimir Krinski
Church interior converted into a factory, early 1920s
Lithograph
David King Collection, London

To complete its liturgical functions, the factory had to be fitted out with iconic images:

> After the death of Lenin, or of 'Him' who died for us, the Leninists must follow 'Him' and in the future suffer for 'Him' in order to commune with 'Him'... Factory hooters must accompany the Leninists into the grave and into life. The body of the person who has died or fallen for Lenin, must be carried to the factory, where there must be a place for the celebration of the requiem and sermon commanded by Him [Lenin]. These are parting words. Later the question arises about the form of the link with 'Him'. This link can be completed through entrance into the cube as eternity. The cube of eternity must be placed as a sign of the union of the dead man with 'Him'.[15]

The 'cube of eternity' is a three-dimensional realisation of the *Black Square* which, as we have seen, Malevich had hung over his own bed at the time of his death (1935, Plate 98), acceding to infinity like a traditional icon. His theory of the death-transcending potential of the cube had also been applied in the case of Lenin: 'The point of view that Lenin's death is not death, that he is alive and eternal, is symbolised in the new object which has the aspect of a cube. The cube is no longer [just] a geometrical body. In this new object we attempt to depict eternity, to create such a circumstance by which the eternal life of Lenin will be affirmed, the eternal life that has overcome death.'[16]

In relation to the broader destiny of the world, in which this new 'eternal life' will be affirmed, the cube takes on apocalyptic associations, as anciently predicated in the Book of Revelation, where the city of paradise is witnessed by St John the Evangelist as being not only square, but cubic in its dimensions: 'And I John saw the holy city, new Jerusalem, coming down out of heaven... And the city lieth four square, and the length is as large as the breadth: and he [the angel] measured the city with the reed... The length and the breath and the height of it are equal.'[17] Malevich's own vision bears a remarkable resemblance to that of St John:

> A new eternity of 'His' [Lenin's] paradise has been created and the symbol of this paradise, of this new eternity, is a cube, it is no longer paradise with trees or in the clouds, but a geometrical paradise. The cube is the completion of all noises and misfortunes which had existed because they were one-dimensional, two-dimensional, or three-dimensional ... they followed all the teachings and in the end, in Communism, they must finally arrive at the last organised cube, the cube of eternity, i.e. of rest.[18]

Consistent with his feeling for the necessary evolution of eternal life in the form of a cube, Malevich's association of the cube with communism echoes the attempt of Bela Uitz (see Chapter 3) to find a geometrical logic underlying the social history of the world:[19] 'In Leninism ... begins the struggle between the pyramid of Cheops and the cube, the form of the burial of Lenin. For this, one has to choose a place and build a pyramid. The triangle is conquered by a quadrangle, hence rectangular culture can be called Communist or classless culture, but ancient, triangular culture cannot'.[20]

Although avant-garde art was eventually suppressed, due to its inaccessibility to the general populace, Malevich's notion of a 'geometrical paradise' did, remarkably, have at least some equivalents at a popular level. René Fülöp-Miller, writing in 1926, recalled one secular missionary of the modern age, a well-travelled sailor, who was determined to free his countrymen from the 'besotting influence of religion'. He reported that:

> For this purpose, he [the missionary] usually stations himself at the entrance to a church, forcibly prevents the faithful from listening to the divine service and, in order to 'enlighten them' reads to them disconnected passages from the gospel of the modern man, the encyclopaedia, say the extract on the isosceles triangle or on similar triangles. Chance put him into possession of this work of reference in twenty volumes, and it became for him the book of books, the epitome of the new truth, which he preaches to everybody, whether they will or not. And in fact, he has succeeded with his dogma of the isosceles triangle, in winning quite a number of adherents, previously true sons of the Orthodox Church, who now regard him as a kind of new saint.[21]

In addition to its own logic, Malevich considered the cube of eternity to be the consummation of the sacred corner shrine, where icons were hung in traditional Russian homes (as discussed, in conjunction with the first exhibition of his *Black Square* in 1915, on pp. 145–7). Whichever route one takes towards the corner, one's path will exist in three dimensions; therefore the cube comprehends all possible approaches to the corner, implicitly containing the possibility of perfection. Inevitably, the corner itself was to be reserved for an image of Lenin:

> The idea has flared up of making Lenin corner shrines. Here is a close analogy to the church, and to the Orthodox Church, which has taken care to arrange corner shrines to Christ and all His saints.[22] ... Every true Leninist ... will make a shrine in his home and dedicate it to 'His' name, and in every village reading-room or in the clubs there will also be 'His' corner shrine from which 'His' teaching (sermon) will be preached. Models of these little corners will be created and others built on the same lines throughout the land of the faithful.[23]

Although Malevich described the parallels between Leninism and Christianity with passionate intensity, he did not ultimately believe in any such form of religiosity or conceptualism; he advocated mere existence ('materialism') without mental abstractions and accretions. The cube of eternity was a contemporary equivalent to the art and religion of the past; but, in relationship to the mere unadorned existence of the 'material' world, even the cube of eternity was simply a conceived construct, added unnecessarily to the fact of reality. 'The cube is nothing but a geometrical conception. In the material world, the cube does not exist. Geometry attempts to metamorphose matter into geometric realism, but geometrical bodies are not [real, material] bodies, they are those same icon-ideas, conceptions. And mathematics is closely linked with geometry and gives birth to numbers, indefinite like angels'.[24]

He claimed that in art, freedom from superfluous symbols, ideas and conceptualisations had been achieved, as 'the dissolution of the cube and the emancipation of consciousness which will have to stand face-to-face with non-objectivity';[25] in a political context, however, the final point had not yet been reached: 'Cubism is the culminating point in the culture of painting, as Communism is the culminating point of Socialist culture, the difference lies only in that the cube in painting already is dissolved in movement, disobjectivised, but the economic cube [still] goes towards the final point of the objective idea [symbolised by Lenin]'.[26]

Malevich stressed that Lenin himself was against the religiosity of images and cultishness; on the contrary, he claimed, Lenin sought to achieve an equivalent to non-objectivity in social culture – i.e. an ultimate realism that was not determined by theories and interpretations:

> All his [Lenin's] life, he fought against the corner shrine [cultishness], freed himself from it and wanted to free others. He wanted to lead everybody out of the icon corner, he fought for reality, he was opposed to both God and the devil, and when he was alive it seemed to go unnoticed that the revolution carries a new cult within itself [Leninism]... In the aspect of an icon, he stands as a testimony to his former material covering, and those who believed in him were told that his spirit would soar above them, that the spirit alone can overcome Satan, Capitalism and the devil of the bourgeoisie.[27] ... Every teacher speaks only of non-objectivity to his disciple, but frequently, after the teacher's death, not one

> disciple understands the teacher and so creates objectivity [a projected realm of concepts], wishing to realise the idea of the teacher in it. Thus a multitude of rituals and objects are created about which the teacher did not speak.[28]

Malevich described how, before people had time to adapt and react to news Lenin's death, there were five minutes of non-conceptual non-objectivity:

> Lenin died and life stopped for five minutes, just as the sun darkened at Christ's death and brought life to a halt. This is an attempt at the grandiose, static state of complete rest, an element of the non-objective. We do not have many minutes for these true signs of non-objectivity for which we can allow ourselves only five minutes. It is five minutes of normal life after an onslaught of worker's objectivity [fantasised veneration]... In fact life stopped not for five minutes but until such time as Leninism begins to exist as a religion.[29]

The 'religion of Leninism' assumed many forms, often associated with the traditional rites of passage – birth, marriage and death – but also with such occasions as graduation. Malevich himself made or observed numerous analogies between the cultishness of Christianity and the cultishness growing up around Lenin. He saw resonances, for instance, between Prince Vladimir I (who introduced Christianity to Russia) and 'Vladimir II' (Lenin, whose socialist vision superseded Christianity), and between Gorki, the place of Lenin's death, and Golgotha, the site of the Crucifixion, because both begin with 'Go';[30] he also compared the survival of Lenin 'in the spirit of the Socialist cause' to the Resurrection of Christ.[31]

Malevich wanted to understand the triumph of Leninism as a progressive, necessary and metaphysical act. In this way, his own vision and identity were, by extension, also authenticated. His will to divest the triumph of Leninism of any hint of the accidental, which would have qualified it and made it open to question, obliged him to formulate it as the fruit of an objective evolutionary force, in a quasi-Hegelian manner. Hence his ability to find signs of its inevitability in otherwise inexplicable resonances with the old order. However, this was not the only model with which to understand the shift from Christian cultural conventions to Soviet ones. Leon Trotsky, for instance, recognised the legitimate function of popular customs both as psychologically expedient (despite their being based on superstition) and as agents of cultural cohesion. In his article 'The Family and Ceremony', published in *Pravda* in July 1923, he advocated that new customs be developed organically, experimentally and freely, in contrast to the extremists who saw them as little more than tools with which to manipulate the religiosity of the masses. He also observed that, although they had already been developed for the public domain, where they were already articulating new social ideals, they had not yet penetrated the homes of individuals:

> The workers' state already has its festivals, processions, reviews, and parades, symbolic spectacles – the new theatrical ceremonies of state. It is true that in the main they are too closely allied to the old forms, which they imitate and perpetuate. But on the whole, the revolutionary symbolism of the workers' state is novel, distinct, and forcible – the red flag, red star, worker, peasant, comrade, International. But within the shut cages of family life the new has not penetrated, or at least, has done so but little, while individual life is closely bound up

> with the family. This explains why in the matter of icons, christenings, church funerals, etc, the balance is in favor of custom. The revolutionary members of the family have nothing to offer in place of them. Theoretical arguments act on the mind only. Spectacular ceremony acts on the senses and imagination. The influence of the latter, consequently, is much more widespread. In the most communist of circles a need has arisen to oppose old practices by new forms, new symbols, not merely in the domain of state life, where this has largely been done, but in the domain of the family.[32]

New customs were, however, beginning to develop around the private occasions of birth, marriage and death, as Trotsky records in the article – though not always in the liberal and ennobling manner that he had envisaged. Many adults, for instance, adopted new first names, submitting to the cause of the Revolution as if it was a monastic commitment. Traditional Christian names commemorating saints or Christian festivals (e.g. Natalia – after the Nativity of Christ) were replaced by names that commemorated socialist heroes, revolutionary concepts or technological symbols. These included Oktyabrina (to commemorate the October Revolution), Ninel (Lenin backwards), Vladelina (a combination of Lenin's first and second names), Rem or Elektrifikatsiya (revolutionary electrification) and even Avangard.[33] Such names were also to be given to new-born children, sometimes collectively to avoid individualism, at 'Red baptisms'. These occasions were administered by the Party secretary at the Party Headquarters and witnessed by the works council. Children were to be 'octobered' rather than christened – 'with the hammer and sickle, the new symbols of the hard and laborious path, which has replaced the cross and thorns' (Plate 112).[34]

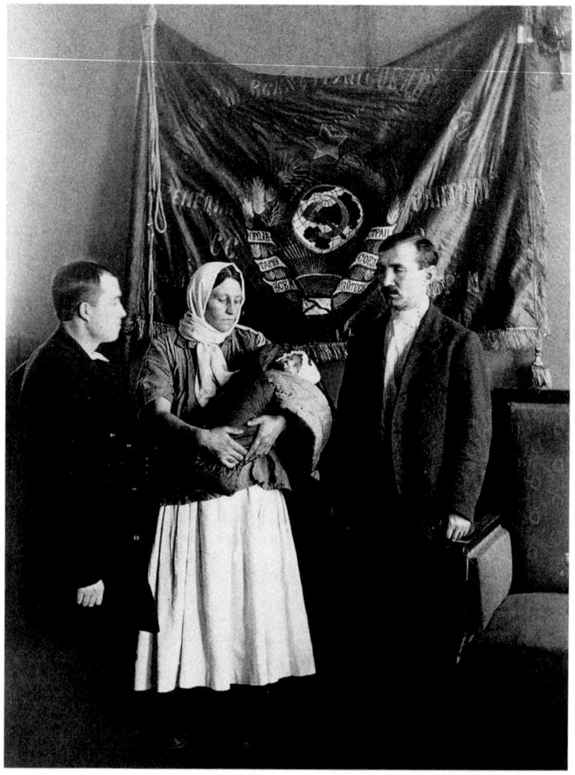

112

Octobering Ceremony, 1927
David King Collection, London

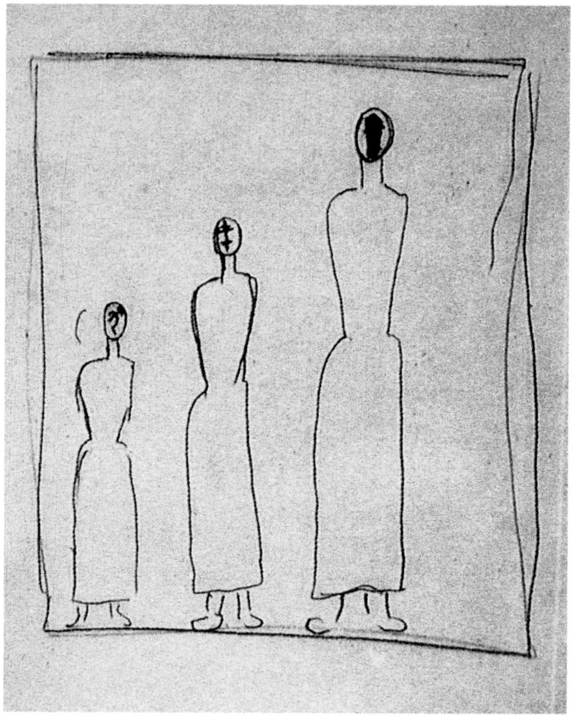

113
Kazimir Malevich

Three figures with Sickle, Cross and Coffin, 1930–1
Pencil on paper
18.5 x 16 cm (7 ¼ x 6 ¼ in)
Private collection

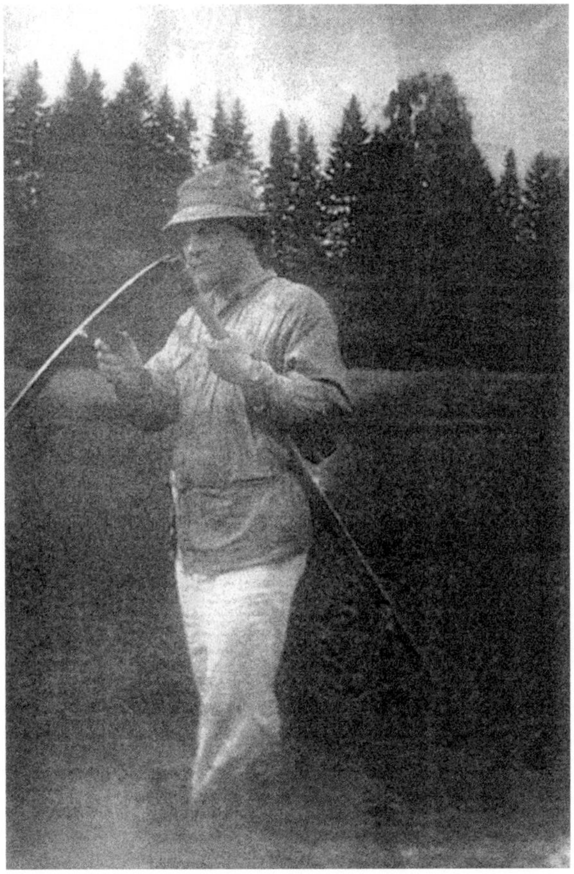

114

Photograph of Kazimir Malevich with scythe, Abramtsevo, 1931
David King Collection, London

The hammer and sickle, erected in place of icons and crosses in churches all over Russia, took on a particular significance for Malevich. Just as he attempted to reconcile the geometrical forms of Suprematism with Leninism (via the square and cube), so – towards the end of his life – did he aim to integrate the Bolshevik hammer and sickle into the abstract metaphysical world of Suprematism. This symbol not only lent itself to Suprematist interpretation at a purely compositional level, i.e. as a highly charged arrangement of forms with a primary axis crossed by a bar,[35] it also has a deeper connection to the cross, by virtue of which it becomes an agent of spiritual transformation. This is most fully suggested in the Suprematist crosses that are composed of intersecting arcs, dating from 1918 (Plate 91).[36] One late drawing prominently juxtaposes the two symbols on a single page, highlighting their formal similarity and suggesting a symbolic equivalence.[37] Another example makes a direct parallel by placing three featureless figures next to each other, their faces occupied by the symbol of the hammer and sickle, the Orthodox many-armed cross and a coffin respectively (Plate 113).[38] Besides seeming to equate the ideals of the Revolution with spiritual transformation, the hammer and sickle may also have had further significance for Malevich. Firstly, the sickle played into the artist's penchant for cutting instruments of all kinds – scissors, swords, knives, bayonets, saws and scythes – which were a recurrent feature of his figurative works throughout his career. It is not inconceivable that this attraction was associated with the Russian notion of a 'cutting truth' (i.e. a very direct and possibly painful truth) and the expression to 'cut truth into another person's face' (or 'eyes' – *rezat pravdu v glaza*), particularly as the motifs are located in the faces of the standing figures.[39] In this context, the motifs can be seen to be both signs of the fact that the truth of a new identity has been 'cut into their faces' and symbols of that new truth – revolutionary self-sacrifice and the consummation of life (in death). The presence of a coffin in the image highlights the apocalyptic implications of the sickle, associating it with the angel of death (harvesting souls) and the final reckoning at the end of time. Photographs from 1931 show the artist holding a scythe (cutting grass at Abramtsevo), as if he was himself a kind of grim reaper, cutting truth into viewers' faces (Plate 114).[40] The coffin may also have had sacramental overtones for Malevich. As he said of Lenin: 'Lenin was buried in a glass coffin for no other reason except that he should be seen as a sacrament'.[41]

A similar translation of ancient behavioural structures into new cultural forms took place in relation to public holidays and festivals. Christian processions had already been usurped by celebrations of revolutionary anniversaries, but Malevich believed that these would now evolve into 'religious' phenomena themselves:

> All feast days celebrating revolutionary victories will become holy Lenin processions (the procession of the Cross or the procession of Christ) with all the relics of the 'orthodox' and all the depictions of the 'non-believers', i.e. devils with frying pans and burning chains, with all the hell of Capitalism, the bourgeoisie has become the contemporary devil which tortures the faithful who believe in 'Him' alone, and those who are with 'Him' will be saved, those who are not with 'Him' belong to the devil or to the bourgeoisie and will suffer eternal damnation.[42]

Malevich's analysis of the similarities between the Lenin cult that he saw growing up around him and Orthodox religiosity was, at times, remarkably detached. The cult itself, however, was always designed to be entirely engrossing. On the one hand, early Soviet propagandists attempted to stamp out religion altogether by demonstrating the absurdity of it on scientific grounds. They demonstrated, for instance, how the relics of saints were bogus and could be easily fabricated. Traditionally believed to be holy on account of their miraculous survival and fragrance, several examples were exhumed and exhibited besides the bones of animals that had been preserved in air-vents, or bones from ancient Egyptian tombs that had survived through mummification. In Kiev, the bones of Saints Antonius, Johannes and Eustachius, martyred in 1344, were displayed next to the bones of a rat and a frog.[43] In the same spirit, Bolshevik pilots also took peasants up into the skies in aeroplanes to show them that there are no angels there; pilots were instructed to wait for cloudy days and to fly into clouds.[44]

The criticisms that were levelled at the clerical exploitation of peasant credulity resembled the criticisms of abuses that led to the Reformation in the sixteenth century. Museums of anti-religion, in which such teachings were expounded, continued to exist in Russia until the end of the Soviet period. On the other hand, the Bolsheviks were also fully appreciative of the persuasive effects of religious ceremony and, both deliberately and spontaneously, they took full advantage of them in promoting their own ideologies. Lenin's body, for instance, was embalmed and put on display – exactly like the relic of a saint – immediately after his death, 'in accordance with the wishes expressed by many workers and peasants' – though not of Lenin's wife who described Lenin's antipathy to such cultishness in *Pravda*. Of course, the parallel made here between Lenin's body and holy relics – which were traditionally authenticated by their physical survival – totally contradicted the simultaneous disbelief in relics, as described above.

The sight of Lenin's physical survival was complemented by elaborate notions that he was also immortalised in his work and in the commitment of the proletariat to the realisation of his vision. Several senior politicians – for instance, Leonid Krassin, the Commissar of Foreign Trade – believed that there would come a time when new technology would enable Lenin to be resurrected bodily. The 'God-building' scientist and philosopher, Alexander Bogdanov, developed a belief that the indefinite prolongation of life – to the point of immortality – could be achieved by blood transfusions, and, in 1926, he succeeded in persuading Stalin to authorise the establishment of the first Institute of Haematology in the world (though ironically he died two years later when an experiment he performed on himself went wrong). His belief that blood transfusion could eventually be used to achieve a kind of 'physiological collectivism' in

115

Malevich and UNOVIS members on their way from Vitebsk to Moscow for the First All-Russian Conference of Teachers and Students of Art, 5 June 1920
David King Collection, London

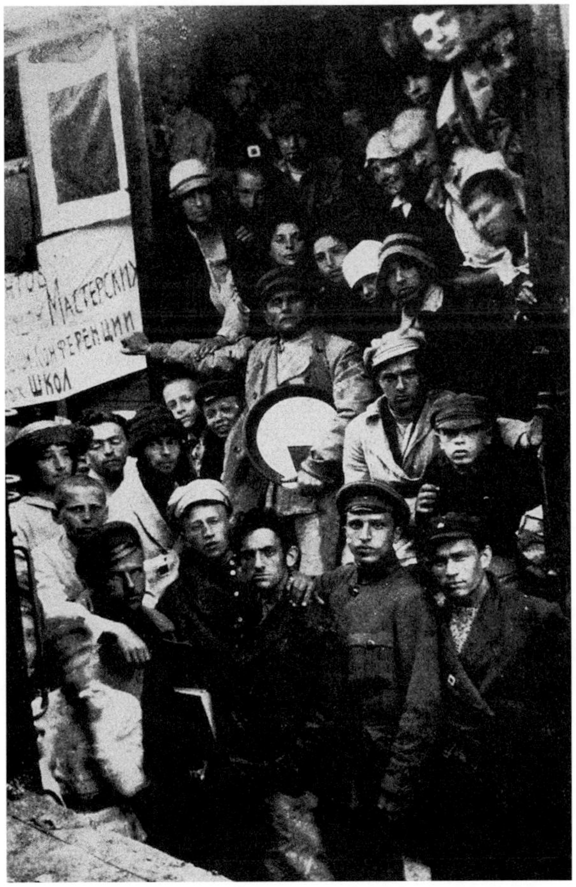

human society resonates powerfully with the sacramental vision of the Church, whereby the identity of the 'holy community' is sustained through 'holy communion'.[45] In this respect, Bogdanov was influenced by the Resurrection theology of the Futuristic philosopher Nikolai Fedorov (1829–1903), who maintained that humanity is evolving towards a state of physical immortality and that the bodies of the deceased will eventually be resurrected. His theory is also consistent with the traditional precedence that the Orthodox Church gives to Easter over other church feasts. Another God-builder, Maxim Gorky (1868–1936), adapted the concept of resurrection to contemporary politics, proposing that the death of the individual self and the emergence of a communal identity in its place amounted to a 'resurrection of God' as the people. In subsequent years, Soviet leaders continued to aspire towards transcendence of bodily decay, and the natural fitness for rule that it seemed to convey, by having wrinkles, blemishes and birthmarks omitted from paintings and airbrushed from photographs.[46] In this way, a new *dvoeverie* – the ancient 'double-faith' that acknowledged that the structures and dynamics of pre-Christian paganism continued to exist and function subliminally within Christianity – developed in Soviet Russia.

Avant-garde posters and banners were paraded at revolutionary demonstrations in much the same way that icons were traditionally carried into battle or paraded through the streets on feast days (Plates 8, 115). Although the Cubist and Futurist imagery of some posters proved incomprehensible to many people (and was eventually suppressed for this reason), the theatrical circumstance of political demonstrations held much the same appeal for the hopeful populous as the processions of icons on feast days held for pre-revolutionary Christians: while the vision of the Mother of God and Christ on the front line harnessed the flailing emotional energy of the masses to the promise of victory in battle, the bravura of avant-garde propaganda harnessed that same energy to the promise of a harmonious and just life in this world.

Agricultural and industrial achievements provided opportunities for celebrations of communal values. In place of priests who, in tsarist Russia, blessed the fields each year in ritual splendour, tractors became the new miracle-workers. They were manufactured in their tens of thousands (as soberly registered by Pavel Filonov in his *Tractor Department at Putilovsky Works*, 1931) and their arrival at the new collective farms was celebrated in a spirit of solemnity and jubilation that links them to icons and Christ's entry onto Jerusalem (plate 46). At the opening of a collective farm in 1931, a triumphal arch in the form of a giant hammer and sickle was erected in a field to greet the stately procession of new tractors (Plate 116). Such celebrations resembled church feasts and processions, with the religious banners and icons (as seen all over tsarist Russia and depicted in such paintings as Ilya Repin's *Religious Procession in Kursk Province*, 1880–3)[47] replaced by Soviet flags and images of Stalin and his colleagues. Many such scenes were also painted on lacquered panels and boxes which had formed a part of the traditional village arts of Russia for two centuries. Although the miniaturist style of these works was largely associated with fairy tales and folk legends, it originated in the style of the sixteenth-century Stroganov school of icon painting, and continued to be used for icons at the beginning of the twentieth century at Kholui, Mstera and Palekh. Following the 1917 Revolution, and the foundation of a state-approved Co-operative 'Artel' (workshop) of Ancient Painting in 1924, many icon painters from these centres turned their hands to painting lacquer boxes. The example illustrated here, the *Village Library*, painted in 1927 by Ivan Bakanov, a conservator of frescos and former icon painter in Palekh, reflects Soviet efforts to eliminate illiteracy from Russia, while also introducing images of Marx, Lenin and Kalinin to a very alien world (Plate 117). Aspects of the distinctive, ancient and iconic style of the Stroganov and Palekh schools – including materials, technique, colour and design – continued to shine through in such works, apparently without any fear of iconic associations. On the other hand, a monumental fresco, *Harvest Festivity*, painted in 1934–5 for the foyer of the Chervonozavods'ky Theatre in Kharkov by the Ukrainian artist Mikhail Boichuk and his followers (the Boichukists) was criticised for being 'too religious' (Plate 118). Even in his Socialist Realist works, Boichuk's style clearly retained elements of the iconic stiffness and stylisation that characterised the early 'Byzantinist' works he exhibited in Paris in 1910–12 (plate 24). Such characteristics were considered to be

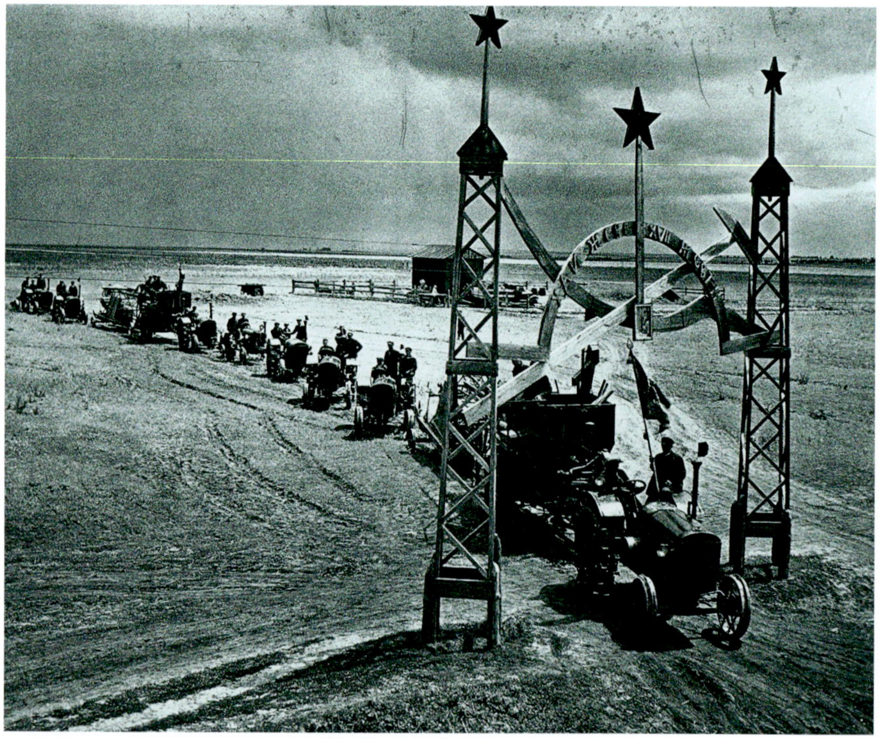

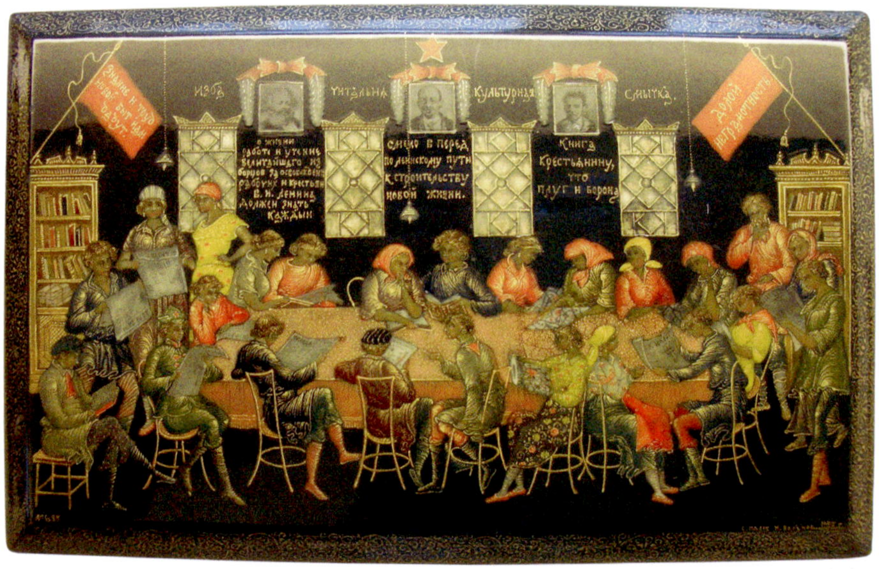

116

Procession of tractors,
late 1920s
David King Collection, London

117
Ivan Bakanov

Lacquer box showing *Village Library*, 1927
8 x 12.5 cm (3 1/8 x 4 7/8 in)
Russian Museum,
St Petersburg

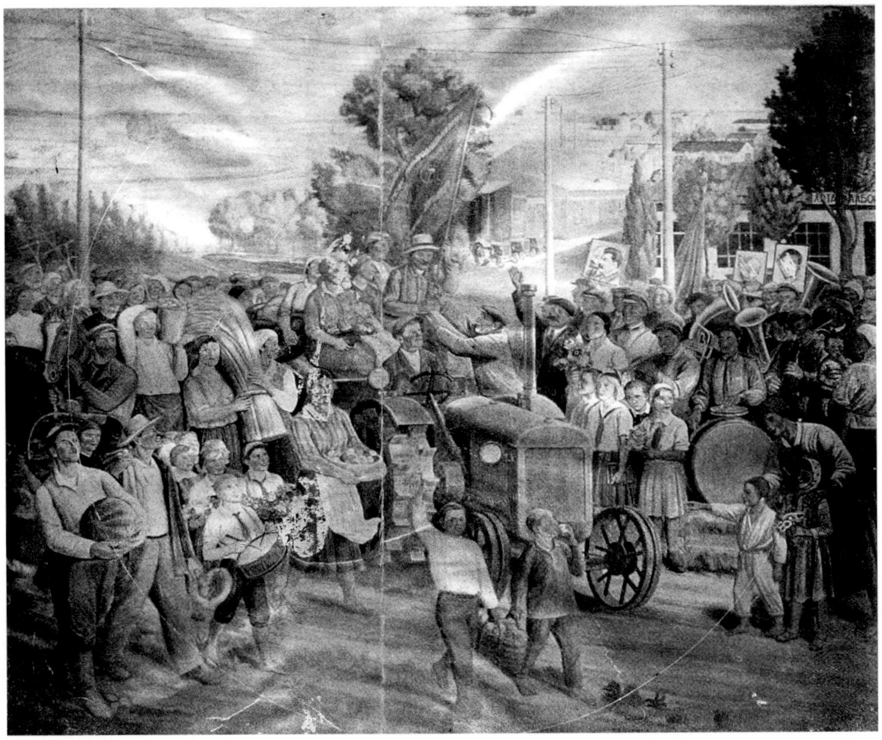

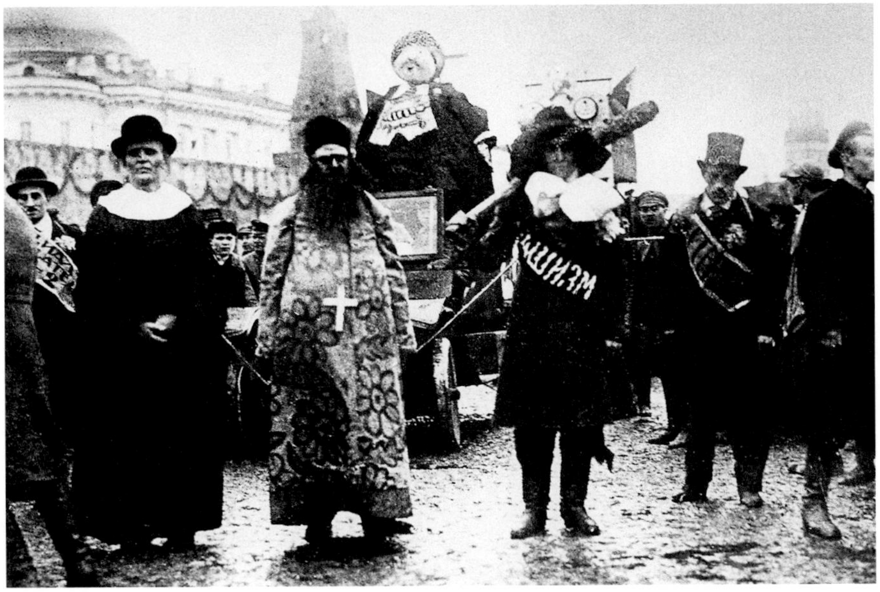

118
Mikhail Boichuk

Harvest Festivity, decoration for the Chervonozavods'ky Theatre, Kharkov, 1934–5
Fresco (destroyed)

119

Anti-religious demonstration, 1920s
David King Collection, London

too nationalistic – too particular to the Ukraine, where Orthodoxy had thrived in its pure Byzantine form before the process of Russification began. As a result, Boichuk was eventually purged for 'counter-revolutionary tendencies' – as indeed were the two senior politicians, Vlas Chubar and Stanislav Kosior, celebrated in the fresco on banners alongside Lenin and Stalin, for their role in the collectivisation of agriculture in the Ukraine. Their faces were erased from the painting (as visible here on the far right) before the fresco itself was destroyed for its own transgressions.[48]

Besides creating new festivals in celebration of revolutionary anniversaries, the Bolshevik government also promoted direct parodies of the traditional Christian festivals. For many believers, religious life consisted not so much in considered subscription to the doctrines of Christianity as in traditional, sanctified participation in seasonal festivals. The Bolsheviks recognised the power of ritual over ideology and, as a result, instituted their own rites. These occasions – including 'red masses' and 'atheist Easters' – took place on the day of the feast that they were ridiculing and usurping, and were performed in front of churches, by mock priests in caricatured vestments, to traditional melodies (often exaggerated) with subverted words (Plate 119). The priests were typically portrayed as being drunk and corrupt, depriving the peasants of their dues. Such performances were intended to be both entertaining and educational – for instance, by pointing to the pagan source of Easter and to the absence of scientific proof for the existence of Christ – but they may also conceal an element of self-mockery at the root of Russian cultural psyche. Dramatised parodies of religious authority and belief had been practised in Russia for many centuries – by Ivan the Terrible, among others.[49] Such practices may have originated in Roman 'saturnalia'

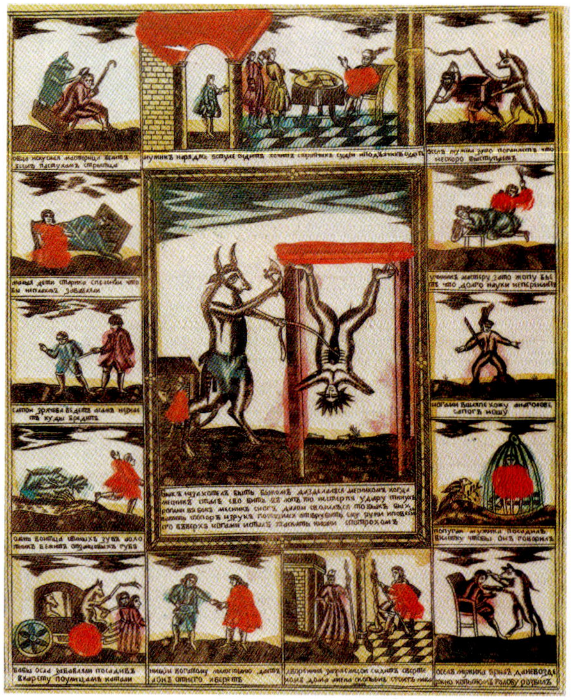

120

'The bull that didn't want to be a bull and became a butcher', late 18th century
Lubok engraving, printed and handpainted in the 1820s
45.5 x 37 cm (17 ⅞ x 14 ⅝ in)
Historical Museum, Moscow

rites and were probably invested with notions of magical powers. An eighteenth-century *lubok* (popular print) shows several scenes of role reversal – such as a cow slaughtering a butcher, and a donkey being pulled in a carriage by its master (Plate 120). In this particular case, the *lubok* itself parodies an icon by placing the various scenes in the border around a central image, like an icon of a saint surrounded by scenes from his life (Plate 70).

Revolutionary strategy also echoed the changes enforced by Peter the Great, who attempted to accomplish radical changes in the self-image of Russia by suppressing the manifestations of cultural life on which the old sense of identity nourished itself. For instance, the Bolshevik attempt to replace the word *spasibo* – 'thank you' in Russian, literally meaning 'God protect you' – with the more secular *merci* resembles Peter's famous abolition of beards from 1698, part of his attempt to replace the retarded traditionalism of Russia with progressive westernisation in one fell swoop. With the exception of the clergy, Old Believers and the lowest class of peasants, men who refused to shave were shaved by force and fined. Peter's command caused an uproar, as beards – worn by all Orthodox Russian men – were a means of identification with saints (as visualised in icons). One man is recorded as having kept his cut beard inside his shirt, for fear of not being recognised when he died and appeared at the gates of heaven. But curiously, besides undermining religiosity, Peter also imitated the Church in his own bizarre range of rituals, in which an *All-Mad, All-Jesting, All-Drunken Assembly*[50] of mock-metropolitans, cardinals and prince-popes, appointed by himself, engaged in mock ordinations, blessings and processions – day-long carnivals of wild drinking and singing, in which the formalities of religious and pagan ritual were parodied to the most extreme degree. Peter participated in the action himself, frequently signing letters 'archdeacon Peter' and administering his outlandish duties dressed up as a cardinal. Significantly, Ivan the Terrible is also known to have engaged in parodies of religious practice.

Peter was relatively free of prejudice against other denominations of Christianity, partly due to his own temperament and partly in order to weaken the hold of the Orthodox Church in Russia. However, while he thought that too much religiosity was harmful both to the development of the nation and to his own authority – as well as being tiresome, irrational and self-indulgent – he evidently recognised the socially cohesive power of ritual. The early Soviet propagandists also acknowledged this power and their re-enactments of recent events (including the storming of the Winter Palace in 1920 using a cast of 10,000) form part of the same quasi-liturgical tradition of re-living identity-affirming experiences. However, they felt no sympathy for religious belief whatsoever. They were happy to inherit the psychological infrastructure of icon veneration, and to make use of its technical devices, but icons themselves were mocked and destroyed in their hundreds of thousands.

The most powerful tool that was used to create and sustain support for the new regime – apart from force – was propaganda. The Bolsheviks quickly realised how important propaganda would be in their struggle to deliver the Revolution to remote areas of the country, inhabited by provincial, uneducated people whose world-view and sensitivities were, broadly speaking, defined by archaic religious ideas. The earliest propaganda took advantage of all the mechanisms of religious psychology, appearing in many forms. In addition to the traditional outlets such as posters, books and journals, more dynamic and experimental media were also developed. The propagandist potential of cinema, in particular, was intensively explored. While experiments in the educational use of film had been undertaken in tsarist times (though Nicholas II himself was not unduly impressed by the medium), it was still sufficiently new and unknown in the 1920s to be seen as unencumbered by bourgeois associations. On the contrary, its non-dependence on literacy, the immediacy of its impact, the communal nature in which it had to be consumed (in mass-viewing – less open to subjective interpretation than the individual experience of paintings) and the inherently technological nature of the manufacturing process all helped to frame it as a cultural form that was perfectly suited to a socialist society. Moreover, both Lenin and Trotsky recognised its particular potential as a propagandist tool. Lenin's statement to Lunacharsky in 1922 that 'of all the arts for us the most important is cinema' is well known.[51] The following year, Trotsky published an article in *Pravda* – 'Vodka, the Church and Cinema' – in which he specifically advocated the promotion of cinema as an alternative to the Church. In so doing, he was tacitly acknowledging a degree of potential equivalence in the disposition of the habitual church-goer to that of the film-watcher. He therefore advocated that film be developed to facilitate a transfer of allegiance from Christian culture, which enslaves the psychology of the individual, to socialist culture, which enlivens it:

> The cinema competes not only with the tavern but also with the church. And this rivalry may become fatal for the church if we make up for the separation of the church from the socialist state by the fusion of the socialist state and the cinema... The workers' relation to the church ... holds mostly by the thread of habit... Icons still hang in the home because they are there ... it would be bare without them; people would not be used to it. A worker will not trouble to buy new icons, but has not sufficient will to discard the old ones... As for church-going, the people do not go because they are religious; the church is brilliantly lighted, crowded with men and women in their best clothes, the singing is good – a range of social-aesthetic attractions not provided by the factory, the family, or the workaday street. There is no faith or practically none. At any rate, there is no respect for the clergy or belief in the magic force of ritual. But there is no active will to break it all... Meaningless ritual, which lies on the consciousness like an inert burden, cannot be destroyed by criticism alone; it can be supplanted by new forms of life, new amusements, new and more cultured theaters. Here again, thoughts go naturally to the most powerful – because it is the most democratic – instrument of the theater: the cinema. Having no need of a clergy in brocade, etc, the cinema unfolds on the white screen spectacular images of greater grip than are provided by the richest church, grown wise in the experience of a thousand years, or by mosque

> or synagogue. In church only one drama is performed, and always one and the same, year in, year out; while in the cinema next door you will be shown the Easters of heathen, Jew, and Christian, in their historic sequence, with their similarity of ritual. The cinema amuses, educates, strikes the imagination by images, and liberates you from the need of crossing the church door. The cinema is a great competitor not only of the tavern but also of the church. Here is an instrument which we must secure at all costs![52]

Although the medium of film was a new one, the religiosity of propaganda was as active in film-making as it was in any other medium. In keeping with a tradition of art theory in Russia that dated back to the first half of the nineteenth century, films were required not merely to entertain their viewers, but above all to serve a social function. From the beginning of the 1920s, the propagandist potential of film was hotly debated, giving rise to many new and conflicting approaches to the medium. Firstly, there were advocates of documentary collage which was intended to convince its audiences with an overwhelming barrage of affirmations of revolutionary accomplishment. From 1918, when the budget for making feature films was at an all-time low, films of this type were circulated on agit-trains to distant parts of the country, where they were most urgently needed, and to troops on the front line to boost their morale. Such trains included a library and bookshop, a printing press, and facilities for making film and radio broadcasts. Their exteriors were boldly decorated with monumental imagery and slogans by the some of the most prominent artists of the day. Earlier attempts had been made to set up mobile cinemas – for instance by travelling projectionists (using projectors called *peredvizhki*), reminiscent of the Wanderers (*Peredvizhniki*), and on barges in the early 1900s.[53] It is not inconceivable that the idea of the agit-train was inspired by the mobile church (a church created in a railway carriage) that was instigated by Nicholas II in 1896 to take Christianity to remote parts of Siberia – a means of missionary transport that the Orthodox Church revived in 2000.

One of the most influential makers of early Soviet documentaries was Dziga Vertov (1896–1054) who experimented with music, science-fiction and sound engineering before becoming involved in the development of propagandist films in 1920. Vertov's *Enthusiasm* (1930), also known as *The Symphony of the Donbass*, is a classic of the documentary genre. Like all of Vertov's work, the film is intensely anti-religious in its content but, at a deeper level, it arguably maintains certain values that are fundamental characteristics of the tradition of representing the sacred in Russia. At the level of its content, the film clearly documents the triumph of heavy industry over the decrepitude of religious belief and despair. This position is explicitly and aggressively stated in numerous sequences of 'montage', in which Soviet celebrations are juxtaposed with superstitious religious practices so as to suggest that the Church is not simply being forgotten or discarded as an outdated tradition of no value; its powers are subsumed and it is consciously superseded. The destruction of churches, for instance, is filmed against the belching smoke of factory chimneys; the toppling of crosses from church domes is followed by a shot of an elevated telegraph pole, in which an echo of the orthodox cross is subjected to having a purely technical application; a five-pointed star is mounted on a church, just as in Vertov's earlier work, *The Man with a Movie Camera* (1929), an image of Lenin is seen over the main entrance of a church, now turned into a Leninist club. Such obvious and clear-cut demonstrations of the supersession of religious belief by communist ideology are complemented by subtler, more manipulated effects. Towards the end of *Enthusiasm*, for instance, the frenetic pace and repetitiveness of the mechanical sequences and the manic application of the workers echo the ritual repetitions and religious fervour of the faithful, shown kissing icons at the beginning of the film – a nuance that is, not deliberately of course, implicit in the very title of the film which derives from the Greek words for 'god within' (*theos* and *en*).

Over and beyond the perception that communist ideology forms an infinitely superior equivalent to Christian belief is Vertov's subscription to certain aesthetic theories that had been validated by centuries of use in the Orthodox Church, albeit in very different social and material circumstances. Vertov's attitude towards the Church was obviously antipathetic in the extreme but his commitment to film-making as a propagandist medium did attract him to patterns of thought that underlay other forms of religious or absolute art in the Russian tradition. His development of Kino-Pravda (Film-Truth), for instance, based on the documentary filming of un-acted real-life action – without actors, invented roles or preconceived narrative – derives from his wish to develop an utterly transparent medium in which the truth of reality, as it is lived, could communicate itself without alteration or enhancement or even interpretation by the director. That is to say, he positioned himself in relation to what he considered to be an objective truth and facilitated the communication of that truth. In this respect, his philosophy resonated not only with that of Malevich, whose Suprematist work was also intended to promote and celebrate the self-communication of reality, but also with icons, for, as we have seen, icons too are conceived as actual extensions of absolute reality, rather than as mere 'representations', 'expressions' or 'depictions' of it. In all three cases, it is reality itself that is believed to be communicated – unmade by human hands – rather than a second-hand, mediated impression of that reality.

Vertov further enhanced the unique and definitive truthfulness of his work by stressing that not only does his use of cinema communicate reality in an unmodified form, but it reveals aspects of that reality that cannot be seen by the naked eye. By using such devices as repetition, montage, slow motion, reverse action, superimposed images, animation and unusual viewpoints (for instance, putting the camera on or under a moving train), he enabled people to see aspects of life that they could not experience without the help of a camera, which became for him 'kino-eye' – a kind of 'superior eye'. In this sense, Vertov believed that his work provided insight into reality. Its purpose was not simply to reproduce the temporal and spatial world that the human eye can already see. On the contrary, as with icons, it revealed a hidden truth – realising 'the possibility of making the invisible visible, the unclear clear, the hidden manifest, the disguised overt, the acted nonacted; making falsehood into truth'.[54] By overcoming the conventions of time and space, and the extended linear frame of reference that they impose on human perception, kino-eye became symbolic of a higher form of human identity, and was objectively realised as such in *The Man with a Movie Camera*, in which the camera is represented as an independent form of perception and at one point even takes on a life of its own.

> I am kino-eye. I create a man more perfect than Adam, I create thousands of different people in accordance with preliminary blue-prints and diagrams of different kinds... From one person I take the hands, the strongest and most dextrous; from another I take the legs, the swiftest and most shapely; from a third, the most beautiful

and expressive head – and through montage I create a new, perfect man. I am kino-eye. I, a machine, show you the world as only I can see it. Now and forever, I free myself from human immobility, I am in constant motion, I draw near, then away from objects, I crawl under, I climb onto them. I move apace with the muzzle of a galloping horse, I plunge full speed into a crowd, I outstrip running soldiers, I fall on my back, I ascend with an airplane, I plunge and soar together with plunging and soaring bodies... My path leads to the creation of a fresh perception of the world. I decipher in a new way a world unknown to you.[55]

Although many experimental documentary films of this kind were based on authentic and therefore seemingly 'indisputable' newsreel – albeit selectively assembled to the point of falsification – they were heavily criticised for being 'formalist' or excessively concerned with the expressive impact of the film medium. At the other end of the scale were the Russian-made feature films that were neglected in the immediate aftermath of the Revolution but received new impetus following the partial stabilisation of the economy in the early 1920s. Such films were as ideologically conformist as educational documentaries and avant-garde agitational films, but they were entirely different in their means, following the formula of an entertaining and exemplary tale with an edifying moral. Although this type of film aimed, like Social Realist painting, to be naturalistic and accessible in its form (which could not always be said of avant-garde film), it was also criticised for indulging in bourgeois fantasising and for capitulation to western (especially Hollywood) values. Such films stood in strict contrast to avant-garde films, such as *Enthusiasm*, where a considerable amount of the intended impact of the film was concentrated in its form and the physiological effect of that form on its viewers. The makers of the new feature films tended to invest the ideological content of their work in their narratives, which were required to advocate and demonstrate the superiority of Soviet values, frequently to the point of deifying their heroes. A key feature was to demonstrate – with an almost scientific sense of cause and effect – the indisputable value of Soviet ideology in the context of daily life.

An unusual product of this approach can be found in the silent film, *Earth*, made by the Ukrainian director Alexander Dovzhenko in 1930. The film tells the story of the collectivisation of agriculture on a Ukrainian farm and the heroic death of the young communist who achieved it in the face of resistance from *kulaks* (rich landowning peasants), one of whom eventually murders him. The plot is a typical example of Soviet propaganda, with built-in inducements to religiosity. The cult of the tractor, for instance, has already been mentioned. In this instance, the excited rush of villagers to greet their new 'steel horse' strongly recalls icons of Christ's Entry into Jerusalem; children in particular can be seen rushing to keep up with it. When it runs out of water, the farmhands replenish the radiator by urinating into it – thereby sealing their symbiotic relationship with it – though, in the version released to the public, this scene was suppressed.[56] More importantly, by dying at the hands of a *kulak*, the protagonist, Vasily, is turned into a martyr, thereby sanctifying the cause for which he was fighting. The emotions aroused in this way – both in the villagers and, hopefully, in the viewers – are then seamlessly and invisibly transformed into emotional support for his cause, as if such support was the only way to assuage the sorrow of the viewer and justify Vasily's death.

Such polarisations of good and evil were typical of the politicised narratives of early Soviet feature films. In the case of *Earth*, however, they were not enough to avert criticism of the sensibility of the film, which was considered to be too reverential towards the old guard and too pantheistic, almost mystical, in its feeling for nature. The paradox is interesting for the light it throws on the differences between form and content in this period of visual culture in Russia: in this instance, the content is overtly anti-Christian (as it was in all Soviet culture), despite certain formulae adapted from Christianity (and sterilised) to stimulate religiosity. The form, however, arguably may be seen to continue pictorial traditions that had been validated in Russia over many centuries, and it is in this capacity that the film may be relevant in the present context. This becomes particularly clear when the film is seen in relation to the films of Dovzhenko's contemporaries. Whereas the films of Sergei Eisenstein and Vertov, for instance, frequently border on the hyperactive – in order to demonstrate, as well as describe, the frenetic energy of their subject matter – the pace of *Earth* is remarkably slow; in fact, it is not only slow, it is frequently static. The first 20 minutes or so of the film resemble a sequence of stills; there is almost no action at all and there is no panning of the camera, which simply rests on the land or on the faces of people, sometimes for up to 10 seconds at a time. The only movement is of the grasses and clouds, and in the occasional slow turning of people's heads. The characters almost never blink; some do not blink at all. Vasily's father in particular simply looks at the camera. The effect would not be so striking were it not occurring in a silent film. Such impressions are of course common in photographs which the viewer can look at for as long as they want to, but in a film the effect is more intense because the duration of the image is prescribed by the director; every moment is deliberate and accounted for. In this instance, the director ignores the unique potential of film to capture movement, but capitalises instead on its ability to capture and hold attention.

As the early encounters in *Earth* are so extraordinarily prolonged, and as nothing is actually happening or being said during them, it is clear that Dovzhenko intended them to be invested with particular significance and meaning. It is arguable that he achieved this effect, whether deliberately or otherwise, by drawing on the tradition of icon painting. Not only did icon painting provide a unique visual language for the type of encounter that Dovzhenko was trying to promote – including for the most part, real life encounters, which are rarely so static, intense and direct – but that language was already universally understood by the populace for whom the film was made. In some ways, Dovzhenko's static face-to-face encounters took the contemplative potential of icon painting to a new level, by accommodating both the 'stillness of the object' and the 'duration of attention' in a single work of art. The combination of stillness and duration is especially iconic in that it is conducive to contemplation – in contrast to the stillness of a photograph which is that of an isolated moment (without duration) or the duration of everyday experience which is without the stillness.

In these moments, *Earth* capitalises on some of the advantages that cinema had over painting, as advocated by Malevich in the 1920s. Particularly as Malevich and Dovzhenko were both Ukrainian by birth, there is every likelihood – although there is no proof that I am aware of – that they knew each other's work. Malevich maintained that, in its highest essence, cinema represented a development of visual art towards the total conveyance of dynamic reality 'as such', and not as mediated through narratives and meaningful subject matter. Prior to the invention of cinema, artists could only reproduce the impression of an object; now they could reproduce it as a moving reality.[57] Partly to consolidate his notion that cinema was rooted in painting (rather than theatre), but also to highlight the conservatism by which contemporary cinema was still afflicted, he commented that the compositions of the stills in many contemporary films were essentially painterly, citing various Old Masters, Wanderers and Impressionists as sources.[58] Dovzhenko, who trained as a painter before working in film, epitomises these tendencies, but he was not the kind of film-maker that Malevich considered to be doing justice to the medium and to the times they were living in. In his article 'Painterly Laws and the Problems of Cinema' (1929)[59] Malevich singled out Dziga Vertov for praise as an example of a director who was working towards non-objective film, and away from outdated representational narratives. On the other hand, Malevich's own work from the period paints a slightly different picture, allowing for more symbolic references to the non-objective world than were present in his Suprematist work. His faceless characters, for instance, depict non-subjectivity without aiming to induce it in the viewer – in contrast to, say, *Black Square*. Various versions of the *Head of a Peasant*, however, occupy a middle ground. They are representational in what can only be seen as a retrogressive manner. One example in the Tretyakov Gallery is also both symbolic (the cross behind the peasant's head obviously symbolises Christ) and iconic in the penetrating, fixative way that it engages the viewer (Plate 104). It is precisely in this 'late-Malevichian' way that Dovzhenko's peasants, which resemble Malevich's transpersonalised peasant heads closely, might also be seen as iconic. Not only have they evidently been composed by the eye of a painter, but they are also able to accommodate the durational quality of contemplation.

Moreover, the parallel raises the question as to how Malevich may have been influenced by film. It is not inconceivable that his late figurative paintings of anonymous and transpersonalised figures may have been facilitated by the rise of this medium. Not only had Suprematism already transcended itself on its own terms, but the political climate in the late 1920s was becoming increasingly hostile to avant-garde art. The ability of film to capture duration (even the duration of a static object, as in *Earth*) may also have enabled Malevich to feel free of the obligation to adhere to a form of art (such as Suprematism) in which time, relativity and the possibility of difference or change were increasingly transcended. In cinema, time was inherently accounted for in the medium, even if no movement was seen; it was therefore unnecessary to abolish movement and relativity as a matter of principle, as it had been in Suprematism. It may well have been the knowledge of the possibilities of film-making that justified Malevich's return to figuration, enabling him to see his late peasant figures with the eye of a film-maker, just as Dovzhenko was seeing his own peasants with the eye of a painter or, at times, the eye of an icon painter.

Alongside the iconic 'manner of seeing', the narrative circumstances of the early part of *Earth* also lend themselves to this iconic treatment. The patriarch of the family, Vasily's grandfather, lies dying in the midst of his family who are gathered round him in solemn reverence. Their heads are bowed, exactly like the heads of saints on an iconostasis. Old Peter, an elderly stooping man with thinning hair and a short white beard, resembles St Peter exactly (Plates 121, 122); Vasily's mother clasps her hands and lowers her eyes with all the sorrow of a Mother of God. The camera moves from one to the other, before alighting on Vasily, the first of the men not to be bearded. The viewer knows immediately, because of Vasily's bright good looks and the positive glint in his eye, that he is the protagonist.

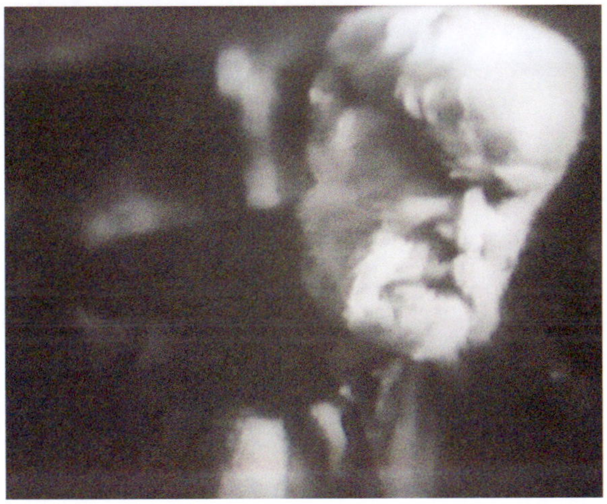

121

A still from Alexander Dovzhenko's film, ***Earth***, 1930, showing Peter

122

St Peter, Vologda region, 16th century
Tempera on wooden panel
85.5 x 36.2 cm (33 5/8 x 14 1/4 in)
Cerepovec Ethnographic Museum

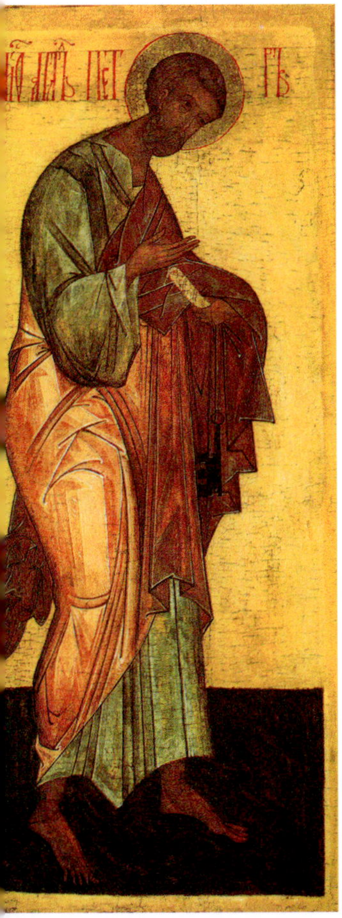

Like the figure of Christ in Majesty at the centre of the iconostasis, towards whom all the saints bow their heads, Vasily is our point of contact, although it takes him time to grow into the role. It is also in relation to him, and to the future that he represents, that speed and narrative action – excitement – are introduced into the film. Indeed, it is his destiny that constitutes the plot and political identity of the film. However, on many occasions, the film falls back into the more iconic mode of dwelling for prolonged periods on scenes of non-narrative movement and action, such as women gathering hay or oxen ploughing. Such scenes seem to forget the didactic message of the plot, and simply drift among impressions of the sufficient fullness of nature, leading critics to comment that Dovzhenko was more interested in the atmosphere and poetry of his work than in the storyline. It was precisely this feeling of contentment, enjoyed in nature and allowed to settle on peasants working in the traditional manner, which was considered to be reactive and controversial about the film, seeming to understate the urgency of reform and leading to accusations of nationalistic separatism. 'Doubts' about Dovzhenko's political priorities ultimately led to a notorious meeting with Stalin in 1944, in which the 'beloved leader', once a supporter of Dovzhenko, now denounced him. As an immediate result of this encounter, Dovzhenko was increasingly excluded from the world of Soviet film and, ironically, from the cultural life of the Ukraine. Significantly, as his estrangement from contemporary culture grew and his life as a film-maker evaporated, his belief in God, which he had jettisoned in 1911 at the age of 17, returned. In 1945, he wrote a story in which he dreamed that God relieved him of his need and talent for film – he could now see reality without it – rather as Malevich had been 'relieved of the need' to paint in 1918. It was as if, in the intervening years, making films – or seeing as a film-maker – had become his way of communing with the world.

The expressive possibilities of film were in their infancy in the early Soviet period, leading to a huge variety of experimental attempts to communicate the new communist ideals. From the early 1930s, such experimentation was thwarted in favour of more accessible, predictable narratives with unambiguous, politicised agendas centrally controlled by the state. During the period of transition, many ancient and traditional processes, associated with the cultural mediation of religious doctrine and experience, were recycled: artistic forms, religious beliefs and practices, deep-seated psychological tendencies, poetic associations and superstitious customs. Yet such qualities were often radically transformed in the process of transmission and the ways in which they were conducted into the new medium were often indirect. The most obvious characteristics of icons, certainly, are not easily transferred to a moving image. The case is not so ambiguous for propagandist posters, in which the parallels with icons – as didactic, awe-inspiring representations of higher truths – are immediately apparent.

With regard to propagandist posters, a long-standing tradition of popular visual culture already existed in Russia and the first Bolshevik propagandists were glad to inherit it. The example of icons was of fundamental importance in this respect. The reassuring familiarity of icons, their impressive graphic effect, their immediacy of impact and their ancient aura of power – not to the mention their deeply ingrained, if now undermined, association with the promise of salvation – were important traditions to bequeath. The religious meaning of icons was, of course, savagely rejected, but the captivating power of their pictorial language, originally developed in conjunction with their religious meaning, was subtly retained and made to serve new ends. The power of association continued to be highly effective. Significantly, the physiological theory of conditioned reflexes was becoming popular at this time; its Russian authors, Ivan Sechenov and Ivan Pavlov (winner of the Nobel Prize for physiology in 1904, and of 'Pavlov's dog' fame), proposed that psychological phenomena are conditioned by purely physiological impulses. Both authors demonstrated that reflexes are not simple responses to stimuli from the outside world, but responses to mental associations made with those stimuli, and that they can be manipulated by controlling the stimuli. In keeping with Pavlov's observation that a dog that had been habituated to associate the sound of a bell with food would salivate whenever it heard a bell ring (whether food was present or not), Sechenov suggested that 'as it was his habit to think of politics before going to bed each night, it might happen that if he were to lie down in the daytime the properties of his bedroom might elicit thoughts of politics in him'.[60] Striking parallels exist between the implications of Pavlov's research and the intentions of Soviet propagandists – the associative power of certain physiological aspects of icon-veneration was known to be familiar and effective and it was put to new use.

The reasons for the artistic appeal of icons to designers of early Soviet propaganda – particularly of posters – are clear. Like propaganda, icons are fundamentally didactic. Both media communicate a single message in a purely visual language and they share a dependence on the rhetorical effect of gesture. Considering the extent of illiteracy in both medieval and post-revolutionary Russia, these are particularly important similarities. When words are incorporated into the images, they are usually simple and direct, often making a graphic contribution to the design. The compositions of both art forms are simple and focused, and their colouring is bold and clear. The temperature of the palette tends to be warm, mostly using red, black, white, green, orange and yellow – earthy colours – with little blue. Many of the most vociferous posters are red hot.

The colour red (*krasnyi*), in particular, is charged with meaning – not least because of its closeness to the Russian word for beauty (*krasivi*). Its use by French revolutionaries and its traditional association with the blood of martyrs in the Christian Church also made it instantly transferable to the new ideology, where it became the romantic cloak of the Bolshevik hero. This is exactly as it appears in icons of St George (Plate 53), the martyr-warrior whose fluttering cape of bright vermilion was frequently given the most exaggerated and agitated shape, and whose victory over the dragon became a prototype for numerous posters of the conquest of communism over capitalism (Plate 123). The colour red also dominates many posters in the form of flags, dramatically unfurled across the sky (Plate 124), like the swathes of vermilion fabric that are draped, apparently gratuitously, over the buildings in the background of many icons (Plates 29, 57, 58). In icons, this enigmatic fabric is the veil of the temple, being woven by the Virgin Mary to cover the Jewish tabernacle at the time of the Annunciation (as represented in icons of the Annunciation, Plate 57) and torn 'in twain' at the time of the Crucifixion. Significantly, the rationale behind this fabric has been largely forgotten, though not knowing its meaning does not render it superfluous. On the

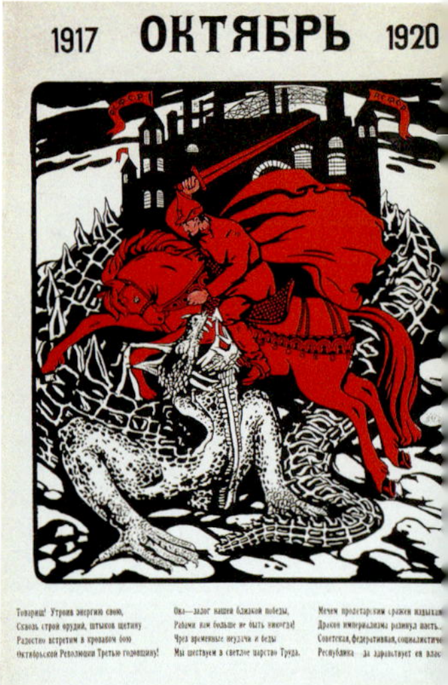

123

Poster celebrating the 3rd Anniversary of the October Revolution, 1920
David King Collection, London

124

Poster of May Day Celebration, 1920
David King Collection, London

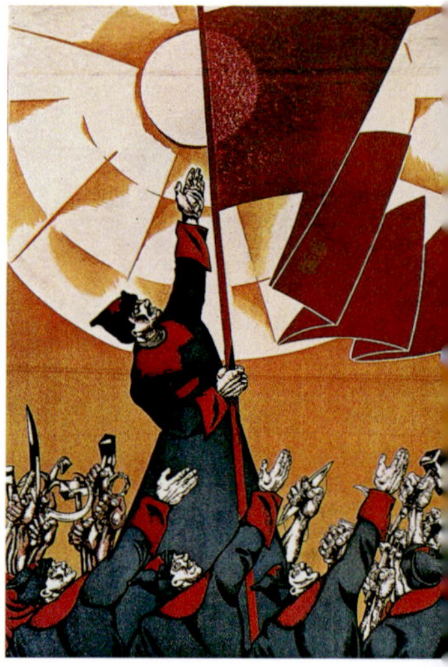

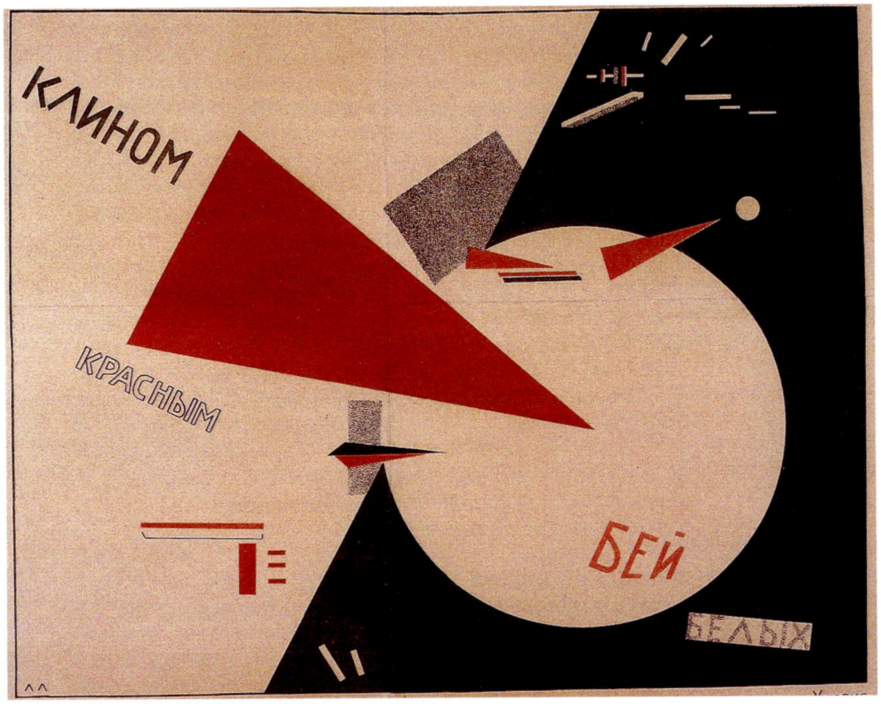

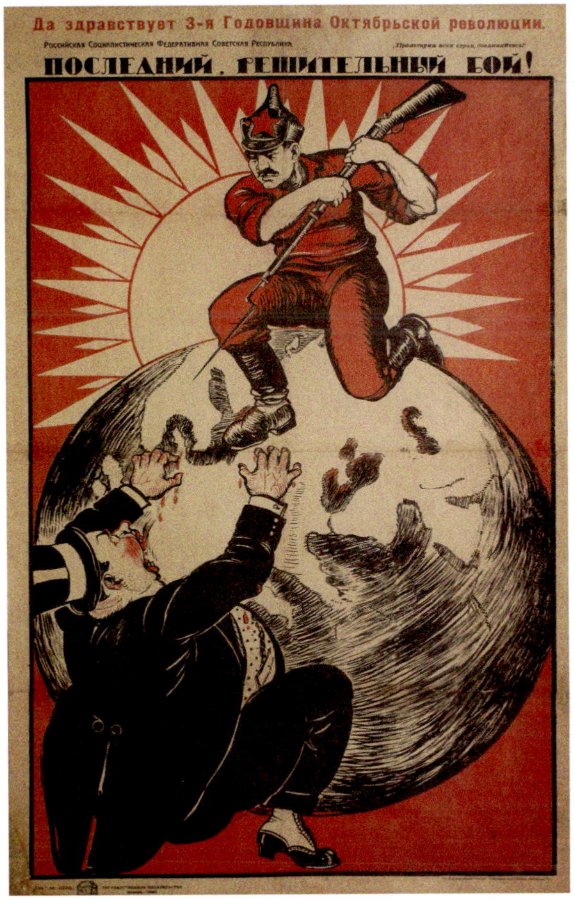

125
El Lissitsky

Beat the Whites with the Red Wedge, 1919–20
Poster
54 x 72 cm (21¼ x 28⅜ in)
David King Collection, London

126
Dmitri Moor

The Last Decisive Battle, 1920
Poster
Dimensions unknown
www.internationalposter.com

contrary, its value has long since been transferred from its meaning to its presence and colour. The same could be said of the aggressive use of the colour red in El Lissitsky's famous poster *Beat the Whites with the Red Wedge* (1919–20, Plate 125), in which the meaning of the jagged shards of red, reminiscent of the fluttering cloak of St George, is self-evident despite being entirely abstract.

One of the most renowned designers of political posters in the early Soviet period was Dmitri Moor (1883–1946). Moor had no formal artistic training and his talent for drawing was discovered by chance. He spent the first ten years of his artistic life producing cartoons for a variety of journals, only turning to the more expressive medium of posters after the Revolution. He considered popular prints (*lubki*) and icons – especially simple early examples – to be the predecessors of poster art and, despite being a committed atheist from the age of 15, he acknowledged in an unpublished autobiography that icons 'lay at the foundation of [his] work'.[61] His sense of colour, stability of compositional structure and simplicity of narrative – freeze-framing highly dramatic incidents as if they were feasts of the Church – bear out this comment. His *The Last Decisive Battle* (1920, Plate 126), for instance, depicting a revolutionary guard wearing red and holding a bayonet, casting a fat black-suited capitalist off the earth, is clearly influenced by icons of the Transfiguration (Plate 26) and Anastasis (Christ's Descent into Hell, Plate 2). As with the figure of Christ in the Transfiguration, the guard is placed against a bright light (in this case, the sun against a red sky), radiating sunbeams. Like the astonished figures of Peter, James and John in the icon, the capitalist is sent tumbling to the ground. A precedent for the cosmic or planetary dimension of the image is provided by the Anastasis in which Christ descends through the heavenly realms,

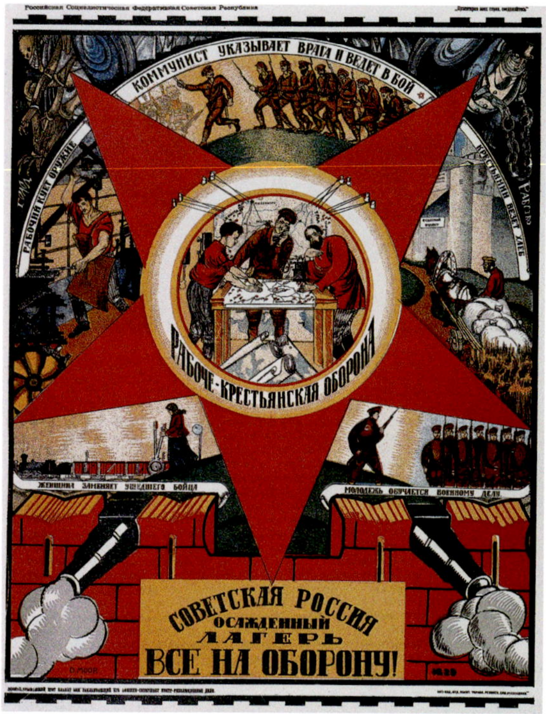

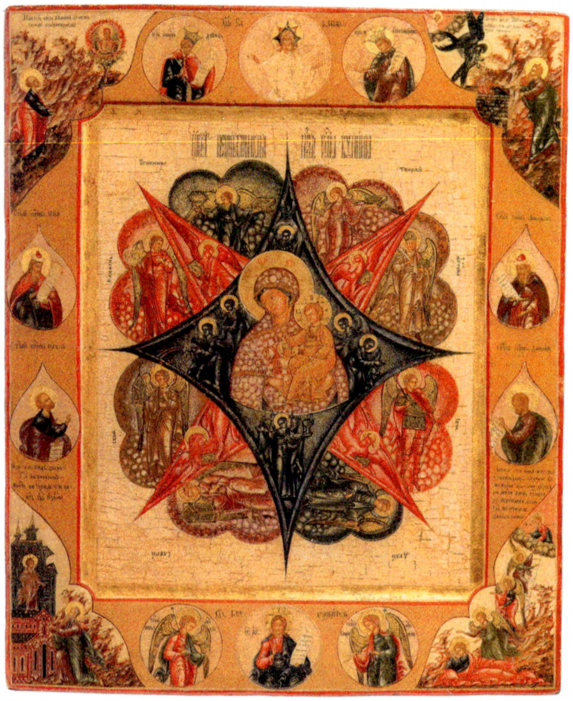

127
Dmitri Moor

Soviet Russia as an Armed Camp, 1919
Lithograph
97 x 73 cm (38 ¼ x 28 ¾ in)
David King Collection, London

128
Palekh School

Virgin of the Burning Bush, 18th century
Tempera on wooden panel
36 x 29.5 cm (14 ⅛ x 11 ⅝ in)
Temple Gallery, London

represented as concentric circles behind him, into Hell where he conquers the black figure of death; in some examples, the figure of death is speared by a host of archangels inhabiting the heavens.

Aspects of the cosmological scope of icons are also present in Moor's coloured lithograph of *Soviet Russia as an Armed Camp* (1919, Plate 127) which adapts the visionary logic of icons of the Virgin of the Burning Bush (Plate 128), not to mention Christ in Majesty (Plate 42), to the communist agenda.[62] According to the Book of Exodus, the Virgin appeared to Moses in a burning bush on Mount Sinai but was not consumed by the flames.[63] This vision was traditionally understood by Christians to anticipate the conception of Christ by the Virgin Mary whose virginity was not consumed when she conceived. In icons of this subject, the Virgin and Child appear at the centre of a four-pointed blue star superimposed over a four-pointed red star, with depictions of Old Testament scenes, believed to be prophetic of the virgin birth, in each of the panel's four corners. Moor appears to have adopted this dogmatic and diagrammatic design for his own image. The red star continues to act as a charismatic visual device but it has acquired a new symbolic significance, its fifth point transforming it into the red star of the Bolsheviks. At the centre, the Virgin and Child have been replaced by three figures – a factory worker, a soldier and a farm labourer – gathered round a table surveying a map of Russian territory which they are protecting for the people. The close resemblance of the figures – identified as the Workers-Peasants-Defence – to the three angels in icons of the Old Testament Trinity (Plate 6) gives them an air of familiarity, investing them with a sense of the consoling and secure, but it also raises them to the level of an archetype, finding roots for them in historical consciousness that make them seem ancient, just and inevitable. Their presence at the sacred centre is further supported by subsidiary images in-between the points of the star, which show how each of them contributes in a fundamental way to the realisation of the whole – just as the miracle of the Virgin of the Burning Bush is implicitly realised in the prophetic signs that were believed to anticipate it.

Moor's ambivalent relationship with icons was noticed by contemporaries. His contributions to the anti-religious journal, *Bezbozhnik u stanka* (*The Godless at the Workbench*), which provided a regular outlet for articles on atheist subjects and which Moor directed from 1923–31, were clearly based on an intimate knowledge of the wide range of icon types. His designs frequently reflect the influence of icons, primarily in their colour, composition and subject matter (albeit violently subverted), but also in their graphic style – sources of inspiration that he also recommended to other artists working for the journal. According to Stephen White, Moor explained (in an unpublished lecture on poster art) how the poster form had a precedent in the traditional woodcut or *lubok* (Plate 120), but was especially indebted to 'the religious paintings in the vestibules of churches and in a certain number of icons, particularly of the fifteenth century'.[64] In response to the suggestion that he depicted the heavenly opponents of materialist atheism too sympathetically, he justified himself by saying 'you have to study your enemy'.[65]

Bezbozhnik u stanka was an official tool of the Central Committee of the Communist Party, tirelessly presenting religion as a pernicious strategy of exploitation, in which capitalists and clergy are cynical and knowing conspirators against the workers. It was originally called *Bezbozhnik* but was changed to *Bezbozhnik u stanka* in 1923 in order to differentiate it from a newspaper of the same name published the previous year.[66] The regular content of the journal included scientific proofs of the absurdity of religion, exposure of the clergy as hypocritical parasites (Catholic as well as Orthodox), stories of conversions to atheism (ideally by priests) and testimonies to the self-sufficient wonders of new technology. It was copiously illustrated with vitriolic, even vicious, caricatures of religion, many of which were created by Dmitri Moor. At its peak, the journal was printed twice a month and had a print run of up to 70,000.[67]

Throughout the pages of *Bezbozhnik u stanka*, the Church and religion (primarily Christianity and Judaism, but occasionally Islam and Buddhism too) are mercilessly lampooned. In one edition, a miserly God is shown 'fishing for souls' from above the clouds, using icons and crosses as bait. In another, Jehovah and a flashily dressed Christ are depicted as suave and cunning partners in a commercial family firm – father and son – selling a range of ecclesiastical items including icons.[68] While these images were developed as new designs, others were subversions of established and instantly recognisable icon types. A caricature of a housewife, represented at the centre of the image as a 'diabolic pot', surrounded by a sequence of cartoon narratives – her creation by God, abuse by her husband and self-abasement in front of a church (in absurd gratitude for being abused) – was clearly based on a typical icon of a 'saint with scenes from his life' (Plates 70, 129). In another case, a despondent Virgin holds a protecting veil over men at war with each other. The image is designed to show how ineffectual she is; significantly, the veil is coloured an ominous blue-black, not the brilliant hopeful red used in icons of the Intercession of the Mother of God on which it is based. In the same way, a manipulated version of the Nativity of Christ (Plate 130) was used to expose the Church's theft of agricultural produce from the peasants (Plate 131). At the centre of the image, the Virgin is shown milking a cow – based on the cow that is habitually shown in icons of the Nativity (together with an ass) in the cave in which Christ was believed to have been born. Christ and angels (shown guiding the shepherds towards Christ in icons) are shown stealing a pig and chickens from a farmyard. In the foreground, two *putti* are decanting milk into large urns – in place of the midwives who wash the new-born Christ by pouring water over him from a ewer. The cover of another edition of the journal depicts a group of disenchanted industrial workers casting Christ into a pit, a treacherous recasting of his descent into hell, surrounded by ministering angels.[69]

Despite their anti-religious message, the extremeness of these caricatures in *Bezbozhnik u stanka* contributed to a polarisation of good and evil that is the very backbone of religious myth. In some cases it was used to promote, rather than undermine, cultish psychology. In 1924, for instance, the editors, positively indulging the religiosity of their readers, issued a brochure on 'How to Build a Godless Corner' with the journal. In a brazen attempt both to ridicule and to appropriate the ancient respect that was traditionally shown to icons placed in the holy corners of Russian homes (Plate 87), the brochure advertised 'Godless Corner Kits', which consisted of 'a Godless Corner banner; two large

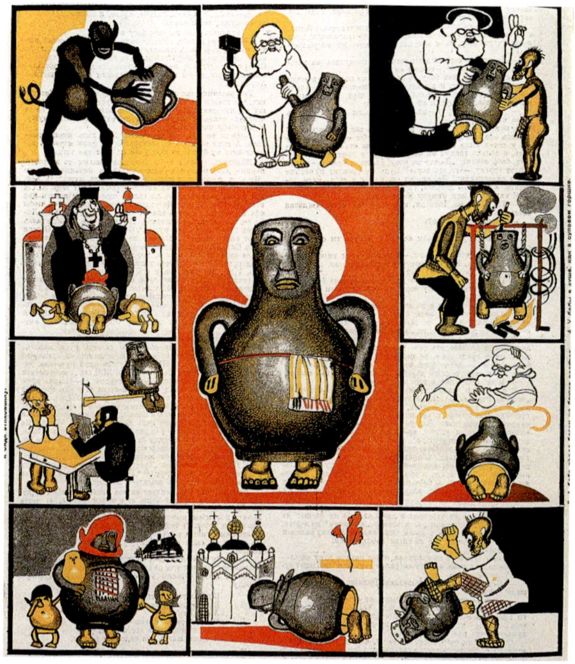

129

'The Diabolic Pot' by A. Deineka, from ***Bezbozhnik u stanka*** (***The Godless at the Workbench***), no.1, 1924, p.8
David King Collection, London

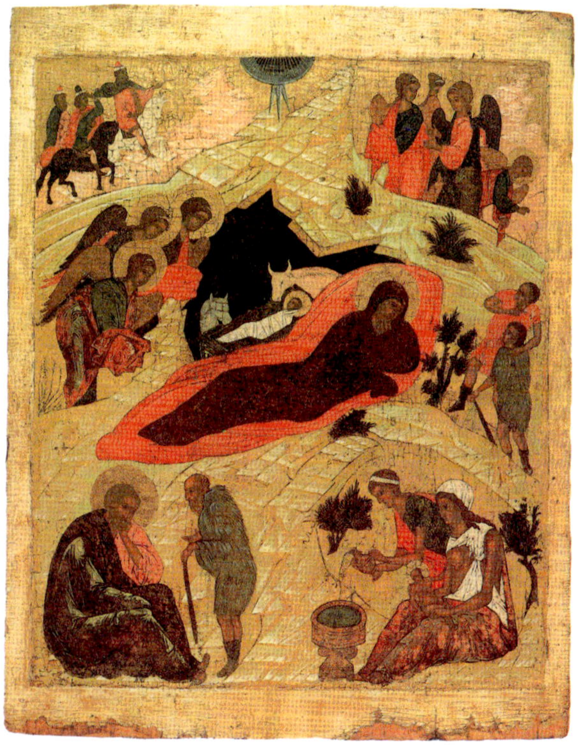

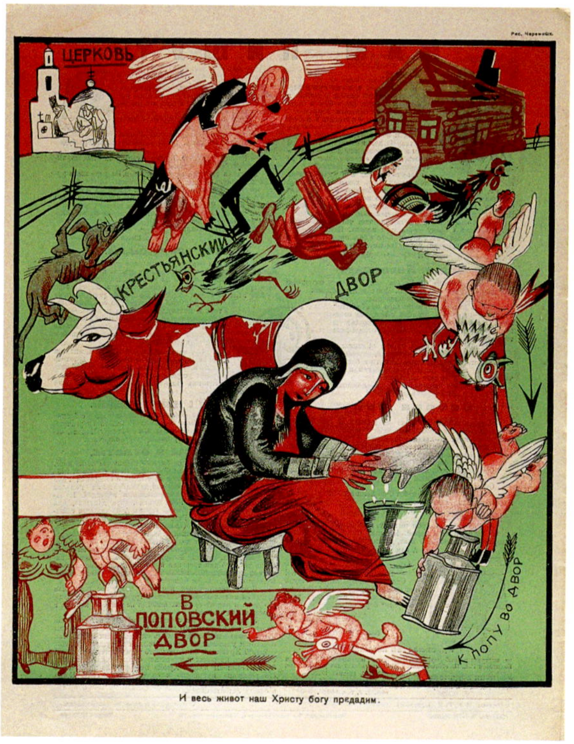

130

Nativity, mid-16th century
Tempera on wooden panel
80 x 60 cm (31 ½ x 23 ⅗ in)
Temple Gallery, London

131

'All goes to the priest's homestead, and we give up our life for Christ', by M. Cheremnykh, from ***Bezbozhnik u stanka*** (***The Godless at the Workbench***), no.4, 1923, back cover
David King Collection, London

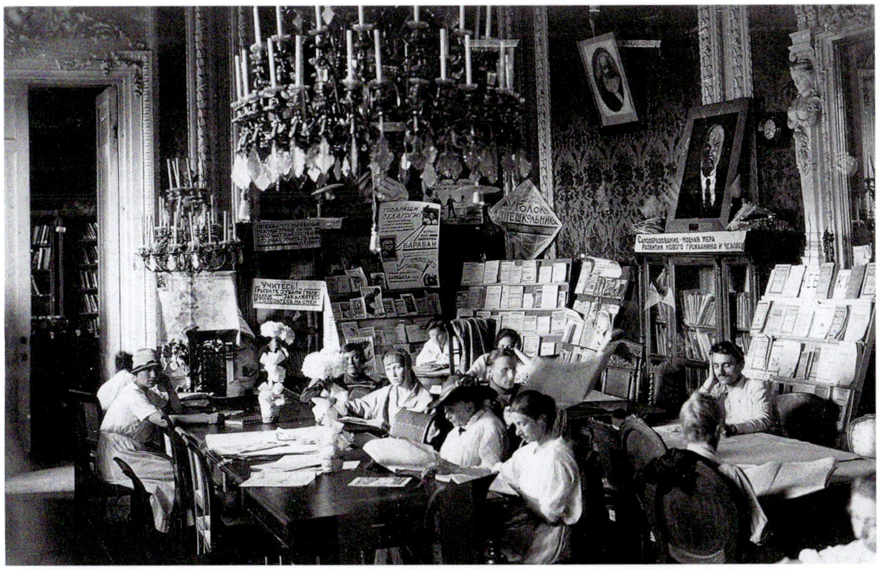

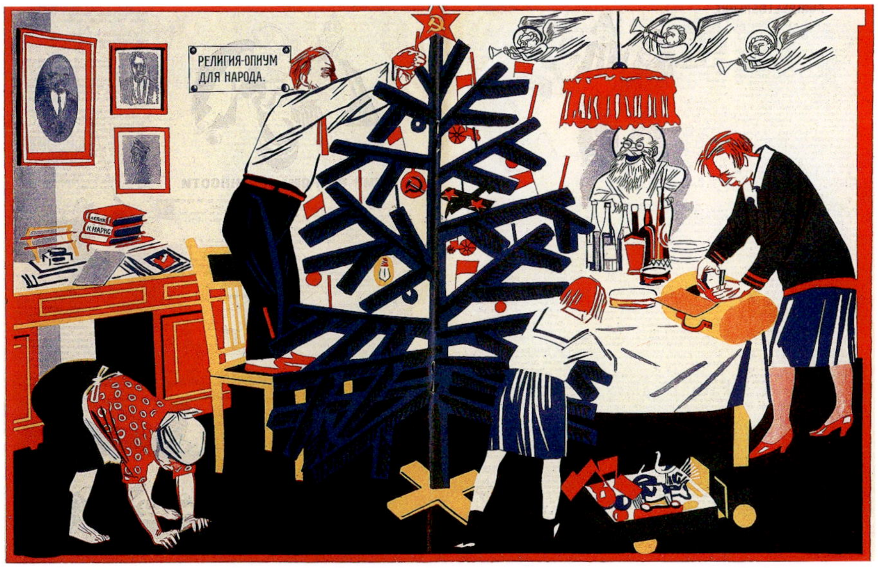

132

The Godless Corner in an Educational Workers' Club, Moscow, *c.*1927
David King Collection, London

133

'Religious spirit in Soviet life. The Soviet person: "Look at our tree. We've liberated it from old superstitions." God: "He! he! New song, same old tune"', by N. Kogout, from ***Bezbozhnik u stanka*** (***The Godless at the Workbench***), no.12, 1928, centrefold
David King Collection, London

posters with anti-religious imagery and slogans; seven outsized brightly coloured humoristic posters; six back issues of *Bezbozhnik u stanka* from which to extract centrefolds and additional images; and visual instructions on how to assemble the corner in an alluringly symmetrical composition'.[70] Such corners were to be established in prominent places in factories – or, for children, in schools – where anti-religious events and discussions could take place (Plate 132).

However, the aping of Orthodox traditions could also backfire, because it facilitated the continuation of Christian religiosity in a new form – rather as the veneration of ancient Slavic spirits had continued as part of a 'double-faith' (*dvoeverie*) under Christianity. In the most extreme cases, parodies of Christianity were entirely counter-productive: some satirical representations of religion resembled icons so closely that illiterate peasants, unable to detect their anti-religious purpose, were known to venerate them as Christian objects.[71] In other cases, the issue was more subtle and psychological, addressing the problem of religious psychology rather than religious belief. A salutary centrespread in *Bezbozhnik u stanka*, for instance, shows a family gathering round a 'Christmas' tree decked with the transformative 'gods' of Soviet culture – a light bulb, a hammer and sickle, and the ubiquitous tractor (Plate 133). A picture of Lenin and a sign reading 'religion is the opium of the people' hang prominently on the walls. At a superficial glance, the image shows the ideal family home, pervaded by Soviet values but, on closer inspection, this is not an image of 'how things should be'. On the contrary, the reader is being warned against the superficial transferral of ritualistic and superstitious thinking to the material trappings of Soviet culture: in smug recognition of the religious psychology that is still at work at such times, the figure of a complacent

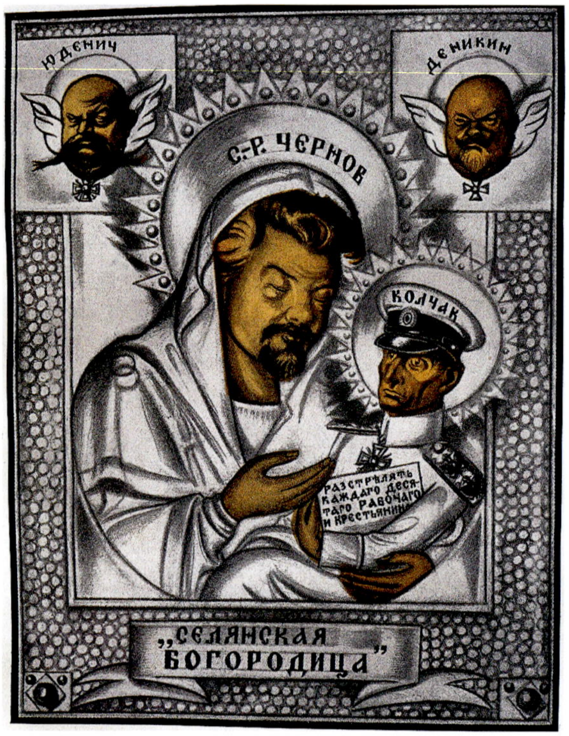

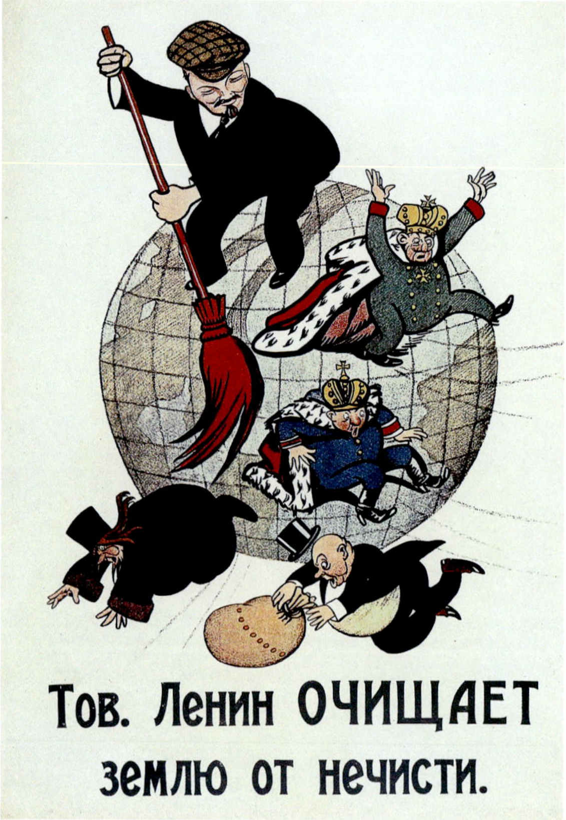

134
Viktor Deni

The Village Virgin, 1919
Coloured lithograph
46 x 33 cm (18 ⅛ x 13 in)
David King Collection, London

135
Viktor Deni

Comrade Lenin Cleans the Earth of Scum, 1920
Coloured lithograph
68 x 44 cm (26 ¾ x 17 ⅜ in)
David King Collection, London

God can be seen secretly smiling in the background.

Moor's posters make use of icons in a subliminal way, subtly appropriating their communicative power but using it is an affirmative way to serve their own purpose – to create and support the communist ideal (rather as Christian missionaries in medieval Russia had sublimated the pagan god of thunder, Perun, in the Christian prophet Elijah). The way in which the image is used remains the same; only its identity as a Christian object (determined by the iconography) is changed. Other posters worked in the opposite way, undermining, rather than affirming, their subject matter. These images were more satirical than heroic and the viewer is invited to laugh at their incongruity, and recoil. In these works, the discredited Christian identity of the image type is deliberately retained, but it is present only to be ridiculed, which in turn serves to trivialise religious belief, especially as manifest in icon veneration.

A classic example of this type of image is Viktor Deni's lithograph of *The Village Virgin* (1919, Plate 134) which mimics an icon of the Hodigitria (Mother of God with Christ, Plate 4) but replaces the faces of the Virgin and Christ with the faces of the White (revolutionary but anti-Bolshevik) leaders Viktor Chernov and Admiral Kolchak. Kolchak holds a placard which reads: 'shoot every tenth worker and peasant'. In the top left and right, the faces of the counter-revolutionary leaders Nikolai Yudenich and Anton Denikin are depicted, winged like seraphim. The image is signed 'icon painter Deni'.[72] Stephen White records that, according to the poet Demyan Bedny, a door-sized replica of this poster was made by artists in Siberia and was carried about in a parody of a religious procession. Ironically, although the icon as a cult object was ridiculed in this way, something of the cultishness of icons was transferred directly to the new type of image. A quasi-religious respect for the posters themselves – and not just their subject matter – was promoted by the discreet inclusion of texts, in the corners of the posters, asserting that to damage a poster (for instance Deni's *Kapital*, 1919) or paste another poster over it would be a counter-revolutionary crime.

A comparison of Moor's *Last Decisive Battle* (Plate 126) with Deni's *Comrade Lenin Cleans the Earth of Scum* (Plate 135) demonstrates the differences between the styles of the two artists. Although both images share a common layout – a good man sweeping the bad men off the earth – Deni's design is simple and humorous rather than dramatic, and uses no supplementary pictorial devices to intensify its impact. The fact that Deni is not working in the heroic mode is clearly reflected in the fact that even Lenin is caricatured, appearing as a squat, jocular character rather than an upright visionary, and holding a domestic broom rather than a bayonet.

Ten years later, such an irreverent image of Lenin would have been impossible. By this time, the cult of Lenin was fully underway and Lenin was revered as a kind of secular saint, with all the trappings of Orthodox religiosity. The attempted assassination of Lenin in 1918, followed by his death in 1924, made him especially vulnerable to projections of belief in the resurrection of Christ. His emergence as a personal cult object was paralleled in poster design, where the original archetype of the revolutionary activist was eventually eclipsed by the image of the recognisable leader, initially Lenin, as a political genius of vision and stature. Alexander Gerasimov's 1929 painting of *Lenin on the Tribune*, reproduced widely in poster form from 1932 (Plate 136), is a classic example of this more personal type of image.[73] Lenin is portrayed as a charismatic seer; like a saint or prophet, he intercedes for his people, transforming their fragile dream of a better future into a vision of destiny. Similar associations have been attached to Isaak Brodskii's famous painting of *V.I. Lenin in Smolny* (1930) in which a seated Lenin, seen from the side in the act of writing, has been compared to icons of the evangelists writing their gospels. A messianic element has also been detected here, associating the empty chair opposite Lenin with the *hetoimasia*, a traditional Byzantine image of a throne prepared for the Second Coming of Christ.[74]

The introduction of a sense of the 'personal' and the 'specific' to poster design represented an overall shift away from the generalised types of hero and rogue – personifications of good and evil forces – that characterised the posters of the Civil War period following the Revolution, towards the use of supposedly 'realistic' depictions of individuals with which the viewer could immediately identify. This shift was to some extent precipitated by the new use of photography in photomontages, but it also reflects a change in the intended impact of propagandist images. The poster designs of Moor and Deni had been highly stylised, often to the point of caricature. They revolved around a generalised type of proletariat warrior-worker-hero, frequently engaged in intense physical action, and they were intended to stimulate feelings of revolutionary fervour in the viewer. Negative characters were exaggerated in their ugliness, encouraging viewers to differentiate themselves and dissociate from what they were seeing. Such art tended to personify ideas (whether in a positive or in a negative light) and, in this respect, it was fundamentally doctrinal. By way of contrast, images of cult personalities from the late 1920s onwards were less concerned to disseminate doctrine as to intensify belief in, adulation of, and submission to the leaders in question (primarily Lenin and Stalin). Such propaganda ceased to operate as a form of political argument, but became a form of religious observance. It focused on the attractiveness of the image, affirming it in an accessible, naturalistic style that enticed the viewer, often illiterate in artistic matters, into identifying with its emotional orientation. Such a style relinquished the

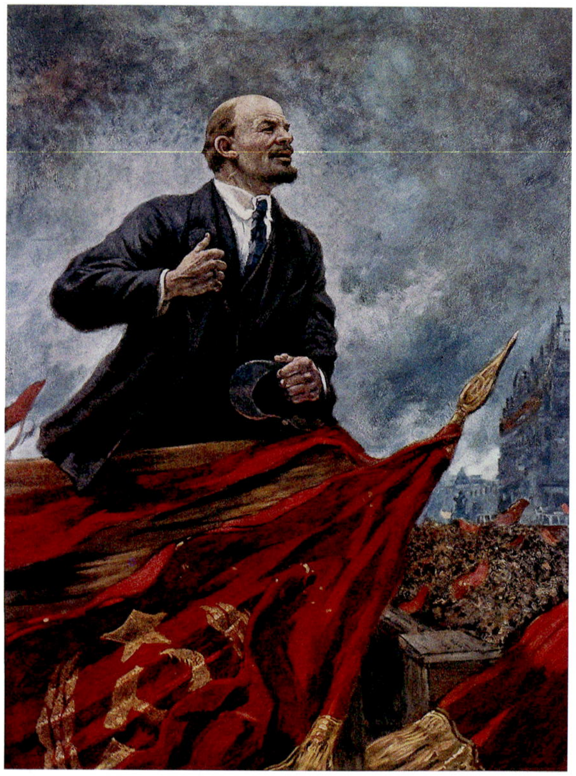

136
Alexander Gerasimov
Lenin on the Tribune (1917), 1929, made into a poster in 1932
Oil on canvas
288 x 177 cm (113 3/8 x 69 5/8 in)
David King Collection, London

uglifying potential of distortion and was therefore – like icons – less well suited to the representation of negative characters. On the contrary, it was designed to convey a sense of political vision and stability, rather than revolutionary fervour, and it set out to stimulate feelings of confidence and passionate commitment in the viewer.

A particularly unusual example of this type of image, clearly intended to attract the kind of attention that was traditionally reserved for icons, was published as a full page in *Red October* in 1922, celebrating the fifth anniversary of the October Revolution (Plate 109). Designed by academician Smolnikov, the picture shows Lenin in a typically iconic head-and-shoulders position. However, far more importantly, the image is created exclusively from tonal differences in the text of Lenin's 1918 constitution for the RSFSR (Russian Soviet Federation of Socialist Republics, absorbed into the USSR in 1922) which covers the page in closely set type. As a result, not only does the reading of the constitution become a meditative perusal of the face of Lenin,but it also relates to the word *pisat* (to write), traditionally used to refer to the making of icons, to contemporary wonder-working imagery. The image recalls Claude Mellan's famous engraving of the *Veil of Veronica* (plate 137) in which the face of Christ is made up from a single line, evenly spiralling out from the tip of his nose, with nothing but variations in its thickness to create the necessary sense of modelling.[75] As if to underline its deliberately iconic posture, the image includes it own frame. Just as icons appear to be 'framed' by the raised borders that remain at their edges when the central area of the wooden panel is recessed (Plates 22, 46), so, in this instance, the border does not *surround* the image; it is itself a part of the image, simply made up of darkened text at the top, sides and bottom of the page.

Another image of Lenin that makes a clear reference to a specific icon-type is a poster from 1929, commemorating the fifth anniversary of Lenin's death (Plate 138). The poster revolves around an image of the leader in his heroic mode of pointing, supplemented by a series of images of memorable scenes from his life. It is clearly based on hagiographical icons in which images of saints are surrounded by scenes from their lives (Plate 70) and it duplicates this model in order to appropriate its associations for Lenin. Exactly as in such icons, the final scene in the narrative of Lenin's life is his funeral procession, surrounded by his followers.

Lenin was vehemently against the development of cultishness among the proletariat and it is significant that his cult only flourished after his death. This was not the case with Stalin who was proactive in the development of the cult of Lenin largely because it paved the way for his own cult. The development of a Lenin cult was of supreme importance to Stalin as it enabled him to direct the religious energy of the people towards the Communist Party without appearing to direct it towards himself. This

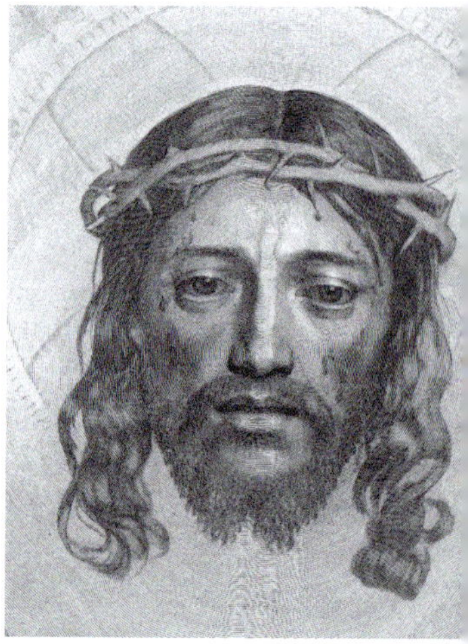

137.
Claude Mellan
The Veil of Veronica, 1649
Engraving
43 x 30.6 cm (17 x 12 in)
Private Collection

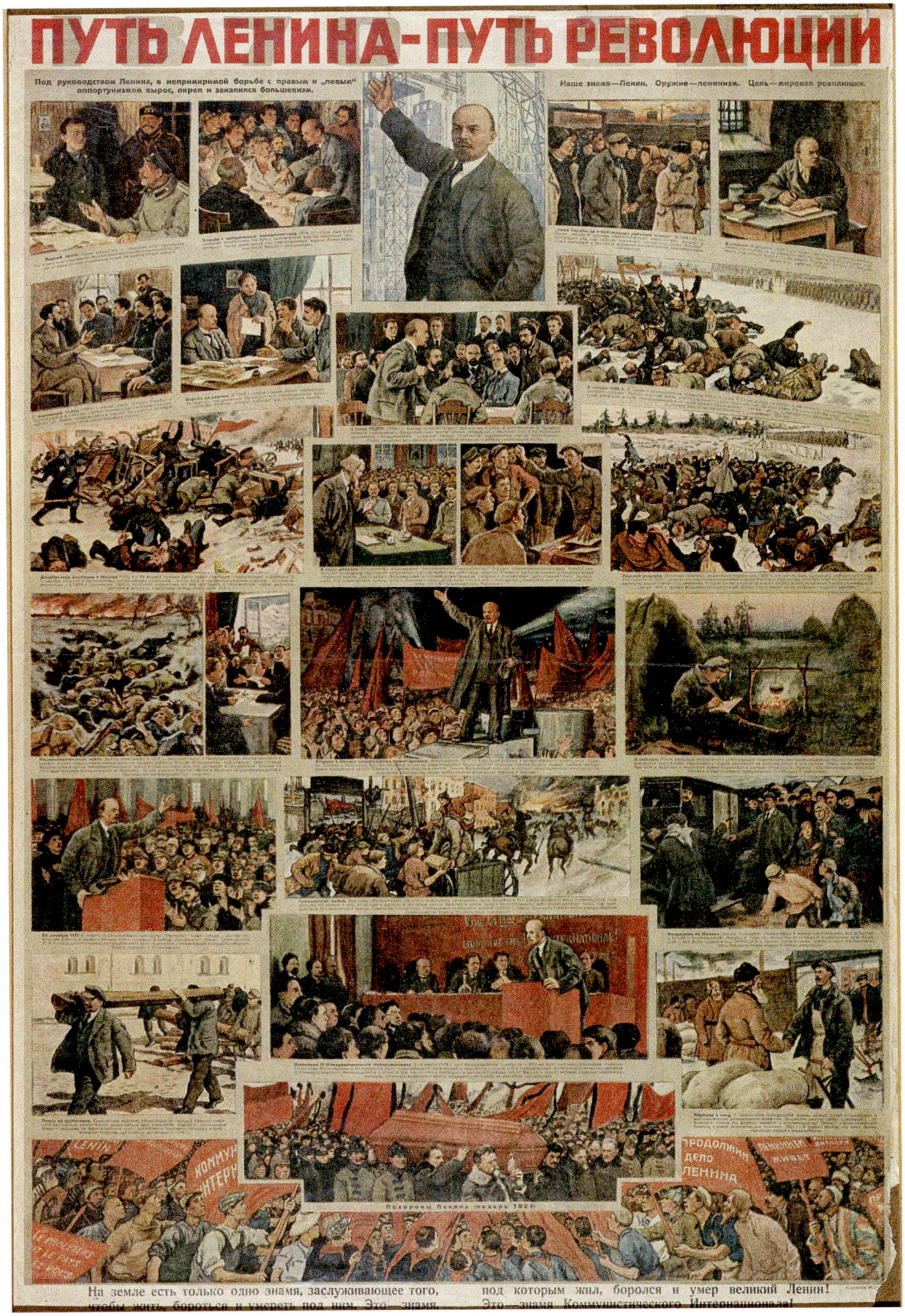

138

The Path of Lenin is the Path of the Revolution, 1929
Poster
103 x 71 cm (40 3/5 x 28 in)
David King Collection, London

shift of focus began to take place at the end of the 1920s when Stalin's defence of the name of Lenin against criticism has the subtle effect of idealising and mythologising Lenin, causing the emotional space that he had previously occupied as a 'beloved leader' to become increasingly vacant. Several images reflect how Stalin began to share and then encroach upon the territory once held sacred for his predecessor. For instance, the poster designed by the one-time Suprematist artist Gustav Klutsis – *Under Lenin's Banner for Socialist Construction* (1930) – in which Stalin's face emerges dramatically from behind Lenin's, or the same artist's *Under the Banner of Marx, Engels, Lenin and Stalin* (1933) – in which Stalin is the only figure making eye contact with the viewer.

The quality of contact with the viewer is important in relation to images of Stalin because it reflects the way in which Stalin had himself presented to his public, not merely as a commemorated ideal, as Lenin had been presented, but as a charismatic and living presence in his own right. Whereas Lenin tended to be represented in the context of his political activism – in the act of proclaiming, discussing or studying the new ideology – Stalin was often portrayed as the implementer of that ideology and the source of its benefits for the Soviet people. Unlike Lenin, who was usually represented in a state of striving towards a future ideal (the promise of which was the ultimate content of the images), Stalin was represented in a state of glowing contentment, firmly conveying the impression that his vision of a transformed Russia had already been realised and that he was responsible for this achievement. Indeed, while he increasingly considered himself to be the heir and consummator of Lenin's legacy, he reacted against the idealist revolutionaries of the early 1920s, with a view to reinstating the hierarchical and autocratic structures,

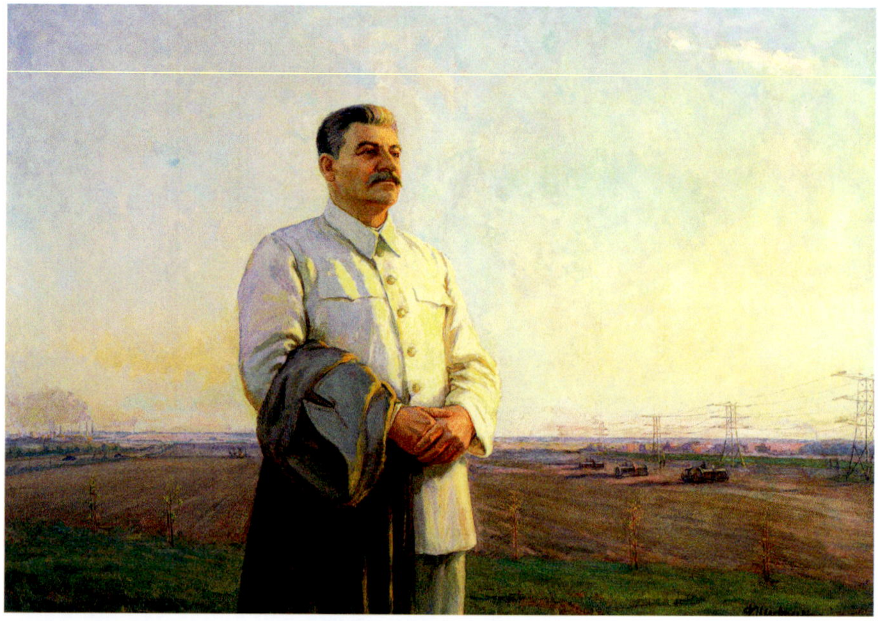

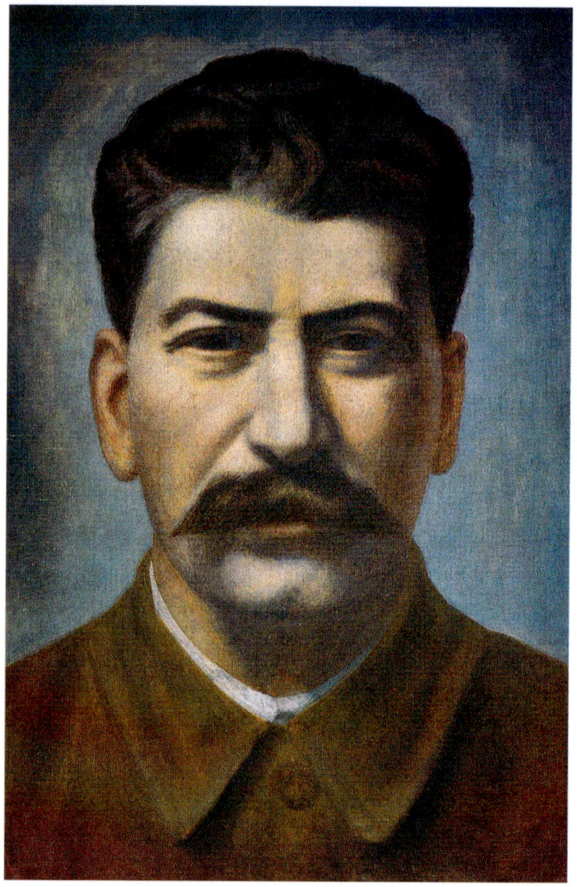

139
Fedor Shurpin

Morning of our Native Land, 1948
Oil on canvas
168 x 231 cm (66 ⅛ x 91 in)
Private collection

140
Pavel Filonov

Portrait of Stalin, 1936
Oil on canvas
99 x 67 cm (39 x 26 ⅜ in)
Russian Museum, St Petersburg

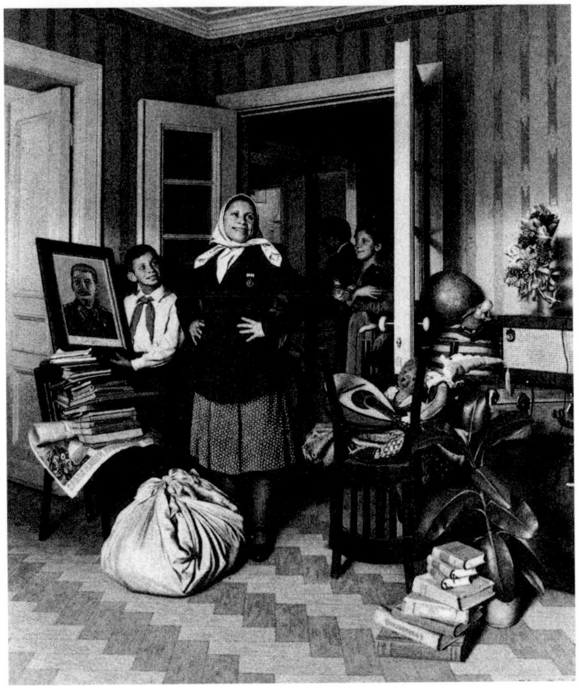

141
Aleksander Laktionov

Into the New Flat, 1952
Oil on canvas
130 x 113 cm (51 ⅛ x 44 ⅕ in)
Donetsk Regional Museum, Russia

paraphernalia and ritual – both Orthodox and tsarist in origin – that they had fought so hard to destroy. In this capacity, propagandist representations of Stalin reveal a fundamental similarity to icons which, according to Orthodox theology, do not express a yearning for redemption through Christ (as in western devotional art) but celebrate the triumph of Christ, already accomplished by the incarnation. Indeed, it could be argued that the wealth of peevish criticism and ultimate suppression of realist details such as sweat on the faces of labourers (on the grounds that sweat suggests that working towards the great motherland is burdensome) amount to a political 'theology of iconography' – recalling Orthodox debates around the heresy or legitimacy of representing the 'hand of God' in icons and other such issues.[76]

This resonance with icons differs significantly from the way in which icons are reflected in the propaganda of the early 1920s, revealing a profound shift of orientation. Where the artists of the revolutionary period had adapted the complex and fragmented dynamics of icon painting to undermine the turgidity and torpor of late imperial aestheticism and the social structures it held in place, Stalin demanded a return to the naturalism of the late nineteenth century. However, the anti-rational cult appeal of icons – and the simplicity of composition (as opposed to the complexity of internal dynamic) that facilitated it – was invoked to articulate his autocracy and to stifle all forms of opposition.

Fedor Shurpin's *Morning of our Native Land* (1948, Plate 139) depicts Stalin in a field tinged by the light of the rising sun, with an industrial site – vast in its own extent but minute in the context of the picture – and a farm, evidently improved by collectivisation, in the remote background.[77] The painting deliberately fuses the notions of morning, the regeneration of Russia and Stalin himself; but, based on the visual evidence of the picture, it is clear that it is not the native land but Stalin, both illumined and enlightened, who is the subject of the painting. As the 'fulfiller of promises' and the 'bringer of a perfect life', he is shown as a quasi-messianic figure, evocative of Christ as Saviour but also recalling Peter the Great, who frequently called his new city of St Petersburg a 'paradise'.[78] The depiction is completely iconic in that its sense of narrative is entirely secondary and that it focuses on the sanctity of its subject. The factories and farm serve only to contextualise the sanctity of Stalin, just as the scenes from the lives of saints in icons – for instance, the foundation of Solovetsky Monastery by SS Zossim and Savvati – serve to identify and honour the figures portrayed. In the most extreme cases, such as Pavel Filonov's *Portrait of Stalin* of 1936 (Plate 140), painted for mass reproduction, the formality of context was dispensed with altogether. The face of the leader, seen close-up and frontally, was entirely decontextualised. As in icons showing only the head of Christ or St Nicholas, not only are there no attributes or narrative details in this image to help and encourage the viewer to imagine a human drama or narrative, but there is no attempt to capture some aspect of the sitter's personality. It is the object itself – the mere fact of Stalin, incarnated in his icon – rather than the object's meaning that has become significant.

While the iconic status of Stalin is clearly manifest in the way Stalin was represented, it is also reinforced by the way that images of Stalin were themselves portrayed in works of art. Aleksander Laktionov's *Into the New Flat* (1952, Plate 141) is an object-lesson in Stalinist attitude-formation.[79] Like a Counter-Reformation representation of a saint in ecstasy before the consecrated host, the painting offers classic instruction on 'how to relate to images of the leader', providing the viewer with a perfect example to follow. The painting shows a literate and cultured family at the moment of their arrival in a new flat. The first and most important object to be placed is evidently the portrait of Stalin, the only possession in the room that has not been casually dumped on the floor. The mother of the family, just about to sigh with relief at having brought in the last of the heavy bags, now looks up to the place on the wall where the portrait of her leader will hang. Her relief comes in the form of contemplating where in the room she will hang the portrait. The fact that she looks upwards indicates that the picture will be given the place of honour, above eye-level opposite the entrance of the room – exactly like the sacred 'icon corner' in traditional homes – but it also communicates a more general sense of admiration and respect. The children are impressed and educated by the devotion of their mother and the viewer is encouraged to be moved to a similar state of respect by all three of them.

Although Stalin was interested in the mechanics of religious psychology rather than the content of religious ideas, his use of 'propaganda' was entirely consistent with the original use and meaning of the concept, which was first developed in a religious context – in connection with the Sacred Congregation for the Propagation of the Faith (*de Propaganda Fide*), the missionary ministry of the Catholic Church, founded by Pope Gregory XV in 1622. Indeed the concept evolved at a time when religious ideas were used to justify political agendas (absolute monarchy and the divine right of kings) more explicitly than ever before. In Russia the sacralisation of the state gathered momentum under Peter the Great whom Stalin may well have regarded as a precedent, despite distancing himself from him. Peter began to disempower the Church by failing to replace Patriarch Adrian at his death in 1700 and by setting up a Church Synod, instead of a Patriarchate, as a kind of Ministry of Ecclesiastical Affairs in 1721. As a result of these changes, the will of the monarch did not so much represent the Church as replace it. This shift is reflected in the way Peter chose to be portrayed. Whereas his father, Alexei I, was typically shown in the full vestments of theocracy (sanctioned by the Church), Peter was independently empowered, and wore the secular dress of the West. His sanctity was not dependent on the Church; it was directly given by God himself. As Stephen Baehr has shown, towards the end of the seventeenth century, tsars increasingly came to be referred to as 'gods and christs'.[80] In 1680, a decree was passed forbidding 'citizens from comparing the tsar to God, though the practice continued – and was encouraged – throughout the eighteenth century'. One of Peter's associates, Kirillov, 'even kept a portrait of Peter in his icon corner, bowed to it, and lit candles in front of it'. According to his son's tutor, Peter was 'so pleased when they equate him with God'.[81] A feeling for Peter's iconic status is reflected in a contemporary description of the rock supporting Étienne-Maurice Falconet's great bronze statue of the tsar (*The Bronze Horseman*, commissioned by Catherine the Great and unveiled in 1782) as a 'mountain not made by human hands'.[82] The description – based, of course, on the miraculous 'icon not made by human hands' – alludes not only to the uncut stone on which the statue rests but also to Peter himself as the rock (*petrus* in Latin) on which Christ said he would 'build his Church'.[83] Like so much of the anti-capitalist imagery of the 1920s, the sculpture itself, which represents the tsar on horseback killing a serpent, incorporates all the semantic devices of a St George and the Dragon icon.

Exemplary characters played an important part in Soviet iconography. As we have seen, in the 1920s, this role was largely taken by highly stylised and politicised types that established bridges of possibility between the viewer and the ideal, and heralded a radiant future. Under Stalin, this sort of romanticised and idealised symbolism was thought to smack of bourgeois fantasy and the role of exemplar came to be taken by more real types with whom the viewer could identify personally. This was by no means the first time that Russian culture had undergone a shift away from what was perceived to be 'dangerous subjectivity' in art, towards a more prescribed mode of representation. Firstly, icon painters had been instructed for centuries not to invent anything according to their imagination or depict the Godhead according to their own concepts, but to submit to the sanctity of objective tradition: 'Let the iconographer's skills resemble those of the ancient models, the first painters, men of divine wisdom... Let him not add anything new himself, not even an iota; even if he thinks he knows many things, let him not dare transgress the tradition of the Fathers.'[84]

More recently, artists of many different persuasions, from the Wanderers to the avant-garde, had railed against the indulgence and random aestheticism of subjective art, a malaise with which the West was particularly badly afflicted. The Wanderers were certainly regarded as the forerunners of the Socialist Realists, despite some radical differences in ideology, and some of the most important Realist painters were taught at the St Petersburg Academy of Fine Arts by Ilya Repin. However, the fact that a precedent for the movement away from the subjective potential of images towards a more literal form of representation also exists in the Orthodox Church raises the question as to whether the inclination away from arbitrariness and subjectivity, towards conformity to (what appears to be) an 'objective truth', may be present as an ancient characteristic of the national identity of the Russian people. At the Orthodox Council in Trullo in 692, symbolic representations of Christ – showing him, for instance, as a lamb – were prohibited, in favour of the more literal and 'objective' depiction of Christ as a man. [85] Although this decree was passed long before Russia was converted to Christianity, it provides a precedent for the literalisation of Socialist Realist representation within an Orthodox context, prompting the speculation that it may have been 1000 years of Orthodox conformism that habituated the Russian psyche to an anti-subjective ideal of creativity. It is arguable that such an anti-subjective tendency existed in the Eastern Church from the earliest times, as suggested by the Byzantine support for a conciliar approach to ecclesiastical authority (ratified democratically in church councils). In contrast to this approach, which aimed to reflect the equality of the apostles, the Roman Church promoted the notion that St Peter was the most senior of the 12 apostles, thereby legitimising the model of papal supremacy (and objectifying the latent individuality in western religiosity). Of course, it may equally well have been a pre-existent potentiality in the psyche of the Slavonic people of Kievan Rus (partly conditioned by historical and geographical conditions) that attracted them to the conformist culture of Orthodox Christianity.

Be this as it may, the realist figure type favoured by Stalin included both generalised characters and specific individuals. Among the most striking demonstrations of the way in which the generalised type was integrated into popular culture – in grandiloquent squares but also in the routine grind of the everyday – are the first metro stations to have been built in Moscow and Leningrad, dating from 1932 and 1940 respectively. The extensive decorative programmes in some of the stations demonstrate how the metro system was conceived, not only for its obvious practical value, but also as a cultural achievement and an ideological triumph, presenting transportation as a form of joyful liberation, just as the electrification of the USSR was presented as a form of enlightenment. In some cases, as when the Church of Holy Sign on Nevsky Prospekt in Leningrad was ostentatiously and controversially replaced by Ploschad Vosstaniya metro station in 1940, the pretensions of technology to be analogous, but superior, to religion were clearly and gleefully stated.[86] Other stations, such as Ploschad Revolutsii in Moscow, which opened in 1938, raised the hero-worker types of the day to the level of a Soviet pantheon, as if they were the angels and saints of the modern world. The 76 figures, designed by the sculptor Matvei Manizer (1891–1966) and executed on a monumental scale in cast bronze, are represented with the tools of their trade – echoing the identificatory 'attributes' held by saints in icons: soldiers with rifles, in place of archangels' lances; aviators with parachutes, in place of angelic wings; and students and scientists with books, resembling the evangelists that crouch with their gospels beneath the domes of orthodox churches (Plates 3, 142).[87]

The combination of militant atheism and politicised religiosity thrived in the USSR until World War II, when Stalin realised that he could not afford to alienate believers. The chief organs of anti-religious propaganda, the journals *Bezbozhnik u stanka* and *Antireligioznik*, were discontinued in 1941. The cult of Stalin, however, only began to subside at the dictator's death in 1953. Stalin's successors, Nikita Khrushchev and Leonid Brezhnev, did not become cult objects in the way that he did. On the contrary, as revelations regarding Stalin's true nature began to emerge, Khrushchev began to undermine his cult status, though he continued to implement his predecessor's virulent anti-religious campaigns until he was himself forced to retire in 1964. New research into the efficacy of propaganda led to a shift away from concentrated personality cults, relocating supreme authority in the Communist Party as a whole, and, as result, the cult of icons ceased to set an effective and meaningful precedent for propagandist imagery. By very slow degrees, a climate of tolerance for dissident culture began to develop. In this context too, the precedent of icons had little to offer. The orientation of icons towards objectivity, absoluteness, ideological significance and national identity – qualities that had inspired avant-garde artists at the beginning of the century – had been so thoroughly hijacked and distorted by the Communist Party that the art form had little left to recommend it. Artists turned away from accessible, doctrinal art towards the personal, suggestive and obscure. However, national indifference towards icons – neither reactive nor appreciative – did enable a market for icons to develop in the West. And although many icons were lost to Russia at this time, many were also saved. Indeed, the international awareness of their significance and interest that has subsequently developed have surely contributed much towards the renewed appreciation of icons that has taken place in Russia since the fall of the Soviet Union in 1991.

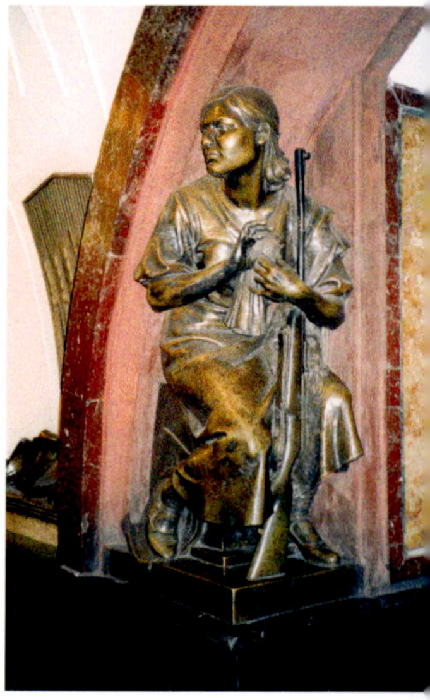

142

Matvei Manizer

Rifler from Ploschad Revolutsii Metro Station, Moscow, 1938
Bronze

NOTES

1. Tartarin, p.577.
2. Stites, pp 101–05; Read, pp 57–94; Kline, pp 103–26.
3. Malevich, 'The Question of Imitative Art' in Andersen (1971), p.170.
4. Malevich, 'The Book on Non-Objectivity' in Andersen (1976), p.336.
5. Ibid p.318.
6. Malevich, 'God is Not Cast Down' in Andersen (1971), pp 202–3.
7. Ibid p.206.
8. Malevich accepted Lenin 'only as one of the active members of the materialistic group of Communists, as a unit with a greater share of energic elements of dynamic force'. Andersen (1976), p.325.
9. Ibid p.332.
10. Ibid pp 320–1.
11. Ibid p.331.
12. Cooke (1990), figs 40, 41. Alexander Vesnin's diploma project drawing is reproduced in Khan-Magomedov (*Alexander Vesnin and Russian Constructivism*, 1986), p.25.
13. Andersen (1976), p.330.
14. Ibid p.331.
15. Ibid p.325.
16. Ibid p.344.
17. Book of Revelation 21 verses 1, 2, 16.
18. Andersen (1976), p.324.
19. See (currently) pp 99–107.
20. Andersen (1976), p.326.
21. Fülöp-Miller, pp 189–90.
22. Ibid p.331.
23. Ibid p.334. See also Tumarkin (1983), p.222; Stites, p.120.
24. Andersen (1976), p.356.
25. Ibid p.355.
26. Ibid.
27. Ibid p.333.
28. Ibid p.349.
29. Ibid pp 337–8.
30. Ibid pp 320, 324.
31. Ibid p.337.
32. Trotsky, L., *Pravda*, 14 July 1923.
33. Ibid. See also Comrie & Stone, p.188.
34. Andersen (1976), p.346.
35. *Kazimir Malevich* (1997), cat.no.51.19, p.110; reproduced the other way up in Nakov (2002), cat.no.S518, p.292.
36. Nakov (2002), cat.nos S501–S506, pp 288–9.
37. The whereabouts of the drawing is currently unknown but it is illustrated in Marcadé, J.-C. (1990), ill.384, p.255.
38. Nakov (2002), cat.no.PS49, p.362. Coffins, as places of transpersonal- or non-identity, appear elsewhere in Malevich's work at this time. Nakov, cat.nos PS72 (the figure's face), PS116, PS219. Also Marcadé, J.-C. (1990), ill.378, p.252.
39. For a linguistic analysis of the Russian phrase 'cutting truth', see Wierzbicka, pp 401–32.
40. Vakar & Mikhienko, vol.2, plates 141, 142.
41. Andersen (1976), p.353.
42. Ibid p.332.
43. Fülöp-Miller, p.187. Also, Wynot.
44. Gabel, p.353.
45. Tartarin, p.570.
46. See Zbarskii & Hutchinson; King.
47. Ilya Repin's *Religious Procession in Kursk Province* (1880–3, Tretyakov Gallery, Moscow) is reproduced in Lebedev, ill.68.
48. My thanks to David King for the likely identification of these figures. For information about their downfall, see Conquest, R., *The Great Terror*, Oxford, 1990, pp 419, 435, and Medvedev, R., *Let History Judge*, Oxford, 1989, p.538.
49. Ryan, p.56.
50. See Hughes, L., pp 249–57, and Zitser.
51. Boltyanski, G.M. (ed.), *Lenin I kino* (*Lenin and Cinema*), Moscow & Leningrad, 1925, pp 16–19, translated in Taylor & Christie, p.57.
52. First published in *Pravda*, 12 July 1923. English translation in Taylor & Christie, pp 94–7.
53. Babitsky & Rimberg, p.53.
54. Vertov, D., 'The Birth of Kino-Eye' (1924) in Michelson (1984), p.41.
55. Vertov, D., 'The Cine-Eyes. A Revolution' in *Lef*, 1923, no.3 (June/July), pp 135–43, translated in Michelson (1984), pp 17–18.
56. Liber, p.111.
57. Malevich, 'The Artist and the Cinema' in Andersen (1971), p.233.
58. Ibid pp 234–5.
59. Tupitsyn, pp 147–59.
60. See Kentridge.
61. White, S., p.7.
62. Ibid plate 3.18, p.53.
63. Exodus, 3, 1–6.
64. White, S., p.6.
65. Ibid p.7.
66. Peris, p.74.
67. Ibid.
68. *Bezhboznik u stanka*, 1924, no.3.
69. *Bezhboznik u stanka*, 1929, no.15.
70. 'Kak Ustroit Ugolok Bezbozhnika' ('How to Build a Godless Corner'), *Bezbozhnik u stanka*, Moscow, 1924, in Gérin, p.41.
71. Pavlov, I.N., *Moya zhizn' I vstrechi*, Isskustvo, Moscow, 1949, p.260, cited in White, S., p.43.
72. White, S., p.6.
73. Cullerne Bown, p.129.
74. Kleberg & Ringbom, pp 306–10; Blomqvist, pp 298–301. Also see Abel, p.158.
75. Mellan's engraving is reproduced in *The Image of Christ*, National Gallery exh.cat, London, 2000, cat.39, p.93.
76. See (currently) p.22.
77. Cullerne Bown, p.238.
78. Baehr (1991).
79. Cullerne Bown, p.275.
80. Baehr (1984), p.156.
81. Cherniavsky M., *Tsar and People*, Yale University Press, 1961, p.78, cited in Baehr (1984), p.157.
82. The comment was made by the poet Vasilii Ruban in 1791 in *Nadpisi k kamniu nakhodiashchemusia v Sanktpeterburghe... v podnozhii konnogo vylitogo litsepodobiia dostoslavnogo Imperatora Petra Velikogo*, St Petersburg, 1791, quoted in Cross, p.399, and Baehr (1984), p.155.
83. Matthew, 16, 18. The etymology of Peter was abundantly used in the same way by the papacy, descended from St Peter, to legitimise its own political aspirations.
84. Ouspensky (1992), vol.2, p.299.
85. See (currently) p.13.
86. The church, completed to designs by Fedor Demertsov in 1804, was the parish church of Nobel prize-winner Ivan Pavlov, who campaigned to save it on artistic grounds until his death in 1938, when it was closed.
87. See http://www.beeflowers.com/Metro/PloshadRevolutia/mainpage.htm.
For a comprehensive range of reproductions of Moscow's metro stations, with details, see http://www.beeflowers.com/Metro/-Startfiles-/index.htm.

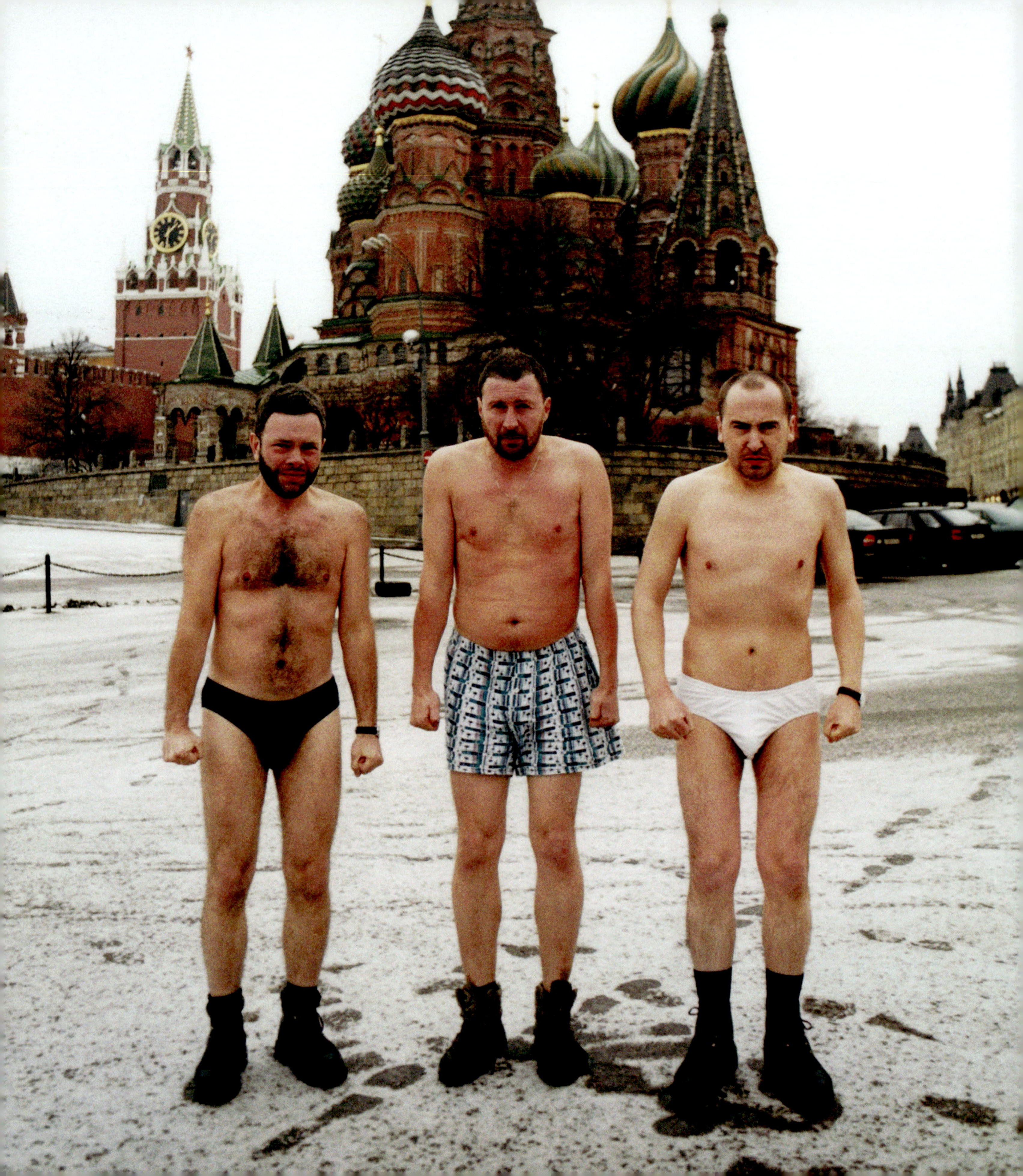

6

Icons and the Destiny of Russia

The role played by icons in the history of modern art in Russia is rich and complex. Although Christian beliefs and the Church hierarchy were strongly criticised throughout the period for being bastions of fear and hypocrisy, icons were commonly felt to retain their identity, though more as an expression of popular feeling than as a sign of allegiance to the Church. The old saying that 'if God doesn't exist, at least we have St Nicholas', might equally have been 'if Christianity doesn't exist, at least we have icons'. And we can console ourselves today with the thought that 'even if art is meaningless, at least we have the *Black Square*'. Although in the context of the history of the avant-garde movement as a whole, the role played by icons is only a small part of the story, it is unquestionable that their influence was both pervasive and profound. In fact, in some cases, it was *only* pervasive and profound, as it was invisible to the naked eye. At every step of the way – whether faced with Nesterov's wistful dream-visions, Goncharova's stolid peasant-workers, Popova's blasts of fragmented planes or Moor's fervent declamations of political beliefs – icons served as catalysts to the new art, providing artists with a benchmark of national identity, popularity and design against which to measure their own work. However, unlike the other forms of traditional culture that also served in this capacity – *lubki* prints, shop-signs, children's' drawings and shamanistic pictograms among others – icons could also claim a rich and sophisticated tradition of artistic wisdom and a depth of spiritual insight that the other crafts could not claim, but which precipitated Suprematist art towards its own perfection.

Although icons made a definitive impact on the avant-garde movement at every stage of its development, the role they played was believed by some to be more than that of mere influence. For such influence to be possible, a new level of receptivity to icons – indeed an entirely new capacity to understand – also had to evolve. By the nineteenth century, the ability to understand and appreciate icons had long since been lost or forgotten. In many cases, the icons themselves – including Andrei Rublev's famous *Old Testament Trinity* (Plate 6) – had been hidden under layers of darkened varnish and metal cladding. It was as if, from the middle of the seventeenth century or so, they had undergone their own 'descent into hell', both into the physical obscurity of darkened varnish and into the spiritual obscurity of human ignorance –

143
Blue Noses

The New Holy Fools, no.4, 1999
Photograph
Guelman Gallery, Moscow

just as Christ is believed, in the Orthodox Church, to have descended into hell after the Crucifixion and before the Resurrection, a miracle that is celebrated in the Orthodox calendar at the feast of the Anastasis (Plate 2). This 'descent' of icons into the underworld, however, was not simply due to human carelessness and neglect. At a deeper level, it was also seen to be an esoteric act that belonged to a higher evolutionary scheme. It was as if the wisdom of icons had deliberately chosen to withdraw itself from the visible world, both in order to protect itself against the corruption of secularised humanity and to subject man – just when he was ready to experience it – to the ordeal of knowing for himself that life without the wisdom of the divine is a barren wilderness. This was exactly the condition that Kramskoi attempted to evoke in his *Temptation of Christ in the Wilderness* (Plate 9), painted in 1872. This striking work was created just as the 'resurrection' of icons – reversing their earlier 'descent into hell' – was beginning to take place. This esoteric occurrence, which was deeply transformative of the psyche of man, was only dimly perceived in the world, where it surfaced as the revival of interest in icon painting. As a further sign that man was emerging from the 'wilderness of godlessness' at this auspicious time, this work (and many others, as explained in Chapter 2) indicated how man's state of dereliction became newly redeemable by virtue of its identification with the suffering Christ.

That the evolution of a truly Russian form of culture was facilitated by, and even accomplished as a function of, the progressive re-evaluation of the ancient tradition of icon painting was appreciated by a number of contemporary writers. Alexander Benois commented on the synchronicity of the revival of icons and the maturation of the avant-garde in his 'Letters on Art: Icons and the New Art' of 1913.[1] Similarly, referring to the rediscovery and restoration of ancient icons, the Symbolist poet, Maksimilian Voloshin, wrote, 'Graves do not open accidentally; these works have been thrust out of the grave at exactly that moment of history when they are needed. In days of profound artistic collapse, in years full of the disorder of aspiration and of purpose, ancient Russian art is revealed in order to give a lesson in the harmonious balance between tradition and individualism, between method and intention, between line and colour.'[2] In his essay 'Russia and Her Icons' (1918), Evgenii Trubetskoi wrote:

> It is as if throughout the bad years an invisible hand preserved the icon for a later generation, which would again be able to understand it. The icon has suddenly appeared to us in all its beauty, almost untouched by time. This alone is like a newly manifested miracle. Surely it is no accident that the icon has come to us during the past ten or fifteen years, that it was discovered just before we were going to need its closeness and would again understand its forgotten language. The icon appeared on the eve of the historic events that would bring us close to it and renew our feeling for it.[3]

Following the great exhibition of icons in 1913, Nikolai Punin went so far as to ask: 'Can we now count the day and the year of the opening of the Moscow exhibition as the day and the year of the beginning of our rebirth?'[4]

Something of the evolutionary logic that underpins the rediscovery of icons in Russia is reflected in the career of Kazimir Malevich. During the course of his career, Malevich was increasingly influenced by icons: initially by their mysterious atmosphere, their social inclusiveness, the boldness and simplicity of their design, the earthiness of their colours and the immediacy of their impact; but eventually by the spiritual significance of their forms, the absolute sanctity of their physical presence and, finally, by their most profound and definitive attribute – the innate self-dislocation of their identity into the identity of the divine. One might almost say of him that the more responsive he became to the deeper levels of meaning in icons, the more drawn he was towards his own centre – to the point at which, intuiting the meaning of icons, he discovered the meaning of his own life and work.

Malevich's discovery was not purely personal. If he had not made it, surely somebody else would have done so. As the radical atonal composer Arnold Schoenberg (who shattered the language of harmony rather as Malevich shattered the language of pictorial form) said, when accused of being the 'notorious Schoenberg': '*well, somebody had to be*'. Nor is Malevich's achievement of purely historical interest. Its impact continues to shape contemporary culture. When Punin wrote that Malevich's *Black Circle* was the 'full stop in the history of art', he did not mean that it was the end of the sentence; he meant that it was the end of the book. When Malevich purified the language of art to such an extent that the creative energy which had shaped it for centuries, and which had in turn been shaped by it for centuries, was completely liberated from it, he did not expect the spirits of artists to hover around its empty shells like ghosts. He expected them to fly into the bright sun of non-objectivity. But, as he realised himself, the renunciation of art presupposes the sacrifice of self, and this is by no means a matter of purely historical or artistic interest; it is matter of life and death for the human ego, today as much as ever.

Malevich exploded the concept of art as a socially meaningful and effective medium for the realisation and transmission of creative energy and depth of imaginative life. In the West, a hundred years of psychoanalysis has further weakened the monopoly of art in this capacity, despite using it abundantly for its own purposes. As a result of this challenge, the crisis of twentieth- and twenty-first-century culture has been to find a new rationale for art – to keep it alive, often for its own sake. To the extent that the scaffolding of mirrors has been dismantled the corollary of this search, less manifest but more significant, has been to find a new legitimising point of reference for the 'artistic self' (whether maker or consumer). Eighty years later, the conventions of art continue to serve as the basic co-ordinates of contemporary cultural life and cultural identity, despite a continuum of self-questioning and irony. As Friedrich Nietzsche said, in anticipation of such a time: 'we need art lest we perish of the truth'.

In the East, a rather different story has unfolded. Following the Revolution, the logic of self-transcendence was subverted into the suppression of individuality and, for the most part, art became an agent of conformity rather than the final adventure into infinity that Malevich had envisaged. Avant-garde art went underground, functioning as a fragile kind of 'Road of Life', for artists under siege, to the unbounded territory of the imagination. At least in public, the religious significance of icons was also forgotten, not for the first time, despite the fact that they contributed to the visual language of Soviet propaganda for many years. Icons exerted a certain amount of influence on individual artists of the 1970s and 1980s, but the issues for which they could set a precedent and lend their weight at the time were few. As a result, the influence that they had on such artists tended to be personal and poetic, and was more visual than conceptual; the work that emerged seems sentimental and

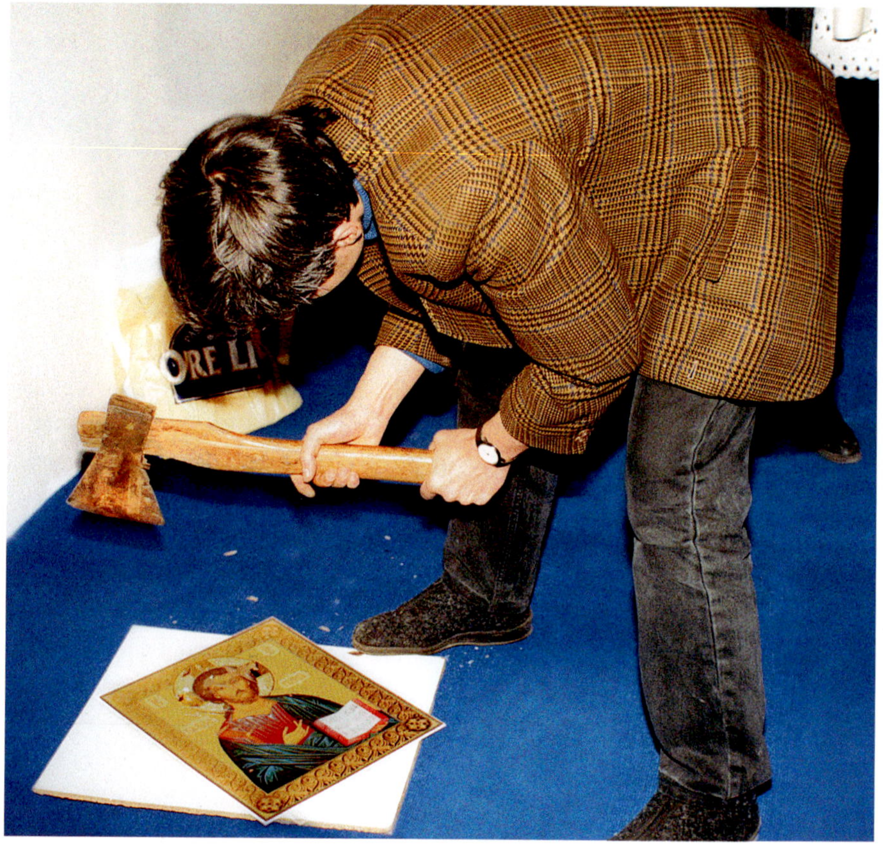

144

Avdei Ter-Oganian destroying an icon, Moscow, 1999
Courtesy of the artist

arbitrary in comparison with the work of the early twentieth century. The value of icons as cultural currency depended on the power that was invested in them by the state and society in general and, as they were largely being ignored by these constituencies (to the great benefit of western museums and collectors), they had little to offer in terms of associative power. It is all the more ironic that, in the meantime, the word 'icon' has crept into the English language, coming to refer to more or less anything that is mesmerisingly fashionable, ranging from supermodels to new designs of kettles, let alone the pictographs that turn our computer-screens into virtual iconostases.

It was not until the break-up of the Soviet Union in 1990, when Christianity became acceptable again in Russia, that icons came again to be charged with cultural value in the public eye. As a result of this shift, they have begun to feature in the discourse of contemporary artists though, as usual, they are used as facilitators for the realisation of contemporary ideas rather than in their original capacity as agents of contemplative awareness. Now that the role of art as an inherently politicised lifeline for a minority has become redundant in Russia, artists have become more preoccupied with the meaning of art *per se* and with the role of the artist, as in the West. It is significant that, in these circumstances, icons continue to represent the ultimate work of art – that which is sacrosanct in itself – and therefore they attract the most aggressive challenges from artists, as metaphors for art itself.

Several contemporary artists in Russia have taken it upon themselves to be the 'holy fools' of the modern world, exempting themselves from the conventions of contemporary society in imitation of the medieval renunciates whose relinquishment of all attachments lifted them above worldly comforts and concerns and empowered them to act in total freedom without fear of the consequences (e.g. St Andrew in Plate 20, bottom right). One such group, the 'Blue Noses', whose work lurches from belligerent non-conformity to absurdist self-mockery, has made this link explicit. Their series of photographs, *The New Holy Fools* (1999, Plate 143) shows three members of the group (Viacheslav Mizin, Alexander Shaburov, Konstantin Skotnikov) standing in front of Russian churches, in the freezing cold, wearing nothing but underpants and heavy-duty boots. Besides referring to the traditional Russian custom of rolling naked in the snow and bathing in icy water, the images are humorous but appreciative references to icons of standing saints (Plate 103) as well as to Malevich's own reference to this tradition (Plate 102). While the artists trivialise their iconic model, they also appropriate some of the impoverished inspiration associated with the saints for themselves. Having said this, they also mock themselves as individuals, foolishly exposing their own feebleness and lack of virility. One of the photographs (No.4) shows them standing in the snow in front of St Basil's Cathedral in Moscow, the resting place of St Basil the Blessed who was renowned for his freedom to insult Ivan the Terrible to his face if he felt so inclined, when others would tremble at the very sight of him.

However, not all artists have managed to transcend the law. Also in 1999, the artist Avdei Ter-Oganian became notorious for setting up a stall in a Moscow art gallery and inviting members of the public to buy cheap reproductions of icons which he then proceeded to deface with abusive slogans or destroy with an axe (Plate 144). The act caused a furore among the Church and public and, although he was spared the fate of his predecessor Foma Ivanov, a barber-turned-Protestant who was burned at the stake for destroying an icon of St Alexius in 1714, Ter-Oganian was eventually charged with 'incitation to religious hatred' and expelled from the country.[5] Notwithstanding the ironic, if obvious, gesture of art destroying itself, Ter-Oganian's act was presented as a comment on the hypocrisy of the Moscow authorities, which were seen to switch overnight from persecuting the Church, in the Soviet period, to defending it for purely political reasons at the current time. The capitalist trade in art objects also came under attack. Ter-Oganian's act was associated with an earlier iconoclastic art action by Alexander Brener, who sprayed a green dollar sign on Malevich's *White Cross* in the Stedelijk Museum in Amsterdam in 1997. Brener, who received a jail sentence for his pains, claimed to be making a constructive comment on the uneasy relationship between the cultural and economic values of art. The fact that he chose a seminal work with obvious religious connotations and that he appropriated the behavioural conventions of iconoclasm by physically attacking it suggest that he was committing a deliberately sacrilegious act. However, he was also claiming to reveal the new 'iconic' value of the image, as reflected in the commercialism of the contemporary art world. The cross (both of Christianity and high modernism) was crossed out by a dollar sign, which is itself a kind of triple-cross – not a million miles from the Russian Orthodox cross! The obvious connection between this act and that of Ter-Oganian may be corroborated, albeit obscurely, by the fact that the wooden panels of icons were originally made with axes and that Malevich, the avant-garde icon-painter, was fascinated by cutting instruments of all kinds, including axes: as with Malevich himself, the iconoclastic iconophile, the destruction of the image was the creation of the art.

Ter-Oganian justified his act on the grounds that mechanical reproductions of icons are not real icons and therefore it is not blasphemous to destroy them. All manner of fascinating, topical and dissembling questions may be raised – as they were in Byzantine times – about the relative values of 'prototypes' and the 'copies'. Yet the sight of an old woman holding a postcard of the *Virgin of Vladimir* against the case of the original icon in the Tretyakov Gallery – in order to charge it with sacred power – silences such art world chatter, reminding one of the remarkable manner in which the 'wisdom of icons' has always found a way, consistent with the language, needs and possibilities of any given time, to keep itself at the heart of the cultural process in Russia.

NOTES

1. Benois (1913).
2. *Apollon*, 1914, no.5, pp 26–9. Quoted in Betz, p.44.
3. Translated into English in Trubetskoi, p.96.
4. *Apollon*, 1913, no.5, pp 41–2. Quoted in Betz, p.44.
5. Michalski, S., p.159.

Bibliography

Abel, U., 'Icons and Soviet Art' in Arvidsson, C., & Blomqvist, L.E., *Symbols of Power: The Esthetics of Political Legitimation in the Soviet Union and Eastern Europe*, Stockholm, 1987, pp 141–62.

Alexeyev, M.P., 'Goethe-Miszellen: Goethe und die altrussische Malerei' in *Germanoslavica*, vol.II, 1932–3, pp 60–4.

Allan, J., *Berthold Lubetkin: Architecture and the Tradition of Progress*, RIBA Publications, London, 1992.

Anders, P., 'The Lenin Institute: Leonidov's Icon of the Future' in *Journal of Architectural Education*, vol.7, no.1, Fall 1983, pp 20–6.

Andersen, T., *Moderne Russisk Kunst 1910–1930*, Copenhagen, 1967, pp 15–26.

Andersen, T., *Malevich*, Amsterdam, 1970, p.24.

Andersen, T. (ed.), *Malevich: Essays on Art 1*, Copenhagen, 1971.

Andersen, T. (ed.), *Malevich: The World as Non-Objectivity – Unpublished Writings 1922–25*, vol.III, Copenhagen, 1976.

Andersen, T. (ed.), *Malevich: Unpublished Writings*, vol.IV, Copenhagen, 1978.

Andersen, T. (ed.), *Art et Poésie Russes: 1900–1930, Textes Choisis*, Centre Georges Pompidou, Paris, 1979.

Apollinaire, G., 'Les Russes' in *Gil Blas*, 22 Apr 1911.

The Art of Holy Russia: Icons from Moscow 1400–1600, exh.cat., Royal Academy of Arts, London, 1998.

L'Art russe dans la seconde moitié du XIXe siecle: en quete d'identité, exh.cat., Musée d'Orsay, Paris, 2005.

Arwas, V. (ed.), *The Great Russian Utopia*, Academy Editions, London, 1993.

Aschenbrenner, M., 'Farben und Formen in Werk von Kasimir Malewitsch' in *Quadrum*, IV, 1957.

Aslanov, G., 'The Photius Fraternity' in *Russian Paris*, Palace Editions, St Petersburg, 2003.

Avant-Garde Hongroise, 1915–1925, exh.cat., Banque Bruxelles Lambert, Brussels, 1999.

Babitsky, P. & Rimberg, J., *The Soviet Film Industry*, New York, 1955.

Baehr, S., 'Regaining Paradise: The "Political Icon" in Seventeenth and Eighteenth Century Russia' in *Russian History/Histoire Russe*, 11, nos 2–3, Summer–Fall 1984.

Baehr, S.L., *The Paradise Myth in Eighteenth-Century Russia: Utopian Patterns in Early Secular Russian Literature and Culture*, Stanford University Press, 1991.

Bajkay, E., *Uitz Bela*, Budapest, 1974.

Bajkay, E., *Uitz Bela*, Budapest, 1987.

Bajkay, E., *Bela Uitz: Arbeiten auf Papier aus den Jahren 1913–1925, Budapest-Wien-Moskau-Paris*, Budapest, 1991.

Bajkay, E., 'Bela Uitz's series *Analysis* in the Scottish National Gallery of Art, Edinburgh' in *Britain and Hungary 3: Contacts in Architecture, Design, Art and Theory in the Nineteenth and Twentieth Centuries*, Hungarian University of Craft and Design, Budapest, 2005, pp 157–65.

Barnard, L., 'The Theology of Images' in Bryer, A. & Herrin, J. (eds), *Iconoclasm: Papers given at the Ninth Spring Symposium of Byzantine Studies*, Birmingham, 1975.

Bartlett, R., 'The Circle and the Line: Eisenstein, Florensky and Russian Orthodoxy', invited paper for the 'Eisenstein at 100: A Reconsideration' conference, Dartmouth College, Nov 1998.

Bartlett, R., 'Stravinsky's Russian Origins' in Cross, J., *The Cambridge Companion to Stravinsky*, Cambridge University Press, 2003.

Batchan, A., 'Oblomovka – Love it or Leave it: A Commentary on Nikita Mikhailkov's Nostalgic Vision of Russia' in *Russian History/Histoire Russe*, 11, nos 2–3, Summer–Fall 1984.

Beckwith, J., *Early Christian and Byzantine Art*, Harmondsworth, 1979.

Belting, H., *Likeness and Presence*, University of Chicago, 1994.

Benois, A., 'Iskusstvo Stelletskogo' ('The Art of Stelletsky') in *Apollon*, 1911, no.4, pp 5–16.

Benois, A., 'Ikony i novoe iskusstvo' ('Letters on Art: Icons and the New Art') in *Rec'*, 5 Apr 1913.

Bering, K., 'Suprematismus und Orthodoxie. Einflüsse der Ikonen auf das Werk K. Malevics' in *Ostkirchliche Kunst*, 2.3, 1986, pp 143–55.

Besançon, A., *L'image interdit: une histoire intellectuelle de l'iconoclasme*, Fayard, Paris, 1994.

Betz, M. 'The Icon and Russian Modernism' in *Art Forum*, XV, 10, 1977, pp 38–45.

Bevan, E., *Holy Images: An Inquiry into Idolatry and Image-Worship in Ancient Paganism and in Christianity*, London, 1940.

Billington, J., *The Icon and the Axe*, London, 1966.

Birnholz, A., 'The Russian Avant-Garde and the Russian Tradition' in *Art Journal*, vol.32–3, Winter 1972–3, pp 146–9.

Birnholz, A., 'El Lissitzky and the Jewish Tradition' in *Studio International*, 186(959):133, 1973.

Birnholz, A., 'On the Meaning of Kazimir Malevich's "White on White"' in *Art International*, XXI, Jan 1977, pp 9–16.

Birnholz, A., 'Forms, angles and corners: On Meaning in Russian Avant-Garde Art' in *Arts Magazine*, 51, Feb 1977, pp 101–9.

Blank, K., 'Lev Tolstoy's Suprematist Icon-Painting' in *Elementa*, vol.2, 1995.

Blomqvist, L.E., 'Some Utopian Elements in Stalinist Art' in *Russian History/Histoire Russe*, 11, nos 2–3, Summer–Fall 1984.

Boersma, L.S., *The Last Futurist Exhibition of Painting*, 0,10 Publishers, Rotterdam, 1994.

Bojko, S., *New Graphic Design in Revolutionary Russia*, Lund Humphries, London, 1972.

Bonnell, V.E., *Iconography of Power: Soviet Political Posters under Lenin and Stalin*, University of California Press, 1999.

Bowlt, J., 'The Failed Utopia: Russian Art 1917–32' in *Art in America*, 59, Jul–Aug 1971, pp 40–51.

Bowlt, J., 'Pavel Filonov' in *Studio International*, 186, Jul 1973, p.30–6.

Bowlt, J., 'The Semaphors of Suprematism: Malevich's Journey into the Non-objective World' in *ARTnews*, 72, Dec 1973, pp 16–22.

Bowlt, J., 'Neo-Primitivism and Russian Painting' in *Burlington Magazine*, 116, 1974, pp 133–40.

Bowlt, J., *The Silver Age: Russian art of the early twentieth century and the 'World of Art' group*, Newtonville, Massachusetts, 1979.

Bowlt, J., *Journey into Non-Objectivity: The Graphic work of Kazimir Malevich and other members of the Russian Avant-Garde*, exh.cat., Dallas Museum of Fine Arts, 1980.

Bowlt, J., *Russian Stage Design: Scenic Innovation, 1900–1930. From the Collection of Mr and Mrs Nikita

D. Lobanov-Rostovsky, Mississippi Museum of Art, 1982.

Bowlt, J., *Russian Art of the Avant-Garde*, Thames & Hudson, London, 1988.

Bowlt, J., 'A Brazen Can-Can in the Temple of Art: The Russian Avant-Garde and Popular Culture' in Varnedoe, K. & Gopnik, A. (eds), *Modern Art and Popular Culture: Readings in High and Low*, Abrams, New York, 1990.

Bowlt, J., 'From Practice to Theory: Vladimir Tatlin and Nikolai Punin' in *Literature, Culture and Society in the Modern Age*, Stanford Slavic Studies, vol.4:2, Stanford, 1992, pp 50–66.

Bowlt, J. & Bann, S. (eds), *Russian Formalism; A collection of articles and texts in translation*, Scottish Academic Press, Edinburgh, 1973.

Bowlt, J. & Drutt, M. (eds), *Amazons of the Avant-Garde*, Guggenheim Museum, New York, 2000.

Bowlt, J. & Matich, O. (eds), *Laboratory of Dreams: The Russian Avant-Garde and Cultural Experiment*, Stanford, 1996.

Bowlt, J. & Misler, N. (eds), *Pavel Filonov: A hero and his fate. Collected writings on art and revolution, 1914–1940*, Austin, Texas, 1983.

Bowlt, J. & Misler, N., *Twentieth Century Russian and East European Painting: The Thyssen-Bornemisza Collection*, Philip Wilson, London, 1993.

Bowlt, J. & Washton Long, R-C., *The Life of Vasilii Kandinsky in Russian Art: a study of 'On the spiritual in art' by Wassily Kandinsky*, Oriental Research Partners, Newtonville, 1984.

Brumfield, W.C., *A History of Russian Architecture*, Cambridge, 1993.

Brumfield, W.C. & Velimirovic, M., *Christianity and the Arts in Russia*, Cambridge, 1991.

Bryer, A. & Herrin, J. (eds), *Iconoclasm: Papers given at the Ninth Spring Symposium of Byzantine Studies*, Birmingham, 1975.

Bullen, J.B., 'Byzantinism and Modernism in Britain, 1900–1914' in *Burlington Magazine*, Nov 1999, pp 665–75.

Bushkovitch, P., *Religion and Society in Russia; The Sixteenth and Seventeenth Centuries*, Oxford, 1992.

Bychkov, V., *The Aesthetic Face of Being: Art in the Theology of Pavel Florensky*, St Vladimir's Seminary Press, New York, 1993.

Bychkov, V., 'Russian Religious Aesthetics' in Kelly, M., *Encyclopaedia of Aesthetics*, New York & Oxford, 1998, pp 195–202.

Chamot, M., *Goncharova*, Paris, 1972.

Chamot, M., *Goncharova: Stage Designs and Paintings*, Oresko, London, 1979.

Chipp, H.B., *Theories of Modern Art*, London, 1968.

Chudovski, V., 'Futurism and the Past' in *Apollon*, no.6, Aug 1913.

Compton, S., 'Malevich's Suprematism – The Higher Intuition' in *Burlington Magazine*, 118, 1976, pp 577–85.

Compton, S., *The World Backwards: Russian Futurist Books, 1912–1916*, British Library, London, 1978.

Compton, S., *Chagall*, Royal Academy of Arts, London, 1985.

Compton, S., *Russian Avant-Garde Books: 1917–1934*, British Library, London, 1992.

Comrie, B. & Stone, G., *The Russian Language since the Revolution*, Oxford, 1978.

Conio, G., *Le Constructivisme russe*, L'Age d'Homme, Lausanne, 1987.

Cooke, C., *Russian Avant-Garde Art and Architecture*, Academy Editions, London, 1983.

Cooke, C. (ed.), *Architectural Drawings of the Russian Avant-Garde*, MOMA, New York, 1990.

Cooke, C., & Ageros, J. (eds), *The Avant-Garde: Russian Architecture in the Twenties*, Academy Editions, London, 1991.

Cormack, R., *Writing in Gold: Byzantine Society and its Icons*, London, 1985.

Cracraft, J., *The Petrine Revolution in Russian Architecture*, Chicago & London, 1988.

Cracraft, J., *The Petrine Revolution in Russian Imagery*, Chicago, 1997.

Cracraft, J. & Rowland, D. (eds), *Architectures of Russian Identity: 1500 to the Present*, Cornell, New York, 2003.

Craft, R. & Stravinsky, I., *Memories and Commentaries*, Faber, London, 1960.

Crone, R. & Moos, D., *Kazimir Malevich: The Climax of Disclosure*, University of Chicago Press, 1991.

Cross, A.G., 'An English Version of a Poem by Vasilii Ruban' in *Study Group on Eighteenth Century Russia Newsletter*, no.7, 1979.

Crowther, P., 'Philosophy and Non-objectivity' in *Malevich, Art and Design*, vol.5, no.5/6, Academy Editions, London, 1989.

Cullerne Bown, M., *Socialist Realist Painting*, Yale, New Haven, 1998.

Curtiss, J.S., *The Russian Church and the Soviet State*, Little, Brown & Co, Boston, 1953.

Dabrowski, M., *Liubov Popova*, MOMA, New York, 1991.

Dabrowski, M., Dickerman, L. & Galassi, P. (eds), *Alexander Rodchenko*, MOMA, New York, 1998.

Davies, I., 'Primitivism in the First Wave of the Twentieth Century Avant-Garde in Russia' in *Studio International*, 186, 1973, pp 80–4.

Douglas, C., 'Birth of a "Royal Infant": Malevich and "Victory over the Sun"' in *Art in America*, no.62, Mar–Apr 1974, pp 45–51.

Douglas, C., 'The New Russian Art and Italian Futurism' in *Art Journal*, 34, 3, 1975, pp 229–39.

Douglas, C., *Swans of Other Worlds: Kazimir Malevich and the origins of abstraction in Russia*, Ann Arbor, Michigan, 1980.

Douglas, C., 'Beyond Reason: Malevich, Matiushin, and their Circles' in *The Spiritual in Art: Abstract Painting 1890–1985*, Los Angeles & New York, 1986.

Douglas, C., *Malevich*, Abrams, New York, 1994.

Duborgel, B., *Malevitch: La question de l'icône*, Publications de l'Université de Saint-Etienne, 1997.

Erenburg, I., 'Russkoje narodnoe iskusstvo v Parize' in *Pariskij Vestnik*, no.20, 17 May 1913, p.3.

Evtuhov, Catherine, *The Cross & the Sickle: Sergei Bulgakov and the fate of Russian religious philosophy*, Cornell, New York, 1997.

Fauchereau, S., *Malevich*, Academy Editions, London, 1992.

Fedotov, G.P., *The Russian Religious Mind. Kievan Christianity: the 10th to the 13th centuries*, Harper Torchbooks, New York, 1946.

Figes, O., *Natasha's Dance: A Cultural History of Russia*, London, 2002

Figes, O. & Kolonitskii, B., *Interpreting the Russian Revolution; The Language and Symbols of 1917*, Yale, New Haven, 1999.

Filonov, exh.cat., Centre Georges Pompidou, Paris, 1990.

Filonov: Seer of the Invisible, Palace Editions, St Petersburg, 2006.

Florensky, P.A., *Iconostasis*, 1922, trans. Sheehan, D. & Andrejev, O., St Vladimir's Seminary Press, New York, 1996.

Florensky, P.A., *La prospettiva ravesciata e altri scritti*, trans. & introduction by Misler, N., Rome, 1983.

Friedman, M., 'Icon Painting and Russian Popular Art as Sources of Some Works by Chagall' in *The Journal of Jewish Art*, vol.V, 1978, pp 94–107.

Friedman, M., 'Prophet Elijah's Ascension in the Work of Chagall' in *The Journal of Jewish Art*, vol.X, 1984, pp 102–113.

Fülöp-Miller, R., *The Mind and Face of Bolshevism*, London & New York, 1926.

Gabel, P., *And God Created Lenin: Marxism vs. Religion in Russia, 1917–1929*, Prometheus Books, New York, 2005.

Gabo: Constructions, Sculpture, Paintings, Drawings, Engravings (introductory essays by Read, H. & Martin, L.), Lund Humphries, London, 1957.

Gabo, N., 'Constructive Art' in *The Listener*, 16, no.408, 4 Nov 1936.

Gabo, N., 'The Concepts of Russian Art' in *World Review*, Jun 1942.

Gabo, N., *Of Divers Arts*, A.W. Mellon Lectures in the Fine Arts, Bollingen Series 8, National Gallery of Washington, 1959.

Galavaris, G., *Constantinople-Moscow-Munich: Byzantium and twentieth-century European painting*, Greek Canadian Association of Constantinople, Toronto, 1994.

Garafola, L. & van Norman Baer, N. (eds), *The Ballets Russes and Its World*, Yale, New Haven & London, 1999.

Gaßner, H., *Alexander Rodschenko Konstruction 1920*, Frankfurt, 1984.

Gates of Mystery: The Art of Holy Russia, exh.cat., London & Texas, 1993.

Gayraud, R. (trans.), *Mikhail Larionov: Manifestes*, Editions Allia, Paris, 1995.

Geldern, J. von, *Bolshevik Festivals, 1917–1920*, University of California, 1993, http://ark.cdlib.org/ark:/13030/ft467nb2w4/.

Gérin, A., *Godless at the Workbench: Soviet Illustrated Humoristic Antireligious Propaganda*, Dunlop Art Gallery, Regina, 2003.

Gough, M., *The Artist as Producer: Russian Constructivism in Revolution*, University of California, 2005.

Gray, C., *The Russian Experiment in Art*, London, 1986.

The Great Utopia: The Russian and Soviet Avant-Garde, 1915–1932, exh.cat., Guggenheim Museum, New York, 1992.

Gregory Palamas: The Triads, trans. Gendle, N., ed. Meyendorff, J., Paulist Press, New York, 1983.

Grishchenko, A., *Russian Icon as the Art of Painting*, Moscow, 1917.

Gritz, T. & Kardzhiev, N., 'Matiss v Moskve' in *Matiss: Sbornik statei o tvorchestve*, Moscow, 1958.

Guerman, M., *Mikhail Vrubel*, Aurora Art Publishers, Leningrad, 1985.

Gurianova, N., *Exploring Color: Olga Rozanova and the Early Russian Avant-Garde, 1910–1918*, G. & B. Arts International, Amsterdam, 2000.

Hamant, Y. (ed.), *The Christianisation of Ancient Russia: A Millennium, 988–1988*, Unesco, Paris, 1992.

Hamilton, G.H., *The Art and Architecture of Russia*, Harmondsworth, 1983.

Henderson, L.D., 'The Merging of Time and Space: "The Fourth Dimension" in Russia From Ouspensky to Malevich' in *The Structurist*, no.15/16, 1975–6, pp 97–108.

Henderson, L.D., *The Fourth Dimension and Non-Euclidean Geometry in Modern Art*, Princeton, 1983.

Hilton, A., 'Matisse in Moscow' in *Art Journal*, vol.29, no.2, 1969–70, pp 166–73.

Hilton, A., *Russian Folk Art*, Indiana University Press, 1995.

Howard, J., *The Union of Youth: An artists' society of the Russian avant-garde*, Manchester, 1992.

Hughes, L., *Russia in the Age of Peter the Great*, Yale, New Haven, 1998.

Hughes, R. & Paperno, I. (eds), *Christianity and the Eastern Slavs, vol.2: Russian culture in modern times*, University of California Press, 1994.

Hungarian Constructivism: 1918–1936, exh.cat., Watari-Um Museum of Contemporary Art, 1994.

Husband, W.B., *Godless Communists: Atheism and Society in Soviet Russia, 1917–1932*, Northern Illinois University Press, 2000.

Hutchings, S.C., *Russian Modernism: The Transfiguration of the Everyday*, Cambridge, 1997.

Isdebsky-Pritchard, A., *The Art of Mikhail Vrubel (1856–1910)*, UMI, Ann Arbor, 1982.

Jackson, D., 'Icons in 19th Century Russia' in *Icons 88*, Veritas Publications, National Gallery of Ireland, Dublin, 1988, pp 75–84.

Jackson, D., 'Western Art and Russian Ethics: Repin in Paris, 1873–76' in *Russian Review*, vol.57, no.3, Jul 1998, pp 394–409.

Jackson, D., *The Wanderers and Critical Realism in Nineteenth-century Russian Painting*, Manchester, 2006.

Kachalova, I., Mayasova, N. & Shchennikova, L., *The Annunciation Cathedral of the Moscow Kremlin*, Iskusstvo, Moscow, 1990.

Kaier, C., *Imagine No Possessions: The Socialist Objects of Russian Constructivism*, MIT, Cambridge MA, 1995.

Kandinsky, Chagall, Malevich e lo spiritualismo russo, exh.cat., Electa, Milan, 1999.

Kandinsky: Oeuvres de Vassily Kandinsky, Centre Georges Pompidou, Paris, 1984.

Kantor, S.G., *Alfred H. Barr, Jr., and the Intellectual Origins of the Museum of Modern Art*, MIT, Cambridge & London, 2002.

Kartsonis, A., *Anastasis: The Making of an Image*, Princeton, 1986.

Kashchenko, S., *Pyotr Demianovich Ouspensky: Moscow-St Petersburg, 1878–1917*, Vyborg & London, 2007.

Kazimir Malevich: Drawings from the Khardzhiev-Chaga Art Foundation, SMA Cahiers, Amsterdam, 1997.

Kazimir Malevich: 1878–1935, exh.cat., Leningrad, Moscow, Amsterdam, 1988.

Kazimir Malevich: 1878–1935, exh.cat., Armand Hammer Museum of Art, Los Angeles, 1990.

Kazimir Malevich e le sacre icone Russe: avanguardia e tradizioni, exh.cat., Electa, Milan, 2000.

Kentridge, B., 'Comparative Psychology: Lecture 2', 1995, www.dur.ac.uk/robert.kentridge/comp2.html.

Khan-Magomedov, S.O., *Alexander Vesnin and Russian Constructivism*, London, 1986.

Khan-Magomedov, S.O., *Rodchenko: The Complete Works*, London, 1986.

Khan-Magomedov, S.O., *Vhutemas: Moscou 1920–1930*, 2 vols, Editions du Regard, Paris, 1990.

King, D., *The Commissar Vanishes: The Falsification of Photographs and Art in Stalin's Russia*, London, 1997.

Kirichenko, E., *The Russian Style*, Laurence King, London, 1991.

Kleberg, L. & Ringbom, S., 'V.I. Lenin in Smolny: an Addendum to Lars Erik Blomqvist's article' in *Russian History/Histoire Russe*, 11, nos 2–3, Summer–Fall 1984.

Kline, G., *Religious and Anti-Religious Thought in Russia*, University of Chicago, 1968.

Klinghoffer, A.J., *Red Apocalypse: The Religious Evolution of Soviet Communism*, New York, 1996.

Kochno, B., *Diaghilev and the Ballets Russes*, New York, 1970.

Kouriltseva, V. & Iavorskaya, N., *Iskusstvo Sovietskoi Oukrainii. Otcherki* (*The Art of Soviet Ukraine. Essays*), Moscow, 1957.

Krieger, V., 'Das Interesse der Avantgarde am Bildkonzept der Ikone' in *Chagall, Kandinsky, Malewitch und die Russische Avantgarde*, Hatje, 1999.

Kudryavtseva, T., *Circling the Square: Avant-Garde Porcelain from Revolutionary Russia*, Fontanka, London, 2004.

Lang, W.K., 'The "Atheism" of Jesus in Russian art: Representations of Christ in Ivan Kramskoy, Vasily Polenov and Nikolai Ghe' in *Nineteenth-century Art Worldwide*, vol.2, no.3, 2003, http://www.19thc-artworldwide.org/autumn_03/articles/lang.shtml.

Larionov, M., 'Les Icones' (*c*.1920) in *Une Avant-Garde Explosive. Textes traduits, réunis, et annotés par Michel Hoog et Solina de Vigneral*, Lausanne, 1978.

Lasko, P., *Ars Sacra 800–1200*, Harmondsworth/New Haven, 1994.

Lassaigne, J., *Marc Chagall*, Paris, 1957.

Lavrentiev, A.N., *Varvara Stepanova: A Constructivist Life*, Thames & Hudson, London, 1988.

Lavrentiev, A.N. (ed.), *Aleksandr Rodchenko. Experiments for the Future: Diaries, Essays, Letters and Other Writings*, MOMA, New York, 2005.

Lavrentiev, A.N. & Nasarov, Y.V., *Russian Design: Traditions and Experiment, 1920–1990*, Academy Editions, London, 1995.

Law, A. & Gordon, M., *Meyerhold, Eisenstein and Biomechanics: actor training in revolutionary Russia*, McFarland, London, 1996.

Lebeau, E., 'Les Manuscrits de Nicolas Obouhow au Department de la Musique de la Bibliotheque Nationale' in *La Revue Musicale*, no.290–1, 1972.

Lebedev, A., *The Itinerants: Russian Realist artists from the second half of the 19th and the early 20th centuries*, Aurora, Leningrad, 1982.

Lemaire, F., *La musique du XXe siecle en Russie et dans les anciennes Republiques sovietiques*, Fayard, Paris, 1994.

Lepowitz, H., *Images of Faith: Expressionism, Catholic Folk Art and the Industrial Revolution*, University of Georgia Press, 1991.

Liber, G.O., *Alexander Dovzhenko: A Life in Soviet Film*, London, 2002.

Liebelt, U., 'Marc Chagall und die Kunst der Ikonen' (unpublished doctoral dissertation), Marburg, Lahn, 1971.

Likhachev, D.S., *Russian Art, from the Middle Ages to the Avant-Garde* (in Russian), Iskusstvo, Moscow, 1992.

Lindsay, K. & Vergo, P. (eds), *Kandinsky: Complete Writings on Art*, Hall, Boston, 1982.

Lobanov-Rostovsky, N., *Revolutionary Ceramics: Soviet Porcelain 1917–1927*, Rizzoli, New York, 1990.

Lodder, C., *Russian Constructivism*. Yale, New Haven, 1987.

Lodder, C., 'The Vkhutemas and the Bauhaus' in Marquadt, V. H. & Roman, G.H. (eds), *The Avant-Garde Frontier: Russia meets the West, 1910–1930*, University Press of Florida, 1992, pp 196–237.

Lodder, C. & Hammer, M. (eds), *Gabo on Gabo: Texts and Interviews*, Artist Bookworks, Sussex, 2000.

Lodder, C. & Hammer, M., *Constructing Modernity: The Art and Career of Naum Gabo*, Yale, New Haven, 2000.

Long, R.-C., *Kandinsky: The Development of an Abstract Style*, Oxford U.P., 1980.

Looper, M.G., 'The Pathology of Painting: Tuberculosis as a Metaphor in the Art Theory of Kazimir Malevich' in *Configurations*, 3.1, 1995, pp 27–46.

Lowden, J., *Early Christian and Byzantine Art*, Phaidon, 1997.

Lunacharsky, A., *On Literature and Art*, Moscow, 1965.

Macdonald, H., *Skryabin*, Oxford, 1978.

Maes, Francis, *A History of Russian Music: from Kamarinskaya to Babi Yar*, trans. from the German by Pomerans, A.J. & Pomerans, E., University of California Press, 2002.

'Malevich', *Art and Design*, London, vol.5, no.5/6, 1989.

Malewitsch: Werk und Wirkung, exh.cat., Cologne, 1995.

Malmstad, J.E., *Andrey Bely: Spirit of Symbolism*, Cornell, New York, 1987.

Mango, C., (ed.), *The Art of the Byzantine Empire: Sources and documents*, University of Toronto, 1997.

Mansbach, S.A. (ed.), *Standing in the Tempest: Painters of the Hungarian Avant-Garde 1908–1930*, Santa Barbara, 1991.

Mansbach, S.A., *Modern Art in Eastern Europe; From the Baltic to the Balkans, ca. 1890–1939*, Cambridge U.P., 1999.

Marc Chagall: The Russian Years, 1906–1922, exh.cat., Frankfurt, 1991.

Marcadé, J.-C. (ed.), *Malévitch, 1878–1978: Actes du Colloque internationale, tenu au Centre Pompidou, Musée national d'Art moderne, les 4 et 5 mai 1978*, Lausanne, 1978.

Marcadé, J.-C., 'L'avant-garde russe et Paris' in *Cahiers du Museé National d'Art Moderne*, Oct–Dec 1979, pp 174–83.

Marcadé, J.-C., *Le Futurisme Russe*, Paris, 1989.

Marcadé, J.-C., *Malévitch*, Paris, 1990.

Marcadé, J.-C., *L'Avant-garde russe, 1907–1927*, Flammarion, Paris, 1995.

Marcadé, J.-C. & V., *L'Avant-Garde au Feminin: Moscou-StPetersbourg-Paris, 1907–1930*, Centre d'art plastique contemporain, Paris, 1983.

Marcadé, J.-C. & Siger, S., *K. Malevitch. La Lumière et la couleur. Textes inédits de 1918 à 1926*, Lausanne, 1981.

Marcadé, V., *L'art d'Ukraine*, L'age d'homme, Lausanne, 1990.

Margolin, V., *The Struggle for Utopia: Rodchenko, Lissitzky, Moholy-Nagy, 1917–1946*, Chicago, 1997.

Marsden, V.E., *The King of the Jews: A Sacred Drama*, Funk & Wagnalls, New York, 1914.

Massat, R., *Antoine Pevsner et le constructivisme*, Paris, 1956.

Massine, L., *My Life in Ballet*, Macmillan, London, 1968.

Matisse, H., 'Le Chemin de la Couleur' in *Art Présent*, Paris, no.2, 1947.

McDuff, D. in *Nikolai Leskov: Lady Macbeth of Mtsensk and Other Stories*, Penguin, Harmondsworth, 1987.

Meyendorff, J., *Byzantium and the Rise of Russia*, St Vladimir's Seminary Press, New York, 1989.

Meyendorff, J., *Rome, Constantinople, Moscow: Historical and Theological Studies*, St Vladimir's Seminary Press, New York, 1996.

Michalski, S., *The Reformation and the Visual Arts: The Protestant Image Question in Western and Eastern Europe*, Routledge, London, 1993.

Michelson, A. (ed.), *Kino-Eye: The Writings of Dziga Vertov*, Pluto Press, London & Sydney, 1984.

Michelson, A., 'The Kinetic Icon and the Work of Mourning: Prolegomena to the Analysis of a Textual System' in Lawton, A. (ed.), *The Red Screen: Politics, Society, Art in Soviet Cinema*, Routledge, London, 1992.

Milner, J., *Vladimir Tatlin and the Russian Avant-garde*, Yale, New Haven, 1984.

Milner, J., *Russian Revolutionary Art*, Bloomsbury, London, 1987.

Milner, J., *The Exhibition 5 x 5 = 25: Its Background and Significance*, Amsterdam, 1992.

Milner, J., *Malevich and the Art of Geometry*, Yale, New Haven, 1996.

Milner, J., *A Slap in the Face! Futurists in Russia*, Philip Wilson, London, 2007.

Milner-Gulland, R., 'Icons and the Russian "Modern Movement"' in *Icons 88*, Veritas Publications, National Gallery of Ireland, Dublin, 1988, pp 85–96.

Milner-Gulland, R., *The Russians*, Blackwell, Oxford, 1997.

Misler, N., *Pavel Florensky: Beyond Vision*, Reaktion Books, London, 2002.

Morrison, S., *Russian Opera and the Symbolist Movement*, University of California Press, 2002.

Nakov, A., *Avant-Garde Russe*, Art Data, London, 1986.

Nakov, A., *Kazimir Malewicz: Catalogue raisonné*, Paris, 2002.

Nash, S.A., 'Naum Gabo: Sculptures of Purity and Possibility' in Nash, S. A., Nakov, A. & Pétris, M., *Le Dernier tableau*, Paris, 1972.

Natalia Goncharova: The Russian Years, exh.cat., State Russian Museum, St Petersburg, 2002.

Nathalie Gontcharova/Michel Larionov, exh.cat., Centre Georges Pompidou, Paris, 1995.

Nemeth, L., *Modern Art in Hungary*, Corvina, 1969.

New Art for a New Era: Malevich's Vision of the Russian Avant-Garde, Booth-Clibburn Editions, London, 1999.

Nichols, R.L., 'The Icon and the Machine in Russia's Religious Renaissance, 1900–1909' in Brumfield, W. & Velimirovic, M., *Christianity and the Arts in Russia*, Cambridge, 1991.

Noever, P. (ed.), *Aleksandr M. Rodchenko, and Varvara V. Stepanova: The Future is Our Only Goal*, Prestel, Munich, 1991.

Oliver, L., *Boris Anrep: The National Gallery Mosaics*, Yale, New Haven, 2004.

One Hundred Years of Russian Art, from Private Collections in the USSR, exh.cat. edited by Elliot, D. & Dudakov, V., Lund Humphries, London, 1989.

Origins of the Russian Avant-Garde, exh.cat., Palace Editions, St Petersburg, 2003.

Ouspensky, L., *Theology of the Icon*, St Vladimir's Seminary Press, New York, 1978.

Ouspensky, L., *Theology of the Icon*, 2 vols, St Vladimir's Seminary Press, New York, 1992.

Ouspensky, L., & Lossky, V., *The Meaning of Icons*, St Vladimir's Seminary Press, New York, 1983.

Paris-Moscou 1900–1930, exh.cat., Centre national d'art et de culture Georges Pompidou, Paris, 1979.

Parton, A., *Mikhail Larionov and the Russian Avant-Garde*, London, 1993.

Passuth, K., *Les avant-gardes de l'Europe Centrale*, Flammarion, Paris, 1988.

Peris, D., *Storming the Heavens: The Soviet League of the Militant Godless*, Cornell, New York, 1998.

Petric, V., *Constructivism in Film: The Man with a Movie Camera: A Cinematic Analysis*, Cambridge, 1987.

Petrov-Vodkin, K., 'Zhivopis' budushchego', lecture, Apr 1912, in *Mastera* VII, p.448.

Petrova, Y. (ed.), *Malevich's Circle: Confederates, Students, Followers in Russia 1920s-1950s*, Palace Editions, St Petersburg, 2000.

Petrova, Y., *The Russian Avant-Garde: Representation and Interpretation. Academic papers from the conference accompanying the exhibition 'Museum in a Museum: the Russian Avant-Garde from the Former Museum of Artistic Culture in the Collection of the State Russian Museum', 1998*, Russian Museum, Palace Editions, St Petersburg, 2001.

Petrova, Y. (ed.), *A Legacy Regained: Nikolai Khardzhiev and the Russian Avant-Garde*, Palace Editions, St Petersburg, 2002.

Petrova, Y., *The Russian Avant-Garde: Personality and School. Academic papers from the conferences accompanying the exhibitions 'Kazimir Malevich in the Russian Museum' and 'Malevich's Circle'*, Russian Museum, Palace Editions, St Petersburg, 2003.

Pevsner: Colloque international Antoine Pevsner tenu au musée Rodin en décembre 1992 sous la direction de Jean-Claude Marcadé, Association 'Les Amis d'Antoine Pevsner', Art Edition, Paris, 1995.

Popova, O., *Russian Illuminated Manuscripts*, London, 1984.

Povelikhina, A. & Kovtun, Y., *Russian Painted Shop Signs and Avant-garde Artists*, Aurora, Leningrad, 1991.

Powell, D., *Anti-Religious Propaganda in the Soviet Union*, Harvard, 1975.

Punin, N., 'K probleme vizantiiskogo iskusstva' ('Towards the Problem of Byzantine Art') in *Apollon*, no.3, 1913, pp 17–25.

Punin, N., 'Vizantiiskaia vystavka rabot' in *Apollon*, 1913, no.4, pp 42–3.

Punin, N., 'Vystavka i khudozhestvennaia zhizn: Vystavka drevne-russkago isskustva' ('Exhibitions and Artistic Life: An Exhibition of Ancient Russian Art') in *Apollon*, no.5, 1913.

Punin, N., 'Puti Sovremennayo Isskusyva i Russkaya Ikonopis' ('The Paths of Contemporary Art and Russian Icons') in *Apollon*, no.10, Dec 1913, pp 44–50.

Punin, N., 'Andrei Rublev' in *Apollon*, no.2, 1915, pp 1–23.

Punin, N., *Tatlin: Protiv kubizma (Against Cubism)*, Petrograd, 1921.

Rakitin, V., *Nikolai Mikhailov Suetin*, Palace Editions, St Petersburg, 1998.

Rakitin, V., *Ilya Chashnik*, Palace Editions, Moscow, 2000.

Rancour-Laferriere, D., *The Slave Soul of Russia: Moral Masochism and the Cult of Suffering*, New York University Press, 1995.

Read, C., *Religion, Revolution and the Russian Intelligentsia, 1900–1912*, New York, 1980.

Reshetylo-Rothe, D.A., *Rilke and Russia: A Re-evaluation*, Peter Lang, New York, 1990.

Riabushinsky, V., 'Russian Icons and Spirituality' in *The Third Hour*, V, 1951, p.48.

Robinson, E., 'The Apophatic Art of Kasimir Malevich' in *Studia Mystica*, vol.II, no.2, 1979, pp 48–55.

Rodley, L. *Byzantine Art and Architecture: An Introduction*, Cambridge, 1994.

Rosenfeld, A., *Defining Russian Graphic Arts, from Diaghilev to Stalin, 1898–1934*, Rutgers U.P. & the Jane Voorhees Zimmerli Art Museum, New Jersey, 1999.

Rosenthal, B.G. (ed.), *The Occult in Russian and Soviet Culture*, Cornell, New York, 1997.

Roslof, E., *Red Priests: Renovationism, Russian Orthodoxy, and Revolution, 1905–1946*, Indiana U.P., 2002.

Roth, C.P. (trans.), *St Theodore the Studite, On the Holy Icons*, St Vladimir's Seminary Press, New York, 1981.

Rowell M. & Wye, D. (eds), *The Russian Avant-Garde Book: 1910–1934*, MOMA, New York, 2002.

Rudenstine, A.Z., *The Guggenheim Museum Collection: Paintings 1880–1945*, vol.I, 1976.

Rudenstine, A.Z., *Russian Avant-Garde Art: The George Costakis Collection*, London, 1981.

Rusakov, Y., 'Matisse in Russia in the Autumn of 1911' in *Burlington Magazine*, no.866, vol.117, May 1975, pp 284–91.

Rusakov, Y., *Petrov-Vodkin*, Leningrad, 1986.

Rusakova, A., *Mikhail Nesterov*, Aurora Art Publishers, Leningrad, 1990.

Russian Paris, exh.cat., Palace Editions, St Petersburg, 2003.

Russian Painting of the Avant-Garde: 1906–1924, exh.cat., Scottish National Gallery of Modern Art, Edinburgh, 1993.

Russians: Larionov, Goncharova, Kandinsky and Others: The Roots of the Avant-Garde, 1900–1920, exh.cat., Brescia Mostre, Palace Editions, St Petersburg, 2000.

Russki Istoricheski Portret: Epocha Parsuni (*Historic Russian Portraits: The Epoch of the Parsuna*), exh.cat., Moscow, 2004.

Ryan, W., *The Bathhouse at Midnight: Magic in Russia*, Sutton, 1999.

Sabaneyeff, L., *Modern Russian Composers*, Martin Lawrence, London, 1927.

Sadykowa, E., 'Kunst-Leben: Der Einfluss des russischen "religiösen Renaissance" auf die Ästhetik und Kubst des Spätsymbolismus zu Beginn des 20. Jahrhunderts in Russland', PhD dissertation, University of Osnabruck, 2004.

Salmond, W., *Arts and Crafts in Late Imperial Russia: Reviving the Kustar Art Industries, 1870–1917*, Cambridge, 1996.

Sarabianov, D., 'Wassily Kandinsky dans le contexte de la culture russe' in *Kandinsky et la Russie*, exh.cat., Fondation Pierre Gianadda, Martigny Suisse, 2000.

Sarabianov, D. & Adaskina, N.L., *Popova*, Thames & Hudson, 1990, pp 14, 137, 139.

Schloezer, B. de, *Scriabin: Artist and Mystic*, trans. Slonimsky, N., Oxford, 1987.

Senkevitch, T.V., 'The Illusive Aesthethic Project of Pavel Florenskii: Space Between Geometry and Religion' in Franz, N., Hagemeister, M. & Haney, F., *Pavel Florenskij: Tradition und modern*, Peter Lang, Frankfurt, 2001, pp 403–22.

Sers, P., *Kandinsky. Philosophie de l'Abstraction: L'image metaphysique*, Skira, Geneva, 1995.

Sharp, J.A., *Primitivism, 'Neoprimitivism' and the art of Natal'ia Goncharova, 1907–1914*, Yale, New Haven, 1992.

Sharp, J.A., *Russian Modernism between East and West: Natal'ia Goncharova and the Moscow Avant-Garde*, Cambridge, 2006.

Shaw-Miller, S., 'Skriabin and Obukhov: *Mysterium* and *La Livre de Vie*, the Concept of Artistic Synthesis' in *Consciousness, Literature and the Arts*, vol.1, no.3, Dec 2000, http://www.aber.ac.uk/cla/archive/skria.html.

Shaw-Miller, S., *Visible Deeds of Music*, Yale, New Haven, 2002.

Shlovsky, V., 'Space in Painting and Suprematism', *Iskusstvo*, no.8, 3 Sept 1919.

Shvidkovsky, O., *Building in the USSR*, New York & Washington, 1971.

Simmen, J., *Kasimir Malewitsch: Das Schwarze Quadrat: Vom Anti-Bild zur Ikone der Moderne*, Frankfurt am Main, 1998.

Simmons, W., 'Kasimir Malevich's "Black Square": The Transformed Self' in *Arts Magazine*, 'Part 1: Cubism and the Illusionistic Portrait', no.53, Oct 1978, pp 116–25, 'Part 2: The New Laws of Transrationalism', no.54, Nov 1978, pp 130–41. 'Part 3: The Icon Unmasked', no.55, Dec 1978, pp 126–34.

Simmons, W., *Kasimir Malevich's 'Black Square' and the Genesis of Suprematism, 1907–1915*, New York & London, 1981.

Sitsky, L., *Music of the Repressed Russian Avant-Garde, 1900–1929*, Greenwood Press, Westport & London, 1994.

Slipko-Moskaltsev, K., *Ukrainske malyarstvo* (*Ukrainian Painting*), Kharkov, 1930.

Smith, T., *Lenin for Sale: The rise and fall of the personality cult of V.I. Lenin in Soviet Russia*, National Library of Canada, Ottawa, 1996.

Smolik, N., 'Der erste postmoderne Künstler' in *Malewitsch: Werk und Wirkung*, exh.cat., Cologne, 1995.

Sokolova, L., *Dancing for Diaghilev*, Mercury House, San Francisco, 1960.

Spira, A., 'Malewicz i ikony' in *Kresy*, no.44, Apr 2000, pp 210–219.

Stanley, A., *The Eastern Church*, London, 1876.

Steiner, E., *Stories for Little Comrades: Revolutionary Artists and the Making of Early Soviet Children's Books*, University of Washington Press, 1999.

Stavrou, T.G. (ed.), *Art & Culture in Nineteenth-Century Russia*, Indiana University Press, 1983.

Stites, R., *Revolutionary Dreams: Utopian Vision and Experimental Life in the Russian Revolution*, Oxford, 1989.

Struve, N., 'Yulia Reitlinger and Russian Emigré Icon-Painting' in *Russian Paris*, Palace Editions, St Petersburg, 2003.

Stuart, J., *Ikons*, Faber & Faber, London, 1975.

Stupples, P., *Pavel Kuznetsov: His life and art*, Cambridge, 1989.

Sytova, A, *The Lubok: Russian Folk Pictures 17th to 19th Century*, Aurora Art Publishers, Leningrad, 1984.

Tanner, N. (ed.), *Decrees of the Ecumenical Councils*, Sheen & Ward, London, 1990.

Tarabukin, N., *Smysl Ikony*, Moscow, 1999.

Tarasov, O., 'The Russian Icon and the Culture of the *Modern*: The Renaissance of Popular Icon Painting in the Reign of Nicholas II' in *Experiment*, 7, 2001.

Tarasov, O., *Icon and Devotion: Sacred Spaces in Imperial Russia*, Reaktion Books, London, 2002.

Tartarin, R., 'Transfusion sanguine et immortalité chez Alexandr Bogdanov' in *Droit et Société*, 28, 1994.

Taruskin, R., *Stravinsky and the Russian Traditions*, University of California Press, 1996.

Tavis, A.A., *Rilke's Russia: A Cultural Encounter*, Northwestern University Press, Evanston, 1994.

Taylor, R., *Film Propaganda: Soviet Russia and Nazi Germany*, I.B. Tauris Press, London & New York, 1998.

Taylor, R. & Christie, I. (eds), *Inside the Film Factory: New Approaches to Russian and Soviet Cinema*, Routledge, London, 1991.

Taylor, R., & Christie, I. (eds), *The Film Factory: Russian and Soviet Cinema in Documents 1896–1939*, London & New York, 2002.

Temple, R., *Icons and The Mystical Origins of Christianity*, Element Books, Longmead, 1990.

Timberlake, C.E. (ed.), *Religious and Secular Forces in Late Tsarist Russia*, University of Washington Press, 1992.

Trubetskoi, E., *Icons: Theology in Color*, St Vladimir's Seminary Press, New York, 1973.

Tumarkin, N., 'Religion, Bolshevism and the Origins of the Lenin Cult' in *Russian Review*, 40–1, Jan 1981, pp 35–46.

Tumarkin, N., *Lenin Lives! The Lenin Cult in Soviet Russia*, Harvard, 1983.

Tupitsyn, M., *Malevich and Film*, Yale, New Haven, 2002.

Turowski, A., *Malewicz w Warszawie*, Krakow, 2002.

Vakar, I. & Mikhienko, T., *Malevich o sebe, sovremenniki o Maleviche: pis'ma, dokumenty, vospominaniia, kritika*, 2 vols, Moscow, 2004.

Valkenier, E.K., 'Il'ia Repin and David Burliuk' in *Canadian-American Slavic Studies*, 20, nos 1–2, 1986.

Valkenier, E.K., *Russian Realist Art*, Columbia University Press, New York, 1989.

Velikanova, O., *Making of an Idol: On uses of Lenin*, National Library of Canada, Ottawa, 1996.

Venturi, L., *Chagall*, Geneva, 1956.

Vezin, A. & L., *Kandinsky and Der Blaue Reiter*, Paris, 1992.

Voloshin, M., 'Chemu uchat ikony?' in *Apollon*, 1914, no.5, pp 26–9.

Vzdornov, G. *Istoriia otkrytiia i izucheniia russkoi srednevekovoi zhivopisi XIX vek*, Iskusstvo, Moscow, 1986.

Wahl, H., 'Goethes Anstoss zur russischen Ikonenforschung' in *Goethe*, (N.F. des Jahrbuches der Goethe-Gesellschaft, 10, Weimar, 1947, pp219–26).

Wedgwood Benn, D., *Persuasion and Soviet Politics*, Blackwell, Oxford, 1989.

Weiss, P., *Kandinsky and Old Russia*, Yale, New Haven, 1995.

Wember, P., 'Von der Einstimmung der Farbe bis zur Einfarbigkeit' in *Pantheon*, 32, 1974, p.164, n.10.

White, E., *Stravinsky: The Composer and his Works*, Faber, London, 1966.

White, S., *The Bolshevik Poster*, Yale, New Haven, 1988.

Wierzbicka, A., 'Russian Cultural Scripts: The Theory of Cultural Scripts and its Applications' in *Ethos*, 30 (4), Dec 2002, pp 401–32.

Wright, C.A., 'Christ Interrogated: Bulgakov and Others' in *Transactions of the Association of Russian-American Scholars in the USA*, vol.24, 1991, pp 163–76.

Wynot, J., 'Russian Orthodox Monasteries' Response to the Relics Exposing Campaign, 1917–1922', http://www.georgefox.edu/academics/undergrad/departments/soc-swk/ree/2003/wynot03.html.

Yablonskaya, M.N., *Women Artists of Russia's New Age*, Thames & Hudson, London, 1990.

Youngblood, D.J., *Movies for the Masses: Popular Cinema and Soviet Society in the 1920s*, Cambridge, 1992.

Zbarskii, I.B. & Hutchinson, S., *Lenin's Embalmers*, Harvill Press, London, 1998.

Zelinsky, B., 'Der Primitivismus und die Anfänge der avantgardischer Malerei und Literatur in Russland' in *Zeitschrift für Aesthetik und allgemeine Kunstwissenschaft*, XXVII/2, 1982, pp 121–41.

Zernov, N.M., *The Russian Religious Renaissance of the Twentieth Century*, London, 1963.

Zhadova, L., *Malevich, Suprematism and Revolution in Russian Art, 1910–1930*, Thames & Hudson, London, 1982.

Zhadova, L.A., *Tatlin*, Rizzoli, New York, 1988.

Ziolkowski, M., 'Pilate and Pilatism in Recent Russian Literature' in Duffin Graham, S. (ed.), *New Directions in Soviet Literature: Selected Papers from the Fourth World Congress for Soviet and East European Studies, 1990*, St Martin's Press, New York, 1992, pp 164–81.

Zitser, E.A., *The Transfigured Kingdom: Sacred Parody and Charismatic Authority at the Court of Peter the Great*, Cornell, New York, 2004.

Zweite, A., *The Blaue Reiter in the Lenbachhaus (Munich)*. Munich, 1989.

Index

NOTE: Page numbers in italics refer to illustrations.

N

O

P

R